MW00616455

SAP PRESS e-books

Print or e-book, Kindle or iPad, workplace or airplane: Choose where and how to read your SAP PRESS books! You can now get all our titles as e-books, too:

- ▶ By download and online access
- ▶ For all popular devices
- ▶ And, of course, DRM-free

Convinced? Then go to **www.sap-press.com** and get your e-book today.

Integrating SuccessFactors™ with SAP®

SAP PRESS is a joint initiative of SAP and Rheinwerk Publishing. The know-how offered by SAP specialists combined with the expertise of Rheinwerk Publishing offers the reader expert books in the field. SAP PRESS features first-hand information and expert advice, and provides useful skills for professional decision-making.

SAP PRESS offers a variety of books on technical and business-related topics for the SAP user. For further information, please visit our website: www.sap-press.com.

Amy Grubb, Luke Marson
SuccessFactors with SAP ERP HCM: Business Processes and Use (2nd Edition)
2015, 644 pages, hardcover
ISBN 978-1-4932-1173-9

Masters, Toombs, Bland, Morgalis
Self-Services with SAP ERP HCM: ESS, MSS, and HR Renewal
2015, 345 pages, hardcover
ISBN 978-1-59229-984-3

Joe Lee, Tim Simmons
Talent Management with SAP ERP HCM
2012, 388 pages, hardcover
ISBN 978-1-59229-413-8

Dirk Liepold, Steve Ritter
SAP ERP HCM: Technical Principles and Programming (2nd Edition)
2015, 863 pages, hardcover
ISBN 978-1-4932-1170-8

Vishnu Kandi, Venki Krishnamoorthy, Donna Leong-Cohen,
Prashanth Padmanabhan, Chinni Reddygari

Integrating SuccessFactors™ with SAP®

Bonn • Boston

Editor Sarah Frazier
Acquisitions Editor Emily Nicholls
Technical Reviewer Steve Ritter
Copyeditor Melinda Rankin
Cover Design Graham Geary
Photo Credit Shutterstock.com/202755718/© hin255
Layout Design Vera Brauner
Production Graham Geary
Typesetting III-satz, Husby (Germany)
Printed and bound in the United States of America, on paper from sustainable sources

ISBN 978-1-4932-1185-2
© 2015 by Rheinwerk Publishing, Inc., Boston (MA)
1st edition 2015

Library of Congress Cataloging-in-Publication Data
Krishnamoorthy, Venki.
Integrating SuccessFactors with SAP / Venki Krishnamoorthy, Donna Leong-Cohen, Prashanth Padmanabhan, Chinni Reddygari.
pages cm
Includes index.
ISBN 978-1-4932-1185-2 (print : alk. paper) -- ISBN 1-4932-1185-4 (print : alk. paper) -- ISBN 978-1-4932-1186-9 (ebook) --
ISBN 978-1-4932-1187-6 (print and ebook : alk. paper) 1. SAP ERP. 2. Personnel management--Computer programs.
3. Manpower planning--Computer programs. 4. Cloud computing. I. Title.
HF5549.5.D37K75 2015
658.300285'53--dc23
2015000991

Contents at a Glance

Dear Reader,

SuccessFactors is on the rise. For HCM customers and consultants familiar with what SuccessFactors is and the advantages it offers, the question of how to jump on this bandwagon and address the best method of integration still remains.

As foreword writer David Ludlow states, the integration of cloud-based and on-premise HCM systems is not just a technical issue, but also a business issue. SuccessFactors consultants, customers, and system integrators need to evaluate where each organization fits into the bigger SuccessFactors picture, and weigh the variables involved in each option for moving to the cloud. By addressing these business issues, they can begin identifying what options meet their technical needs.

Written by experts with decades of SAP ERP HCM and SuccessFactors experience, this book walks through the different integration stages and enables you to make informed decisions about your company's integration strategy. Delivering in-depth coverage on the packaged integrations for each deployment model and real-world case studies to provide a roadmap for implementation, this resource will help you make more educated choices and continue your SuccessFactors journey.

What did you think about *Integrating SuccessFactors with SAP*? Your comments and suggestions are the most useful tools to help us make our books the best they can be. We encourage you to visit our website at *www.sap-press.com* and share your feedback.

Thank you for purchasing a book from SAP PRESS!

Sarah Frazier
Editor, SAP PRESS

Rheinwerk Publishing
Boston, MA

sarahf@rheinwerk-publishing.com
www.sap-press.com

Contents

PART II SuccessFactors Deployment Models

PART III SuccessFactors Integration Models

Foreword

When SAP acquired SuccessFactors in 2012, SuccessFactors was—and now continues to be—a leading HCM solutions provider to organizations both within and outside of the SAP install base. Many existing SAP customers showed immediate excitement about the acquisition, but also had questions about integrating the SuccessFactors cloud solutions with the SAP on-premise solutions. From day one that we knew we would have to assume some responsibility of this integration by identifying key scenarios and providing integration content to help our customers deploy these solutions quickly, with low cost and risk.

From my over 10 years' experience gained by leading the HCM product management team at SAP, and by meeting hundreds of customers over that time, I have learned that integrations are not just a technical issue, but also a business issue. Data mapping, data synchronization, real-time vs. batch, understanding the system of records for each data element, creating end-to-end processes without regard to the backend system, where to do reporting and analytics—these are just some of the items to consider when thinking about integrations. Customers who pay early and adequate attention to the topic of integration are far more likely to increase their chances of completing their projects on time and on budget to deliver on the needs of their businesses in an effective and timely manner.

Recognizing these needs, we have built and delivered packaged integrations, integration tools, templates, and application programming interfaces; which we continue to maintain and add more to all the time. This productized integration content and integration technologies help customers connect the SuccessFactors cloud and SAP on-premise worlds, and determine when and how they will leverage cloud solutions while still maximizing their, often significant, on-premise investments.

To date, these integrations have focused on three primary deployment models: Talent Hybrid, Full Cloud HCM, and Side-By-Side HCM. Under the Talent Hybrid deployment model, customers run core HR processes (such as Personnel Administration [PA], Organizational Management [OM], and SAP Payroll) on-premise with SAP ERP HCM, connecting it with cloud-based SuccessFactors talent solutions (such as employee performance management, SuccessFactors Learning, and SuccessFactors Recruiting) and, optionally, Workforce Analytics. Under the Full Cloud HCM deployment model, customers run all of their HR processes in the cloud, but need to connect HR processes and data with third-party systems and on-premise SAP ERP. The Side-By-Side HCM deployment model is for customers who use SAP ERP HCM to deliver core HR processes for a subset of their employees and use Employee Central to deliver core HR processes for another subset of their employees. These three deployment models have been carefully designed to meet the varying needs of customers in their journey to the cloud.

The integration packages, timelines, technology, and roadmap have generated many questions from our customers. We have also received many questions about the real-world experiences of customers who have successfully implemented the packaged integrations. In their book, *Integrating SuccessFactors with SAP*, Venki Krishnamoorthy, Donna Leong-Cohen, Prashanth Padmanabhan, Chinni Reddygari, Vishnu Kandi, and many more expert contributors provide valuable content and insight that can guide consultants, customers, and partners through the evaluation, design, and implementation phases of all three deployment models. The authors and contributors are a combination of SAP employees, partners who created best practices content for integrations, partners who implemented the various deployment models for large global customers, and technical architects who have implemented both packaged and custom integrations for thousands of customers. I am sure that you will benefit from their collective wisdom.

David Ludlow
Group Vice President
Line of Business Solutions — HR
SAP

Preface

In a January 2014 article in the *Wall Street Journal*, Marc Andreessen, an Internet pioneer and venture capitalist, compared the cost of starting a technology company today to the cost of starting a technology company in the 1990s. He said that if you wanted to build an Internet company in the 90s, you needed to buy Sun servers, Cisco networking gear, Oracle databases, and EMC storage systems, and spend a ton of money just to get up and running. Andreessen stated that today's companies can go to Amazon Web Services and pay per use to get the same services for about 1,000 times cheaper. Such a reduction in cost is speeding up the progress of technology and the pace of innovation. This innovation has revolutionized the consumer software industry and is spilling over into the enterprise software industry starting with customer relationship management, procurement, travel and expense management, and HCM. Today, almost all innovations in the areas mentioned above are being done by vendors who provide their software as a service rather than as a package that can be installed behind the firewalls of an organization.

Book Goals

The journey to the cloud, for most areas of enterprise software, is inevitable. However, unlike most consumer software, where the costs are low and switching technology vendors is easy, enterprise software investments are huge and costly to abandon. So, while the journey to the cloud for some customers will be swift, for others it will be in stages. This is one area where integration plays an important role. Integration can help organizations start their journey to the cloud at their own pace.

In this book, we attempt to explain the evolution of enterprise software and how integration content and technologies from SAP and SuccessFactors can help with the move to the cloud. Each chapter addresses the needs of a specific audience and a specific set of topics. We'll begin by looking at the target audience for this book and the structure that can be expected.

Target Audience

The target audience of this book includes SAP and SuccessFactors functional consultants, cloud solution architects, integration designers, and integration middleware consultants who implement packaged integrations that connect SuccessFactors to SAP and third-party applications, or create custom integrations to suit their needs. In addition, this book can also be a valuable guide for senior executives such as chief information officers, chief HR officers, and chief financial officers who have the need to move their HCM software to the cloud.

How This Book is Structured

This book is divided into the following 3 parts and 11 chapters:

► **Part I: What Does the Cloud Mean for You?**
This portion aims to introduce the current HCM environment in which customers are moving to the cloud and certain considerations that should be made in getting there.

We begin with a discussion of the fundamentals in **Chapter 1**, introducing the evolution of HCM architecture, the current trends in enterprise software, and SAP's strategy to respond to those trends. If you are a chief financial officer, chief information officer, chief people officer, vice president of human resources, or director of information technology, this chapter is for you. We also provide an overview of what is happening in the HCM technology industry and describe how the technology landscape is evolving. We then discuss SAP's strategy to respond to this evolution and talk about how SAP is helping you move to the cloud with various software deployment options supported by integration content and tools.

Next, in **Chapter 2**, we look at how information technology teams within organizations and software technology service providers can help customers make their journey to the cloud. If you are a chief information officer, director of information technology, a partner in a software consulting firm, a solution architect, or vice president of professional services in a technology service firm, this chapter is for you. We start by discussing who is moving their HCM software to the cloud and elaborate on the factors driving this movement. We then talk about the three main stages that play out in the decision-making phase of cloud migration. These three stages include: the business architecture review stage, the product review stage, and the solution architecture review stage. We end the chapter by providing an in-depth case study of a customer's journey to the cloud.

- ▶ **Part II: SuccessFactors Deployment Models**
  This part looks at the three SuccessFactors deployment models which provide different pathways to the cloud. They include Full Cloud HCM, Talent Hybrid, and Side-By-Side HCM.

  Chapter 3 looks at the Full Cloud HCM deployment model, discussing its architecture, target audience, and technology options for integration. We then go into detail about the supported packaged integrations for this deployment model. We then cover the user experience integrations and rapid-deployment solution related integrations that are involved with Full Cloud HCM. Finally, we apply real-world application with the use of two in-depth case studies that follow the implementation of this deployment model. Ultimately, this chapter can tell you how you can take a huge jump in technology and user experience innovation while reducing the total cost of ownership for HCM software at the same time.

  Chapter 4 discusses the Talent Hybrid deployment model. We start by looking at its architecture, target audience, and the various technology options that can be utilized during implementation. We then provide details about the supported packaged integrations for this deployment model, followed by a look at the user experience and rapid-deployment solutions related integrations. Finally, we discuss two case studies about customers who made their move from on-premise talent management systems to SuccessFactors Talent Solutions in the cloud, while keeping their core HR and payroll on-premise.

  Finally, in **Chapter 5** we look at the newest deployment model by SuccessFactors and SAP, Side-By-Side HCM. We start by discussing the target audience for this deployment model and the two available beta packaged integrations: consolidated and distributed. We then go into detail about the user experience, process, and reporting integrations, along with the different business processes that this integration supports. Finally, we end by discussing two case studies about the packaged integrations supported by Side-By-Side HCM.

- ▶ **Part III: SuccessFactors Integration Models**
  Integration plays a critical part in the various deployment models. Chapter 6 through Chapter 8 explore the different integration scenarios, templates, and applications that will need to be integrated. Chapter 9 and Chapter 10 then go over instructions for various integration scenarios for the Full Cloud HCM and Talent Hybrid deployment models. Finally, in Chapter 11, we address the data migration concerns that may arise during integration.

Starting in **Chapter 6**, we introduce SuccessFactors' integration layers and APIs. After reviewing this chapter, you will better understand SuccessFactors' logical integration architecture as well as the capabilities of its various APIs to integrate with SuccessFactors modules. If you are an integration designer, HR business analyst, integration consultant from a customer or a partner organization, you will find this chapter useful.

Chapter 7 then discusses the standard integration templates available with SuccessFactors. This chapter also talks about the standard data imports available which can be used to integrate with systems that don't have a packaged integration.

Moving on to **Chapter 8**, we look at integrating an instance of SuccessFactors Talent Suite with some of the leading cloud-based, third-party service providers. Providers such as PeopleAnswers, First Advantage, VLS, Questionmark, and more will be discussed in conjunction with SuccessFactors Recruiting, Onboarding, and Learning integrations.

The next two chapters look at applying the packaged integrations for Full Cloud HCM and Talent Hybrid.

Chapter 9 starts by outlining the target audience for the Full Cloud HCM deployment model, where customers run all their HCM applications in the cloud and connect them with on-premise business applications and other cloud service providers. It then talks about implementing the packaged integrations that support the Full Cloud HCM model. In this chapter, we discuss specific examples of how SuccessFactors modules are integrated. The chapter will also contain specific examples and best practices to following during implementation, while providing sample code in places. This chapter is meant for HCM functional consultants who configure SAP and SuccessFactors Employee Central, technical consultants who configure middleware technologies to implement the packaged integrations, and ABAP programmers who wish to extend the integrations to suit customer needs.

Chapter 10 starts by outlining the target audience for the Talent Hybrid deployment model's packaged integrations. It then walks through the step-by-step process of implementing the available packaged integrations that support the Talent Hybrid deployment model in the form of case studies. If you are an integration designer, HR business analyst, talent solutions integration consultant from a customer or a partner organization, you will find this chapter very handy.

Finally, in **Chapter 11**, we look at the procedures for proper data migration. All cloud deployment models start with a one-time migration of foundational data. Obtaining, cleansing, and migrating data to a core HR system is critical to the success of an implementation and integration projects. The key to a successful data migration is standardized and engineered rapid data migration content for a fast and simple go-live with valid and clean data. In this chapter, we'll explain the migration of data from an SAP ERP HCM or third-party system into Employee Central by leveraging the rapid-deployment solutions paradigm. This chapter is meant for HCM functional consultants who configure SAP and SuccessFactors Employee Central and technical consultants who migrate employee data as part of an implementation. The chapter also provides insight for implementation project managers who need to plan an Employee Central implementation.

In summary, this is a good source of insight and information for executives who are planning their journey to the SuccessFactors HCM suite in the cloud, partners who are advising customers on such a move, HR professionals who want to understand why integration matters, HR functional consultants who configure the software, HR IT professionals who want to plan the integration between SuccessFactors and other systems, integration architects who design integrations, middleware consultants who configure the integration, and ABAP programmers who extend the integrations to suit customer needs.

Acknowledgments

We would like to thank the following people for their contributions to this book:

- David Ludlow, Group Vice President of SAP Cloud Solutions Marketing for his insight, support, and encouragement.

- Our friends at Rheinwerk Publishing for their guidance, patience, and support. We would especially like to thank Emily Nicholls, who made this book possible and has encouraged us to get the words onto the printed page. A huge thanks to Sarah Frazier, our project manager, for her patience and support in editing our content, and working with us to get the content in the desired format.

- Our contributors for providing content in the book. This includes Frank Densborn, Kevin Chan, Seng-Ping Gan, Rachel Leonard, Dina Hermosillo-Burrus, Bhargav Gogineni, Anoop Kumar Garg, Kiran Vuriti, Ritesh Mehta, and Raja Thukiwakam.

- All the product managers, product owners, and solution managers of SAP SuccessFactors integration for sharing their insight and time with us. These individuals include Wolfgang Dittrich, Yamini Polisetty, Ganesh Kudva, Parvathy Sankar, Jean Handel-Bailey, and David Hock. In addition we also would like to thank SuccessFactors Recruiting product owners Paige Cherny, Meghan Wilson, and Megan Sensenbaugh.

- A special thanks to SAP's Packaged Solutions and SAP Education team, who were kind to answer our queries and provide valuable inputs. The team includes: Elvira Wallis, Oren Shatil, Nir Rostoker, Janusz Smilek, Sapna Subramaniam, Hilmar Dolderer, Timm Schmalfuss, Jens Baumann, Sevil Rende, Arvind Prasad, Karsten Martin, Anja Weiss, Andreas Holle, Andrea Cottino, Marian Harris, Miguel Anthony Dietz, Shweta Walaskar, Theresa Reinke, Monica Reidl, Jamie Fall, Joshua Steele, Bill McKinlay, Regina Gama, and Dave Winters.

- SAP Mentor Luke Marson and our technical reviewer Steve Ritter, for reviewing the content and providing valuable input.

▸ Arun Kumar Timalapur, Yasmine Abdallah, Vivek Mahajan, Nithyananthan Thangaraj, Darien Cohen, Ken Bowers, Brandon Toombs, Kim Lessley, Amy Grubb, Sugie Liao, Alan Yang, Joe Zhao, Jennifer Endres, Dominique Wang, Wally Hayes, Scott Lemly, and Mary Battle Stump for their help with this book.

PART I
What Does the Cloud Mean for You?

Human Capital Management (HCM) customers are moving to the cloud to take advantage of its innovation, agility, and lower total cost of ownership. SAP is responding to this by making the cloud central to its strategy, with integration as a key enabler.

1   SAP Cloud Integration Strategy

One major trend in the realm of HCM software is the transition that companies are making by moving to the cloud. In this chapter, we provide an overview of what is happening in the HCM technology industry and how the technology landscape is evolving. From there, we will look at SAP's strategy to respond to this evolution and talk about how SAP is helping companies move to the cloud with various software deployment options supported by integration content and tools.

To begin, we will look at the current shift in software design that is changing the IT landscape. Then, we will discuss SAP's response to the growing needs of their customers through integrations and cloud deployment models.

1.1   The Consumerization of IT

Consumerization describes the primary driving force behind product and service design as catering to the needs of the individual customer. This concept represents a major shift in the IT industry.

Most SAP customers who run SAP ERP on-premise are experiencing this shift in employee expectations. Such organizations are adopting cloud solutions, among other things, to take advantage of faster innovation, provide consumer-grade user experience to their employees, and lower their total cost of software ownership.

Lines of businesses (LOBs) such as human resources, procurement, finance, sales, service, and marketing are adopting the cloud to respond to changing customer expectations faster without having to rely entirely on internal information technology teams and without having to undertake large, high-cost, high-risk, on-premise software implementations. They are also turning to the cloud because of the superior user experience that engages all generations of employees who expect enterprise software to function like consumer apps they use every day. For example, an industry that is struggling to attract and retain new college graduates can implement onboarding solutions that attract and engage a new generation of employees during the critical new-hire onboarding period.

The cloud is an attractive option for information technology teams, too. IT teams are adopting the cloud because it helps them deliver solutions to their internal customers faster, at a lower cost, while freeing up time and money to invest in projects that help the core business of their companies. For example, banking customers that run SAP for Banking can move human resource management, procurement, and travel management to the cloud while retaining on-premise software to run their bank.

Executives such as CEOs, CFOs, and CIOs are moving subsidiaries or newly acquired companies to the cloud and connecting cloud systems with their on-premise SAP ERP systems to reduce the cost of information technology, gain better insight into the business, and reduce the time it takes to integrate the systems and cultures of newly acquired companies.

When LOBs move their software applications to the cloud, they sometimes incorrectly assume that these applications are self-contained and do not need to share data with other business applications that may be on-premise and other supporting applications that may be in the cloud. Such an assumption is costly and may lead to the failure of cloud implementations.

Many Critical Business Applications Need Employee Data

SAP product teams studied thousands of cloud implementations and learned that on average LOB HR cloud applications are connected to over 15 critical business systems using at least 60 integrations. For large businesses, this number could be in the hundreds.

SAP's cloud integration strategy was developed in response to these challenges, desires, and ground realities. Although SAP's cloud applications are designed to provide complete self-contained functionality, they are also well integrated with a customer's on-premise SAP systems to support an end-to-end business process. SAP provides first the necessary technology and content to connect its cloud applications to third-party cloud applications and second a set of tools and technologies that enables customers and partners to build their own custom integrations. For customers who may not have the know-how, SAP provides fixed-price professional services packages to implement the integrations.

1.2   SAP's Response to Customer Needs

SAP recognized that cloud solutions need to be a central part of the strategy devised to meet the customer demands of faster innovation, consumer-grade user experience, and lower total cost of ownership. Traditionally, the IT department and executives made IT decisions with little or no influence from LOB managers and users. Now, with cloud solutions that can be bought as subscriptions, LOB managers have more say in enterprise software purchasing decisions.

Recognizing this shift in demand and buying patterns, SAP has developed or acquired cloud solutions to meet the needs of LOBs. For human resource management, SAP acquired SuccessFactors. For procurement in the cloud, SAP acquired Ariba. For customer engagement, SAP developed an in-house cloud solution and augmented it with the acquisition of Hybris. For travel and expense management, SAP developed an in-house application called SAP Cloud for Travel. In 2014, SAP announced its intention to acquire Concur, the leading travel and expense management provider in the cloud, becoming SAP's go-forward solution for travel and expense management in the cloud. For acquiring and managing contract employees and projects, SAP acquired Fieldglass. For finance, SAP developed SAP Cloud for Financials. It has extended cloud options to small businesses and subsidiaries of large companies with Business ByDesign, SAP's cloud business suite.

What's the goal behind these acquisitions and developments? To have a unified cloud platform for all LOB applications (see Figure 1.1).

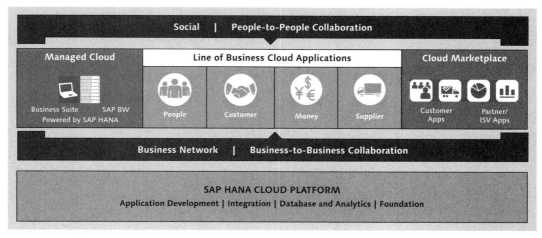

Figure 1.1 Unified Cloud Platform for Line of Business Applications

However, to achieve this vision, SAP has to come up with workable solutions for the over 35,000 customers using SAP ERP HCM solutions to run their businesses. In many cases, these customers have invested tens of millions of dollars into their on-premise solutions. Many of these customers have large teams of employees or partners skilled in deploying and managing HR business processes using these applications.

Such customers need a path to the cloud that does not require discarding all their investment in on-premise LOB applications. They also need guidance and assistance in retraining their IT teams to make the move from deploying and managing on-premise applications to deploying, configuring, customizing, integrating, and extending cloud-based applications. Cultural barriers within organizations and government regulations also play an important role in the journey of LOBs to the cloud.

Keeping such factors in mind, SAP product managers have devised and executed an integration strategy and direction that enables SAP ERP customers move their LOB applications to the cloud at a pace that suits their needs and their organizations while respecting their company culture and the information security laws of the countries in which they operate.

To this end, to help customers rapidly and flexibly integrate SAP's cloud solutions with other systems (whether they are SAP, non-SAP, or custom applications), SAP has adopted the following framework:

▶ Identify and prescribe cloud deployment models for all products (see Section 1.3)

▶ Support each cloud deployment model through the following (see Section 1.4) options:

   ▷ Packaged integrations (see Section 1.4.1)

   ▷ Standard integration templates (see Section 1.4.2)

   ▷ Professional services packages and rapid-deployment solutions for implementation (see Section 1.4.3)

   ▷ Application program interfaces (APIs) to enable custom integrations (see Section 1.4.4)

   ▷ Integration middleware technology in the cloud and on-premise (see Section 1.4.5)

Let's walk through each of these pillars of the integration framework by first looking at the three cloud deployment models offered by SAP and SuccessFactors.

1.3   Cloud Deployment Models

Cloud and on-premise products can be deployed in many different ways. To enable
productive conversations about architecture, meaningful decision-making, and
fast implementation, SAP has identified and documented the most common
deployment patterns of cloud and on-premise products that cater to specific scenarios. SAP refers to these patterns as *cloud deployment models* (see Figure 1.2).

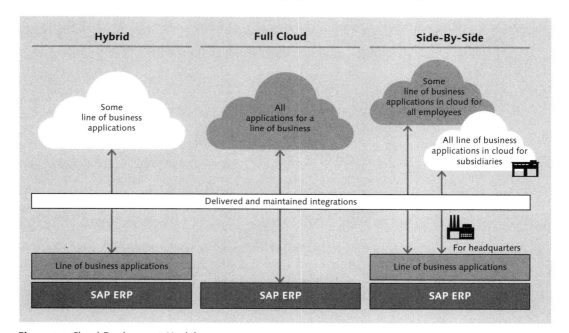

Figure 1.2 Cloud Deployment Models

Some customers prefer to move all applications supporting an LOB such as human
resource management, procurement, travel management, customer engagement
or finance to the cloud while using their on-premise SAP ERP applications to run
their core businesses, such as banking, manufacturing, and retail. Such customers

can move applications supporting one or more one of more of their lines of businesses to the cloud and integrate them with their SAP ERP application on-premise. This deployment model is called the *Full Cloud deployment model*.

There is also a recommended path to the cloud for customers currently using LOB software applications in SAP ERP. Such customers can move one or more applications to the cloud while continuing to use SAP ERP for the remaining applications. Business processes might cut across cloud and on-premise applications. This deployment model is called the *Hybrid deployment model*.

A third set of customers might want to run business applications supporting a subsidiary or a newly acquired company in the cloud while using SAP ERP to support the needs of LOBs in the parent company. In other words, they want to bring together two systems of record side-by-side. For such customers, SAP has put together a cloud deployment model called the *Side-By-Side deployment model*.

While engaging with a customer, SAP solution architects prescribe a deployment model for the customer after studying their current business needs and system landscapes. Once a customer picks a deployment model, SAP implementation experts conduct a workshop to identify the productized integration components and services available from SAP that could reduce the cost and risk of the overall integrations.

For example, according to the SAP solution management team, there are over 14,000 customers using SAP ERP HCM for their employee administration needs. Over 700 of those customers are using—and many others are debating using—one or more SuccessFactors talent solutions in the cloud while keeping employee administration (often known as core HR) on-premise. Solution architects have designed the Talent Hybrid deployment model to help such customers.

The Full Cloud HCM deployment model is designed for another crowd. There are over 35,000 SAP ERP customers using SAP ERP to run their businesses. Most of these customers use HR management systems on-premise, and some of these systems are built on outdated technologies that cost a lot of money to maintain. Such customers are choosing to move all their HCM applications to the cloud while integrating them with SAP ERP, which they use to run their core businesses, such as banking, retail, or manufacturing.

Finally, many SAP customers who use SAP ERP HCM for core HR and SuccessFactors talent solutions frequently grow their companies through acquisitions. Such acquired companies most often use a different system for managing their employees. The cost of migrating employees of such acquisitions to the parent company's SAP ERP HCM system, while necessary, is expensive, disruptive, and time-consuming; in terms of HR, integration of core business systems such as finance, supply chain, or customer relationship management systems always gets prioritized over integration of HCM systems. For this reason, organizations end up maintaining tens of different HR management systems for the same organization. This leads to inefficiencies, increased cost, decreased productivity, and poor talent management.

Such customers are choosing to move their acquisitions' HR management systems to the cloud to migrate them faster, reduce operating expenses, provide a unified employee experience, and perform integrated workforce planning. In many cases, this model enables customers to try out the cloud for employee administration for a small number of employees and experience new ways to deploy software before embarking on company-wide deployment of cloud software for human resource management. The Side-By-Side HCM deployment model is designed to meet the needs of such customers and can act as a stepping stone to the Full Cloud HCM deployment model. The packaged integrations supporting the Side-By-Side HCM deployment model are designed to enable customers to run core HR in the cloud and on-premise for different sets of employees at the same time.

1.3.1 Full Cloud HCM Deployment Model

The Full Cloud HCM deployment model is applicable when an organization wants to run all people management applications in the cloud. As shown in Figure 1.3, this means moving completely away from on-premise HCM and into cloud HCM, even if other SAP ERP applications (Sales and Distribution, Plant Maintenance, etc.) remain "on the ground." All applications in the talent solutions suite, employee administration applications, and payroll applications are run in the cloud.

More information on the Full Cloud HCM deployment model can be found in Chapter 3.

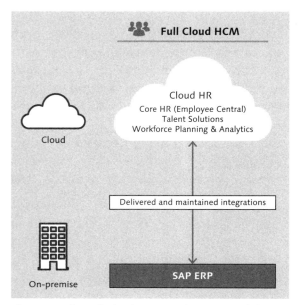

Figure 1.3 The Full Cloud HCM Deployment Model

Consumers

The Full Cloud HCM deployment model is for customers who want to run all people management applications in the cloud. Customers who run very old versions of core HR systems are good candidates for the Full Cloud HCM deployment model. Rather than invest in new on-premise SAP ERP HCM, they could invest in moving all HCM software to the cloud.

Packaged Integrations

The Full Cloud HCM suite integrates with SAP ERP using multiple packaged integrations. The following sections look at these integrations at greater length. For more information on these integrations and how to integrate them, see Chapter 9.

Employee Central Integration with SAP ERP

As shown in Figure 1.4, organizational data and employee data is sent from Employee Central to SAP ERP. Cost center data is sent from SAP ERP to Employee Central.

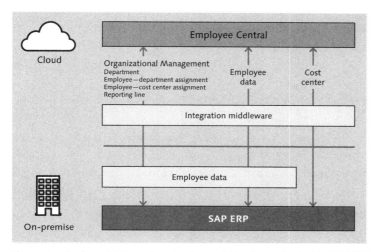

Figure 1.4 Packaged Integrations to Connect Employee Central to SAP ERP

Employee Central Integration with SAP Payroll

Another packaged integration connects Employee Central with SAP Payroll. In this scenario (as illustrated in Figure 1.5), the SAP on-premise payroll system receives cost center data from SAP Financials and employee master data from Employee Central. As an optional integration, UI integration between SAP ERP HCM and Employee Central is offered for selected country payroll versions.

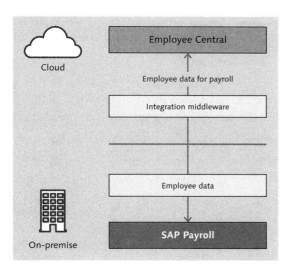

Figure 1.5 Packaged Integration to Connect Employee Central with SAP Payroll On-Premise

> **Employee Central Integration with Employee Central Payroll**
>
> Please note that in addition to the payroll integration with SAP Payroll, Employee Central also integrations with Employee Central Payroll.

Employee Central Integration with Third-Party Applications

Most organizations use one or more third-party applications for payroll, benefits, and time management purposes. Sometimes, subsidiaries in different countries use local benefits, time, and payroll systems. Employee Central can be integrated with such third-party systems. You can connect Employee Central with third-party applications with packaged integrations, standard templates, custom integration services, and a library of APIs (see Figure 1.6).

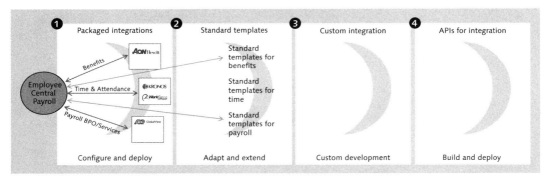

Figure 1.6 Productized Integration Components for Connecting Employee Central with Third-Party Applications

Integration Technology Options

The current integration technology for the Full Cloud HCM deployment model is Dell Boomi AtomSphere. Figure 1.7 illustrates how Dell Boomi AtomSphere works as the middleman for integration.

SAP is working on supporting SAP HANA Cloud Integration (HCI) middleware technology as an alternative for Dell Boomi AtomSphere. No release dates have been announced (as of spring 2015).

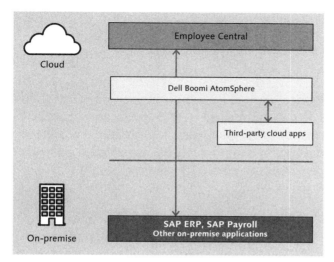

Figure 1.7 Integration Technology for Full Cloud HCM

1.3.2 Talent Hybrid Deployment Model

Simply put, the Talent Hybrid deployment model shown in Figure 1.8 comes into play when customers use one or more SuccessFactors Talent Solutions applications in the cloud while using SAP ERP HCM for their employee administration needs and payroll needs.

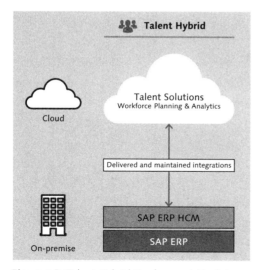

Figure 1.8 Talent Hybrid Deployment Model

For more information on the Talent Hybrid deployment model, see Chapter 4.

Consumers

The Talent Hybrid deployment model is for customers who want to run talent solutions in the cloud while keeping employee administration on-premise. Usually, customers who run SAP ERP HCM for all their HCM application needs start by moving one or more talent management applications to the cloud to access innovation fast without a huge investment in implementation or custom development.

Packaged Integrations

As shown in Figure 1.9, the SuccessFactors Talent Solutions suite integrates with SAP ERP HCM via multiple packaged integrations. Figure 1.9 shows all the current and planned packaged integrations. These packaged integrations are part of the Integration Add-on for SAP ERP HCM and the SuccessFactors HCM suite.

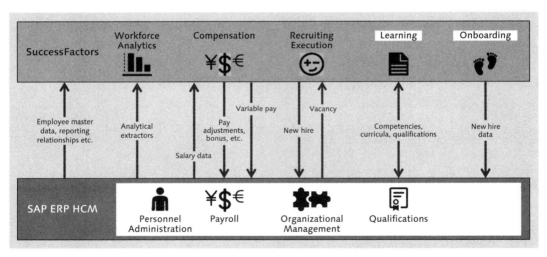

Figure 1.9 Packaged Integrations for the Talent Hybrid Model

Packaged data integrations are available for integrating employee data from SAP ERP HCM with SuccessFactors Talent Solutions and SuccessFactors Analytics, and process integrations are available for integrating SuccessFactors Compensation and SuccessFactors Recruiting with SAP ERP HCM.

More information on the packaged integrations for this deployment model can be found in Chapter 10.

Integration Technology Options

As shown in Figure 1.10, there are three technology options for the Talent Hybrid deployment model: FTP, SAP Process Integration (PI), and SAP HANA Cloud Integration (HCI). SAP PI is the most commonly used integration technology to implement the packaged integrations that support the Talent Hybrid deployment model. This is because more than 4,000 customers have SAP PI in their organizations and have skilled people to implement the integrations using SAP PI.

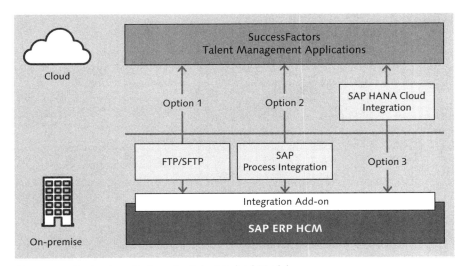

Figure 1.10 Technology Options for Talent Hybrid Model

1.3.3   Side-By-Side HCM Deployment Model

The Side-By-Side HCM deployment model is perhaps the trickiest to conceptualize. In it, SAP ERP HCM on-premise serves as the system of record for employee and organizational information for some employees, while Employee Central in the cloud serves as a system of record for other employees, usually from a subsidiary company. Remember that some organizations use the Side-By-Side HCM deployment model to begin migration to SuccessFactors before committing the bulk of their existing workforce's employee and organizational data.

In this model, all employees in the organization use SuccessFactors Talent Solutions in the cloud (see Figure 1.11).

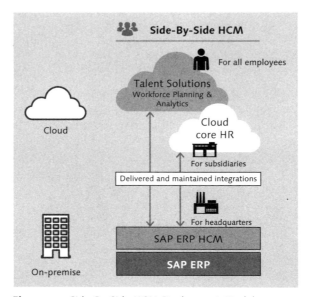

Figure 1.11 Side-By-Side HCM Deployment Model

For more information on the Side-By-Side HCM deployment model, see Chapter 5.

Consumers

The Side-By-Side HCM deployment model is for customers who want to administer part of their employees in the cloud and part of their employees on-premise. This model is suitable for customers who want to move certain countries to the cloud while keeping their on-premise investment in core HR software in other countries or geographies.

Packaged Integrations

The packaged integrations for the Side-By-Side HCM deployment model are divided into two broad categories: Side-By-Side HCM consolidate and Side-By-Side HCM distributed. These categories currently support an employee master data integration.

Other packaged integrations supporting the Side-By-Side HCM deployment model are planned for late 2015 (as of the writing of this book, spring 2015).

Integration Technology Options

Dell Boomi AtomSphere is the enterprise application integration technology supported by the Side-By-Side HCM deployment model.

1.4   Productized Integration Components Provided by SAP

To support every deployment model, SAP delivers and maintains a set of productized integration components—the second pillar of the integration framework.

Moving from standard integrations to more custom integrations, as shown in Figure 1.12, productized components of integration include packaged integrations, standard integration templates, custom integrations from SAP's professional services teams, and APIs. Although packaged integrations cover common integrations needed by most customers and take very little time to implement (usually about 20% of what it would take to build and implement a custom integration), let's take a look at the other customer integrations as well.

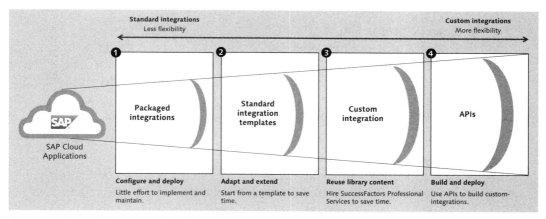

Figure 1.12 Productized Integration Components

1.4.1   Packaged Integrations

SAP has invested in identifying, developing, documenting, delivering, and maintaining a library of functionally rich integrations that most customers need to connect SAP cloud solutions to on-premise applications and third-party applications. Such an approach makes it faster, easier, and cheaper for customers to implement integrations.

Each packaged integration is designed by SAP software architects utilizing data gleaned by studying thousands of customer implementations and in collaboration with dozens of co-innovation customers. Like any other software product, packaged integrations are managed by SAP product managers and are subject to the same product design, testing, documentation, and release rigor as any other SAP product, with the goal of enabling success and reducing the risk of business interruption for customers. With packaged integrations, customers get access to SAP's deep domain knowledge and best practices for hybrid deployments of on-premise and cloud applications. Packaged integrations cover most foundational integrations required by SAP's applications in the cloud.

The packaged integrations from SAP and SuccessFactors fall into three main categories:

- **Data integration**
  Packaged data integration builds the data foundations required by SAP and SuccessFactors applications. The employee master data, organizational data (such as reporting relationships), and data used for workforce analytics are examples of data integration.

- **Process integration**
  Packaged process integration supports system integration for end-to-end business processes across the two systems. Such integration supports users executing business processes that span SAP and SuccessFactors systems when data needs to flow back and forth between the two systems (e.g., maintaining salary data in the SAP system, planning compensation in SuccessFactors, and then making payouts for employees in SAP).

- **User experience integration**
  User experience integration focuses on providing access to both SAP and SuccessFactors systems from one portal. Employees and managers using both SAP and SuccessFactors systems will be able to access them via the Employee Self-Service portal and the Manager Self-Service portal, respectively. They do not have to switch systems or log into multiple systems.

The SuccessFactors home page could also act as a unified portal for both cloud and on-premise systems from SAP, SuccessFactors, and other software providers.

Difference between Migration and Integration

Data migration is usually done once during the life of a software product. Integration happens on an ongoing basis at regular time intervals during the life of a software product.

1.4.2 Standard Integration Templates

Standard integration templates are built to connect SAP cloud products with third-party software vendors in multiple categories. For example, there is a standard integration template to connect Employee Central with third-party time management software vendors.

More information on standard integration templates can be found in Chapter 7.

1.4.3 Rapid-Deployment Solutions and Custom Integration Services

SAP recognizes that packaged integrations cannot realistically cover every integration scenario. To address this need, SAP provides best practices templates and content for most packaged integrations that customers and partners can use to implement the integrations in a predictable manner. SAP calls these best practices *rapid-deployment solutions*.

SAP consulting teams provide custom integration services to build integrations unique to customers. SAP consulting teams have deep expertise in connecting SAP cloud products to third-party solutions and maintain a library of reusable code that can be used to significantly reduce the risk and cost of implementation for customers.

1.4.4 APIs for Customer-Specific Integrations

SAP has learned that customers and partners strive to build unique integrations that differentiate themselves from their competitors. To help customers build integrations that are unique to their needs, SAP offers a rich set of open standards-based APIs that customers can leverage to build custom integrations. SAP customers and partners have already built thousands of custom integrations using cloud APIs to meet their unique needs.

1.4.5 Enterprise Application Integration Technologies

Over a period of years, even decades, organizations buy business software (such as supply chain management applications, enterprise resource planning systems, customer relationships management applications, business intelligence applications, payroll systems, and HR systems) from multiple software vendors. Normally, such software applications typically cannot communicate with one another directly in order to share data or business rules.

Such systems that need to be linked together may reside on different operating systems and may use different database solutions, programming languages, and date and time formats. In some cases, they could also be older systems that are no longer supported by the vendor who originally created them. Some of these systems could be single-tenant systems managed by the customers within their firewalls, and some could be cloud-based, multitenant systems delivered as a service.

All organizations using enterprise software today face this challenge every day, irrespective of the software vendors they buy from. To address such challenges, SAP has developed and delivered enterprise application integration technologies, sometimes called *integration middleware* technologies. The on-premise version of SAP's enterprise application integration technology is SAP PI. The cloud version of SAP's enterprise application integration technology is called SAP HANA Cloud Integration. Some LOB cloud applications from SAP bundle third-party cloud enterprise application integration software, such as Dell Boomi AtomSphere.

What's the takeaway here? Every packaged integration from SAP is built using one or more of the enterprise application integration technologies shown in Figure 1.13. In some cases, the packaged integrations are delivered using FTP- or SFTP-based technologies, in which a data file is generated and sent to the target system via a simple periodic, automated file upload.

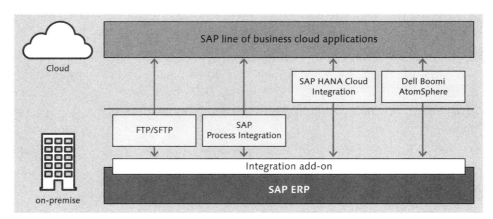

Figure 1.13 Integration Technologies Used by Cloud Products

Although using enterprise application integration technologies supported by the packaged integrations from SAP will save customers time and money, customers are free to use any enterprise application integration middleware technologies of their choice, either on-premise or in the cloud. Almost all SAP customers who integrate their applications use more than one enterprise application integration technology to suit their business needs. Some customers choose to implement the packaged integrations from SAP using a non-SAP enterprise application integration technology for business reasons.

1.5   Summary

The world of enterprise software is becoming consumerized, with the individual consumer as the primary driver behind the design of products and services. Most SAP customers are experiencing this shift in their organizations, particularly in LOBs such as sales, human resource management, procurement, travel management, and finance. Such LOBs are adopting cloud software, which is delivered to them on a subscription basis, rather than purchasing software that is licensed once and then having it installed on-premise.

SAP is responding to this shift by providing software as a subscription-based service, sometimes referred to as cloud software, for all LOBs. Although SAP sees cloud software as the direction for all LOBs, it also recognizes that not all customers are able or willing to move their software to the cloud right away due to business, cultural, or technology reasons. To help customers move to the cloud at a pace suitable to them, SAP has devised three main cloud deployment models. For the human resource LOB, these models are called Full Cloud HCM, Talent Hybrid, and Side-By-Side HCM. SAP supports every such cloud deployment model with productized integration components. SAP also provides the necessary integration technologies both on-premise and in the cloud to support these productized integrations.

In the next chapter, we will learn that the journey to the cloud is not the same for all customers. We will also look at the cloud journeys of two customers and understand why they chose their different paths to the cloud.

Choices made when moving to the cloud vary among organizations. Factors such as company culture, industry, government policy, business challenges, recent investments in technology, current landscapes, and in-house skills play an important role in shaping the journey to the cloud.

2 Journey to the Cloud

In the previous chapter, we looked at the various cloud deployment models available for SAP and SuccessFactors HCM suites. In this chapter, we will discuss when, where, and how the cloud deployment models for SuccessFactors and SAP are adopted by IT executives in customer organizations.

We will discuss the cloud migration of two customers and discover why they took their chosen routes to the cloud. This chapter will also serve as a guide for enterprise architects, HR solution architects, and cloud technology solution engineers on how to advise their HR line of business (LOB) colleagues on cloud adoption and the effective use of packaged integrations.

In the next section, we will look at some of the drivers and business requirements that arise when deciding to move to the cloud and the various scenarios that come into play when choosing these different deployment models.

2.1 Business Architecture Review

Cloud application decisions are mostly driven by LOB decision-makers rather than IT decision-makers. Cloud applications provided by SuccessFactors help customers to start with any one application in the suite and expand to the entire suite of applications. For example, a customer in the oil and gas industry facing talent retention problems can start with recruitment management and then adopt the SuccessFactors Performance and Goals Management modules. Another customer who wants to promote employee development and engagement may choose to start with SuccessFactors Learning and SAP Jam before adopting other modules in the SuccessFactors suite of applications. Customers can do this irrespective of the core HR application that they are currently using.

This flexibility in business architecture provides a unique opportunity for LOB decision-makers who want faster results and may have to show some successes before adopting the complete suite in the cloud. Choosing the first application to adopt and implement might be a challenge. This is where the business architecture review workshop plays an important role. This workshop is conducted by experienced HR professionals who uncover the business problems of an organization and map those problems with people management tools. This workshop can be conducted by SuccessFactors or another HCM consulting partner to uncover, understand, and document the business and associated talent management challenges faced by the company.

If a full-fledged business architecture workshop is not feasible, then the next best alternative is to ask the HR and human resources information technology (HRIT) leaders to list the top three business challenges or opportunities defined by the leadership of the company and the associated talent management challenges perceived or anticipated by the HR and HRIT teams.

In the next three sections, we will look at the different scenarios that may play out when an organization chooses a deployment model.

2.1.1 Scenario 1: Full Cloud HCM Deployment Model

Organizations looking to run all of their HCM applications in the cloud will choose the Full Cloud HCM deployment model.

Customers choosing this option will move their HCM to the cloud in a large-scale project, usually lasting up to a year. These are usually customers who are not happy with their current core HR systems and tend to have multiple core HR systems or very old core HR systems. These customers will take advantage of the packaged integrations associated with the Full Cloud HCM deployment model. Figure 2.1 illustrates a current scenario landscape, with the resulting future landscape of the Full Cloud HCM deployment model.

Customers who move talent management and core HR applications to the cloud have two choices when it comes to deployment of payroll applications: they can keep payroll on-premise or they can choose to move payroll to the cloud.

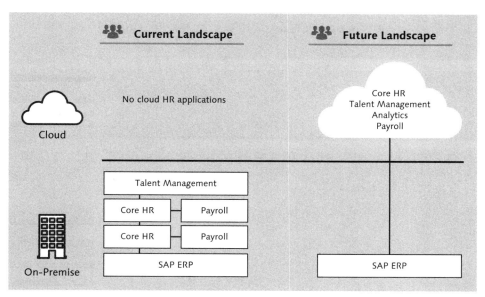

Figure 2.1 Candidates for the Full Cloud HCM Deployment Model

As stated previously, no two customers are the same. Therefore, variations in the commonplace deployment scenarios will arise. Two of these are discussed next.

Employee Central Payroll

Some customers may decide to move payroll applications to the cloud. In this case, they will choose Employee Central Payroll.

Employee Central Payroll is SAP's global payroll solution and is provided as a hosted option that comes integrated with Employee Central. For organizations that wish to manage payroll in-house via a cloud-based solution, Employee Central Payroll offers all the same features and benefits as SAP's on-premise payroll solution, but it is hosted and delivered by SAP. Employee Central Payroll is available as an option for Employee Central customers only.

Although the Employee Central Payroll software is provided as a service, the payroll administration has to be managed by the customer's personnel. Figure 2.2 displays the resulting landscape when moving payroll to the cloud.

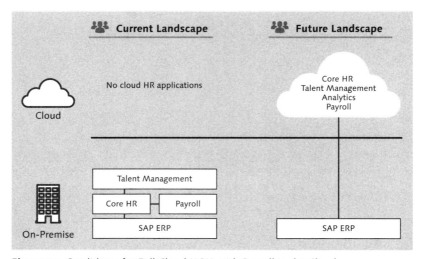

Figure 2.2 Candidates for Full Cloud HCM with Payroll in the Cloud

SAP Payroll

Some customers may decide to keep payroll applications on-premise. In many companies, payroll is managed by finance departments that run their applications on-premise behind firewalls. They tend to be more conservative in their approach to the cloud compared to sales or HCM departments. Figure 2.3 displays the resulting landscape of an on-premise payroll system.

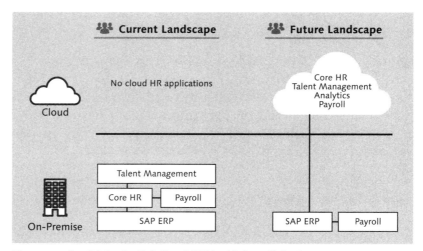

Figure 2.3 Candidates for Full Cloud HCM with Payroll On-Premise

2.1.2 Scenario 2: Talent Hybrid Deployment Model

An organization that wishes to run SAP ERP HCM for its core HR needs on-premise while using the SuccessFactors Talent Management suite for its talent management needs in the cloud will employ the Talent Hybrid deployment model.

Customers who move talent management applications to the cloud normally start with a talent management application that solves an immediate problem area. For example, for customers in the fast-growing oil and gas industry in Canada, attracting and recruiting new employees is a big problem area. Such customers start with the recruiting and onboarding applications first and expand to other applications.

In addition, certain other customers—from the mining industry, for example— may have grown by acquiring other, smaller companies. They may have a need to analyze data from multiple acquisitions. Such customers choose to start with the Workforce Analytics application and then chose to expand to other talent management applications.

Figure 2.4 displays the current and future landscapes of customers choosing the Talent Hybrid deployment model.

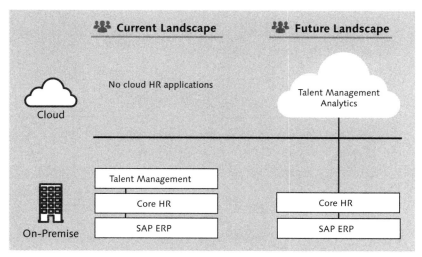

Figure 2.4 Candidates for Talent Hybrid Deployment Model

In many cases, such customers start the project to move core HR for all employees to the cloud one year after they start the project to move talent solutions to the cloud.

Comfort Level of Internal IT Team Members

Moving HCM applications to the cloud is a stressful project for HRIT team members. Moving a small but important application, usually from the talent management suite of SuccessFactors, is a good way to test the waters and see how such a move changes the responsibilities of internal HRIT team members. In almost all projects, there is a clear and important role for HRIT team members, even when HCM moves to the cloud.

2.1.3   Scenario 3: Side-By-Side HCM Deployment Model

The Side-By-Side HCM deployment model is employed when SAP ERP HCM on-premise serves as the system of record for employee and organizational information for some employees, but Employee Central in the cloud serves as a system of record for other employees, usually from a subsidiary company. In this deployment model, all employees use talent management solutions in the cloud.

Figure 2.5 illustrates the current and future landscapes for candidates choosing the Side-By-Side HCM deployment model.

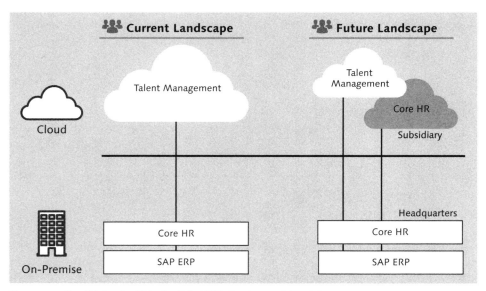

Figure 2.5 Candidates for Side-By-Side HCM Deployment Model

Customers in this scenario have chosen to move only a portion of their employees. They do this for one of two reasons: to test the waters in the cloud or to avoid a large-scale implementation for integrating a newly acquired subsidiary into their information technology landscapes. The success of these deployment models depends on the suitability of the model for the business needs of the customer. The business architecture workshop, usually offered by a HCM consulting expert, is a good exercise to uncover such business needs.

After this evaluation has been completed, the chosen deployment model drives the product review and purchasing decisions. This will be discussed in the next section.

2.2   Product Review

When should an SAP executive or an executive partner start the cloud migration conversation with a customer?

The right time to start conversations about the cloud deployment model, technology landscape, and associated packaged integrations is about six months before the product decision is made and the implementation is kicked off. If you are an SAP account executive or an account executive from a partner organization, then plan to start the conversation about moving to the cloud a year before the anticipated start date of the move.

A discussion about deployment models should not be afterthoughts once the product review is done and the purchasing decisions are made. Instead, the deployment model chosen should drive the product review and purchasing decisions. The solution architecture review workshop is a good forum for such conversations.

2.3   Solution Architecture Review

The solution architecture review is an important step in moving to the cloud. This workshop is valuable for customers who buy the service, account executives who sell the service, and implementation partners who implement the service. This is usually a two-hour workshop conducted before product purchasing decisions are made.

The solution architecture review workshop has multiple objectives. The sections that follow describe the various objectives of a solution architecture review.

2.3.1 Understanding the Current Landscape

The first objective of the solution architecture review workshop is to understand the current landscape of the customer. Almost all organizations will have this document in Microsoft Visio or Microsoft PowerPoint. The document author is usually someone from the IT team who is responsible for enterprise application integration. Normally, this diagram will be more complex than necessary for this workshop and will include items that may not be relevant for this workshop. It is advisable to get the diagram from the IT team member beforehand and to create a simplified version of the diagram for use during the workshop. In some cases, the solution architect conducting the workshop may have to oversimplify the diagram for discussion purposes.

2.3.2 Mapping the Future Landscape

The second objective is to map the future landscape along with any intermediate landscapes. In almost all cases, the eventual landscape for any customer will be the Full Cloud HCM deployment model, even if it takes years to reach that goal. Therefore, it is advisable to assume this goal and to mention it to the customer. The next step in this process is to identify the intermediate landscapes. For example, some customers might adopt the Talent Hybrid deployment model before moving to the Full Cloud HCM deployment model.

2.3.3 Identifying the Available Packaged Integrations

The third objective is to identify the packaged integrations available to support the chosen landscapes. Packaged integrations reduce the cost and time required to build integrations by about 80%. Therefore, identifying the available packaged integrations will help with building the project timeline and calculating the cost of integration. See Chapter 9 and Chapter 10 for further information on the packaged integrations for the Full Cloud HCM deployment model and the Talent Hybrid deployment model.

2.3.4 Identifying Standard Integration Templates

The fourth objective is to identify the standard templates available to support the chosen deployment models. The SAP product team provides standard templates to connect with third-party time, benefits, and payroll providers.

2.3.5   Identifying Reusable Integration Templates

The fifth objective is to identify available reusable templates. SAP professional services teams have performed hundreds of custom integrations. They maintain a library of these integrations and use them when appropriate. Therefore, it is good to verify with them whether there are reusable templates available to integrate with a particular benefits vendor, for example.

2.3.6   Identifying the Need for Custom Integrations

The sixth objective is to identify the custom integrations that might have to be built. It is important to note that 80% of all integrations built will be specific to a customer and hence have to be custom built. The cost associated with this is significant. It is important to identify these integration requirements and plan for them.

2.3.7   Determining the Need for Intermediate Integrations

The seventh objective is to identify the intermediate integrations that need to be built. Integrating two systems is similar to building a bridge across a river. While building a new bridge, traffic may have to be routed through to another path. Civil engineers usually build a temporary bridge to keep traffic moving while they build a new, permanent bridge. IT architects have to do the same when they move the on-premise systems to the cloud. They may have to build temporary integrations between their systems to keep them running while new systems are implemented. In some cases, these intermediate integrations could take a significant amount of time and money to build.

In the next section, we will look at a case study of how a customer can adopt these deployment models in response to his or her organization's business needs.

2.4   Case Study

In this section, we will look at the journey taken by a customer moving some, or all, of his or her HCM solutions to the cloud. During this process, we will see how the customer's solution architects guided him or her through the process by asking the right questions and helping him or her make the right decisions through appropriate input and insight.

Let's begin by looking at the parameters of our case study.

2.4.1 Case Study Parameters

Janet Lee is an information technology executive at a company in the fast-growing oil and gas industry.

Although her industry's growth has opened up many opportunities for the company and its employees, it has also created several talent management challenges. Her industry struggles to attract engineering graduates critical to the growing operations of the company. The chief people officer, Louisa, is keen on adopting all the innovative cloud and mobile applications.

Janet is under tremendous pressure from her senior leadership to cut information technology costs and introduce innovation at a faster pace. She also clearly sees the trend of HCM software moving to the cloud. Her human resource management colleagues demand software that can attract a new generation of employees to the organization and keep them engaged. However, Janet and her organization are not in a position to drop all of their on-premise software and move all HCM to the cloud.

Our solution architect in this situation is James, an SAP solution architect who has been working with Janet and Louisa to help them choose the right cloud applications that will address their business challenges.

Some of the business challenges faced by Janet and Louisa's company include the following:

- **Challenge of recruitment marketing**
  The human resource management team is struggling to attract people to the available opportunities and is not sure about the markets to source future employees from. Their recruitment marketing budget is spent without any insight into the return on such investment.

- **Onboarding experience is inconsistent**
  Even when they are able to attract employees, it is becoming hard to retain them in the critical first three months. New hires are either leaving the industry or leaving to work for competitors who are able to attract them by showcasing more millennial-friendly work environments and career prospects.

- **Timely workforce analytics are hard to gather**
  The HR team is struggling to keep track of headcount due to a lack of analytics tools integrated with the core HR system.

The HR team believes that the turnover rate in the company is the same as the turnover rate in the industry, but has no way of proving that to their colleagues and senior executives. The team did put some new employee incentives in place to address the problem of turnover, which they believe is helping to reduce turnover. However, once again, there is no reliable way of verifying that. The HR team also designed a new hire mentoring program as a strategy to retain new hires in the critical first 90-day period. That program has helped, but the team cannot scale that mentoring program to all new hires because it does not have insight into employees with mentoring skills available in the company.

Packaged Integrations Address Specific Business Challenges

Packaged integrations supporting SuccessFactors HCM suite integration with SAP are designed to address specific challenges faced by organizations. Solution architects can and should be able to identify and pick appropriate talent solutions and the associated packaged integrations that can address specific business challenges.

For example, the SuccessFactors recruiting integration with SAP ERP HCM brings information about new hires to the SAP ERP HCM system for timely employee administration and payroll purposes.

2.4.2 Stage 1: Understanding Business Challenges

A discussion about integration should always start with a look at business objectives and the current technology landscape of an organization. Therefore, James starts by asking Janet about her current technology landscape for human resource management software and how it is connected to SAP ERP and other business applications.

They then discuss the business challenges faced by the human resource management team. Janet points out that her human resource management colleagues have identified attracting and retaining talent as the top business challenge for the next five years. They are using homegrown performance management applications, multiple recruitment management, and recruitment marketing tools in the cloud. However, multiple tools in multiple countries and organizations have not solved the problem of talent acquisition.

James also determines that employee administration and payroll are not big problem areas for Janet's organization at this time. He then comes up with a high-level recommendation for the cloud deployment model that Janet can start with.

James draws a quick diagram of the various SuccessFactors cloud deployment models for Janet. The clear and simple diagrams help Janet grasp the cloud deployment models without reading elaborate documents and sitting through long presentations (see Figure 2.6).

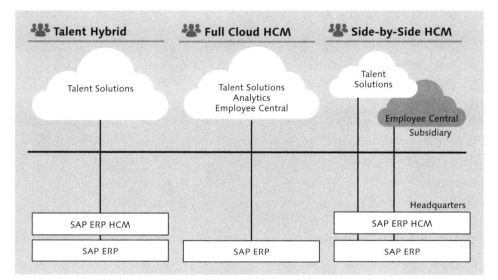

Figure 2.6 James Explains the Deployment Options to Janet

Make a Recommendation for the Deployment Model

The partner or SuccessFactors solution architect should have a hypothesis about the cloud deployment model before conducting a workshop for the larger HRIT and HR business teams. The solution architect should make a clear recommendation to the customer.

James recommends that Janet start with the Talent Hybrid deployment model. He points out that because most of the company's challenges are in the talent management area the ideal first step would be to move talent management applications to the cloud while retaining SAP ERP HCM for core HR applications (see Figure 2.7).

James then points out that there are several packaged integrations provided by SAP to support this deployment model and outlines the packaged integrations available (see Figure 2.8). He also talks about the time and money those packaged integrations can save for Janet.

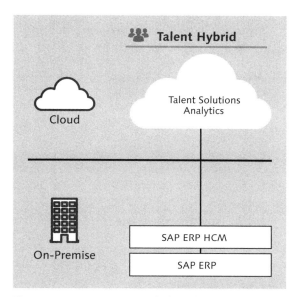

Figure 2.7 James Recommends the Talent Hybrid Deployment Model

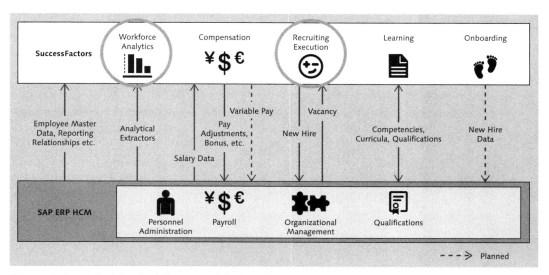

Figure 2.8 James Explains the Talent Hybrid Packaged Integrations to Janet

2.4.3   Stage 2: Executing the Talent Hybrid Deployment Model

Janet likes James' recommendations and starts with the Talent Hybrid deployment model. She understands the importance of bringing the leadership team, the human resource management team, and the information technology team together to the table in order to understand their concerns and address them early on.

The concerns of the leadership team involve return on investment, costs, and the risks involved. The CFO wants to make sure that the recent large investment in implementing the on-premise SAP ERP HCM system is not wasted. He also wants to make sure that the team understands the risks involved in moving employee data to the cloud and takes the appropriate measures to minimize business risk.

The HR business team that supports all managers and employees in the company are interested in understanding what the unified user experience looks like to managers and employees. They also want to understand if the SAP ERP HCM user interface will stay for core HR processes, because they have made many modifications to the user interface.

The SAP technical experts in the team want to understand if they have a role to play in the integration in a scenario in which many applications are moving to the cloud. The in-house SAP ERP HCM functional consultant is a bit concerned about all the new things he has to learn and is wondering if he can bring any value to his organization when many applications on which he is an expert are moving to the cloud.

Janet understands all the questions and concerns and proactively arranges a conversation with James, the SuccessFactors solution architect.

Career Transition to the Cloud

In many cases, the colleagues who are managing SAP ERP HCM in a customer's organization have been doing so for years, if not decades. It is important to point out to these colleagues that this migration to the cloud benefits their career as well. Their skills in the HCM area are valuable, transferrable skills. Embracing SuccessFactors solutions is a good way to make the career transition to the cloud.

Let's look at some of the concerns raised and how James addresses them.

Addressing the Concerns

James starts by explaining to David, the CFO, that the current investment in recent upgrades to SAP ERP HCM will not be lost. He points out to the CFO that the packaged integrations are designed to ensure that the SuccessFactors Talent Solutions modules integrate and function well with existing SAP ERP HCM solutions. He points out that the packaged integrations can be extended to work with the customizations made on the customer's SAP ERP HCM system.

He then turns to Steve, the SAP HCM functional expert, and explains that the packaged integrations map SuccessFactors fields to corresponding infotypes in SAP ERP HCM. He points out that Steve can modify or extend the field mapping to accommodate additional infotypes that Steve has created in the SAP ERP HCM system to suit the needs of his organization.

Alexis, the manager of HRIT, wonders about the source of truth for employee master data. James points out that in the Talent Hybrid deployment model SAP ERP HCM will be the source of truth for employee master data. Changes to the master data will be made in the SAP ERP HCM system. Therefore, Alexis does not need to maintain the data in multiple places, nor does he need to worry about data inconsistency.

Sharon, the HR analyst, supports managers and employees with their self-service questions for core HR processes. She wonders if the user experience of employees and managers will change when SuccessFactors Talent Solutions are added to SAP ERP HCM. James points out that employees and managers will access the same SAP ERP HCM screens from the portals they are currently using. There will be no change to the experience when it comes to core HR processes that are delivered by SAP ERP HCM. He points out that SuccessFactors does not become the user interface for core HR processes. However, employees and managers will access SuccessFactors screens for all talent management applications. He talks about the SuccessFactors theming tool that enables administrators to modify the look and feel of all SuccessFactors screens to match the look and feel of their corporate portal and business applications.

Sharon asks James if they can they can continue to use the Employee Self-Service (ESS) and Manager Self-Service (MSS) portals. James responds that employees and managers can continue to use the ESS and MSS portals to launch SAP ERP HCM and SuccessFactors applications.

Employee Self-Service and Manager Self-Service

Thousands of SAP customers use ESS and MSS portals to provide self-service capabilities for HR and other business applications. It is important to point out that they do not have to discard those portals when they move to the Talent Hybrid deployment model.

Ethan, the SAP ERP administrator, asks James if he has a role to play in the Talent Hybrid deployment model. James says that the SAP ERP administrator does have a role to play in implementing the integrations, given that all packaged integrations rely on an SAP ERP add-on that needs to be installed as a support package by an SAP ERP administrator. These supports packages are made available to SAP ERP administrators from the SAP Service Marketplace, the web site from which all SAP support packages are made available to customers.

This conversation answers most of the questions from Janet's colleagues and gives them an idea of their roles and the road ahead.

The Integration Workshop

Once the initial questions and concerns are addressed, Janet arranges a two hour integration workshop in which the SuccessFactors solution architects and Janet's HRIT colleagues discuss the current and future technology landscapes for HR applications.

Documenting the Current Landscape Is Very Valuable

Most information technology organizations have a diagram showing the integrations between systems in their landscape. Usually, this diagram attempts to document all aspects of the landscape for multiple LOBs and attempts to capture the network and security architecture. The goal of the solution architect should be to simplify the diagram and depict the integrations between HR and business systems without making the diagram too complex to understand.

After studying the current technology landscape, James draws a simplified version of the current landscape on a whiteboard and confirms that his understanding of the landscape is accurate. The HRIT team members point out that there are some systems not documented in the landscape diagram and suggest that James add those systems to the diagram.

The collaborative effort to document and depict the current landscape brings a common understanding of the current state and lays the foundation for a conversation about the future desired landscape.

Talent Hybrid Deployment Model Implementation

Janet starts the implementation of the Talent Hybrid solution. With the strong support of her CFO, the chief human resource officer, and the HRIT team, she significantly increases the probability of an on-time, on-budget implementation. The integration workshop conducted by SuccessFactors solution architects and Janet's HRIT teams creates a common understanding of the current and future technology landscapes and provides a strong foundation of knowledge to plan the implementation.

In about six months, Janet's team completes the successful implementation of all necessary modules in the SuccessFactors Talent Solutions suite.

> **Talent Solutions Suite Implementation**
>
> Even when customers buy the entire talent solutions suite of applications from Success-Factors, they may not implement all the solutions in the first phase. They usually choose to implement two to three applications in the first phase and expand later. The architecture of the SuccessFactors HCM suite enables customers to do so.

2.4.4   Stage 3: Acquiring a Smaller Competitor

After the SuccessFactors Talent Management solutions implementation was complete, Janet's company acquired another smaller, innovative competitor. The CEO decides to run the new acquisition as a separate legal entity for business reasons. Even though the new acquisition is a separate business, executives and managers need to have a unified view of all employees for talent management, workforce planning, and workforce analytics purposes.

This is a practical situation. When a company acquires another company, in some cases the parent company runs the acquired company as a subsidiary for a while. Over a period of months or even years, they may integrate the acquired company into the parent company. However, for workforce planning, workforce analytics, and talent management purposes, human resource management professionals need to look at the entire workforce in one place within a few weeks after the acquisition is complete.

In this situation, the employees from the new company had to be combined with the employees from the parent company for talent management needs but kept separate for employee administration needs, compensation planning purposes, and payroll purposes.

In Janet's case, employees of the acquired company were already using multiple software solutions in the cloud and were not very inclined towards using an on-premise core HR system. Janet's analysis also found out that implementing a separate SAP ERP HCM system for the acquired company would be a multiyear, multimillion dollar implementation. She reaches out to James for his advice on the best way to handle this challenge. James points out that this might be a good opportunity for Janet to test the waters for core HR in the cloud.

Employee Management

Forcing employees of a smaller, innovative company to switch to systems they consider old and cumbersome to use is not a good way to retain talent. This challenge could become an opportunity for the parent company. Rather than force the employees of the acquired company to use older systems, the parent company could implement cloud solutions for the new employees and learn from the experience.

Side-By-Side HCM Deployment Model

In the Side-By-Side HCM deployment model, organizations run core HR in the cloud for some employees, usually from a subsidiary, and core HR on-premise for other employees, usually from the parent organization. In this model, all talent management for all employees is performed via cloud applications.

James suggests that Janet should use Employee Central for core HR for employees of the acquired company. This will give Janet an opportunity to address all her business needs while keeping overall project costs lower. This approach also gives Janet an opportunity to do a relatively small project for core HR in the cloud before moving core HR for all employees to the cloud. James points out that this deployment model is called the Side-By-Side HCM deployment model and that there are several packaged integrations planned to support this deployment model (see Figure 2.9).

James points out that in this deployment model Janet will use SuccessFactors in the cloud for talent management processes and workforce analytics. She will run Employee Central in the cloud to deliver core HR processes for employees of the newly acquired company and will run SAP ERP HCM to deliver core HR processes for employees of the parent company. She will have a unified view of the employees for workforce planning and workforce analytics purposes while maintaining two different core HR solutions for two sets of employees.

Side-By-Side HCM Deployment Model

The Side-By-Side HCM deployment model helps customers with specific business needs, such an integrating a newly acquired company or employees from a geographical region that was not previously part of the HR landscape. However, the Side-By-Side HCM deployment model requires more time, money, and skills to implement. When possible, customers should consider moving to the Full Cloud HCM model directly.

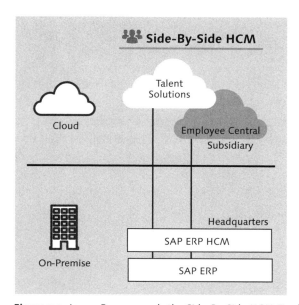

Figure 2.9 James Recommends the Side-By-Side HCM Deployment Model

Janet understands that this is a good solution to the current business challenges she faces and decides to implement the solution. It takes about a year to implement Employee Central for the newly acquired company. Because the acquired company had very few employees, Janet and her team were able to manage the risks and understand what it takes to move core HR to the cloud without undertaking a high-cost, high-risk project.

Data Migration

Migration of data from an on-premise core HR system to a cloud-based core HR system is a critical and yet often overlooked part of a core HR project. Fortunately for Janet, SAP provides a data cleansing and migration service that she utilizes to cleanse data before it is loaded into Employee Central, the cloud-based core HR system from SuccessFactors. Cleansing the data using proven best practices and migrating the data using tried and tested tools lays a good foundation for the move of core HR to the cloud for Janet. The core HR in the cloud project was completed successfully in a year.

> **Data Migration from SAP ERP HCM to Employee Central**
>
> The enterprise information management experts at SAP have designed the data migration package to move data from one or more SAP ERP HCM systems to Employee Central. The details of this data migration service are explained later in Chapter 11.

Employees of the newly acquired company were glad that they were provided with a new and innovative core HR and talent management system in the cloud. The project improved employee engagement and helped retain key talent from the acquired company. The project became a success story not just for the information technology team but also for the mergers and acquisitions team and the company executives.

2.4.5   Stage 4: Moving to Full Cloud HCM

Completing the Side-By-Side HCM deployment model gives Janet and her team the confidence and the clear metrics required to plan the movement of core HR to the cloud for all employees (see Figure 2.10).

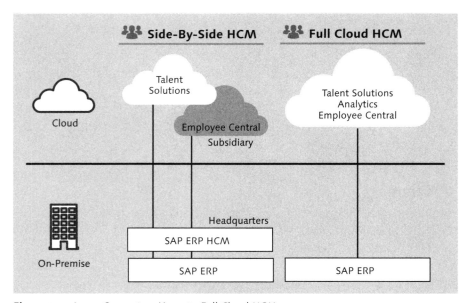

Figure 2.10 James Suggests a Move to Full Cloud HCM

The success of this project becomes instrumental in securing the budget approval for moving core HR for all employees to the cloud.

James explains the packaged integrations that support the Full Cloud HCM deployment model. He points out that the packaged integrations fall into three broad categories: employee data, organizational management data, and cost center data (see Figure 2.11).

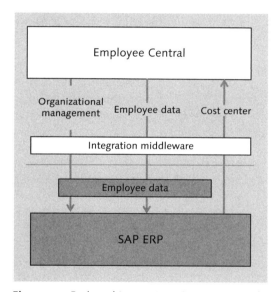

Figure 2.11 Packaged Integrations Connecting Employee Central to SAP ERP

As previously stated, James indicates that these packaged integrations may save the company time and money in the transition. This helps with the budgetary concerns for the project, allowing the company to move forward successfully.

2.5 Summary

The journey to the cloud may not be the same for all customers. Based on factors such as company culture, government policy, recent technology investment, and business challenges, different customers may choose different paths to the cloud.

SuccessFactors solution architects need to study the customer's business challenges, recent investments in information technology, and current human resource management technology landscape and then suggest an appropriate deployment model to start with. Every direction should assume that sooner or later customers may move to the cloud, even if they have no plans to do so today. It is the belief of industry experts that competitive pressures and relentless innovation in the cloud will make the move to the cloud for HCM inevitable for most organizations in the world.

In the next chapter, we will look at the Full Cloud HCM deployment model and discuss the packaged integrations and other tools available to connect HCM applications in the cloud with on-premise SAP ERP applications and third-party cloud applications.

PART II

SuccessFactors Deployment Models

New providers of HR software in the cloud and cloud offerings from traditional HR software providers dominate the market. Sooner rather than later, moving all HCM to the cloud will become a competitive necessity for almost all organizations. In this chapter, we will discuss the deployment model that will allow the customer to do just that.

3 Full Cloud HCM Deployment Model

SAP ERP customers are simplifying their HCM technology landscape by moving all the people management applications to the cloud using the SuccessFactors HCM suite. They are doing this to simplify their current technology landscape, reduce total cost of ownership, and adopt rapid innovation that is happening in the cloud. The deployment model that enables customers to do this is called the Full Cloud HCM deployment model (see Figure 3.1).

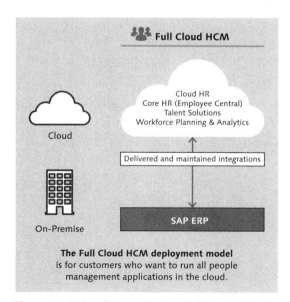

Figure 3.1 SAP and SuccessFactors Full Cloud HCM Deployment Model

In this chapter, we will discuss the packaged integrations that connect HCM applications in the cloud with on-premise SAP ERP applications, third-party payroll, time applications, and benefits applications. We will also discuss the user experience integration that makes this deployment model unique. To wrap the chapter up, we will look at two case studies that display the use of these packaged integrations at work.

Let's begin by looking at the type of audience this deployment model would attract.

3.1 Target Audience

The Full Cloud HCM deployment is for customers who want to run all people management applications in the cloud while connecting them with on-premise business applications and third-party cloud business applications.

In the Full Cloud HCM deployment model, customers run Employee Central, SuccessFactors Talent Solutions, and Workforce Planning and Analytics in the cloud and integrate them with on-premise SAP ERP applications. With this deployment model, you can move all your HCM applications to the cloud while providing employee information to all critical applications that run your business.

Normally, customers who are struggling with employee administration prefer to move to this deployment model. Such customers fall into two main categories.

The first category of customers might be running a very old core HR system to manage their employees. These customers may be struggling with employee administration due to a lack of modern features, lack of support from the vendor who provided the software, and excessive customization that is difficult to maintain.

The second category of customers may be running multiple core HR systems. Some of these customers run about ten different core HR systems to administer their employees. Such distribution of data and administration creates problems that can be addressed by moving to the Full Cloud HCM deployment model and customizing it via its various packaged integrations.

3.2   Technology Options

Before we begin looking at the Full Cloud HCM integrations themselves, it is important to understand the technology options that are available to facilitate them.

Dell Boomi AtomSphere is the enterprise application integration technology for the Full Cloud HCM deployment model. Dell Boomi AtomSphere acts as a single hub in the cloud for all integrations originating or ending in Employee Central, thus making the management and administration of these packaged custom integrations efficient and cost-effective (see Figure 3.2).

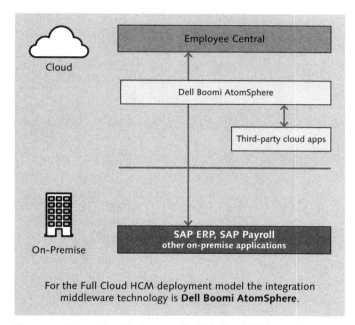

Figure 3.2 Integration Technology for Full Cloud HCM Deployment Model

The cost of licensing a cloud-based integration technology could run into millions of dollars per year for a large organization. The license cost usually increases with the number of integrations built on that integration technology. To address this problem and free customers from the cost burden, SAP bundles the license for the Dell Boomi AtomSphere enterprise application integration technology with the Employee Central license. Customers can use it to connect Employee Central with not only on-premise SAP ERP but also with any third-party cloud or on-premise application. Several Employee Central customers have taken advantage of this offer and have built hundreds of custom integrations over and above the packaged integrations provided by SAP.

The Dell Boomi AtomSphere integration technology is hosted by SAP in the same data centers as SuccessFactors and is secured the same way SuccessFactors applications are secured.

Via these technology options, the SuccessFactors HCM suite integrates with SAP ERP and third-party applications using multiple packaged integrations. These packaged data integrations are available for three areas:

▸ Integrating Employee Central with SAP ERP

▸ Integrating Employee Central with on-premise SAP Payroll and cloud-based Employee Central Payroll

▸ Connecting Employee Central with third-party cloud applications in the areas of payroll, time management, and benefits administration

The following sections look at these integrations in further detail.

3.3   Packaged Integrations for Employee Central and SAP ERP

There are multiple packaged integrations to connect Employee Central with SAP ERP. Most of the current packaged integrations fall into the following categories (see Figure 3.3):

▸ Employee Central employee data integration (see Section 3.3.1)

▸ Employee Central organizational management data integration (see Section 3.3.2)

▸ SAP ERP Financials cost center data integration with Employee Central (see Section 3.3.3)

Let's begin with the integration of employee data between Employee Central and SAP ERP.

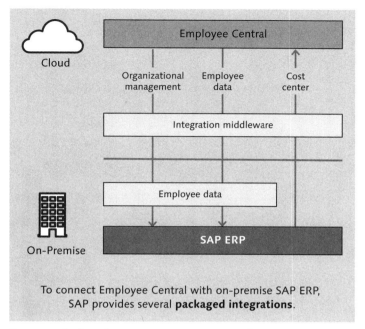

To connect Employee Central with on-premise SAP ERP, SAP provides several **packaged integrations**.

Figure 3.3 Packaged Integrations to Connect Employee Central with SAP ERP

3.3.1 SAP ERP Employee Data Integration

The integration of employee data between SAP ERP and Employee Central replicates basic employee information from Employee Central to SAP ERP. This integration enables the execution of business processes in the connected SAP ERP systems that customers use to run their businesses.

Additional Information

Implementation and integration information is provided in a document titled *Employee Central and SAP ERP: Employee Master Data Replication*. This document can be downloaded from *http://help.sap.com/cloud4hr*.

When customers move all people management applications to the cloud, the cloud becomes the source of truth for employee data. However, systems that run the business of a customer require such employee data. Employee data, such as name and gender, are extracted from Employee Central and transferred to SAP

ERP, to make it available for the systems that run a customer's business. The process flow of this packaged integration is depicted in Figure 3.4.

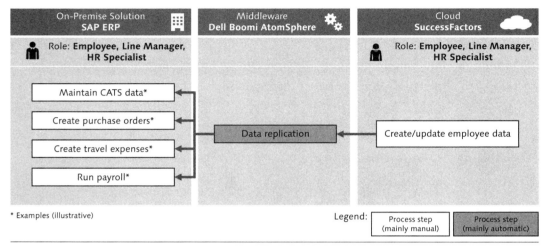

Figure 3.4 Employee Central Data Integration with SAP ERP

SAP provides predefined integration content for this scenario via the SuccessFactors Integration 1210 Add-on for SAP ERP. The integration of employee data from Employee Central to SAP ERP is performed via a web service periodically. The transfer of data can be done in near real time, if required. The amount of (historical) data to be transferred can be controlled. The integration supports loading of initial data as well as delta integration that replicates only changed data. Time dependency is also considered.

The built-in extensibility options allow data integration to be enhanced to include customer-specific attributes required at the job level or personal information level without the need to change code; it can be realized simply through configuration.

Prerequisites

The following prerequisites must be met:

▸ This Integration 1210 Add-On for SAP ERP 6.0 or higher. The current version of the SuccessFactors HCM suite is required.

▸ The Employee Central Integration Add-On for SAP ERP 6.0 is required.

▸ Dell Boomi AtomSphere enterprise application integration technology is required.

3.3.2   SAP ERP Organizational Management Data Integration

In this integration, organizational data and an employee's relationship with such organizational data is replicated from Employee Central to SAP ERP.

In the Full Cloud HCM deployment model, Employee Central is the system of records for the enterprise structure, which includes departments, business units, and divisions. Information about this enterprise structure and an employee's relationship to the elements in that structure are required by systems that run the business. For example, many business systems will require information about an employee's cost center association.

Employee Central is the system of record for HR-related organizational data and organizational assignments, and the integration replicates these objects to SAP ERP. This includes the following data integration points:

▶ **Data integration for enterprise structure information**
This integration is realized through several web services that replicate enterprise structure data such as business units, divisions, and departments. In addition, the scenario ensures the synchronization of the respective employee assignments to these objects from Employee Central to SAP ERP organizational management. The enterprise structure information in Employee Central is interpreted as organizational unit information in SAP ERP.

▶ **Data integration for reporting lines**
The reporting line information shows the relationship of an employee and the responsible manager. This replication takes place via a web service. The job information in Employee Central is mapped to the organizational management in SAP ERP. In SAP ERP's organizational management, the information is interpreted as a relationship between the employee's and the line manager's positions. If a position does not exist in SAP ERP, then the system automatically generates technical positions in SAP ERP's organizational management. Employee Central position management is not required to make use of this integration.

▶ **Data integration for employee cost center assignments**
SAP provides a web service for the data replication of employees and their cost center assignments from Employee Central to SAP ERP's organizational management. In SAP ERP's organizational management, the information is interpreted as a relationship between the employee's position and the cost center.

SAP recommends that you first implement the cost center data integration scenario before using the scenario for organizational data.

The process flow of the packaged integration to connect organizational data from Employee Central to SAP ERP is depicted in Figure 3.5.

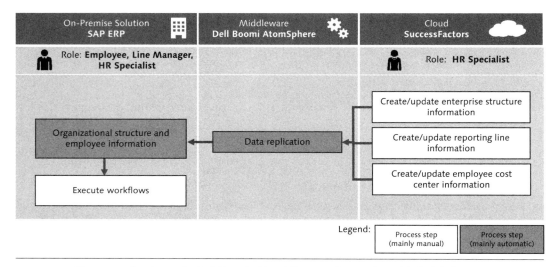

Figure 3.5 Employee Central Organizational Structure Integration with SAP ERP

Prerequisites

The following prerequisites must be met:

▸ SAP ERP EHP 6.0 or higher

▸ Employee Central HCM suite latest version

▸ Employee Central Integration 1210 Add-on for SAP ERP

▸ Dell Boomi AtomSphere (delivered with the Employee Central solution)

3.3.3 SAP ERP Financials to Employee Central Cost Center Data Integration

This packaged integration sends cost center data from SAP ERP Financials to Employee Central. Employee Central requires information about available cost centers to be able to assign employees to appropriate cost centers. Cost centers maintained in SAP ERP Financials are integrated with Employee Central.

The cost center integration enables cost distribution maintenance in Employee Central, which could be leveraged for payroll purposes. The integration supports the loading of initial data as well as delta integration that replicates only changed data. Time dependency is also considered. The built-in extensibility options allow data integration to be enhanced through the implementation of a Business Add-In (BAdI), to take into account customer-specific requirements.

The process flow of the packaged integration to connect cost center data from SAP ERP to Employee Central is depicted in Figure 3.6.

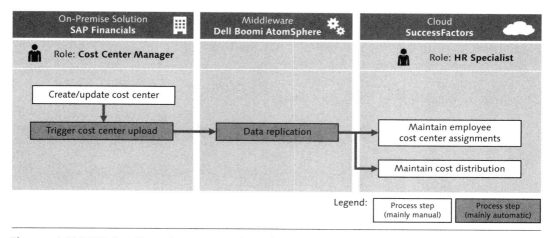

Figure 3.6 SAP ERP Cost Center Integration with Employee Central

Prerequisites

The following prerequisites must be met:

- SAP ERP EHP 6.0 or higher
- Employee Central (HCM suite) latest version
- Employee Central Integration 1210 Add-on for SAP ERP
- Dell Boomi AtomSphere (delivered with the Employee Central solution)

Now that we've looked at the different packaged integrations between Employee Central and SAP ERP, let's turn our attention to the use of packaged integrations in connecting to on-premise SAP Payroll and cloud-based Employee Central Payroll.

3.4   Packaged Integrations for Employee Central and Payroll

This section discusses the Employee Central integration with both on-premise SAP Payroll (see Section 3.4.1) and Employee Central Payroll (see Section 3.4.2). Integration of the employee administration system with the payroll systems is one of the most common and foundational integrations in HCM.

3.4.1   SAP Payroll Integration

There are over 7,000 installations of on-premise SAP Payroll. Even when customers move all HCM applications to the cloud, they may continue to use SAP Payroll on-premise. To enable such customers to reduce cost and business risk, SAP provides a packaged integration to connect Employee Central with on-premise SAP Payroll.

Payroll Ownership

In some organizations, payroll is managed by the finance department rather than the HR department. Such organizations tend to keep payroll on-premise, even when all other people management applications are moved to the cloud.

In this scenario, customers run SAP Payroll on-premise and integrate it with Employee Central in the cloud. The payroll system receives cost center data from SAP ERP Financials and employee master data from Employee Central. You can also integrate the UI of SAP Payroll into the UI of Employee Central for the selected country payroll version.

This integration comprises predefined content and documentation based on best practices for integrating both SAP Payroll systems with Employee Central. The packaged integration to connect Employee Central to on-premise SAP Payroll uses Dell Boomi AtomSphere as the integration middleware.

In this packaged integration, multiple types of data are sent between the systems. The following types of data will be sent:

▸ **Cost center**
   Cost centers are replicated from SAP ERP Financials to SAP Payroll. The integration is based on intermediate documents (IDocs). The integration is automated.

IDocs

IDoc, short for *intermediate document*, is an SAP document format for business transaction data transfers.

► **Employee data**

Basic employee data is transferred from Employee Central to the payroll system. The integration utilizes a web service and then transfers the data periodically. The amount of (historical) data transferred can be specified. The integration supports the loading of initial data as well as the replication of changed data. Extensibility options allow data integration to be enhanced to include customer-specific requirements.

The process flow of the packaged integration to connect payroll-relevant data from Employee Central to on-premise SAP Payroll is depicted in Figure 3.7.

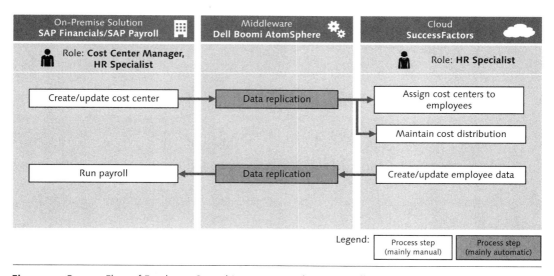

Figure 3.7 Process Flow of Employee Central Integration with SAP Payroll On-Premise

SAP provides predefined integration content for this scenario with the Employee Central solution and the Employee Central Integration 1210 Add-on for SAP ERP.

HR Renewal

HR Renewal is an add-on for SAP ERP enhancement packages that contains new capabilities for some HR areas. The HR Renewal shipments contain functional and user experience improvements and aims to increase the productivity of HR professionals and the overall HR efficiency. HR Renewal documentation is available from *https:// help.sap.com/hr_renewal*. SAP recommends that you always implement the latest feature pack of HR Renewal, because SAP continuously delivers new country versions and updates to support integration with Employee Central.

▸ **User interface**
The user interface integration enables pay statement look-up for employees in Employee Central. The user interface integration also enables HR administrators to maintain payroll data in SAP ERP HCM without leaving the Employee Central user interface.

Prerequisites

The following prerequisites must be met:
▸ SAP ERP EHP 6.0 or higher
▸ Employee Central (HCM suite) latest version
▸ Employee Central Integration 1210 Add-on for SAP ERP
▸ Dell Boomi AtomSphere (delivered with Employee Central)
▸ Optional: HR Renewal 1.0

3.4.2 Employee Central Payroll Integration

In this scenario, customers run Employee Central Payroll in the cloud and integrate it with Employee Central in the cloud. The payroll system receives cost center data from SAP ERP Financials and employee master data from Employee Central.

The process flow of the packaged integration to connect Employee Central with Employee Central Payroll is depicted in Figure 3.8. In this packaged integration, multiple types of data are sent between the systems. Integration of cost center data, employee data, and the user interface is done exactly the same way as when integrating Employee Central with on-premise SAP Payroll (see Section 3.4.1).

Prerequisites

The following prerequisites must be met:

- ► SAP ERP EHP 6.0 or higher
- ► Employee Central (HCM suite) latest version
- ► Employee Central Integration 1210 Add-on for SAP ERP 6.0
- ► Dell Boomi AtomSphere (delivered with Employee Central)

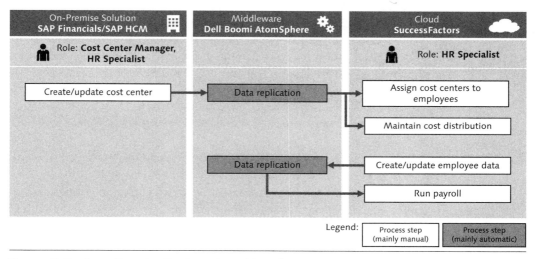

Figure 3.8 Employee Central to Employee Central Payroll Integration

Having looked at the packaged integrations for Employee Central and payroll, let's now look at the different packaged integrations available between Employee Central and third-party applications.

3.5 Packaged Integrations for Employee Central and Third-Party Applications

Employee Central makes use of multiple third-party cloud applications in the areas of time management, benefits management, and payroll (see Figure 3.9).

SAP provides packaged integrations to connect Employee Central with time management applications, such as those from Kronos and WorkForce Software. Employee Central is integrated with benefits providers, such as Aon Hewitt, Benefitfocus, and Thomons Online Benefits, via packaged integrations. For payroll, Employee Central is integrated with ADP and NGA.

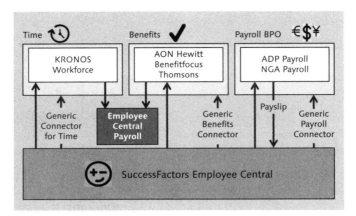

Figure 3.9 Packaged Integrations for Employee Central to Third-Party Cloud Applications

Kronos, Workforce Software, Aon Hewitt, Benefitfocus, Thomons Online Benefits, ADP, and NGA are service providers who partner with SAP. However, customers can also use providers who are not SAP partners for their time management, benefits management, and payroll needs. To cater to the needs of such customers, SAP provides standard integration templates for time management integration, benefits management integration, and payroll integration (see Chapter 8).

The following sections look at these integrations in closer detail.

3.5.1   Kronos Time Management Integration

Kronos Time Management is a time and attendance management solution. Kronos Time Management provides employers with a cloud-based solution to manage time- and labor-related information. Kronos Time Management receives information from employee administration (core HR) systems, such as Employee Central, and uses that information for time and attendance management purposes. Kronos Time Management then sends periodic updates to employee administration systems and payroll systems that require time data for legal reporting and payroll purposes.

Employee data is extracted from Employee Central and sent to Kronos Time Management periodically. The integration middleware technology maps the employee data to a format provided by Kronos Time Management. It then sends the employee data to Kronos Time Management, which accepts the data and populates necessary systems.

Employees enter time- and attendance-related data in Kronos Time Management, which then makes such data available. This data is fetched by the integration middleware technology and provided to Employee Central Payroll, which uses the information for payroll purposes (see Figure 3.10).

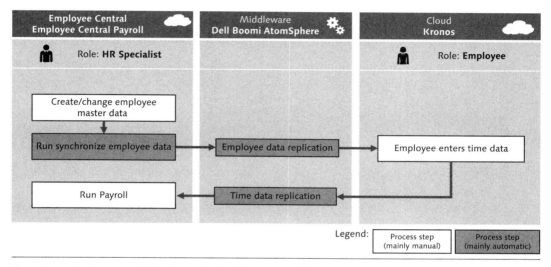

Figure 3.10 Employee Central to Kronos Time Management Integration

Employees using Employee Central can navigate to Kronos Time Management to enter time- and attendance-related information without having to provide a separate user name and password. SAP implementation guides provide information about configuring such access as Single Sign-On (SSO).

Prerequisites

The following prerequisites must be met:

▶ A license to use Kronos Time Management

▶ Dell Boomi AtomSphere integration middleware, licensed along with Employee Central

3.5.2 WorkForce Software Integration

WorkForce Software EmpCenter is a third-party, cloud-based time management provider. WorkForce Software EmpCenter can be integrated with Employee Central as well as with Employee Central Payroll. WorkForce Software EmpCenter receives information from employee administration (core HR) systems such as Employee Central and uses that information for time and attendance management purposes. It then sends periodic updates to employee administration systems and payroll systems that require time data for legal reporting and payroll purposes.

Employee data is extracted from Employee Central and sent to WorkForce Software EmpCenter periodically. The integration middleware technology maps the employee data to a format provided by WorkForce Software EmpCenter. It then sends the employee data to WorkForce Software EmpCenter, which accepts the data and populates the necessary systems (see Figure 3.11).

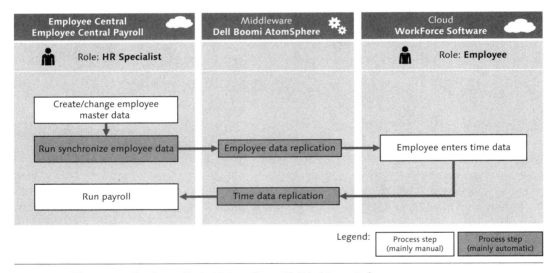

Figure 3.11 Employee Central Integration with WorkForce Software

Employees using Employee Central can then navigate to WorkForce Software EmpCenter to enter time- and attendance-related information without having to provide a separate user name and password. SAP implementation guides provide information about configuring such access as SSO.

Prerequisites

The following prerequisites must be met:

▶ A license to use WorkForce Software EmpCenter

▶ Dell Boomi Atomsphere integration middleware, licensed along with Employee Central

3.5.3   Aon Hewitt Integration

Aon Hewitt provides employers, consumers, and insurance carriers with cloud-based technology to shop, enroll, manage, and exchange benefits information. Employees can choose their benefit plans in an online portal and such information is then sent to payroll systems and other providers (see Figure 3.12).

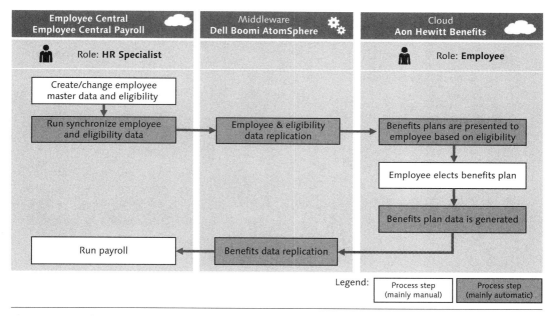

Figure 3.12 Employee Central Integration with Aon Hewitt

Employees using Employee Central can navigate to Aon Hewitt to elect benefit plans without having to provide a separate user name and password. SAP implementation guides provide information about configuring such access as SSO.

Prerequisites
The following prerequisites must be met:
▸ Aon Hewitt benefits license
▸ Dell Boomi AtomSphere integration middleware, licensed along with Employee Central, is required.

3.5.4 Benefitfocus Integration

Benefitfocus provides employers, consumers, and insurance carriers with cloud-based technology to shop, enroll, manage, and exchange benefits information. Employees can choose their benefit plans in an online portal, and such information is then sent to payroll systems and other providers (see Figure 3.13).

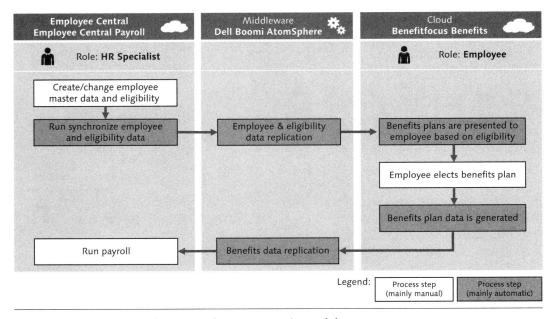

Figure 3.13 Employee Central Integration with Benefitfocus

Employee data and benefits eligibility data is sent from Employee Central to Benefitfocus. Based on the eligibility information and personal data of an employee, benefits plans are offered to an employee by the benefits provider. Employees then elect a benefit plan by logging into the provider's application. Benefitfocus will then process the benefit plans based on the election information of an employee and send the pay deduction information to the payroll system to be accounted in calculations of remuneration.

Employees using Employee Central can then navigate to Benefitfocus to elect benefit plans without having to provide a separate user name and password. SAP implementation guides provide information about configuring such access as SSO.

The following prerequisites must be met:
- ▶ Benefitfocus license
- ▶ Dell Boomi AtomSphere integration middleware, licensed along with Employee Central

3.5.5 Thomons Online Benefits Integration

Thomons Online Benefits provides employers, consumers, and insurance carriers with cloud-based technology to shop, enroll, manage, and exchange benefits information. Employees can choose their benefit plans in an online portal, and such information is then sent to payroll systems and other providers.

Employee data and benefits eligibility data is sent from Employee Central to Thomons Online Benefits. Based on the eligibility information and personal data of an employee, benefits plans are offered to an employee by the benefits provider. Employees then elect a benefit plan by logging into the provider's application. Thomons Online Benefits will then process the benefit plans based on the election information of an employee and send the pay deduction information to the payroll system to be accounted in calculations of remuneration (see Figure 3.14).

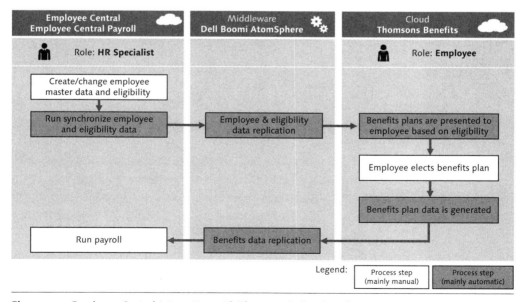

Figure 3.14 Employee Central Integration with Thomons Online Benefits

Employees using Employee Central can navigate to Thomons Online Benefits to elect benefit plans without having to provide a separate user name and password. SAP implementation guides provide information about configuring such access as SSO.

Prerequisites

The following prerequisites must be met:

▶ Thomons Online Benefits license

▶ Dell Boomi AtomSphere integration middleware, licensed along with Employee Central

3.5.6 ADP Integration

Many Employee Central customers plan to leverage ADP GlobalView for their global payroll. They want to eliminate duplicate keying and the risk of employee master data being out of sync. The packaged integration between Employee Central and ADP GlobalView provides data replication services from Employee Central to ADP GlobalView (see Figure 3.15).

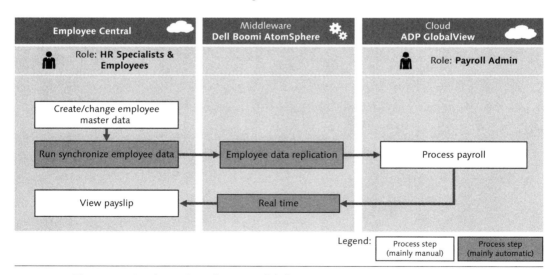

Figure 3.15 Employee Central to ADP GlobalView Integration

How does it work? Data for new hires, rehires, or master data changes in Employee Central is extracted via the SuccessFactors API and replicated to ADP GlobalView.

Employee master data and organization assignment information, including personal information, addresses, work schedules, basic pay, bank information, recurring payments, and nonrecurring payments, is sent from Employee Central to ADP GlobalView.

Prerequisites

The following prerequisites must be met:

▶ ADP GlobalView license

▶ Dell Boomi AtomSphere integration middleware, licensed along with Employee Central

3.5.7 NGA Integration

Many Employee Central customers plan to leverage NGA euHReka for their global payroll. They want to eliminate duplicate keying and the risk of employee master data being out of sync. The packaged integration between Employee Central and NGA euHReka provides data replication services from Employee Central to NGA euHReka.

Data for new hires, rehires, or master data changes in Employee Central is extracted via the SuccessFactors API and replicated to NGA euHReka. Employee master data and organization assignment information, including personal information, addresses, work schedules, basic pay, bank information, recurring payments, and non-recurring payments, is sent from Employee Central to NGA euHReka (see Figure 3.16).

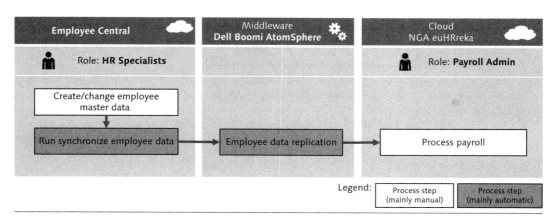

Figure 3.16 Employee Central to NGA euHReka Integration

Prerequisites
The following prerequisites must be met: ▸ NGA euHReka license   ▸ Dell Boomi AtomSphere integration middleware, licensed along with Employee Central

Now that we've looked at the packaged integrations for the Full Cloud HCM deployment model, let's turn our attention to another important integration: user experience.

3.6 User Experience Integration

In addition to data integration, user integration is provided in three areas:

▸ Administrators and employees can sign into ADP GlobalView without providing additional user names and passwords. This can be enabled by configuring the systems for SSO.

▸ HR administrators can update infotype data specific to payroll in ADP GlobalView seamlessly from within the Employee Central user interface.

▸ Employees can view their pay slips stored in ADP GlobalView pay slip information from within Employee Central.

All systems are in the cloud and already use the same user interface. Therefore, the integration teams have added limited value in this area for this deployment model.

So far, we have seen the available packaged integrations that support the Full Cloud HCM deployment model. Many customers choose to implement these integrations on their own or with the help of a partner. Some customers like to have a clear idea of the implementation timeline and costs associated with their projects for budget and planning purposes.

To help such customers, SAP has put together content and services. Together, they are called rapid-deployment solution packages, and there are rapid-deployment solution packages that support the implementation of the packaged solutions for the Full Cloud HCM deployment model. Let's take a look at them next.

3.7 Rapid-Deployment Solutions

Many SAP customers are wary of the uncertainty associated with the implementation of hybrid solutions. To address these concerns, SAP provides an integrated delivery approach designed to fix scope, contain costs, and streamline schedules for implementation of these packaged integrations. SAP calls this delivery approach rapid-deployment solutions. Rapid-deployment solutions enable customers to quickly and affordably deploy SAP solutions for specific business requirements at a low service-to-software ratio.

There is a rapid-deployment solution available for integrating employee data, organizational management data, and cost center data. Employee data and organizational management data is sent from Employee Central to SAP ERP. Cost center data is sent from SAP ERP to Employee Central.

Rapid-deployment solutions are available to cover the following packaged integrations (see Figure 3.17):

▶ Transfer of basic employee data from Employee Central to SAP ERP. This allows you to extract personnel administration and organization management data flexibly and to perform full and delta uploads.

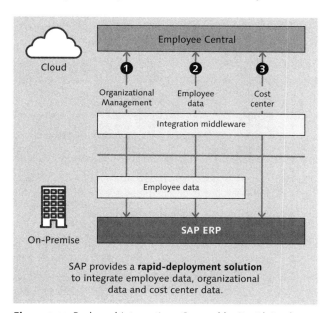

Figure 3.17 Packaged Integrations Covered by Rapid-Deployment Solutions

► Transfer of organizational management data from Employee Central to SAP ERP.

► Transfer of cost center data from SAP ERP to Employee Central.

3.7.1 Employee Data Migration to Employee Central

A rapid-deployment solution to migrate data to Employee Central from a customer's current core HR system covers the migration of foundational data, employee data, time off data, and position data from current core HR systems to Employee Central.

This data migration solution enables customers to do several things. First, it helps customers analyze existing data from virtually any source system. Second, it enables customers to cleanse the data and transform the data to the required format. Third, the data is validated against specific customer business rules and loaded to Employee Central. Finally, the data is reconsolidated against the source data and a report of all migration activities is generated. Data migration is discussed in more detail in Chapter 11.

3.7.2 Delivering Rapid-Deployment Solutions via Partners

Partners who want to deliver these rapid-deployment solutions to customers get free access to all the content from the SAP Service Marketplace. Content for all rapid-deployment solutions from SAP can be accessed from *http://service.sap.com/rds*.

> **Helpful Documentation for Customers**
>
> The following are some helpful resources for customer integration questions:
> ► Visit *http://help.sap.com/cloud4hr* for help documentation.
> ► Visit *http://service.sap.com/public/hybrid* for a good place to start to download administration guides (customer login required).

3.8 Case Studies

As discussed in Section 3.1, the Full Cloud HCM often applies to two types of customers: those who are running an old core HR system and need to invest in a modern core HR system and those who are running multiple on-premise core HR systems and need to consolidate them into a modern, unified, cost-effective core HR system. In the case studies that follow, we will look at one customer from each type and see how that customer made the move to the Full Cloud HCM deployment model and how the integration technologies and tools from SAP helped the customer on the way.

3.8.1 Case Study 1

In this case study, we will look at a company in the financial services industry that uses SAP to run its business. The customer has invested heavily in software that manages its business for decades. However, its HCM software investment has fallen behind for many reasons. We will discuss how the customer addressed this situation by adopting the Full Cloud HCM deployment model. Let's start with a look at the company and the business problems it faces.

Client Scenario

In the following case study, we will look at the company AlphaBeta Co., a financial services company of about 5,000 employees that provides banking, financial, and wealth management services to individuals and businesses.

Currently, AlphaBeta Co. uses SAP ERP to run its company and SAP for Banking to run its banking business. The company uses other SAP Business Suite solutions, such as SAP Customer Relationship Management (CRM), to manage its customer information and SAP Supplier Relationship Management (SRM). It also uses a 20-year-old HCM solution provided on-premise. The company customized it heavily during the initial deployment and modified it to suit AlphaBeta Co.'s needs over the years. The vendor that provided that solution does not support the software any longer, and therefore the system is hard to maintain, costly to upgrade, and no longer meets AlphaBeta Co.'s business needs.

The company's current HCM system is connected to 15 different business systems. These include several business applications, such as SAP Financials, SAP CRM, and SAP SRM, as well as multiple payroll and benefits providers. Most of this integration is done via file-based data transfer on a daily basis. In the case of some payroll providers, information is uploaded via data entry to service center teams, which receive this information via Microsoft Excel files.

In addition, AlphaBeta Co.'s recruiting system is in the cloud, and employee information from its current core HR system is sent via FTP every week. Figure 3.18 shows a simplified version of the company's current landscape.

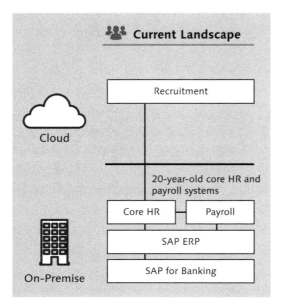

Figure 3.18 Current Landscape of AlphaBeta Co., Running an Old Core HR System

Given that AlphaBeta Co. is in the financial services industry, finding and retaining top-quality talent is very important to their bottom line. However, the company currently struggles to attract young, talented people, due in large part to their technological shortcomings described previously. The result is that the company is seen as a traditional organization that doesn't embrace new technologies and processes used by younger workers today. AlphaBeta Co. uses a cloud-based recruiting system to attract and recruit employees, but the processes to bring these new employees into the company and motivate and retain them are paper-based and rely too heavily on managers who themselves are not trained in the use and adoption of new technologies and processes. Young interns and entry-level employees, put off by the paper-based processes and old technology used by the company, are being driven to rivals with newer technology and modern business processes.

To remedy its shortcomings, AlphaBeta Co. has chosen to move its entire HCM solution to the cloud via the Full Cloud HCM deployment model.

Process Steps

Having chosen the Full Cloud HCM deployment model, the company is moving its HCM solution to the cloud, including all talent management solutions from

SuccessFactors, such as Performance and Goals Management, Succession Planning, Learning Compensation, SAP Jam, and SuccessFactors Analytics. For employee administration, the company adopted Employee Central and Employee Central Payroll.

Even though the company licenses SuccessFactors Recruitment Management and SuccessFactors Onboarding, it has chosen to continue to use its current third-party recruiting system with which everyone is familiar. To integrate the third-party recruiting system with Employee Central, AlphaBeta Co. created a custom integration using the APIs provided by Employee Central. Using Dell Boomi AtomSphere as the enterprise application integration technology, the company will send vacancy data to its third-party recruiting system and bring back new hire data to Employee Central.

The following list describes the individual steps taken to successfully implement these choices:

1. The company starts by migrating employee data from its legacy system to Employee Central. It then uses the rapid-deployment solution provided by SAP to handle the migration process. For detailed information about employee data migration to Employee Central, see Chapter 11.

2. The company moves its payroll data to Employee Central Payroll to get payroll up and running.

3. The company builds the necessary integration of Employee Central with SAP ERP and third-party payroll, time management, and benefits providers. For detailed implementation information about the packaged integrations between Employee Central and SAP ERP, see Chapter 10.

4. Once Employee Central is up and running along with payroll, the company implements the SuccessFactors Performance and Goals Management, Succession Planning, and Compensation systems.

5. Next is the implementation of SuccessFactors Learning for formal learning and SAP Jam for informal learning and collaboration. The company implemented the packaged integrations available to connect SuccessFactors learning to Adobe Connect for virtual learning and PayPal Payflow Pro for payment processing.

6. The company builds a custom integration to connect its on-premise Active Directory with the cloud-based HR system, using the middleware Dell Boomi AtomSphere. For this integration, the company relies on the integration template

provided by the SAP professional services team and utilizes these services to take advantage of the team's expertise in this area.

7. The company integrates its third-party recruiting system with Employee Central to bring new hire data in near real time to Employee Central.

The entire implementation process of the Employee Central module takes Alpha-Beta Co. a year, plus another six months for the implementation of the Success-Factors Talent Solutions modules.

Using Packaged Integrations and Integration Technology

Even after HCM is completely moved to the cloud, employee information is still required by the company's business applications, which it plans to run on-premise behind a firewall for years to come. This means that the company has to provide employee information and organizational information from Employee Central to SAP ERP and SAP for Banking. It will also have to provide cost center information from SAP Financials to Employee Central. The company will continue to use its current payroll and benefits providers. To do so, it has to build packaged integrations for every one of those payroll and benefits providers. In addition, it will have to build several custom integrations to other homegrown systems that manage several business processes unique to the company.

Dell Boomi AtomSphere, the enterprise applications integration technology, is made available for all Employee Central customers as part of their Employee Central license. Customers can connect Employee Central with any number of SAP or third-party applications for no additional license fee. Taking advantage of this license offering, this customer integrates Employee Central with an existing third-party recruiting application. This saves a significant amount of money in license costs over the life of the software.

AlphaBeta Co. will also use the rapid-deployment solutions for data migration and integration. Using rapid-deployment solutions provided by SAP enables the company to define the budget and timeline clearly and without any budget overruns and enables the company to access SAP experts who have experience implementing multiple data migration and integration projects.

Figure 3.19 shows AlphaBeta Co.'s landscape after the implementation.

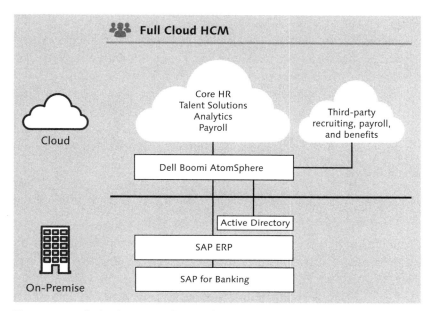

Figure 3.19 Full Cloud HCM Landscape after Adopting a Rapid-Deployment Solution

Let's now look at another type of customer with different business needs.

3.8.2 Case Study 2

In this case study, we will look at a company in the retail industry that uses SAP to run its business. The company has invested heavily in software that manages its business and its people. The company grew its business by building new stores and by acquiring other, similar businesses. Because HCM is critical for the retail industry, even the acquired companies have their own implementations of on-premise SAP ERP HCM for managing their employees. Because every newly acquired company has customized SAP ERP HCM to suit its culture and its own needs, the company decided to continue using a separate instance of SAP ERP HCM for every acquired business. However, over the years the management of multiple instances of SAP ERP HCM has become costly and time-consuming. We will now discuss how this customer addressed this situation by adopting the Full Cloud HCM deployment model. Let's start with a look at the company and its business problems.

Client Scenario

In the following case study, we will look at the company IndustryShopper Inc., a retail center selling industrial supplies that has about 30,000 employees. The company distributes various types of supplies, such as material handling, safety and security, cleaning and maintenance, pumps and plumbing, electrical, lighting, ventilation, tools, metal working, fluid power, heating and air-conditioning products, motors, and power transmissions. The company has physical stores that require different numbers of employees and temporary workers depending upon demand and runs online and mobile stores that require the company to attract and retain very talented employees. There is a separate division that analyses the data provided by all stores and derives insight from that data, which then drives hiring decisions in these stores.

Currently, IndustryShopper Inc. uses SAP ERP to run its company and SAP for Retail Solution to run its retail business. It uses other SAP Business Suite solutions, such as SAP CRM to manage its customer information and SAP SRM. It also uses nine SAP ERP HCM systems on-premise and a data store to combine the employee information from these nine systems. In addition, talent management needs are handled via SuccessFactors Talent Managment.

The company's current nine HCM systems are connected to a data store via custom integrations. There are nine different integration points, and they all run at different times depending on the availability of the source system. The combined employee data is integrated with SuccessFactors Talent Management in the cloud via a file-based integration. This data is uploaded every night. Figure 3.20 shows a simplified version of the customer's HR technology landscape.

The company's current business problem involves the multiple core HR systems and instances that have become costly and time-consuming. As noted previously, IndustryShopper Inc. currently runs nine different core HR systems, all powered by SAP ERP HCM. Employee data is distributed across these nine different systems. When employees transfer between divisions or stores, their data is manually entered in the target system and is sometimes duplicated across systems. This causes errors in payroll and delays in transferring employees across stores and divisions that need their skills. It has also led to employee dissatisfaction and a higher than normal employee attrition rate. While planning store locations and office space for employees, the facilities management team struggles to get an accurate headcount of employees and their current work locations. To solve this problem, the company custom built a very expensive data store that combines data from all nine systems for reporting and analytics purposes. This data store addressed the problem of reporting, but the system's user interface was command-line driven and required highly specialized experts. To access the data, HR professionals, managers, and employees were required to rely on these experts. This caused huge delays in decision-making and in many cases forced mangers to make decisions that were not supported by reliable data.

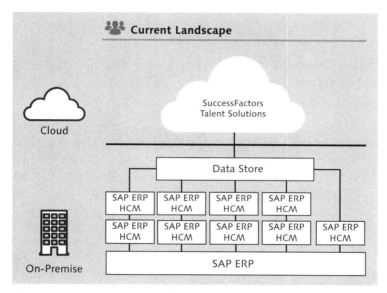

Figure 3.20 Current Landscape of IndustryShopper Inc., Running Multiple Core HR Systems

To resolve these issues, the company has chosen to use the Full Cloud HCM deployment model to eliminate the need for nine different SAP ERP HCM systems.

Process Steps

The company currently runs some talent management solutions from SuccessFactors in the cloud. With the Full Cloud HCM deployment model, it has chosen to use all talent solutions in the cloud. This includes all talent management solutions from SuccessFactors, such as Performance and Goals Management, Succession Planning, Learning Compensation, SAP Jam, and SuccessFactors Analytics. For employee administration, the company adopted Employee Central and Employee Central Payroll. In this way, the company hopes to eliminate the need for nine different SAP ERP HCM systems on-premise and the expensive data store it had custom built.

The following list describes the individual steps taken to successfully implement these choices:

1. The company starts by migrating employee data from the employee data store to Employee Central. The company uses the rapid-deployment solution provided by SAP to handle the migration process. This is followed by the configuration of Employee Central to suit its needs.

2. The company discontinues all the current integrations of the SuccessFactors Talent Solutions module with SAP ERP HCM.

3. The company moves payroll data to Employee Central Payroll to get payroll up and running.

4. The company implements the packaged integrations connecting Employee Central to SAP ERP, using Dell Boomi AtomSphere enterprise application integration technology.

5. The company builds the necessary integration of Employee Central with third-party payroll, time management, and benefits providers, using Dell Boomi AtomSphere as the integration technology.

6. The company uses Dell Boomi AtomSphere enterprise application integration technology to build the necessary custom integrations of Employee Central to third-party cloud systems.

Using Packaged Integrations, Integration Technology, and Services

Just as in the previous case study, this company must also develop packaged integrations, because it has to provide employee information and organizational information from Employee Central to SAP ERP and SAP for Banking, provide cost center information from SAP Financials to Employee Central, and continue to use current payroll and benefits providers. In addition, IndustryShopper Inc. will have to build several custom integrations to other homegrown systems that manage several business processes unique to the company.

Like the customer in the previous case study, this customer also took advantage of the Dell Boomi AtomSphere license offering to integrate Employee Central with multiple third-party applications. This saved a significant amount of money in license costs over the life of the software. The company also used the rapid-deployment solutions provided by SAP for migrating data in a predictable manner.

Figure 3.21 shows the company's landscape after having simplified it by moving core HR to the cloud.

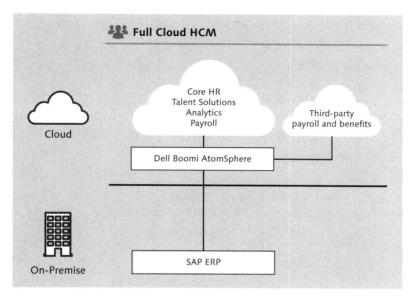

Figure 3.21 Full Cloud HCM Landscape after Implementation

3.9 Summary

The Full Cloud HCM deployment model is for customers who want to run all people management applications in the cloud. In this deployment model, customers run Employee Central, SuccessFactors Talent Solutions, and SuccessFactors Workforce Planning and Analytics in the cloud and integrate them with on-premise SAP ERP applications. SAP and SuccessFactors provide packaged integrations to enable easier and better integration between SAP ERP and the SuccessFactors HCM suite.

In this chapter, we discussed how customers who are having trouble maintaining and analyzing their employee data are good candidates to adopt the Full Cloud HCM deployment model. There are multiple packaged integrations to connect Employee Central with SAP ERP that are customized to address these different customer needs.

In addition, we explored how Employee Central makes use of multiple third-party cloud applications in the areas of time management, benefits management, and payroll. SAP provides packaged integrations for these applications. To connect with other time, benefits, and payroll providers, SAP provides standard integration templates.

We examined two case studies. First, we saw how a customer using a 20-year-old core HR system implemented the Full Cloud HCM deployment model to create a modern HCM suite in the cloud and how the packaged integrations and integration technologies from SAP helped. Then, we looked at a customer struggling with multiple core HR systems on-premise; the company used the Full Cloud HCM deployment model to cut costs while improving efficiency and user experience.

In the next chapter, we will take a look the Talent Hybrid deployment model, which is aimed at customers who are happy with their employee administration tools but need help with talent management and analytics.

In this chapter, you'll learn about the Talent Hybrid deployment model, in which the talent modules are in the cloud and the core HRMS is on-premise. We'll also discuss the packaged integrations that are available with this deployment model.

4   Talent Hybrid Deployment Model

The Talent Hybrid deployment model is a combination of talent modules (Performance and Goals Management, Learning Management, Compensation Management/Variable Pay, Succession Management, Recruiting Management) that are in the cloud, while the core HCM systems continue to be on-premise. When you have the talent solutions in the cloud (either all of the talent modules or some of them), data still needs to be passed between the on-premise SAP ERP HCM applications and the cloud-based talent applications.

After the acquisition of SuccessFactors by SAP, SAP and SuccessFactors became invested in developing packaged integrations between the different talent modules of SuccessFactors and SAP ERP HCM. These packaged integrations facilitate the exchange of data between the on-premise HCM applications and the cloud-based talent applications.

Data Transfers

When data is transferred from SAP ERP HCM to SuccessFactors HCM, the data in the fields identified for integration are transferred to SuccessFactors HCM. Unless you have defined that the data residing in SuccessFactors HCM is the system of record, do not make any changes to the transferred data in SuccessFactors. Any changes made to those fields might be overwritten during the next data transfer for the same integration scenario.

In this chapter, we will discuss what the Talent Hybrid deployment model is, the different integration techniques that can be implemented with it, and an overview of the available packaged integrations. To conclude, we will look at two detailed case studies to see how an integration strategy is developed and how customers can extract the employee data for transfer to their cloud-based Success-Factors Performance and Goals Management application.

Let's begin by looking at who the core audience is for this deployment model.

4.1 Target Audience

The Talent Hybrid deployment model helps customers maintain their investments in the core SAP ERP HCM applications and move their talent processes to SuccessFactors talent applications.

Often, customers are already introduced to the concept of Software as a Service and might have one or more cloud-based applications. These applications will need be integrated with the on-premise SAP ERP HCM solution. In some cases, customers might have already integrated with the on-premise SAP ERP HCM solution by developing their own integration processes, possibly through flat file transfers or developing custom web services.

In the next section, we will look at the options available for customers looking to take advantage of the integration options for the Talent Hybrid deployment model.

4.2 Technology Options

Before we begin looking at the integrations themselves, it is important to understand the technology options that are available to facilitate them.

As shown in Figure 4.1, the customer can perform the integrations by using the flat file method (option 1) or via the middleware integration method. The middleware used for the integration can be SAP PI (or any third-party middleware tool; option 2) or SAP HANA Cloud Integration (option 3).

The customer and the implementation team should discuss and develop an integration strategy. The strategy should leverage the option best suited for the customer.

In the Talent Hybrid deployment model (see Figure 4.2), the cloud application will require the employee details to be made available inside the application. Hence, the employee details (employees' PERNR, their line manager, the employee

HR Manager, etc.) will be transferred from the on-premise HCM application to the cloud application. The cloud application will then transfer the processed data (for example, if SuccessFactors Performance Management and Goal Management application is deployed, the employees' final appraisal scores) to the on-premise SAP ERP HCM application for further processing (if required).

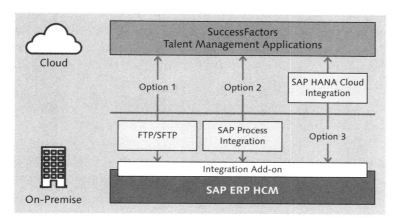

Figure 4.1 Talent Hybrid Integration Technology Options

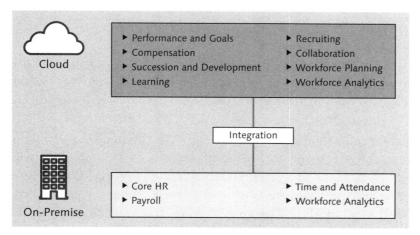

Figure 4.2 Talent Hybrid Deployment Model

Now that you know the options available for deploying these integrations, let's begin looking at the packaged integrations.

4.3   Packaged Integrations for the Talent Hybrid Deployment Model

The following packaged integrations are available from SAP and SuccessFactors for the Talent Hybrid deployment model:

▶ **Employee master data integration**
In this integration, the employee and organizational data are transferred from SAP ERP HCM to SuccessFactors HCM to support the talent modules and the associated talent-related processes (see Section 4.3.1).

▶ **Workforce Analytics/Analytical extractors integration**
For this integration, all the data required to support workforce planning and analytics is transferred from SAP ERP HCM to SuccessFactors Workforce Analytics (see Section 4.3.2).

▶ **Compensation process/Pay-for-performance process integration**
During this integration, compensation data can be transferred from SAP ERP HCM to SuccessFactors HCM to support compensation planning in SuccessFactors. The completed planning data can be transferred from SuccessFactors HCM to SAP ERP HCM, and this data can be included in the payroll run (see Section 4.3.3).

▶ **Recruiting process integration**
In this integration, the position-related data (positions for which requisitions are created) is transferred from SAP ERP HCM to SuccessFactors HCM to enable the creation and maintenance of requisitions in SuccessFactors. Applications can be transferred from SuccessFactors HCM to SAP ERP HCM to enable the HR administrator to perform hiring actions in SAP ERP HCM (see Section 4.3.4).

▶ **SuccessFactors Competencies integration with SAP ERP HCM qualifications**
In this integration, the competency catalog in SuccessFactors is integrated with the qualifications catalog in SAP ERP HCM, and the employee competencies maintained in SuccessFactors are integrated with the employee qualifications maintained in SAP ERP HCM. The qualifications catalog residing in SAP ERP HCM and the assigned employee qualifications are uploaded manually into SuccessFactors. After the initial upload, the employee competencies are maintained in SuccessFactors and are replicated back to SAP ERP HCM through the middleware (see Section 4.3.5).

▶ **SuccessFactors Learning curricula integration with SAP ERP HCM qualifications**

In this integration, the learning curricula is integrated with the SAP ERP HCM qualifications catalog, and each employee's course completion status is integrated with the employee's profile in SAP ERP HCM.

The curriculum catalog is transferred from SuccessFactors LMS to SAP ERP HCM. The curriculum type and curriculum in SuccessFactors LMS is mapped to the qualification group and qualification in SAP ERP HCM. The curriculum status of the employee is transferred to SAP ERP HCM as the employee qualification (the employee's qualification will be displayed in SAP ERP HCM as the employee profile). The employee's curriculum status will have a rating scale of 0 (incomplete) or 1 (complete) (see Section 4.3.6).

▶ **Variable Pay integration**

You can use this integration to transfer employee history records from SAP ERP HCM to SuccessFactors Variable Pay to determine an employee's bonus eligibility and calculate the employee's variable pay. The calculated variable pay is transferred back to SAP ERP HCM for payouts (see Section 4.3.7).

SAP ERP Version
SAP ERP 6.0 SPS 15 is the lowest version on which the Integration Add-on can be implemented.
Refer to SAP Note 1708986 (Installation of SFIHCM01600) to understand the prerequisites, installation process, and the follow-up for installing the Integration Add-on.

In a SuccessFactors project, it is a common occurrence that you might end up using more than one of these integration scenarios. Table 4.1 explains the sequence in which the integration scenarios need to be implemented, as well as any dependencies that exists.

Sequence	Integration Scenario	Dependencies
1	Employee master data	No dependencies.
2	Compensation	Employee master data must exist in SuccessFactors HCM to support compensation planning.

Table 4.1 Sequence and Dependencies in the Integration Scenario Implementation

Sequence	Integration Scenario	Dependencies
3	Recruiting	Employee master data must exist for internal candidates in SuccessFactors HCM.
4	SuccessFactors Competencies integration with SAP ERP HCM qualifications	Employee master data must exist in SuccessFactors to support employee competency integration with SAP ERP HCM qualifications.
5	SuccessFactors Learning curricula integration with SAP ERP HCM qualifications	Employee master data must exist in SuccessFactors HCM.
6	Variable Pay	Employee master data must exist in SuccessFactors HCM.
Not Applicable	Evaluation data	No dependencies exist between evaluation data and other integration scenarios.

Table 4.1 Sequence and Dependencies in the Integration Scenario Implementation (Cont.)

No dependencies exist between recruiting and compensation data integration scenarios. You can implement either of the two scenarios (compensation or recruiting data) in any order you wish.

The following sections look at these different packaged integrations in greater detail.

4.3.1 Employee Master Data Integration

The employee master data packaged integration enables the transfer of employee and organizational data using SAP Process Integration (SAP PI) or SAP HANA Cloud Integration (SAP HCI) as the middleware bus (see Section 4.2).

This integration fully supports the transfer of all employee and organizational data, as well the changed data records (delta) after the initial transfer. It also allows you to transfer future employees from SAP ERP HCM to SuccessFactors HCM, enabling future employee access to groups such as SAP Jam and participation in onboarding activities. When future employees are transferred to SuccessFactors HCM, their status is set to ACTIVE; therefore, it is important that future-dated employees do not have access to SuccessFactors HCM, do not participate in any business processes, and are not visible to their future managers.

You can define an indicator in the CUSTOMER-SPECIFIC field in the flat file that is generated from SAP ERP HCM to SuccessFactors HCM to identify somebody as a future-dated employee. You can use the report RH_SFI_PREHIRE_EMPL_DATA (Sync Employee Data with SuccessFactors in Prehire Period) for extraction of data related to future-dated employees. The extracted data can be transferred to SuccessFactors HCM using the middleware.

To determine an employee's manager in SAP ERP HCM, choose one of the following options:

▶ The relationship B012 (Is Managed by) between the employee's organizational unit and the manager's position

▶ The relationship A002 (Reports to) between the employee's position and the manager's position

The data extracted will be used in the MANAGER field in SuccessFactors HCM.

As shown in Figure 4.3, you can use the packaged integration to do an initial transfer of basic personnel administration and organizational data using SAP PI or SAP HANA Cloud Integration as the middleware bus.

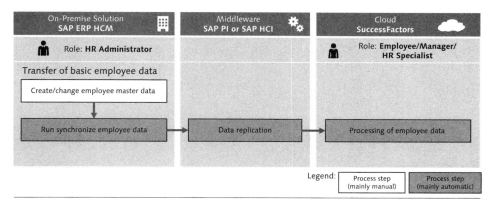

Figure 4.3 Employee Master Data Integration

The data is also transferred due to a business-process-driven event, such as new hire, rehire, termination (voluntary or involuntary), transfer, or any changes that are made in the employee data.

We will discuss more about employee master data integration and the configuration settings that need to be made in an SAP ERP HCM system in Chapter 10, Section 10.2.

Prerequisites

The following prerequisites should be met for the employee master data integration to function:

► Employee profiles are set up and maintained in SuccessFactors

► Employees are hired and their master data exists in the SAP ERP HCM system with at least the following infotypes:

   ► 0000—Actions

   ► 0001—Organizational Assignment

   ► 0002—Personal Data

   ► 0105 (Subtype: Email)—Communication

4.3.2 Workforce Analytics/Analytic Extractors Integration

The analytical extractors integration supports the extraction of reporting data required for SuccessFactors Workforce Analytics from SAP ERP HCM using SAP PI or SAP HANA Cloud Integration as the middleware integration bus. This integration also supports the preparation of the extracted data for upload to Success-Factors HCM.

As shown in Figure 4.4, the extractors enable you to extract the required reporting data from SAP ERP HCM into a flat file and use SAP PI to store these files in an SFTP server. The file mappings are done on the middleware, and the data files are pushed into an SFTP server. Using a prescheduled job, SuccessFactors HCM will read this file and upload into the tables.

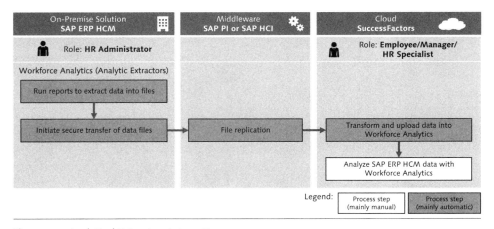

Figure 4.4 Analytical Extractors Integration

Absence reports and aging workforce analytics containing birth date, location, and position are just a few examples of the data that can be extracted.

Table 4.2 provides a listing of SAP ERP HCM transaction codes and reports that are used for data extraction.

Report Name	Transaction Code	Expected Results
Data Provisioning—Organizational Objects/SuccessFactors Analytics (RH_SFI_HRP1000)	HRSFI_AR_HRP1000	Extract Infotype 1000 (DB Table Organizational Objects)
Data Provisioning—Relationships/SuccessFactors Analytics (RH_SFI_HRP1001)	HRSFI_AR_HRP1001	Extract Infotype 1001 (DB Table Object Relationships)
Data Provisioning—Personnel Actions/SuccessFactors Analytics (RH_SFI_PA0000)	HRSFI_AR_PA0000	Extract HR Master Record: Infotype 0000 (Actions)
Data Provisioning—Org. Assignments/SuccessFactors Analytics (RH_SFI_PA0001)	HRSFI_AR_PA0001	Extract HR Master Record: Infotype 0001 (Org. Assignment)
Data Provisioning—Personal Data/SuccessFactors Analytics (RH_SFI_PA0002)	HRSFI_AR_PA0002	Extract HR Master Record: Infotype 0002 (Personal Data)
Data Provisioning—Planned Working Time/SuccessFactors Analytics (RH_SFI_PA0007)	HRSFI_AR_PA0007	Extract HR Master Record: Infotype 0007 (Planned Working Time)
Data Provisioning—Basic Pay/SuccessFactors Analytics (RH_SFI_PA0008)	HRSFI_AR_PA0008	Extract HR Master Record: Infotype 0008 (Basic Pay)
Data Provisioning—Contract Elements/SuccessFactors Analytics (RH_SFI_PA0016)	HRSFI_AR_PA0016	Extract HR Master Record: Infotype 0016 (Contract Elements)
Data Provisioning—Appraisals/SuccessFactors Analytics (RH_SFI_PA0025)	HRSFI_AR_PA0025	Extract HR Master Record: Infotype 0025 (Appraisals)
Data Provisioning—Date Specifications/SuccessFactors Analytics (RH_SFI_PA0041)	HRSFI_AR_PA0041	Extract HR Master Record: Infotype 0041 (Date Specifications)

Table 4.2 Listing of Transaction Codes and Reports Used in Data Extraction

Report Name	Transaction Code	Expected Results
Data Provisioning—Personnel Actions/SuccessFactors Analytics (RH_SFI_PA0077)	HRSFI_AR_PA0077	Extract HR Master Record: Infotype 0077 (Additional Personal Data)
Data Provisioning—Additional Actions/SuccessFactors Analytics (RH_SFI_PA0302)	HRSFI_AR_PA0302	Extract HR Master Record: Infotype 0302 (Additional Actions)
Data Provisioning—Company Code/ SuccessFactors Analytics (RH_SFI_T001)	HRSFI_AR_T001	Extract Company Codes
Data Provisioning—Personnel Area/ Subarea/SuccessFactors Analytics (RH_SFI_T001P)	HRSFI_AR_T001P	Extract Personnel Area/ Subarea
Data Provisioning—Personnel Areas/SuccessFactors Analytics (RH_SFI_T500P)	HRSFI_AR_T500P	Extract Personnel Areas
Data Provisioning—Employee Group/SuccessFactors Analytics (RH_SFI_T501T)	HRSFI_AR_T501T	Extract Employee Group Names
Data Provisioning—Employee Subgroup/SuccessFactors Analytics (RH_SFI_T503T)	HRSFI_AR_T503T	Extract Employee Subgroup Names
Data Provisioning—Ethnic Origin/ SuccessFactors Analytics (RH_SFI_T505S)	HRSFI_AR_T505S	Extract Ethnic Origin Texts
Data Provisioning—Pay Scale Type/SuccessFactors Analytics (RH_SFI_T510A)	HRSFI_AR_T510A	Extract Pay Scale Types
Data Provisioning—Pay Scale Area/ SuccessFactors Analytics (RH_SFI_T510G)	HRSFI_AR_T510G	Extract Pay Scale Areas
Data Provisioning—Wage Type/ SuccessFactors Analytics (RH_SFI_T512T)	HRSFI_AR_T512T	Extract Wage Type Texts
Data Provisioning—Appraisal Criterion/SuccessFactors Analytics (RH_SFI_T513F)	HRSFI_AR_T513F	Extract Appraisal Criteria Texts

Table 4.2 Listing of Transaction Codes and Reports Used in Data Extraction (Cont.)

Report Name	Transaction Code	Expected Results
Data Provisioning—Organizational Key/SuccessFactors Analytics (RH_SFI_T5270)	HRSFI_AR_T5270	Extract Organizational Key Validation
Data Provisioning—Actions/ SuccessFactors Analytics (RH_SFI_T529T)	HRSFI_AR_T529T	Extract Personnel Action Texts
Data Provisioning—Status/Success-Factors Analytics (RH_SFI_T529U)	HRSFI_AR_T529U	Extract Status Values
Data Provisioning—Action and Action Reason/SuccessFactors Analytics (RH_SFI_T530T)	HRSFI_AR_T530T	Extract Reason for Action Texts
Data Provisioning—Work Contract/ SuccessFactors Analytics (RH_SFI_T542T)	HRSFI_AR_T542T	Extract Employment Contracts
Data Provisioning—Corporation/ SuccessFactors Analytics (RH_SFI_T545T)	HRSFI_AR_T545T	Extract Corporation Texts
Data Provisioning—Date Types/ SuccessFactors Analytics (RH_SFI_T548T)	HRSFI_AR_T548T	Extract Date Types
Data Provisioning—Payroll Area/ SuccessFactors Analytics (RH_SFI_T549T)	HRSFI_AR_T549T	Extract Payroll areas
Data Provisioning—Absence/Atten-dance/SuccessFactors Analytics (RH_SFI_T554T)	HRSFI_AR_T554T	Extract Absence and Attendance Texts
Data Provisioning—Jobs (PA)/ SuccessFactors Analytics (RH_SFI_T5U13)	HRSFI_AR_T5U13	Extract Jobs
Data Provisioning—EEO Occup. Categories/SuccessFactors Analytics (RH_SFI_T5UEE)	HRSFI_AR_T5UEE	Extract EEO Occupational Categories
Data Provisioning—Public Holiday/ SuccessFactors Analytics (RH_SFI_THOC)	HRSFI_AR_THOC	Extract Public Holiday Calendar
Data Provisioning—Public Holiday Text/SuccessFactors Analytics (RH_SFI_THOL)	HRSFI_AR_THOL	Extract Public Holidays

Table 4.2 Listing of Transaction Codes and Reports Used in Data Extraction (Cont.)

Prerequisites

The following prerequisites should be met prior to the extraction of analytics data:

▶ Employees are hired, and their master data exists in the SAP ERP HCM system with at least the following infotypes:

  ▶ 0000—Actions

  ▶ 0001—Organizational Assignment

  ▶ 0002—Personal Data

4.3.3 Compensation Process/Pay-for-Performance Integration

The compensation process, or pay-for-performance integration enables the bidirectional transfer of employees and their salary data to support compensation processing in the SuccessFactors Compensation module. In a typical pay-for-performance environment, managers will consider the employee's performance and their salary band during the compensation payout process.

As shown in Figure 4.5, the process for the pay-for-performance integration begins with the transfer of employee data, organizational data, and salary details from SAP ERP HCM to SuccessFactors HCM.

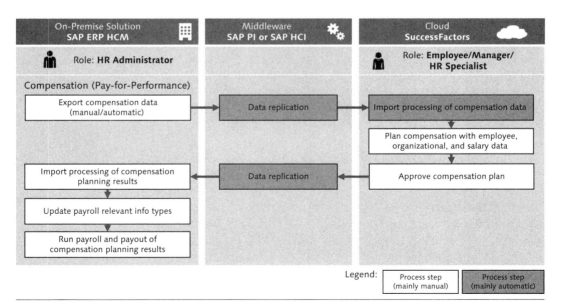

Figure 4.5 Pay-for-Performance Process Integration

Any changes made in the compensation data for the employee, such as salary change, bonuses (lump sum payment), or LTI (Long-Term Incentive), is transferred from SuccessFactors to SAP ERP HCM for processing by SAP Payroll.

For the compensation processing, the following data are extracted from SAP ERP HCM:

▸ **Salary information**
  The employee's salary information (annual, monthly, bimonthly, or hourly)

▸ **Additional organizational information**
  Start date at the current position and the pay grade

▸ **Additional personal information**
  If required, additional employee-related data (eligibility, job title, job level, etc.)

This data is extracted from SAP ERP HCM using the standard extraction logic. You can enhance the BAdI to include custom logic, if any. One of the reasons that you might want to enhance the delivered BAdI will be to determine the employee's eligibility to participate in the compensation process in SAP ERP HCM. You can also determine the employee's eligibility in SuccessFactors. There are no best practices as to where the employee's eligibility should be determined.

What is required, however, is that employee-related data (current salary, current job title, job grade, etc.) must be transferred to SuccessFactors HCM prior to the start of the compensation process. This will ensure that the managers have accurate and up-to-date information about the employees.

Prerequisites

The following prerequisites should be satisfied prior to implementing the pay-for-performance process integration:

▸ Integration Add-on 1.0 SP 02 for SAP ERP HCM and SuccessFactors HCM is implemented.

▸ An initial compensation template is set up in SuccessFactors to enable compensation related evaluation.

▸ Employee data interface is implemented, and employee-related data is transferred from SAP ERP HCM to SuccessFactors HCM for employees who require being part of the compensation process.

▸ Field groupings are configured for data export from SAP ERP HCM to SuccessFactors.

▸ Field groupings are configured for data import from SuccessFactors to SAP ERP HCM.

▸ An ad hoc report for export is configured in SuccessFactors.

4.3.4 Recruiting Process Integration

The recruiting process integration enables the transfer of newly hired candidate data from SuccessFactors HCM to SAP ERP HCM. Once the new hire data is transferred to SAP ERP HCM, the hiring process is initiated and executed in SAP ERP HCM (see Figure 4.6).

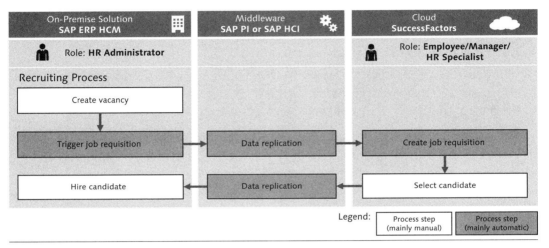

Figure 4.6 Recruiting Process Integration

As shown in Figure 4.6, the process for integration is as follows:

▶ Employee, organizational data, and vacancy information are transferred from SAP ERP HCM to SuccessFactors Recruiting. With these data, the requisition process is initiated in SuccessFactors Recruiting.

▶ Even if the integration is implemented, if the customers desire, they can initiate the requisition creation in SuccessFactors Recruiting without these data.

▶ Once the candidate accepts the offer, the new hire data is transferred from SuccessFactors Recruiting to SAP ERP HCM and is maintained as a new employee.

▶ Status of candidate data transfer is uploaded to SuccessFactors HCM.

▶ Candidate is marked as HIRED and linked to the employee data.

▶ Now the employee (newly hired candidate) can execute the talent management processes (for example, search for jobs as an internal candidate).

Prerequisites

The following prerequisite should be satisfied prior to implementing the recruiting process integration:

▶ Integration Add-on 1.0 SP 02 for SAP ERP HCM and SuccessFactors HCM is implemented.

When the vacancy data is transferred from SAP ERP HCM to SuccessFactors Recruiting, position details such as position description and location of the position are also transferred. When the identified candidate is hired in SAP ERP HCM, the information is sent back to SuccessFactors Recruiting, and the candidate information is updated with the employee ID. Now, the newly hired candidate will be identified in SuccessFactors Recruiting as an internal candidate. The hiring action in SAP ERP HCM can be a new hire, a rehire, or a transfer, depending on whether the identified candidate is a new candidate, an alumni of the organization, or an existing employee.

When the identified candidate has accepted the offer, SuccessFactors Recruiting will initiate an action to hire (or rehire or transfer) the candidate to the identified position. This transfer of information is initiated automatically in the system.

We discuss more about recruiting process integration and the configuration settings that need to be made in SAP ERP HCM system in Chapter 10, Section 10.3.

4.3.5 SuccessFactors Competencies Integration with SAP ERP HCM Qualifications

This packaged integration enables automated uploading of the qualifications catalog maintained in SAP ERP HCM to the SuccessFactors competency library.

The competency library in SuccessFactors is used to maintain an employee's competences. Modules such as Succession Management, Performance and Goals Management, and Learning Management access this competency library for their talent-related business processes. Similarly, many customers maintain a qualifications catalog in SAP ERP HCM. The qualifications catalog is used to track an employee's competencies, learning requirements, and other talent-related processes. Figure 4.7 illustrates the SuccessFactors Competency integration.

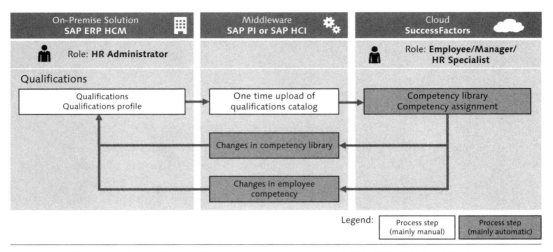

Figure 4.7 SuccessFactors Competencies Integration with SAP ERP HCM Qualifications

When customers implement SuccessFactors talent modules, they sometimes prefer to leverage the qualifications catalog maintained in SAP ERP HCM. They also prefer a single system of truth to maintain the competency library and track the competencies of their employees.

Table 4.3 explains the terminology used in SuccessFactors and in SAP ERP HCM.

SuccessFactors	SAP ERP HCM	Description
Competency library	Qualifications catalog	A set of competencies available for use by the enterprise. You can maintain multiple catalogs in the library.
Competency type	Qualification group	A grouping of similar types of competencies.
Competency	Qualification	An individual competency that can be assigned to an employee.
Curriculum	Qualification	An individual competency that can be assigned to an employee.
Employee competency	Employee skills (competency)	A relationship between a competency and an employee. This relationship will have an associated rating.

Table 4.3 Terminologies Used in SuccessFactors and in SAP ERP HCM

SuccessFactors	SAP ERP HCM	Description
Employee curriculum status	Employee skills (competency)	A relationship between a competency and an employee. This relationship will have an associated status, such as Completed.

Table 4.3 Terminologies Used in SuccessFactors and in SAP ERP HCM (Cont.)

Customers who maintain the qualifications catalog in SAP ERP HCM can export the qualifications into a flat file and populate the SuccessFactors competency library. This is a one-time upload only, and no middleware is used.

In SAP ERP HCM, if you maintain an employee's competency using the qualification catalog, then the data can be migrated from SAP ERP HCM to SuccessFactors using this packaged integration. The migrated competency data of the employees can be viewed in the competency profile. Once these uploads are completed, the customer is required to maintain the competency library in SuccessFactors only. Any changes made to the competency library or to an employee's competency profile in SuccessFactors are updated in SAP ERP HCM on a periodic basis.

The SuccessFactors Competencies integration with SAP ERP HCM qualifications packaged integration has the following limitations:

▶ The competency data object in SuccessFactors has relationships with multiple objects. This packaged integration only supports the relationship between a competency and an employee.

▶ The competency library in SuccessFactors has objects such as skills, behaviors, teasers, and tuners. These are not supported with this integration.

▶ The packaged integration does not support competencies based on the Metadata Framework (MDF).

▶ If you delete a competency in the SuccessFactors competency library, then this deletion is not replicated to SAP ERP HCM qualifications catalog.

▶ In SuccessFactors, an employee's competency rating from multiple sources is stored individually. However, in SAP ERP HCM only one rating is stored for each qualification assigned to an employee. If you want to replicate the employee's competency rating from SuccessFactors to SAP ERP HCM, then customers need to convert the multiple ratings to a single rating prior to replication.

Prerequisites

Prior to implementing the SuccessFactors Competencies integration with SAP ERP HCM qualifications, the following prerequisites should be met:

▸ Ensure the employee master data is available in SuccessFactors HCM.

▸ In SAP ERP HCM, you can maintain qualifications in either the Personnel Administration (PA) or the Personnel Development (PD) modules. Where required, in SAP ERP HCM you can migrate qualifications from one module to another. However, if you do this migration after the implementation of this integration, then you must re-implement the integration.

4.3.6 SuccessFactors Learning Curricula Integration with SAP ERP HCM Qualifications

Many customers use sources other than the competency library to track the competencies of their employees. This packaged integration is specifically useful to SAP ERP HCM customers who have implemented SuccessFactors Learning Management System and use the curricula feature instead of the competency library to track the competencies of their employees.

Any changes made in SuccessFactors curricula will be sent to SAP ERP HCM for updating the qualification catalog maintained there. Similarly, any changes in the employee competency profile will be replicated to the employee profile maintained in SAP ERP HCM. Figure 4.8 illustrates the integration process in detail.

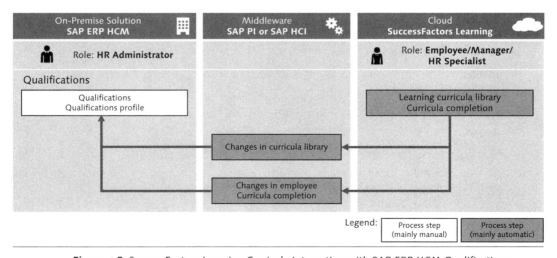

Figure 4.8 SuccessFactors Learning Curricula Integration with SAP ERP HCM Qualifications

The following are the assumptions and limitations that need to be considered while implementing this packaged integration:

▸ No support is currently available for the one-time flat file upload of the SAP ERP HCM qualifications catalog to SuccessFactors Learning Management System.

▸ If a curricula is deleted in SuccessFactors Learning Management System, this deletion is not replicated to the qualifications catalog.

▸ Although the SuccessFactors Learning curricula is mapped to SAP ERP HCM qualifications, SuccessFactors Learning items are not mapped to SAP ERP HCM qualifications.

▸ The SuccessFactors Learning curricula might contain items that have an expiration date. Each item can also have a separate expiration date. To arrive at the valid end date of a curriculum, all the items within a curriculum are processed. The earliest expiration date among these is interpreted as the curriculum end date. If items do not have an end date specified, then it is assumed that the skills will never expire. There is no start date supplied either. The current date is considered to be the valid start date. In every replication, the data for employee skill is updated to start with the current date.

Prerequisites

Prior to implementing learning curricula integration with SAP ERP HCM Qualification, ensure the following prerequisites are met:

▸ The employee master data integration is implemented and the employee master data is available in SuccessFactors HCM.

▸ In this packaged integration, no data will be sent from SAP ERP HCM to SuccessFactors Learning. The curriculum is created and maintained in SuccessFactors LMS.

4.3.7 Variable Pay Integration

As seen in Figure 4.9, the employee history data is extracted from SAP ERP HCM and transferred to Variable Pay in SuccessFactors.

Review Notes

Prior to implementing the integration scenario for Variable Pay, review the following SAP Notes:

▶ **1841471 (Release strategy for ABAP Add-on SFIHCM03 600)**
This note describes the prerequisites, the installation process, and the follow-up for installing the Integration Add-on.

▶ **2017123 (Prerequisite corrections in SFIHCM02 600 for Variable Pay)**
This note includes corrections for the package interface and enhancements to domain fixed values used by the Variable Pay integration.

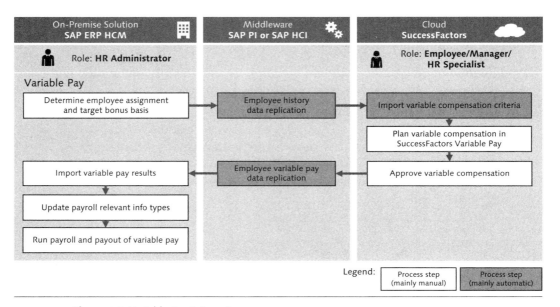

Figure 4.9 Variable Pay Integration

The integration requires the employee history data, which is used as input for bonus calculations and planning.

Using this packaged integration, you can select eligible employees from SAP ERP HCM and load them into the SuccessFactors Variable Pay application. You can select the eligible employees based on certain criteria, such as location or department. You can further apply business rules to filter the selected employees and select only employees who meet the conditions of these business rules. In addition, you can modify the business logic (used to develop the business rules) to suit the specific requirements of your enterprise.

The following elements should be considered while implementing the Variable Pay packaged integration:

▶ The packaged integration assumes that you are currently not using or do not have SAP ERP HCM Compensation Management in your landscape.

▶ The effective date for Variable Pay is determined by user input. This effective date information does not exist in the processed result.

▶ It is important to note that after the Variable Pay data is transferred to SuccessFactors no changes should be made in SAP ERP HCM. Any and all changes after the data transfer should be made only in SuccessFactors.

▶ The variable pay result that you generated using an ad hoc report is based on the completed Variable Pay process.

▶ If you set up the transfer of an employee history record as a scheduled job, then there might be instances when you might have to delete certain records in the staging area. (This will occur when the data is wrong or corrupted.) As a best practice, it is suggested that you schedule a job to update the calculated information in all Variable Pay forms.

SuccessFactors will use the transferred employee data to process Variable Pay for the employees. After the Variable Pay is processed in SuccessFactors, the calculated bonus of each employee is transferred back to SAP ERP HCM to be included in the payroll run.

Prior to the transfer of Variable Pay data from SAP ERP HCM to SuccessFactors, it is important that employee-related data are present in SuccessFactors HCM.

Calculated Variable Pay

Currently, the packaged integration does not support the transfer of the calculated variable pay from SuccessFactors to SAP ERP HCM. As a suggested practice, you can use flat files to transfer the calculated variable pay from SuccessFactors to SAP ERP HCM for payroll processing.

The add-on for Variable Pay must be implemented on SuccessFactors release b1408 or later. The b1405 release also supports the integration, but variable pay for inactive employees is not supported. The integration scenarios are fully supported using the middleware. The current release of the Integration Add-on supports SAP PI, and support for SAP HANA Cloud Integration is planned for the future.

The following general services are used for the Variable Pay integration scenario:

▶ `SFSFSessionHandlingLoginQueryResult_Out`

▶ `SFSFSessionHandlingLoginQueryResult_In`

- `SFSFAPIDictionaryListSFObjectsResult_Out`

- `SFSFAPIDictionaryListSFObjectsResult_In`

- `SFSFAPIDictionaryDescribeSFObjectsExResult_Out`

- `SFSFAPIDictionaryDescribeSFObjectsExResult_In`

- `SFSFGenericUpdateRequestConfirmation_Out`

- `SFSFGenericUpdateRequestConfirmation_In`

- `SFSFGenericDeleteRequestConfirmation_In` (new)

- `SFSFGenericDeleteRequestConfirmation_Out` (new)

- `SFSFGenericInsertRequestConfirmation_In` (new)

- `SFSFGenericInsertRequestConfirmation_Out` (new)

- `SFSFUserQueryRequest_In` (new)

- `SFSFUserQueryRequest_Out` (new)

- `SFSFSessionHandlingLogoutQueryResult_Out`

- `SFSFSessionHandlingLogoutQueryResult_In`

You can monitor the errors by executing the transaction code SLG1 in SAP ERP for object `SFSF_INTEGR_BIZX` and subobject `VARPAY-EXPORT`, and then check for messages, if any.

Prerequisites

The following components are mandatory for implementing the Integration Add-on for the Variable Pay integration scenario:

- Integration Add-on 3.0 SP 01 for SAP ERP HCM and SuccessFactors HCM suite (product version SUCCESSFACTORS HCM INTEGR 3.0, software component versions SFIHCM01 600 with SP 09, SFIHCM02 600 with SP 05, and SFIHCM03 600 with SP 01)

- SAP ERP 6.0 SPS 15 or above (with version 600 of SAP ERP software components; SAP ERP 6.0 SPS 15 comprises SP 38 for software component version EA-HR 600)

- SAP PI 7.11 SP 12 or above

- SAP PI Connectivity Add-on 1.0 SP 01 or above

- ESR Content for software component versions SFIHCM01 600, SFIHCM02 600, and SFIHCM03 600

- SAP Gateway 2.0 SP 07 or above (and in the backend, software component IW_BEP SP 07 or above)

4.4 User Experience Integration

When SAP ERP HCM customers implement SuccessFactors on-premise, one of their big requirements is to access SuccessFactors modules directly from within SAP Enterprise Portal, which provides a unified user experience for the end user.

In this section, we will provide an overview of how unified access can be implemented.

4.4.1 Unified Access for SuccessFactors and SAP Applications

Using Single Sign-On (SSO), SuccessFactors modules can be called directly from SAP Enterprise Portal. The advantage of providing this integration is that it enables end users to access all of the applications (SuccessFactors applications and different SAP applications that are available as iViews in SAP Enterprise Portal) from a single portal. In this section, we will discuss how to set up SSO and provide a unified user experience to the users. We will also discuss setting up Security Assertion Markup Language (SAML) 2.0 as the SSO security token. It is important to remember that SuccessFactors supports other security tokens, such as MD5, SHA1, DES, and 3DES encryption of the username and/or password.

In this section, we discuss the integration between SuccessFactors and SAP Enterprise Portal, but you can integrate SuccessFactors with any identity provider solution, such as SharePoint.

Prerequisites

The following information should be obtained for your SuccessFactors HCM system from SuccessFactors Customer Success:

- Digital certificate in the X.509 standard format
- SuccessFactors entity ID
- URL of the consuming service
- URL of the global logout response handler (optional)
- Relay state (relative path of the application to which the incoming SAML assertion should be redirected)

First, you need to access SuccessFactors Provisioning to complete the provisioning-related setup (see Figure 4.10).

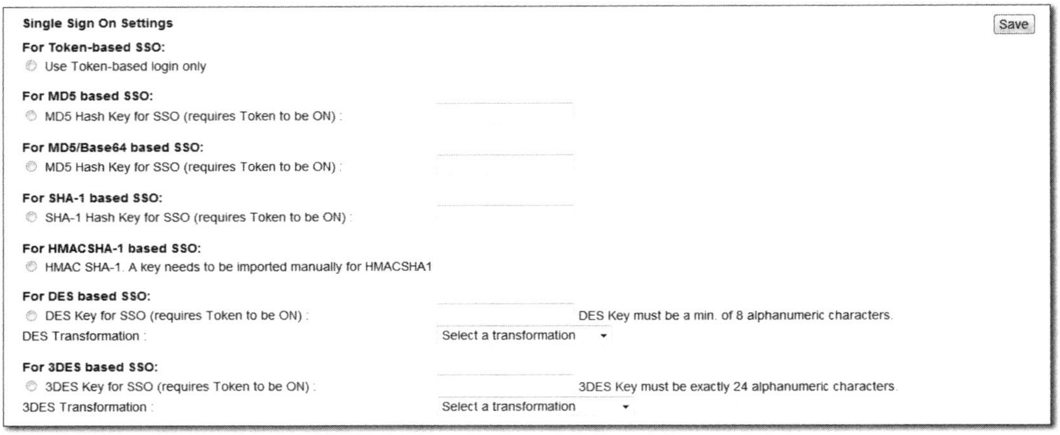

Figure 4.10 SSO Settings to Be Made in SuccessFactors Provisioning

You then need access to SAP Enterprise Portal with sufficient authorization to make changes in the CONTENT ADMINISTRATION area.

When you set up SSO, SuccessFactors requires the user first to be authenticated on the customer side and then to be directed to the SuccessFactors home page (or any other application that you might have set up). With this procedure, the number of user logins is reduced, helping to provide a seamless user experience.

A trust mechanism will pass the identify information between the customer and SuccessFactors servers. This trust mechanism is based on encryption, timestamp, and other relevant data, such as the username and password. HTTPS is the preferred protocol for the transport of this trust mechanism, because SuccessFactors requires an HTTPS post from the customer's SSO environment.

For security reasons, SuccessFactors recommends that all parameters that are passed should be an HTTPS post instead of a GET. A HTTPS post prevents sniffing when information is passed through the network. A HTTPS connection ensures that all information is encrypted when transmitted through the network. SuccessFactors supports HTTPS GET if the customer prefers this protocol.

Prior to data being sent to SuccessFactors, the data packet must be encrypted. When SuccessFactors receives the packet, it will check the timestamp attached to the packet. If the timestamp is more than the predefined period, the user login will be rejected. This predefined expiration period is configured in SuccessFactors Provisioning.

SSO Expiration

If SSO expiration is activated, then there is an option to specify the time zone that can be used for the expiration check. If a time zone is not specified, then it will default to the SuccessFactors server (datacenter) time zone. As a best practice, we suggest that you pass the time zone as part of the HTTPS POST/GET. If you pass the time zone, then it will be considered for the SSO expiration check.

4.4.2 Configuration in SuccessFactors Provisioning

To continue the process of unified access, the following configuration steps must be undertaken in SuccessFactors Provisioning:

1. Click on the SINGLE SIGN-ON SETTINGS (SSO) configuration option. In the displayed page, select the SAML v2 SSO radio button.

SuccessFactors HCM User ID

The SuccessFactors HCM user ID (UID) must be available as a user attribute in the User Management Engine of the identity provider (IdP).

2. The SAML ASSERTING PARTIES (IdP) section is displayed (see Figure 4.11). Enter the following details in the fields:

   ▶ SAML ASSERTING PARTY NAME: Enter a unique identifier.

   ▶ SAML ISSUER: This should be the provider name you have identified.

   ▶ RELAYING PARTY DESCRIPTION: The value will be LOCALHOST.

   ▶ REQUIRE MANDATORY SIGNATURE: The possible values are a) ASSERTION b) RESPONSE (CUSTOMER GENERATED/IdP/ADP) c) BOTH, or d) NEITHER. Check with your admin what values need to be used.

   ▶ ENABLE SAML FLAG: Choose ENABLED.

   ▶ SAML VERIFYING CERTIFICATE: Paste in the SAML certificate you downloaded. Remember to enter the BEGIN CERTIFICATE text above the pasted certificate and the END CERTIFICATE text below the pasted certificate.

Figure 4.11 Configuring SAML 2.0 in SuccessFactors Provisioning

3. Now, click on the ADD AN ASSERTING PARTY button. The asserting party that you created is now available in the picklist attached to the SAML ASSERTING PARTIES (IDP) field.

4. To activate the integration, in the RESET TOKEN field enter a user-defined token. Click on SAVE TOKEN to save the entries.

Disable SSO

To disable SSO, leave the RESET TOKEN field empty and click on the SAVE TOKEN button.

4.4.3 Integrating SuccessFactors HCM with SAP Enterprise Portal

Next, you need to create an iView to call SuccessFactors HCM from the SAP Enterprise Portal. To do so, follow these steps:

1. In the CONTENT ADMINISTRATION area of SAP Enterprise Portal, create an URL portal and enter the following details:

   ▸ URL: Specify your SAP Enterprise Portal and add "/saml2/idp/sso" at the end of the portal.

   ▸ SAML2SP: Specify the entity ID provided by SuccessFactors, which will be similar to *https://www.successfactors.com*.

   ▸ RELAYSTATE: Specify the relay state provided by SuccessFactors.

Tip

The URL can also be created manually by specifying the PORTAL, ENTITY, and RELAY-STATE as *https://<portal>/saml2/idp/sso?saml2sp=ENTITY&RelayState=RELAYSTATE*.

As a best practice, it is recommended that you use a URL encoder to encode the parameters.

2. You can test this by logging in as a user who has credentials set up in Success-Factors HCM and SAP Enterprise Portal. Navigate to the iView, and check whether SuccessFactors HCM opens in a new window.

You might have business requirements that necessitate the user be directed to the landing page of SuccessFactors HCM rather than to specific applications. In such a circumstance, you can use deep links to direct the users to the appropriate SuccessFactors applications.

To embed the deep links, follow this procedure:

1. Create the URL, as mentioned previously in this section.

2. If you would like the user to be taken to the SuccessFactors Recruiting Careers landing page, then RELAYSTATE will have a value of RELAYSTATE=/SF/CAREERS. Table 4.4 lists deep links and the corresponding landing pages.

Base URL (SAML)	Description	Parameters	Add to Login URL (Non-SAML)
/sf/pmreviews/	Takes user to the PERFORMANCE tab to see all PM review forms.	N/A	*pm_actstr= pmreviews*
/sf/processforms/	Takes user to the PROCESS tab to see all process forms.	N/A	*pm_actstr= processforms*
/sf/goals/	Takes user to the GOALS tab to see all goals.	N/A	*pm_actstr= goals*

Table 4.4 Listing of Deep Links

Base URL (SAML)	Description	Parameters	Add to Login URL (Non-SAML)
/sf/liveprofile/	Takes user to the live profile page in employee files (V11 only).	selecteduser (optional) = user sys id.	*pm_actstr= liveprofile or pm_actstr= liveprofile? selecteduser= lhadley1*
/sf/scorecard/	Takes user to the scorecard in employee files (V11 only).	N/A	*pm_actstr= scorecard*
/sf/smorgchart/	Takes user to the succession org chart.	N/A	*pm_actstr= smorgchart*
/sf/express/	PE Express.	N/A	*pm_actstr= express*
/sf/pmaddla/	Use only for SumT 7x LMS integration. Takes user to the ADD LEARNING ACTIVITY dialog box.	docid = the form ID, not the folder map ID	*pm_actstr= pmaddla? docid=42*
/sf/pmaddla/	Use only for SumT 7x LMS integration. Takes user to the ADD RECOMMENDED LEARNING ACTIVITY dialog box.	docid = form ID, not the folder map ID primarykey = learning activities GUID specified by the LMS as recommended for the user	*pm_actstr= pmaddla? docid=42& primarykey=1,2*
/sf/pmdocsummary/	Use only for SumT 7x LMS integration. Takes user to the DOCUMENT SUMMARY.	docid = form ID, not the folder map id	*pm_actstr= pmdocsummary? docid=42*
/sf/pmaddresult/	Use only for SumT 7x LMS integration. Takes user to the DOCUMENT RESULT.	docid = form ID, not the folder map ID	*pm_actstr= pmaddresult? docid=42*
/sf/compforms	Compensation/Forms.	N/A	*pm_actstr= compforms*

Table 4.4 Listing of Deep Links (Cont.)

Base URL (SAML)	Description	Parameters	Add to Login URL (Non-SAML)
/sf/execreview	Compensation/ ExecReview.	N/A	pm_actstr= execreview
/sf/budgetassignment	Compensation/ BudgetAssignment.	N/A	pm_actstr= budgetassignment
/sf/devplan	CDP/DevPlan.	N/A	pm_actstr= devplan
/sf/careerworksheet	CDP/CareerWork-sheet.	N/A	pm_actstr= careerworksheet
/sf/orgchart	CompanyInfo/ Orgchart.	N/A	pm_actstr= orgchart
/sf/directory	CompanyInfo/ Directory.	N/A	pm_actstr= directory
/sf/companyresources	CompanyInfo/ Resources.	N/A	pm_actstr= companyresources
/sf/employmentinfo	Takes user to the Employee Central EMPLOYMENT INFOR-MATION page.	selecteduser (optional) = user sys id.	pm_actstr= employmentinfo or pm_actstr= employmentinfo? selecteduser= lhadley1
/sf/personalinfo	Takes user to the Employee Central PERSONAL INFORMA-TION page.	selecteduser (optional) = user sys id.	pm_actstr= personalinfo or pm_ actstr= personalinfo?select-eduser= lhadley1
/sf/employeeupdate	Takes user to the Employee Central UPDATE EMPLOYEE RECORDS page.	selecteduser (optional) = user sys id.	pm_actstr= employeeupdate or pm_actstr= employeeupdate? selecteduser= lhadley1
/sf/learning	SuccessFactors LMS.	N/A	pm_actstr= learning
/sf/inform	Workforce Analytics.	N/A	pm_actstr= inform

Table 4.4 Listing of Deep Links (Cont.)

3. Typically, when SSO is activated, the SuccessFactors password maintenance functionality is turned off. This prevents users from changing their passwords directly in SuccessFactors. You can switch off the SuccessFactors password maintenance functionality directly in Admin Tools.

4. In Admin Tools, click the COMPANY SYSTEM AND LOGO SETTINGS option. In the displayed page, select the HIDE THE PERSONAL PASSWORD TAB FROM USERS checkbox option. This will prevent the system from asking users to update their passwords.

5. Again in Admin Tools (see Figure 4.12), click the PASSWORD & LOGIN POLICY SETTINGS option. In the displayed page, enter -1 in the MAXIMUM PASSWORD AGE (IN DAYS) field. A value of -1 will keep the password from expiring.

Figure 4.12 Password & Login Policy Settings in Admin Tools

If you decide to disable SSO, then you must rollback these settings as needed for your business requirements.

4.5   Rapid-Deployment Solutions

To ease the pressure of uncertainties involved in implementing integrations in the Talent Hybrid deployment model, SAP provides preconfigured integration solutions referred to as rapid-deployment solutions (RDS).

Rapid-Deployment Solutions Download

Customers can download the required RDS integration option from the SAP Service Marketplace. Each RDS integration option has detailed configuration documents that list the prerequisites and the required configurations that need to be completed by the customers.

The following sections discuss the RDS-related integration options currently available for the Talent Hybrid deployment model.

4.5.1 Recruiting Integration between SuccessFactors and SAP ERP HCM

The recruiting RDS integration solution supports two process scenarios:

- **Job requisition**
  In this scenario, requisition-related data, such as job description, hiring manager details, position title, job location, country, and so on, are transferred from SAP ERP HCM to SuccessFactors Recruiting. The requisition ID is also stored in Infotype 1107 (SuccessFactors Job Requisition) in SAP ERP HCM.

- **Candidate selection**
  In this scenario, qualified users can search for qualified candidates for a specific requisition. The identified candidate data is transferred to SAP ERP HCM for hiring as an employee.

4.5.2 User Authentication Integration

The user authentication integration provides the ease and capabilities of signing on to multiple applications at once via one authentication access point.

When SSO is installed, this RDS integration solution enables users to access both SAP ERP HCM applications and SuccessFactors applications through SAP Enterprise Portal without having to sign in multiple times.

4.5.3 Compensation Integration

The compensation integration facilitates the transfer of salary-related data from SAP ERP HCM to SuccessFactors. For the employee, when there is a salary change or bonus payment the changes are transferred from SuccessFactors to SAP ERP HCM for payroll processing. This integration is primarily used in pay-for-performance business processes.

Now that we've looked at the different integration technologies for the Talent Hybrid deployment model and an overview of the user experience integration and rapid-deployment solutions, let's turn our attention to the two case studies that will provide real-world applications of this content.

4.6   Case Studies

The following two case studies will walk through the implementation of Success-Factors cloud applications using flat files and the implementation of SuccessFactors Succession Management using the MDF.

4.6.1   Case Study 1

In this case study, we will see a customer implement SuccessFactors cloud applications for the first time using the flat files integration method to transfer employee-related data from SAP ERP HCM to SuccessFactors HCM.

The case study will walk through the process of how to use the SuccessFactors-provided data templates and will cover the settings that need to be completed in SuccessFactors Provisioning to automate the data integration.

Client Scenario

In the following case study, we will look at the company ABC Inc., a large consumer goods manufacturer with over 20,000 employees present in 18 countries, headquartered in the United States.

ABC Inc. has an existing SAP on-premise solution and uses all modules from SAP ERP HCM. The company's employee data is maintained in the SAP ERP HCM application. Employees can update their personal info by using Employee Self-Service, made available through the SAP Enterprise Portal.

To improve HR processes to better support enterprise-level talent strategies, ABC Inc. is implementing SuccessFactors Performance and Goals Management and Succession Management. To do this, they have chosen the flat file integration strategy due to the simplicity of the process. The company believed it would be overwhelmed with the change management activities during the rollout of SuccessFactors and did not want to spend time or money implementing SAP PI. It is also important to note that ABC Inc. is an existing TIBCO user and has not been interested in developing APIs or web services to integrate SAP ERP HCM and SuccessFactors with TIBCO as the middleware broker.

> **Important!**
>
> Even though flat files are used for the data integration, no SAP-delivered add-ons were implemented during this customer project.

Now that we have discussed the client scenario and the integration strategy chosen, let's begin looking at the process steps that must be undertaken for a successful implementation.

Process Steps

To begin, the company team develops an ABAP interface to get a listing of active employees, the managers they report to, their HR representatives, and other relevant data from the on-premise SAP ERP HCM application.

The data that is derived from the SAP ERP HCM application then needs to be entered in the SuccessFactors-delivered employee data template and uploaded into SuccessFactors HCM.

As shown in Figure 4.13, the ABAP interface will extract employee demographic data from SAP ERP HCM through the following process:

1. Read an employee's current PA0000 record.

2. Output a CSV file and save it in a predetermined SAP HR network drive.

3. Use an SAP PI file-watcher job to trigger a job that will send the file to the SuccessFactors secure FTP site.

4. A scheduled job will upload the employee demographic file into SuccessFactors HCM.

Figure 4.13 Extraction of Data for Upload into SuccessFactors HCM

Inactive and Active Employees

For the talent modules, it is not required to upload an inactive employee's demographic data (i.e., the PA0000/STAT2 field will have a value of 0 or 2) into SuccessFactors HCM. Hence, we suggest that you upload only active employees into SuccessFactors HCM (i.e., the PA0000/STAT2 field will have a value of 1 or 3).

HTTP protocol is no longer supported; SuccessFactors supports SFTP and HTTPS protocols only. Hence, you do not need to encrypt the file.

If you are still interested in encrypting the file, you can use Pretty Good Privacy (PGP) protocol to encrypt the files.

5. Consult Table 4.5 for the list of fields that are required for the data transfer of the basic employee data. In the table, R = Required, O = Optional, and Re = Recommended.

Header1	Header 2	R/O/Re	Data type/ Length	SAP ERP HCM Info- type/Subtype/Field ID
STATUS	STATUS	R	String/32	0000/STAT2
USERID	USERID	R	String/100	0000/PERNR
USERNAME	USERNAME	R	String/100	0105/USRID
FIRSTNAME	FIRSTNAME	R	String/128	0002/VORNA
NICKNAME	Can be PREFERRED FIRST NAME	O	String/128	0002/RUFNM
LASTNAME	LAST NAME	R	String/128	0002/NACHN
MI	MIDDLE NAME	O	String/128	0002 /MIDNM
GENDER	GENDER	R	String/2	Q00022/GESC2
EMAIL	EMAIL	R	String/100	0105/USERID_LONG
MANAGER	MANAGER UserID	R	String/100	0000/PERNR
HR	HR UserID	R	String/100	0105/PERNR
DIVISION	Can be COMPANY NAME	Re	String/128	T0001/BUTXT
DEPARTMENT	Can be ORGANIZATION NAME	Re	String/128	T527X/ORGTX
LOCATION	Can be PERSONNEL AREA	Re	String/128	T500P/NAME1
JOBCODE	JOB CODE	Re	String/128	P1000/STEXT
TIMEZONE	Can be TIME ZONE	R	String/64	
HIREDATE	LATEST HIRE DATE	O	Date	0041/DAT0#
EMPID	PERSONNEL NUMBER	O	String/255	
TITLE	POSITION TITLE	O	String/255	P1000/STEXT
BIZ_PHONE	BUSINESS PHONE	O	String/255	
FAX	FAX	O	String/255	0105/0020/USRID
ADDR1	Employee's OFFICE ADDRESS	O	String/255	T500P/STRAS
ADDR2		O	String/255	T500P/PFACH

Table 4.5 Structure of the Employee Data File Template

Header1	Header 2	R/O/Re	Data type/ Length	SAP ERP HCM Info-type/Subtype/Field ID
CITY	CITY where the office is located	O	String/255	T500P/ORT01
STATE	STATE where the office is location	O	String/255	T500P/REGIO
ZIP	ZIP of the office address	O	String/255	T500P/PSTLZ
COUNTRY	COUNTRY where the office is located	O	String/255	T500P/LAND1
REVIEW_FREQ	REVIEW FREQUENCY	O	String/255	
LAST_REVIEW_DATE	LAST REVIEW DATE	O	Date	0041/ZG/DATO#
CUSTOM01-CUSTOM15				
MATRIX_MANAGER	MATRIX MANAGER	O	String/100	
DEFAULT_LOCALE	DEFAULT LOCALE	O	String/100	
PROXY	PROXY	O	String/100	
CUSTOM_MANAGER	CUSTOM MANAGER	O	String/100	
SECOND_MANAGER	SECOND MANAGER	O	String/100	
LOGIN_METHOD	LOGIN METHOD	O	String	
PASSWORD	PASSWORD	O	String	0105/USRID

Table 4.5 Structure of the Employee Data File Template (Cont.)

6. When consulting Table 4.5, note the following elements:

  ▶ STATUS: This must be the first field in the template and is used to define the status of the employee. The employee can have either an ACTIVE status or an INACTIVE status. The mapping of the status in the SAP ERP HCM application to SuccessFactors is as follows: If the status in SAP = 0 (employee is separated), then the status in SuccessFactors is translated as INACTIVE. If the status in SAP = 1 (employee is on unpaid leave), then the status in SuccessFactors is translated as ACTIVE. If the status in SAP = 2 (employee has retired), then the status in SuccessFactors is translated as INACTIVE. If the status in SAP = 3 (employee is on paid leave), then the status in SuccessFactors is translated as ACTIVE.

▶ USERID: This must always be the second field in the template. If your organization is based off a single SAP ERP HCM system, then the employee's PERNR can be mapped as the USERID in SuccessFactors. If you have multiple SAP ERP HCM systems or have implemented concurrent employment or global employment, then as a best practice the employee Business Partner (BP) number is mapped as the USERID in SuccessFactors. The USERID is unique to the employee and should not be changed during the employee's tenure with the company. As a best practice, do not reuse the USERID for another employee. The USERID of the employee is visible in the SuccessFactors system to other employees; do not use any PII data as the USERID.

▶ USERNAME: Users use the values stored in this field to log in to the system. USERNAME is visible to other users in the system and should not contain any PII data. USERNAME must be unique, but can be changed during the employee tenure. As a best practice, you can use the employee network login or the SAP account as the value for USERNAME.

▶ FIRSTNAME: This field contains the employee's first name.

▶ NICKNAME: This field can be used to display the employee's preferred first name. Often, employees use a preferred name and would like to be addressed by that name.

▶ LASTNAME: This field contains the employee's last name.

▶ MI: This field is used to display the employee's middle initial.

▶ GENDER: This field contains one of two values: F (Female) or M (Male). The value contained in this field is used by other applications, such as Writing Assistant (to refer to the user as "he" or "she").

▶ EMAIL: In this field, the system will use the stored value to deliver system-generated notifications.

▶ MANAGER: The value in this field helps create the organization hierarchy. The USERID of the manager the employee reports to is stored in this field. Usually, the head of the organization will have a NO_MANAGER value displayed in this field. The employee whose USERID is stored in this field should have an ACTIVE status in the system.

▶ HR: The value in this field displays the USERID of the assigned HR representative. If HR does not need to be maintained, then enter a value of NO_HR in the field.

▶ DIVISION: This field can be used to display the company name. The value in this field is typically used in reporting and in permissions. If data does not exist for an employee, then a value of N/A can be used. As a best practice, ensure that the value stored in this field is made visible to the user.

▶ DEPARTMENT: This field can be used to display the organization name. The value in this field is typically used in reporting and in permissions. If data does not exist for an employee, then a value of N/A can be used. As a best practice, ensure that the value stored in this field is made visible to the user.

▶ LOCATION: This field can be used to display the personnel area. The value in this field is typically used in reporting and in permissions. If data does not exist for an employee, then a value of N/A can be used. As a best practice, ensure that the value stored in this field is made visible to the user.

▶ JOBCODE: This field refers to the job code entered in FAMILIES AND ROLES. Entries are case and space sensitive and must match exactly what is maintained in MANAGING COMPETENCIES AND SKILLS—FAMILIES AND ROLES.

▶ TIMEZONE: The value stored in this field is used for maintaining internal date and time stamps for a specific user. If the field is blank, then the system will default to Eastern Standard Time. To enable the system to automatically adjust for daylight savings time, you will need to use the time zone ID instead of the short name.

▶ HIREDATE: The format for the value stored in this field will be mm/dd/yyyy.

▶ EMPID: You can use this field to store a value other than the USERID stored in the USERID field. If you are using the USERID field to store values other than the employee's PERNR (such as the employee's Business Partner ID), then you can use this field to store the employee's PERNR.

▶ TITLE: This field is used to display the employee's job title.

▶ BIZ_PHONE: SuccessFactors uses the data stored in this field to display the employee's business contact information.

▶ FAX: SuccessFactors uses the data stored in this field to display the employee's business fax information.

- ADDR1: SuccessFactors uses the data stored in this field to display the employee's business address.

- ADDR2: SuccessFactors uses the data stored in this field to display the employee's business address.

- CITY: SuccessFactors uses the data stored in this field to display the city of the employee's business address.

- STATE: SuccessFactors uses the data stored in this field to display the state of the employee's business address.

- ZIP: SuccessFactors uses the data stored in this field to display the zip code of the employee's business address.

- COUNTRY: SuccessFactors uses the data stored in this field to display the country of the employee's business address.

- REVIEW_FREQ: This field is not required and can be left blank.

- LAST_REVIEW_DATE: In this field, the date format is mm/dd/yyyy. If it is not required, then you can leave it blank.

- CUSTOM01 to CUSTOM15: These fields are used to capture employee details that cannot be maintained in the SuccessFactors-delivered fields. Use these custom fields very cautiously. You can only maintain 15 custom fields for all the applications that leverage SuccessFactors HCM. (For modules that leverage MDF, you can create up to 200 custom fields.)

- MATRIX_MANAGER: This field is used to specify the Matrix Manager for the employee. The value will be the USERID of the Matrix Manager for the employee. If your organization does not have Matrix Managers, then you can leave this field blank.

- DEFAULT_LOCALE: The value stored in this field defaults to the system language for the user. For example, if a user is employed in a US office, then the value in DEFAULT_LOCALE will be EN_US.

- PROXY: The identified proxy for the employee will be stored in this field.

- CUSTOM_MANAGER: The USERID of the CUSTOM_MANAGER for the employee is stored in this field. Customers use this field to populate the identified mentor for the employee. If there are multiple CUSTOM_MANAGER values for the employee, then use the "|" symbol to separate the values.

▶ SECOND_MANAGER: You can use this field to develop a second planning hierarchy. This field is used primarily in Compensation.

▶ LOGIN_METHOD: This field is primarily used to track whether the employee is set up to use SSO or the password authentication method. If the field USERNAME is filled with a value, then you can leave this field blank

▶ PASSWORD: Usually, this field is populated during the testing phase only. We strongly recommend not populating this field in production files. If the column is included in the template and if it does not contain a value, then it will force employees to change their passwords.

In the test files, you can consider populating this field with the value contained in the USERID field.

7. In the SuccessFactors SFTP site (see Figure 4.14), click on the INCOMING folder to upload the EMPLOYEE DEMOGRAPHIC data file. You must also create a scheduled job that can read this file and populate the BizX data dictionary. In SuccessFactors Provisioning, in the MANAGING JOB SCHEDULER group, click on MANAGE SCHEDULED JOBS (see Figure 4.15).

> **Important!**
>
> As a suggested practice, do not use any SFTP client to access the SuccessFactors SFTP/HTTPS websites. Access the SFTP website directly from your web browser. The SFTP clients are known to store connection information in an unencrypted format. Hence, we recommend that you access SuccessFactors SFTP/HTTPS sites directly.

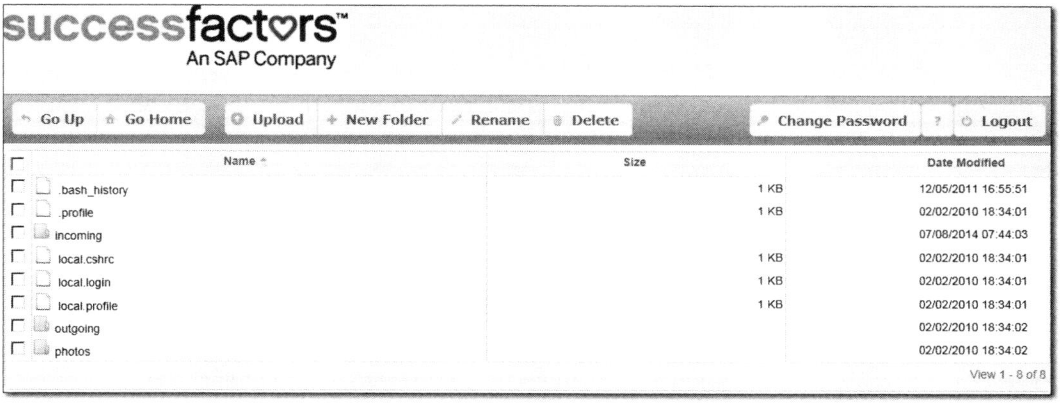

Figure 4.14 SuccessFactors SFTP Website

Figure 4.15 SuccessFactors Provisioning—Create Scheduled Jobs

8. If you are creating jobs for the first time, then click on the Create New Job link displayed in the page (see Figure 4.16).

Figure 4.16 Create a Scheduled Job to Upload the Employee Demographic File

9. In the Create Job page, in the Job Definition group, enter the Job Name and Job Owner. In the Job Type picklist, select Employees Import (see Figure 4.17). In the Job Parameters group, select the values for each field that meet your business requirements.

10. Figure 4.18 shows settings that are made by a customer. However, you might have different requirements for processing the file, so set these parameters accordingly. In the Server Access group, in the Host Address field, enter the URL provided by SuccessFactors to access the SFTP server.

Port 21

Note that Port 21 is default for FTP and Port 22 is default for SFTP. Enter the login ID and password in the fields FTP Login and FTP Password. Click on the Test Connection button. Once you receive the success message, click on the Test File Put Permission button. This will put a .txt file in the FTP server to test write permission.

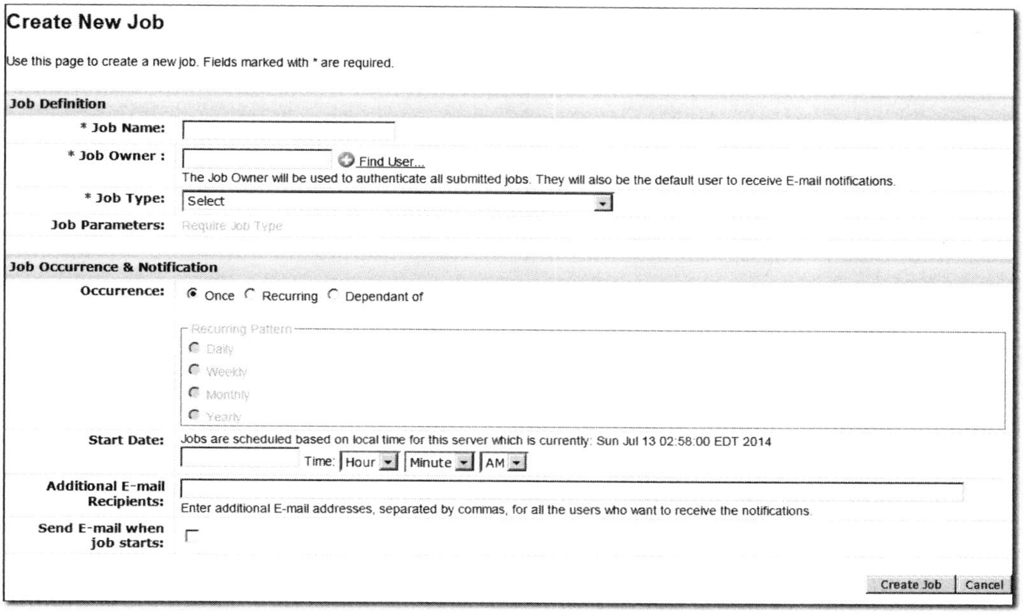

Create New Job

Use this page to create a new job. Fields marked with * are required.

Job Definition

* **Job Name:**

* **Job Owner :**   ⊙ Find User...
The Job Owner will be used to authenticate all submitted jobs. They will also be the default user to receive E-mail notifications.

* **Job Type:** Select

Job Parameters: Require Job Type

Job Occurrence & Notification

Occurrence: ⊙ Once ○ Recurring ○ Dependant of

Recurring Pattern
○ Daily
○ Weekly
○ Monthly
○ Yearly

Start Date: Jobs are scheduled based on local time for this server which is currently: Sun Jul 13 02:58:00 EDT 2014
Time: Hour ▾ Minute ▾ AM ▾

Additional E-mail Recipients:
Enter additional E-mail addresses, separated by commas, for all the users who want to receive the notifications.

Send E-mail when job starts: □

Create Job   Cancel

Figure 4.17 Create a New Job to Upload the Employee Demographic File

Job Parameters: Default value for a new user's password: ○ Username ○ USERID ○ Email ⊙ System Generated

□ Send Welcome Message to New Users.

☑ Validate Manager and HR fields.

□ Process inactive Employees

Automatic Manager Transfer.

□ Automatic insertion of new manager as next document recipient if not already.

□ Automatic Inbox Document Transfer To New Manager

□ Automatic En Route Document Transfer To New Manager

☑ Automatic Completed Document Copy to New Manager

    ☑ Manager
    □ Matrix Manager

□ Automatic Process Owner Change To New Manager For In-Progress Documents When Old Manager is Process Owner (Only for 360)

□ Automatic Process Owner Change To New Manager For Completed Documents When Old Manager is Process Owner (Only for 360)

Automatic Document Removal

□ Remove Inactive Employees' In-Progress Documents

□ Remove Inactive Employees' Completed Documents

□ Remove Inactive Employees' 360 Evaluation Documents

Character Encoding: Western European (Windows/ISO) ▾

Compensation specific options for import

□ Update Compensation Worksheets

□ Update Variable Pay Worksheets

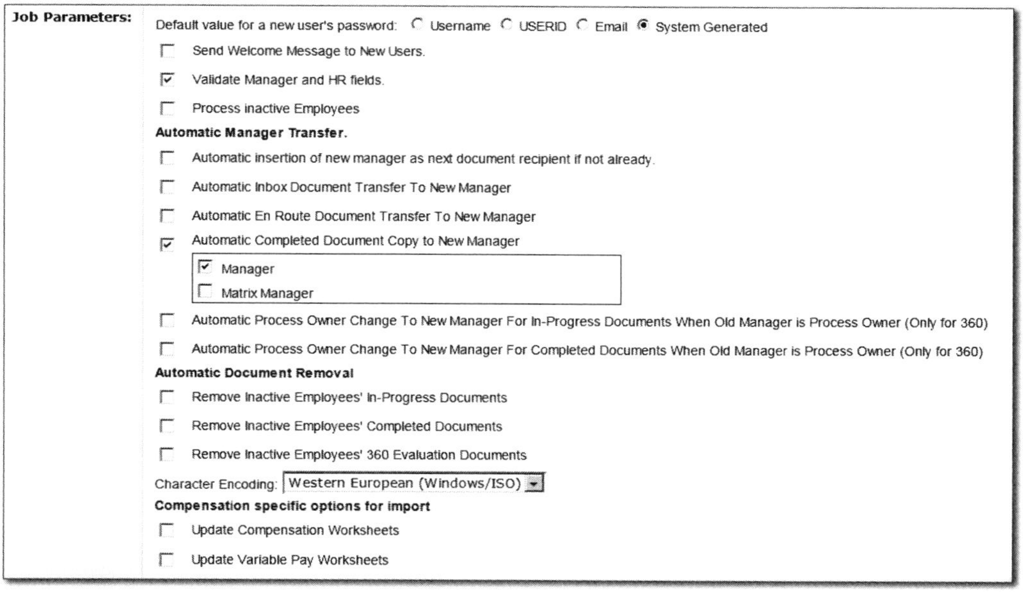

Figure 4.18 Setting Up Parameters for Processing the Employee Demographic File

11. In the FILE ACCESS group (see Figure 4.19), in the FILE PATH field, enter "/incoming", which is the folder in the SFTP host server where the data file will be available for uploading into the SuccessFactors HCM dictionary. In the FILE NAME field, enter the file name as "*<yourcompany_id>_EMP_.csv*". *The yourcompany_id* referenced in the file name is the SuccessFactors instance ID.

12. As a suggested version control practice, it is a good idea to append the date to the file name. In the DATE FORMAT field, select the date format you want to use.

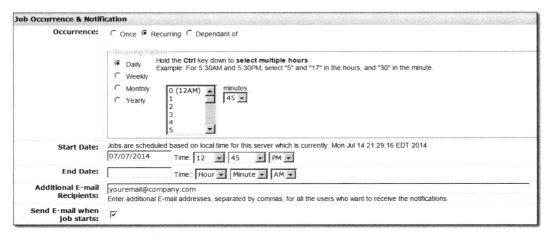

Figure 4.19 Configuring the File Path and File Name in SuccessFactors Provisioning

13. In the FILE ENCRYPTION field, select the option NONE. Because the SFTP host server is being used, you do not need encrypt the files. If you still prefer to encrypt the files, then select the option PGP.

File Naming

The name of the file in the SFTP server should be similar to the file name format you configure in provisioning. For example, if your company name is ABC Corporation, your instance ID is ABCPrd, and you have included date format in the file extension, then you would have configured the file name as "*ABCPrd_EMP_<dateformat>.csv*".

On the SFTP server side, the file will be named *ABCPrd_EMP_140706.csv*.

If the file names do not match, then you will get an error message when the job is executed. The SuccessFactors notification will have a message similar to this: FTP TRANSPORT FAILED TO GET DATA FILE FROM FTP SERVER: SFTP4-INT.SUCCESSFACTORS.COM. If files are encrypted, then add .pgp to the end of the file name. In Provisioning, you will configure the file name as "*<yourcompany_id>_EMP_.csv.pg*".

Both CSV and TXT file formats are supported. If you are using TXT file format, then the values need to be separated by a comma.

14. In the JOB OCCURRENCE & NOTIFICATION group, choose whether this job is a recurring job, a one-time job, or dependent on another job. Choose the start date of the job and an end date if the job is to be terminated in a date range. If there is no end date for the job, then you can leave it blank.

15. If you want email notifications to be generated and sent when the job starts, select the SEND EMAIL checkbox. The owner of the job by default will receive all email notifications related to this job. If you want notifications to be generated for additional recipients, then enter those recipients' email addresses in the ADDITIONAL E-MAIL RECIPIENTS field.

16. Click on the CREATE JOB button to execute the job. You will receive a notification when the job is started. A notification will also be sent when the job is completed.

With this process completed, ABC Inc. has successfully implemented their integration.

4.6.2 Case Study 2

In this case study, we will see how a customer implementing SuccessFactors Succession Management using MDF Position Management uses the flat file to upload the identified key positions. The customer is using the flat file to upload the legacy performance management ratings into SuccessFactors.

The case study will walk through the process of how to use the SuccessFactors-provided data templates to upload the data one time only.

Client Scenario

In the following case study, we will look at the company RapidGrow Co., a large retail store with more than 700 stores nationwide and over 27,000 employees on its payroll. RapidGrow Co. is currently headquartered in Mexico City, Mexico.

RapidGrow Co. is an existing SAP on-premise customer and uses the core modules of SAP ERP HCM, maintaining its employee data in the SAP ERP HCM application. Except for a third-party recruiting solution, the customer uses pen and paper for other talent-related processes.

To convert a pen-and-paper processes into a technology-driven process aligned to current HR trends, RapidGrow Co. is implementing SuccessFactors Performance and Goals Management and Succession Management.

To do this, the company is implementing an integration strategy that is a mixture of flat files, Dell Boomi AtomSphere (the integration tool to integrate Employee Central and on-premise SAP applications), and SAP PI. For this particular scenario, the customer decided to use flat files, because this data upload is one time only.

Now that we have discussed the client scenario and the integration strategy chosen, let's begin looking at the process steps that must be undertaken for a successful implementation.

Process Steps

To begin, two data files need to be uploaded to support Succession Management processes in SuccessFactors. The first data file is the performance ratings of the last five years. The second data file is an upload of the key positions of the organization.

Import Performance Ratings

RapidGrow Co. would like their performance ratings for the last five years to be uploaded into the system. They have never rated an employee on potential, and therefore no historical data is available. Because the historical performance data is maintained via pen and paper, the HRIS team pulled the data into an Excel sheet.

To begin this process, perform the following steps:

1. As seen in Figure 4.20, in Admin Tools you can download the template that can be used to populate performance ratings data by clicking on IMPORT EXTENDED USER INFORMATION.

Figure 4.20 Import Extended User Information

2. In the displayed page (see Figure 4.21), you can download the data file template by clicking on DOWNLOAD DATA IMPORT FILE TEMPLATE.

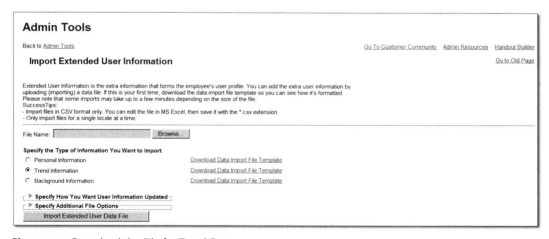

Figure 4.21 Download the File for Trend Data

3. Figure 4.22 shows the format of the data file template that will be used to populate data and upload it into SuccessFactors. The same template can be used to upload historical ratings for POTENTIAL, OBJECTIVES, and COMPETENCIES. For this case study, we will upload historical ratings for PERFORMANCE only.

^UserId	sysOverallPotential	start-date	end-date	name	description	rating	label	min	max
^UserId	sysOverallPerformance	start-date	end-date	name	description	rating	label	min	max
^UserId	sysOverallObjective	start-date	end-date	name	description	rating	label	min	max
^UserId	sysOverallCompetency	start-date	end-date	name	description	rating	label	min	max

Figure 4.22 Trend Information Data Format

4. Table 4.6 lists the fields that are required for the data transfer of the basic employee data.

Field	Required	Recommended	Valid Value
USERID	Yes	Yes	varchar (Max: 100 characters)
SYSOVERALL PERFORMANCE	Yes	Yes	"SYSOVERALLPERFORMANCE"
START-DATE	Yes, if END-DATE is blank	Yes	date (MM/DD/YY or MM/DD/YYYY)
END-DATE	Yes, if START-DATE is blank	Yes	date (MM/DD/YY or MM/DD/YYYY)
NAME	No	No	varchar (Max: 256 characters)
DESCRIPTION	No	No	varchar (Max: 1024 characters)
RATING	Yes	Yes	Float
LABEL	No	Yes	varchar (Max: 1024 characters)
MIN	No	Yes	Float
MAX	No	Yes	Float

Table 4.6 Structure of the Trend Information Data File Template

Data Template

In the data template, a start date or end date is required, but not both. If you provide only the end date, then the system will populate the start date with the same value as the end date, and vice versa.

The current release of SuccessFactors (b1405) does not support the NAME and DESCRIPTION fields. These two fields are included in the template for future use. Providing min and max values enables SuccessFactors to normalize the rating to 100%.

The performance ratings are used in the calibration grid report, live profile data, succession org chart data, in analytics/dashboard reports, and are searchable via a query tool.

The performance ratings are then captured via the OVERALL SUMMARY section in the annual appraisal document, import of the performance ratings, and/or entered manually by the permissioned user in the live profile.

5. Populate the template with the required data (see Figure 4.23) and save it as a CSV file.

6. In Admin Tools, you can now upload the CSV file by clicking on IMPORT EXTENDED USER INFORMATION. In the displayed page, upload the file by clicking on the BROWSE button then selecting the TREND INFORMATION radio button. In SPECIFY ADDITIONAL FILE OPTIONS, select the options that meet your requirements.

^UserId	sysOverallPotential	start-date	end-date	name	description	rating	label	min	max
aaaa	sysOverallPotential	1/1/2004	12/31/2004			3	High	1	3
bbbb	sysOverallPotential	1/1/2004	12/31/2004			2	Medium	1	3
cccc	sysOverallPotential	1/1/2004	12/31/2004			2	Medium	1	3
^UserId	sysOverallPerformance	start-date	end-date	name	description	rating	label	min	max
aaaa	sysOverallPerformance	1/1/2004	12/31/2004			4	Excellent	1	5
bbbb	sysOverallPerformance	1/1/2004	12/31/2004			3	High	1	3
cccc	sysOverallPerformance	1/1/2004	12/31/2004			2	Medium	1	5
^UserId	sysOverallObjective	start-date	end-date	name	description	rating	label	min	max
aaaa	sysOverallCompetency	1/1/2004	12/31/2004			4	Excellent	1	5
bbbb	sysOverallCompetency	1/1/2004	12/31/2004			3	High	1	3
cccc	sysOverallCompetency	1/1/2004	12/31/2004			2	Medium	1	5
^UserId	sysOverallCompetency	start-date	end-date	name	description	rating	label	min	max
aaaa	sysOverallObjective	1/1/2004	12/31/2004			4	Excellent	1	5
bbbb	sysOverallObjective	1/1/2004	12/31/2004			3	High	1	3
cccc	sysOverallObjective	1/1/2004	12/31/2004			2	Medium	1	5

Figure 4.23 Trend Data Template Populated with Data

7. Click on IMPORT EXTENDED USER DATA FILE. SuccessFactors will queue the file for upload, and a SuccessFactors generated notification will be sent once the file is uploaded.

Position Management

The customer has implemented MDF Position Management for Succession Management. MDF Position Management for Succession Management provides benefits such as a dedicated landing page for talent pools and effective dating of any changes being made in identifying key positions in the organization.

The talent team makes an annual review of the key positions in the enterprise. Year after year, very few changes are made to the key positions identified in earlier cycles.

The HRIS team will do once per year uploads of the key positions in the organization, and any updates to the key positions will be maintained in SuccessFactors. If the key positions are updated in SuccessFactors, then a flat file containing the changes will be uploaded into the SAP ERP HCM application.

Because the key positions updates are a once-per-year process, the HRIS team decided to use flat file integration. To initiate this process, perform the following steps:

1. In Admin Tools, search for the configuration step POSITION MANAGEMENT: EXPORT POSITIONS. In the displayed page, click on EXPORT TEMPLATE (see Figure 4.24) to download a copy of the data file template that we will populate with data and upload into SuccessFactors.

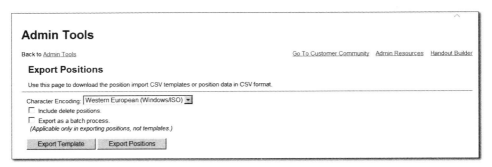

Figure 4.24 Download a Copy of the Positions Data File Template

2. Consult Table 4.7 which lists the fields that are required for the data transfer of the basic employee data.

Column Header	Required	Description	Sample Value
MODEL	Yes	This is retained for future use by SuccessFactors. As of the b1408 release, the value must always be 1.	1

Table 4.7 Structure of the Position Data File Template

Column Header	Required	Description	Sample Value
POSITIONCODE	Yes	This is a unique identifier for the position record. If the customers are maintaining position records in their HRMS, then this field can be populated with that position number or it can be autogenerated (numeric). If this field is blank, then the system will always create a new position. If the field has a value, then the system will use it to check for an existing position first and then update it if found.	40025690 OR SALESREP1234
POSITION_TITLE	No	In the succession org chart, you have the option to display POSITION TITLE or EMPLOYEE TITLE. If you have configured the succession org chart to display EMPLOYEE TITLE, then this field can be blank.	CHIEF FINANCIAL OFFICER
USERID	Yes	This is the incumbent's user ID. The value in this field must match an existing active employee record (if the value is a nonexistent or inactive user ID, then the system will generate an error). If left blank and if there is an incumbent, then that incumbent will be removed from the position, leaving the position marked as TBH.	AAAA
MANAGERPOS	Yes (for new records)	This field should contain the value of the position code of the position that this position reports to. If a position has no manager, then use the value NO_MANAGER. Note: If you are updating existing positions, this field is optional, but we recommend that it be included. Blank or invalid position codes will result in errors.	40000097

Table 4.7 Structure of the Position Data File Template (Cont.)

Column Header	Required	Description	Sample Value
KEYPOSITION	No	The value in this field indicates if the position is key, or it can display a level of criticality. The most common options to indicate a key position are 1 (YES) and 0 (NO). For criticality, you can use any numeric value that corresponds to a criticality rating. If this field is not included, then values for existing positions will not be changed. If the field is included and is blank, then the system will default to a value of 0.	1
JOBCODE	No	See bulleted list ahead.	
TITLE	No	See bulleted list ahead.	
DEPARTMENT	No	See bulleted list ahead.	
DIVISION	No	See bulleted list ahead.	
MANAGER	No	See bulleted list ahead.	
ACTION	No	The supported values are as follows: ▶ Blank (null) Performs an insert or update with the PositionCode and Incumbent ID as the key fields. ▶ DELETE This is a soft delete of the position record. It will disappear from the succession org chart and the position export file. This is equivalent to deleting a position manually on the succession org chart. ▶ REACTIVATE This will restore a position that was deleted with the DELETE action or deleted manually on the succession org chart. If the position had successors, then they will reappear as well.	PURGE

Table 4.7 Structure of the Position Data File Template (Cont.)

Column Header	Required	Description	Sample Value
ACTION	No	▸ PURGE This is a permanent deletion of the position record. This action is irreversible. You will need to recreate the position if you want to restore the position. Note: If the position is deleted or purged, then it will have no effect on the incumbent employee record.	PURGE

Table 4.7 Structure of the Position Data File Template (Cont.)

3. As referenced in Table 4.7, note the following optional information that can be entered:

   ▸ The fields JOBCODE, TITLE, DEPARTMENT, MANAGER, HR, MATRIX_ MANAGER, CUSTOMMANAGER, and CUSTOM 1 to CUSTOM 15 fields only update TBH (to be hired) positions. If the position has a valid incumbent, then these fields will be ignored. Any changes to these fields for a position occupied by an active incumbent can be changed by employee import or by updating it in the system.

   ▸ As a suggested best practice, have valid values for these fields to ensure proper permission controls and display of TBH position records. The permission controls determine who can do succession planning for these positions or for which positions you can do succession planning.

   ▸ For these fields, use the same header and value format that you use in the employee import data file.

   ▸ If a TBH position has no manager, then you can use the value NO_MANAGER (similar to the format you use in the employee import data file).

4. Table 4.8 lists the common error codes that you might encounter while importing the position data file.

Error Code	Description
-5	Invalid Manager ID
-7	Invalid UserID

Table 4.8 Common Error Codes while Importing Position Data

Error Code	Description
-10	Manager Cycle Detected
-15	Invalid Matrix Manager ID (this error appears only for TBH positions)
-17	Invalid Custom Manager ID (this error appears only for TBH positions)
-18	Invalid Second Manager ID (this error appears only for TBH positions)
-19	Second Manager Cycle Detected (this error appears only for TBH positions)

Table 4.8 Common Error Codes while Importing Position Data (Cont.)

In the position's import data file, the MODEL, POSITIONCODE, USERID, MANAGER-POS, and KEYPOSITION fields are stored in the SuccessFactors position record. All other fields are held in user records.

In this case study, we discussed how to use flat files to upload data to support the Succession Management process in SuccessFactors and successfully completed the steps for RapidGrow Co.

4.7   Summary

In this chapter, we discussed the Talent Hybrid deployment model and the packaged integrations available for integrating SuccessFactors talent modules and SAP ERP HCM. We also discussed the employee master data integrations using flat files and MDF-based Position Management in the case studies.

In Chapter 5, we will discuss the Side-By-Side HCM deployment model, which is particularly useful for customers who are implementing SuccessFactors Employee Central and who continue to maintain portions of employee and organization master data records in SAP ERP HCM.

Organizations that have invested in on-premise HR software want to leverage their investment while transitioning to the cloud. This chapter details the Side-By-Side HCM deployment model and defines scenarios that would best suit this integration choice.

5   Side-By-Side HCM Deployment Model

Although customers are eager to move to the cloud, some larger customers may have difficulty transitioning in one single implementation. Instead, these customers adopt a more cautious approach while maintaining full functionality during implementation for employees housed both in the cloud and on-premise. The Side-By-Side HCM deployment model enables this phased and cautious approach to the cloud (see Figure 5.1).

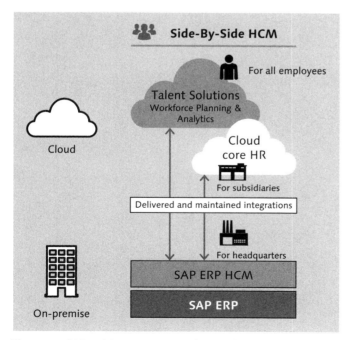

Figure 5.1 SAP and SuccessFactors Side-By-Side HCM Deployment Model

As of the time of writing (spring 2015), the Side-By-Side HCM deployment model is still an evolving model with more scenarios being identified. A phased customer implementation of the Full Cloud HCM deployment model, based on region or subsidiaries, can be considered for a Side-By-Side HCM deployment between the first and final phases. As such, this model is always an intermediate deployment and never a final state model. Customers planning to move to the cloud typically employ this model to start the journey at their own pace. The final model will most likely be Full Cloud HCM deployment.

In this chapter, we will look at the various packaged integrations that are currently available with the Side-By-Side HCM deployment model, along with the user experience integration offered. In addition, details about exclusive features and business processes for this deployment model will be examined. To conclude the chapter, two case studies will be discussed that provide real-world application.

5.1 Target Audience

The Side-By-Side HCM deployment model is for customers who want to transition their HCM systems to the cloud while still leveraging investments into employee administration on-premise. It comprises the coexistence of Employee Central and on-premise SAP core HR.

Easing into the Cloud

In should be emphasized that this deployment model is for those customers that are *easing into* the cloud. It allows businesses to make the transition without large-scale disruption during the process.

In the Side-By-Side HCM deployment model, customers run core HR on-premise for a majority of employees with SuccessFactors Talent Management solutions in the cloud. Simultaneously, the customer also runs Employee Central and talent solutions for employees that belong to a specific region or LOB.

Customers looking to employ the Side-By-Side HCM deployment model may be facing some of the following issues: they are struggling with employee administration for parent and subsidiaries, legal entities in other countries have the need to implement different workflows, or there are branches or subsidiaries that have different rules from the rest of the organization. Such customers fall into two main categories:

▶ The first category of customers might want to implement the SuccessFactors cloud business application for subsidiaries that are either legally separate entries or have different cultures, workflows, and approvals, while still maintaining the rest of their employees on-premise.

▶ The second category of customers may be running multiple, local core HR systems with specialized functionality catering to local population, where Employee Central is used for general functionality for all employee populations and includes Employee and Manager Self-Service (ESS and MSS) functions.

Legal Ramifications

For some US-based companies, there may be governmental-based legal ramifications when exposing foreign nationals' information online in the cloud. The Side-By-Side HCM deployment model would enable companies to keep foreign employees on the on-premise system to avoid exposing sensitive data that may result in penalties and fines.

5.2   Technology Options

Before looking at the packaged integrations that come with the Side-By-Side HCM deployment model, it is important to understand the technology options that are available to facilitate them.

Dell Boomi AtomSphere is the enterprise application integration technology for the Side-By-Side HCM deployment model. Dell Boomi AtomSphere acts as a single hub in the cloud for all integrations originating from or ending in Employee Central. For more information on the use of this technology option, see Chapter 3, Section 3.2.

Via this technology option, the Side-By-Side HCM deployment model's functionality is complemented and extended in the customer's on-premise software, helping customers to move their business to the cloud at their own pace and terms.

Many customers run a majority of their employees on SAP ERP HCM but may have employee populations in other systems as a result of acquisitions, geographic expansions, or "phase 2" implementation projects that never happened. This model enables an organization to achieve a single view of its workforce and allows single access for managers by connecting existing SAP ERP HCM deployments with new Employee Central deployments for those employee populations that are not on SAP ERP HCM. This will enable customers to extend existing SAP on-premise investments while planning a move to the cloud now.

With the SuccessFactors b1408 quarterly release, SAP provided the capability to run Employee Central in parallel with the SAP ERP HCM system that customers might have already deployed. Such a scenario is currently supported with packaged integrations developed and maintained by SAP. The result is an overall reduction of operational costs, minimizing the manual effort necessary to keep distributed system landscapes synchronized and delivering the lowest possible total cost of ownership. Typically, this scenario falls into one of the following two broad categories (see Figure 5.2):

▶ Side-By-Side HCM consolidated packaged data integration (see Section 5.3)

▶ Side-By-Side HCM distributed packaged data integration (see Section 5.4)

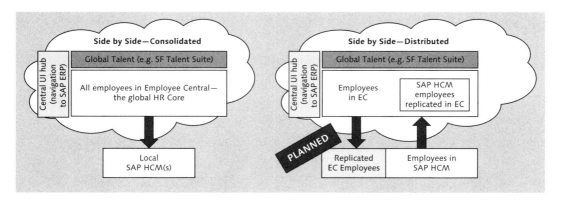

Figure 5.2 Side-By-Side HCM Deployment Model Packaged Integrations

Let's begin with the integration of employee data using the Side-By-Side HCM consolidated approach and its packaged integration.

5.3 Packaged Integrations for Side-By-Side HCM Consolidated

The Side-By-Side HCM consolidated deployment model uses packaged integrations released for the Full Cloud HCM, with the SuccessFactors homepage as the global UI hub for all employee, manager, and payroll mashups. Using the Side-By-Side HCM consolidated deployment approach, Employee Central is established as the single system of record for all global core HR processes, while keeping existing HCM systems for running local and country-specific HR processes and integrations already built with business-critical systems. This scenario is most generally available across customers.

For example, consider a business case in which a customer currently uses multiple core HR systems for different countries or legal entities. However, there is no global template yet established. In this case, eventually there is no real consolidation layer in the customer landscape to feed global HR processes or run analytics in place. Using the Side-By-Side HCM deployment, customers benefit from having Employee Central as the global core HR, setting up global processes (like hiring and talent), establishing a global HR template, gaining insights into the workforce (particularly head count globally), and providing global ESS and MSS (including access to local processes but without modifying country-specific local HR processes or integrations already in place).

Again, Figure 5.3 illustrates the Side-By-Side HCM consolidated approach.

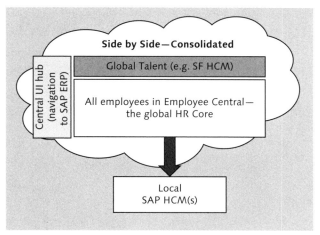

Figure 5.3 Side-By-Side HCM: Consolidated Deployment Model

The integration of employee data between SAP ERP and Employee Central replicates basic employee information from Employee Central to SAP ERP. The integration enables business process execution in the connected SAP ERP systems customers use to run their business.

The following section discusses the packaged integration from Employee Central to SAP ERP HCM for employee data synchronization. This packaged integration is applicable only for the Side-By-Side HCM consolidated deployment model. A consolidated scenario implies that Employee Central is leveraged as the system of record for all global core HR processes, whereas SAP ERP HCM is used for local HR processes.

Employee Master Data from Employee Central to SAP ERP HCM Integration

SAP provides packaged integration content for this scenario via the SuccessFactors Integration 1210 Add-on for SAP ERP. The integration of employee data from Employee Central to SAP ERP is performed periodically via a web service. The transfer of data can be performed in near real-time if required. In addition, the amount of (historical) data to be transferred can be controlled. The integration supports the loading of initial data, as well as a delta integration that replicates only changed data (time dependency is also considered). The built-in extensibility options allow data integration to be enhanced to include customer-specific attributes required at the job or personal information level without the need to change code; this can be realized simply through configuration.

To begin, the HR specialist enters employee- and employment-related data into Employee Central. Data must be manually extracted for employees (for instance, once a day) from the middleware to SAP ERP HCM.

The employee enters his or her private contact data, biographical data, payment information, or direct deposit information in Employee Central. The HR specialist then enters payroll-related information—for example, pay group and compensation information or salary and pay rate—in Employee Central.

> **Additional Information**
>
> Refer to the implementation and integration information provided in a document titled *Employee Central and SAP ERP: Employee Master Data Replication*. The latest version can be downloaded from the SAP Service Marketplace at *http://service.sap.com/ec-ondemand* or directly from *http://help.sap.com/cloud4hr*.

Figure 5.4 illustrates the flow of data from Employee Central to the SAP ERP system through Dell Boomi AtomSphere.

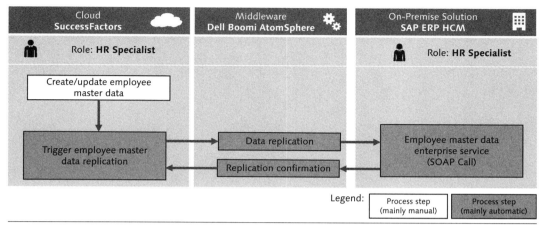

Figure 5.4 Flow of Data from Employee Central to SAP ERP HCM

This packaged integration can be used to perform data transfer from Employee Central to SAP ERP HCM. As part of this packaged integration, the following employee data is sent over to SAP ERP HCM:

- Actions (Infotype 0000)
- Organizational Assignment (Infotype 0001)
- Personal Data (Infotype 0002)
- Addresses (Infotype 0006)
- Planned Working Time (Infotype 0007)
- Basic Pay (Infotype 0008)
- Bank Details (Infotype 0009)
- Recurring Payments/Deductions (Infotype 0014)
- Additional Payments (Infotype 0015)
- Cost Distribution (Infotype 0027)
- Date Specifications (Infotype 0041)
- Communication (Infotype 0105)

After processing the replication, the enterprise service sends a confirmation message that shows the replication status. The entire process is discussed in detail in Chapter 3, Section 3.4.1.

Prerequisites

The following prerequisites must be met prior to this integration:

▶ This integration is an add-on for SAP ERP 6.0 or higher. The current version of the SuccessFactors HCM suite is required.

▶ Employee Central Integration 1210 Add-on for SAP ERP 6.0 is required.

▶ Dell Boomi AtomSphere enterprise application integration technology is required.

Now that we've looked at the consolidated packaged integration version for the Side-By-Side HCM deployment model, let's turn our attention to the distributed approach.

5.4 Packaged Integrations for Side-By-Side HCM Distributed

Using the Side-By-Side HCM distributed deployment approach, the workforce is split up between two or more systems of record (i.e. Employee Central and one or more SAP ERP HCM systems), and all of the changes are made in the system to which the employee is assigned or in which his country of assignment is configured.

When customers plan for a multiyear core HR transition to the cloud using Employee Central, they start with certain legal entities or regions that are smaller in size and then transition the remaining pieces as evaluated from a business perspective, with an end goal of moving the entire organization to the cloud. This approach provides the time and flexibility to reorganize employee data and move to the cloud at their own pace. However, during the interim stage, customers will want to have continued unified access for end users to all HCM processes, regardless of which system houses their core HR data.

To achieve this, a central UI navigation hub will need to be leveraged via UI mashups in Employee Central for ESS/MSS cases in which administrators need to centrally utilize the HR data throughout the company. Despite HR processes running on their respective system of records, employee data still needs to be kept in sync across the distributed HCM system landscape. This necessitates the transfer of employee–manager relationship data (employee data maintained in on-premise HCM to Employee Central for synchronization with the UI hub). In addition, it should be noted that the data of employees mastered in SAP ERP HCM shouldn't be editable in Employee Central and access controlled by RBP. This type of integration is only available as a public beta shipment as of the writing of this book (spring 2015).

Figure 5.5 further illustrates the Side-By-Side HCM distributed approach.

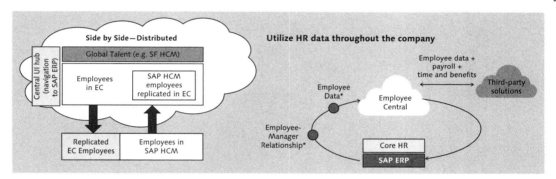

Figure 5.5 Side-By-Side HCM: Distributed Deployment Model

Employee Data Integration

With the SuccessFactors b1411 release, the employee data integration from one SAP ERP HCM system to Employee Central is only generally available for new customers leveraging Performance Management, platform features, and reporting.

With the b1502 release, SAP ERP to Employee Central employee data integration is available for existing SuccessFactors Talent Hybrid customers enabling employee master data replication from SAP ERP HCM to Employee Central with the Side-By-Side HCM deployment model for customers.

The following section discusses the packaged integrations for the Side-By-Side distributed model. This includes information on the on-premise SAP ERP HCM to Employee Central system integration for employee data synchronization that makes use of a single UI for global HR data maintained across systems within the customer landscape, and the enhancements of the SAP ERP HCM to Employee Central Talent Hybrid integration for the Side-By-Side HCM deployment model.

Employee Master Data from SAP ERP HCM to Employee Central

A large number of customers have a global business presence via on-premise SAP ERP HCM systems. When such enterprises with a global footprint embark on their cloud journey, they plan the global rollout of Employee Central to occur in phases. In such circumstances, depending on the country, region, or legal entity, you might have SAP ERP HCM and Employee Central coexisting as a system of records. While the deployment of Employee Central is happening, customers can still leverage their on-premise SAP ERP HCM applications for employee administration.

To reduce cost and business risk for these customers, SAP has provided a packaged integration to connect on-premise SAP ERP HCM with Employee Central in the Side-By-Side HCM distributed scenario.

> **Current Release**
>
> The current release of the Side-By-Side HCM deployment model supports employee data replication from a *single* SAP EPR HCM system to Employee Central.
>
> You can make required configuration settings in SAP ERP HCM by following the menu path IMG • PERSONNEL MANAGEMENT • PERSONNEL ADMINISTRATION • INTERFACES AND INTEGRATION • INTEGRATION OF SAP ERP HCM TO SUCCESSFACTORS EMPLOYEE CENTRAL SIDE BY SIDE.

With this deployment, you will notice the following points:

▸ The application administration of the workforce is split between SAP ERP HCM and Employee Central, depending on the country, region, or legal entity that the employee is attached to.

▸ HR-related processes are executed in their respective systems of record. However, the employee records need to be kept in sync across the distributed HCM system landscape.

▸ Mashups available within Employee Central provide accesses to HR records that are mastered in Employee Central as well in the on-premise SAP ERP HCM.

You can use either synchronous web service calls or CSV-based flat files and the manual import framework to transfer employee master data from SAP ERP HCM to Employee Central (see Figure 5.6).

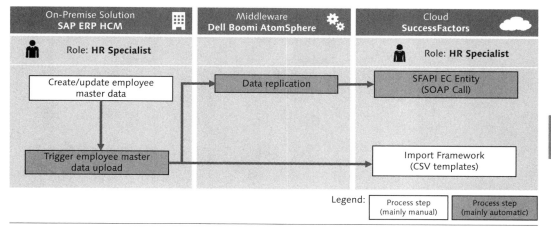

Figure 5.6 Employee Master Data Replication between SAP ERP HCM and Employee Central

---

Prerequisites

The following prerequisites must be met for this integration:

▶ This integration is an add-on for SAP ERP 6.0 or higher. The current version of the SuccessFactors HCM suite (b1408 & above) is required.

▶ The Employee Central Integration 1210 Add-on for SAP ERP 6.0 is required, with software component version PA_SE_IN100 SP 08 or above.

▶ Dell Boomi AtomSphere enterprise application integration technology (provided with Employee Central) is required.

Enhancement of SAP ERP HCM to Employee Central Data Integration

The packaged integration to integrate employee data from SAP ERP HCM to SuccessFactors for the Talent Hybrid deployment scenario, discussed in Chapter 4, Section 4.3.1, is enhanced with new capabilities to be used with Employee Central for the Side-By-Side HCM deployment model. Additional data fields derived from organizational management are now part of the packaged integration. Support is available for integration of more Employee Central entities, such as compensation, recurring payment, nonrecurring payment, new MDF-based payment information, addresses, and terminations. This integration also supports global processes such as concurrent employment, including transfer of data for employees who are concurrently employed within SAP ERP HCM to Employee Central.

More information about employee integration between SAP ERP HCM and SuccessFactors is available at *http://help.sap.com/cloud4hr*.

Now that we've looked at the different packaged data integrations provided for the Side-By-Side HCM deployment model, let's look at another integration this model employs.

5.5 User Experience Integration

The user experience integration for the Side-By-Side HCM deployment model enables employees and managers to launch self-service applications in SAP ERP from Employee Central and is now available as a packaged integration. Users can easily access all HR data independent of systems and leverage the Employee Central experience, including mobile support, by using the Side-By-Side HCM deployment model. Employees can use the SuccessFactors home page as a global UI hub for all HR-related processes and data. Employee Central acts as a display only in cases of local fields, and maintenance of these fields is performed in the system in which they are mastered, such as SAP ERP HCM.

The use of Employee Central as the central UI hub for Side-By-Side HCM deployment customers has been offered as beta functionality in release 1405 of SuccessFactors and SAP. It is currently available in a public beta version as well. Here are some use cases for this feature:

▸ If a global manager has team members, and some are mastered in Employee Central, and others are mastered in SAP ERP HCM, then the manager can navigate to SAP ERP HCM-mastered employees through the Employee Central UI. This approach requires the data integrations discussed earlier in Section 5.4.

▸ The UI navigation for employees replicated from SAP ERP HCM to Employee Central allows menus to adjust automatically for replicated employees.

▸ It can be used to view job information of replicated employee data from SAP ERP in Employee Central.

▸ It can switch from Employee Central to SAP HCM processes and forms for selected replicated employees.

▸ It can trigger workflow creation in SAP HCM.

This feature allows Employee Central customers to leverage Employee Central's UI as a central entry point for managers while still connecting to SAP ERP HCM-mastered employees and/or processes for core HR. Figure 5.7 shows a transaction using Employee Central as the UI hub for employees mastered in SAP ERP HCM and those mastered in Employee Central.

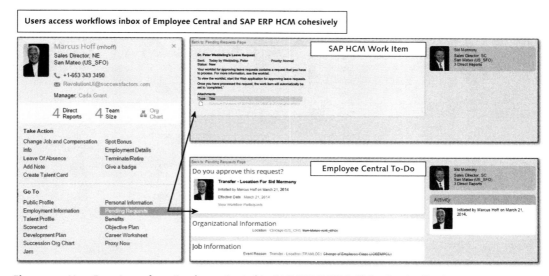

Figure 5.7 User Experience from Employee Central to SAP ERP HCM Self-Service Applications

Managers of employees mastered in SAP ERP can navigate from the SuccessFactors home page via UI mashups to the SAP ERP screen to trigger changes of employee data (MSS). The employees mastered in SAP ERP can navigate from the SuccessFactors home page via the UI mashups to SAP ERP screens to trigger changes of their employee data (ESS). The SuccessFactors home page shows the team members from various master systems, such as Employee Central and SAP ERP (see Figure 5.8).

In addition, the TAKE ACTION & GO TO menu in SAP ERP-mastered Employee Central shows links for viewing employment information, personal information, and other details, including links to change employee data.

The CHANGE EMPLOYEE DATA screen also shows options to change time off-related information, initiation of transfer, termination, and other related changes, whereas the CHANGE OF WORKING TIME screen shows an Adobe form displaying relevant fields that can be updated directly in the SAP ERP system.

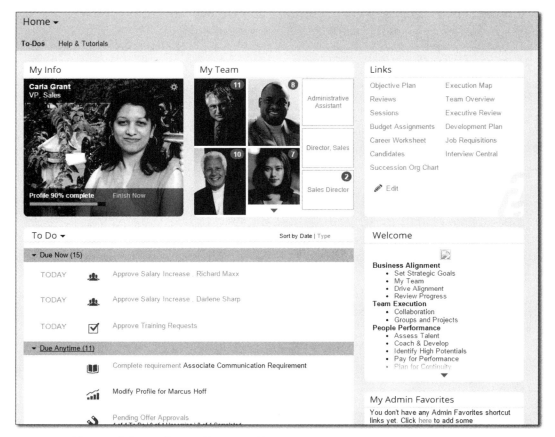

Figure 5.8 SuccessFactors Homepage View

5.6 Process and Reporting Integration

In a Side-By-Side HCM deployment model, it is imperative to have superior process implementation and reporting, even if the systems of record for user data are different. This section details the key features of the Side-By-Side HCM deployment model that make this situation possible.

The Side-By-Side HCM deployment model provides the ability to seamlessly run core HR processes across systems while employee data is kept in sync from the distributed HR system landscape, where the workforce may be split across systems (see Figure 5.9).

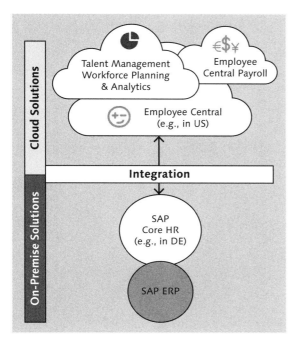

Figure 5.9 Workforce Split among Systems by Country

For example, an on-premise SAP ERP HCM system can be configured to manage a company's employee master data. However, the HR processes can continue running in this system. The employee master data can be synced with Employee Central so that the cloud-based system can be leveraged by global managers. Customers find this function appealing when they are moving certain data to the cloud while keeping some on-premise.

When using the Side-By-Side HCM deployment model, Employee Central supports a range of predelivered standard reports that can be adapted based on the individual need. Reporting requirements on workforces maintained on separate systems can leverage the central view and access. An example of this can be seen in a company looking to get a headcount for employees across multiple branches, departments, geographies, and subsidies.

Now that we have looked at the various features involved in this deployment model, let's see how business processes operate in the Side-By-Side HCM deployment model.

5.7 Business Processes

In the Side-By-Side HCM deployment model, HR processes can be executed with similar efficiency as in standalone systems. This offers convenience for customers who are shifting data to the cloud while keeping some information on-premise.

Prerequisites

Prior to discussing some common HR processes in this deployment model, ensure that the following prerequisites are fulfilled:

▶ Employees are replicated from SAP ERP HCM to Employee Central, but not from Employee Central to SAP ERP HCM.

▶ The number ranges (primarily used for generating Employee PERNRs, Organizational Object IDs, etc.) used in SAP ERP HCM and Employee Central must not overlap.

▶ You defined the system in which the employee is mastered. (The employee is mastered in SAP ERP HCM or in Employee Central; the same employee cannot be mastered both in SAP ERP HCM and Employee Central.) Common rules you can use to define in which system an employee is mastered center on country, regions, and other such factors.

▶ RBPs are defined to control maintenance access.

▶ Employee Central is used as the global HCM system to store all employee master data, including for employees who are mastered in SAP ERP HCM.

▶ SAP ERP HCM stores the master data of employees who are mastered in SAP ERP HCM only.

▶ The following data mappings should been implemented:

  ▶ The Central Person (CP) from SAP ERP HCM is mapped to the `person_id_external` field in Employee Central.

  ▶ The Personnel Number (PERNR) from SAP ERP HCM is mapped to the `user_id` field in Employee Central.

The following sections will discuss employee data considerations for transactions performed in Side-By-Side HCM deployment on employees mastered in SAP ERP HCM and those mastered in Employee Central.

5.7.1 Hire

In this deployment model, when an employee is hired in SAP ERP HCM, the new employee is replicated to Employee Central.

In Employee Central, the employee's PERNR (an employee's personnel number assigned to the employee in SAP ERP HCM) is mapped to the Employee Central `user_id` field and the employee's CP ID is mapped to `person_id_external`. The employee's data is stored in Employee Central as per the mapping you have defined.

In SAP ERP HCM, using the feature RULES FOR DETERMINING ENTRY DATE (ENTRY), you can define how the hire date is determined. The hire date as determined by this feature is replicated to Employee Central.

> **Concurrent and Global Employment Scenarios**
>
> The current release (b1408) of the Side-By-Side HCM deployment model does not support concurrent employment or global employment scenarios.
>
> The current release of the Side-By-Side HCM model does not support the scenario to replicate global assignments of an employee with multiple PERNRs attached to one CP ID stored in SAP ERP HCM to Employee Central.

If you have been using the SAP ERP HCM system for several years and are migrating to Employee Central, then you can replicate the employee master data from SAP ERP HCM to Employee Central at a certain point in time by defining the cutover date. If the cutover date is defined, then the fields HIRE DATE and ORIGINAL START DATE in Employee Central are filled differently, depending on whether the employee's hire date is before or after the cutover date.

The following considerations should be made when dealing with the cutover date for hiring (see also Figure 5.10):

- If the cutover date is before the HIRE DATE in SAP ERP HCM, then the fields HIRE DATE and ORIGINAL START DATE in Employee Central are both filled with the SAP ERP HCM HIRE DATE.

- If the cutover date if after the HIRE DATE in SAP ERP HCM, then the ORIGINAL START DATE field in Employee Central is mapped to the SAP ERP HCM HIRE DATE, and HIRE DATE in Employee Central is mapped to the cutover date.

- If the HIRE DATE is before the cutover date and the employee master data in SAP ERP HCM is changed before the cutover date, then the ORIGINAL START DATE field in Employee Central is mapped to the HIRE DATE in SAP ERP HCM, and the HIRE DATE in Employee Central is mapped to the cutover date. Therefore, the employee will have only have one job info record in Employee Central, which represents the data that is valid on the cutover date.

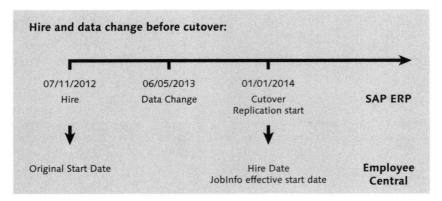

Figure 5.10 Hire and Data Change before Cutover Date

Hiring in Employee Central

In the Side-By-Side HCM deployment model, if the employee is hired directly in Employee Central, then the new hire process in Employee Central will work as usual. Employees mastered in Employee Central are never replicated to SAP ERP HCM.

5.7.2 Rehire

In SAP ERP HCM, it is possible to rehire an employee and assign the same PERNR and CP ID to the rehired employee. After an employee has been rehired, the employee master data is replicated to Employee Central via the Side-By-Side HCM deployment model.

When an employee is rehired in SAP ERP HCM, you'll want to verify that the rehired employee is not mastered in Employee Central. This verification has to be manually done in Employee Central. If you've been using an SAP ERP HCM system for several years and are migrating to Employee Central, then you can replicate the employee master data from SAP ERP HCM to Employee Central at a certain point in time by defining the cutover date.

If the cutover date is defined, then the fields HIRE DATE and ORIGINAL START DATE in Employee Central are filled differently depending on whether the employee's rehire date is before or after the cutover date (see Figure 5.11).

The following considerations should be made when dealing with the cutover date for rehiring:

▶ If the employee was hired, terminated, and rehired in SAP ERP HCM before the cutover date, then the first hire date is mapped to ORIGINAL START DATE in Employee Central. The cutover date is mapped to HIRE DATE in Employee Central. When a rehire is replicated to Employee Central, the special event reason PSEUDO_HIRE is used. In this scenario, the date stored in the ORIGINAL START DATE (the date the employee was first hired into the company) is used to calculate the seniority of the employee.

▶ If the cutover date is between termination and the rehire dates in SAP ERP HCM, then the first hire date in SAP ERP HCM is mapped to ORIGINAL HIRE DATE in Employee Central, and the rehire date is mapped to HIRE DATE in Employee Central. The event reason PSEUDO_HIRE is used in Employee Central.

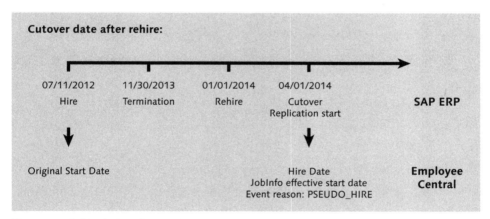

Figure 5.11 Rehire before Cutover Date

Rehiring in Employee Central

If the employee is rehired directly in Employee Central, then the rehire process in Employee Central will work as usual. Employees mastered or rehired directly in Employee Central are never replicated to SAP ERP HCM.

If you hire an employee in Employee Central and this employee already exists in Employee Central (because the employee either was mastered in Employee Central or was replicated from SAP ERP HCM), then the system will perform a duplicate check and will display a message. You will then be required to initiate a rehire event in Employee Central using the same user_id and person_id_external data.

> The current release of the Side-By-Side HCM deployment model does not support the scenario in which an employee who was previously mastered in Employee Central cannot be rehired in SAP ERP HCM.

5.7.3   Transfers

For employees who are mastered in SAP ERP HCM, an organization reassignment would mean changes in Infotype 0001 (Organizational Reassignment). For any organizational reassignment, the employee's country assignment and personnel number must remain unchanged. (The current release of the Side-By-Side HCM deployment model supports only scenarios in which an employee can have only one personnel number.) Any changes made in Infotype 0001 are replicated to Employee Central. In Employee Central, the system creates a new record in the job information object. The date these changes were made in SAP ERP HCM is used as the EFFECTIVE START DATE for this newly created record in the job information object. The event reason DATAREORG is used in Employee Central.

> **Transfers in Employee Central**
>
> If the employee is mastered in Employee Central, then transfers or the organizational reassignment process in Employee Central works as usual. Employees mastered in Employee Central are never replicated to SAP ERP HCM.

International Transfer

When dealing with international transfers in this Side-By-Side HCM deployment model integration, the following considerations should be made:

▸ **Transferring an employee from a country mastered in SAP ERP HCM to another country mastered in SAP ERP HCM**
  When an employee is transferred from one country to another (mastered in SAP ERP HCM in both countries), a LEAVING action is executed in the original country, and a HIRING action is executed in the new country. The employee will get a new personnel number (PERNR) in the new country, and this PERNR will be attached to the same CP.

  The employee master data extraction program ECPAO_EMPL_EXTRACTION merges data from different personnel numbers of the employee assigned to the same CP ID, and the data associated with the different PERNRs are transferred to the job information and job history records in Employee Central if the following conditions are fulfilled:

▸ The PERNRs assigned to the employee are assigned in different countries.

▸ Only one PERNR is active.

▸ Leaving and hiring actions are completed for the employee record.

▸ **Transferring an employee from a country mastered in Employee Central to another country mastered in Employee Central**
There are no changes in the process in Employee Central when an employee is transferred from one country to another. Employee records mastered in Employee Central are not transferred to SAP ERP HCM.

▸ **Transferring an employee from a country mastered in SAP ERP HCM to a country mastered in Employee Central**
When an employee mastered in SAP ERP HCM is transferred from a country to a country mastered in Employee Central, then you are required to execute a *future-dated* leaving action in the original country.

The specific employee's master data is replicated to Employee Central. In Employee Central, carry out a TERMINATION EVENT for the original country, and future-date the employee status as INACTIVE. Now, in Employee Central, create an additional employment for that employee in the hiring country. A new user needs to be created in Employee Central for the new employment.

5.7.4 Termination

For the Side-By-Side HCM deployment model, when an employee is mastered in SAP ERP HCM, if that employee is terminated in SAP ERP HCM, the information about that termination is replicated to Employee Central. When the employee is terminated in SAP ERP HCM, the employee record is set to the WITHDRAWN status.

The replication of the termination status from SAP ERP HCM to Employee Central ensures that the employee is terminated in Employee Central and that master data in Employee Central is set to the INACTIVE status. When the terminated employee records are replicated to Employee Central, a new record is created in the job information object using a termination event and event reason.

> **Terminations in Employee Central**
>
> If the employee is mastered in Employee Central, then the termination process of employees in Employee Central works as usual. Employees mastered in Employee Central are never replicated to SAP ERP HCM.

5.8   Case Studies

As discussed in Section 5.1, the Side-By-Side HCM deployment model applies to the customers that want to keep their on-premise HR system for catering to local needs and have employee and manager actions performed in a modern, unified, cost-effective core HR system. In the case studies that follow, we will look at customers implementing the Side-By-Side HCM deployment model in consolidated and distributed variants.

5.8.1   Case Study 1

In this case study, we will look at a company in the semiconductors industry that uses different SAP deployments to run its business around the globe. They invested heavily in software that manages their business for decades. However, their HCM software could not provide a single system to manage their global workforce. We will discuss how this customer addressed this situation by adopting the Side-By-Side HCM consolidated deployment model.

Client Scenario

ReliableBoards Co., a semiconductors industry of about 9,000 employees that designs, develops, and manufactures flash memory microcontrollers and mixed-signal and analog products, uses multiple HR systems for global human resource management. The company uses other SAP Business Suite solutions, such as SAP CRM, to manage its customer information and SAP SRM system. As a result, it has implemented multiple HCM systems to meet requirements across the globe.

However, these HCM systems are connected to 25 different business systems. These include several business applications, such as SAP ERP, multiple payroll providers, and benefits providers. Most of these integrations were done via file-based data transfer on a schedule. In the case of some payroll providers, information was uploaded via data entry by service center teams that received this information in Microsoft Excel files.

Their multiple HR systems do not provide a global employee count or cross-location reporting and have become hard to maintain and costly to upgrade; as a result, these systems do not meet their business needs. In addition to the difficulty in connecting multiple HCM systems to different business systems, this has pushed the company to use the Side-By-Side HCM consolidated deployment model to implement a single HCM system.

Process Steps

Having decided to implement a single HCM system for the entire organization via the Side-By-Side HCM consolidated model, ReliableBoards Co. adopted Employee Central for employee administration and Employee Central Payroll to run payroll for each of the regions.

This transition to the cloud was executed in multiple phases. Employee Central housed all employee data at the end of the transition, and integrations were implemented for payroll, benefits, time, and attendance systems. ReliableBoards Co. integrated Employee Central with SAP ERP for local workflow management. The following are the individual steps taken to successfully implement consolidated Side-By-Side HCM deployment:

1. In phase 1, ReliableBoards Co. implemented Employee Central for North America. The company migrated North American employees' data from an on-premise HCM system to Employee Central.

2. Then, the company implemented and migrated its payroll data to Employee Central Payroll for processing payroll.

3. Next, the company used Dell Boomi AtomSphere as the middleware platform to integrate Employee Central with on-premise SAP ERP in North America, Employee Central Payroll, Workforce Time Management, and Benefitfocus. To implement these integrations, they used packaged integrations provided by SAP and executed the procedures defined in each of the integration handbooks available at *http://help.sap.com/cloud4hr*.

4. Next, the company used Dell Boomi AtomSphere again as middleware, this time to integrate Employee Central with Active Directory by utilizing the integration template provided by SAP Professional Services. The company then went live with Employee Central for the North America region.

5. ReliableBoards Co. then implemented Employee Central for its European region in phase 2 and for Asia in phase 3, following the same process outlined for phase 1. In each case of these phases, the company integrated Employee Central with its on-premise SAP ERP, Employee Central Payroll, and Workforce Time Management.

6. After phase 3, the company has all its employees in Employee Central but still executes some local processes in its on-premise system. However, Employee Central is the company's global system of record for employee data.

Let's now look at a company that has decided to use the Side-By-Side HCM distributed option.

5.8.2 Case Study 2

In this case study, we will look at a company in the software industry that uses SAP to run its business. The company has invested heavily in its current HR system that manages its business for decades. The company acquired a new business but does not want to bring data for the subsidiary into SAP. We will discuss how the customer addressed this situation by adopting the Side-By-Side HCM distributed deployment model. Let's start with a look at the company and the business problems it faces.

Client Scenario

Gloplex International, a software services industry with over 30,000 employees, provides business transformation and software consulting services to large businesses. Gloplex International acquired Cyberdin Software to expand its services in Asia.

Currently, Gloplex uses SAP ERP to run its company and SAP Payroll for processing payroll for its global employee population. It also uses an HCM solution but has heavily customized it. Recently, the company implemented SuccessFactors Talent Management suite for its global employee population in a record time of six months.

As the industry changes, so do the processes at Gloplex. To keep up with these growing changes, the company decided to move to the cloud and benefit from the advantages. However, the company is hesitant to make this transformation, fearing it could disrupt business. Cyberdin Software, on the other hand, built its own HR system and outsourced payroll processing. Cyberdin conducts performance reviews and learning delivery using homegrown software.

Immediately after the acquisition, Gloplex and Cyberdin formed teams comprising of people from both organizations. This resulted in some employees from Gloplex reporting to middle managers in Cyberdin, who reported to executives in Gloplex. However, without a single employee database containing all users, there were challenges in managing employees effectively across both organizations.

To remedy these shortcomings, the company has chosen to move its entire HCM solution to the cloud, but it wants to move at its own pace. It plans to adopt Employee Central as Cyberdin's core HR system and implement packaged integrations for the Side-By-Side HCM distributed model with Gloplex's SAP ERP HCM, thereby enabling employee transactions for both companies using the same Employee Central instance.

Process Steps

Having chosen the Side-By-Side HCM distributed deployment model, the company is retiring Cyberdin's homegrown HR solution and implementing its HCM solution in the cloud, including all talent management solutions from SuccessFactors, such as Performance Management and Goal Management, Succession Planning, Learning Compensation, SAP Jam, and SuccessFactors Workforce Analytics. For employee administration, the company adopted Employee Central and SAP Payroll.

Because Gloplex had the SuccessFactors Talent Management suite implemented before, all employees of Cyberdin are added to the same SuccessFactors Talent Management suite instance and are provided instant access. The company then embarked on implementing Employee Central for Cyberdin employees and set up Side-By-Side HCM integrations with SAP on-premise.

The following are the individual steps taken to successfully implement these choices:

1. Employee Central was configured using a global template design that would work not just for Cyberdin employees but also for Gloplex employees, because the goal for Gloplex is to use Employee Central for all its employees in the future.

2. While defining the global template, it was ensured that all fields required for employee replication from Employee Central to SAP ERP were defined. These

fields can be found in the Employee Master Data Replication implementation guide available at *http://help.sap.com/cloud4hr*.

3. All Cyberdin employee data was migrated from Cyberdin's legacy system to Employee Central. The company used SuccessFactors migration tools to load this data into Employee Central.

4. The company then enabled employee replication from Employee Central to SAP ERP, following the steps from the Employee Master Data Replication implementation guide. This will allow the company to run SAP Payroll for Cyberdin employees in Gloplex's SAP ERP. This integration needs not be implemented if employees mastered in Employee Central do not use any on-premise applications.

5. The HRIS sync job is turned on for Cyberdin employees from Employee Central to SuccessFactors Talent Management suite, enabling data synchronization between core employee data and talent modules.

6. Next, the company set up and enabled replication of employee master data from SAP ERP to Employee Central for Gloplex employees. The process is documented in Employee Central and SAP ERP in the Side-By-Side HCM Deployment Model implementation guide available at *http://help.sap.com/cloud4hr*.

7. Finally, the integration of Employee Central UI with on-premise SAP ERP enabled managers and employees to use the SuccessFactors home page as a global UI hub was implemented. They can view data or trigger data changes for employees whose data is mastered in SAP ERP HCM using the navigation on the Employee Central UI. This is possible because all employees whose data is mastered in SAP ERP HCM are replicated to Employee Central using the employee data integration of the Side-By-Side HCM deployment model.

5.9   Summary

The Side-By-Side HCM deployment model is for customers who want to segment employee population and run people management applications in the cloud as well as on-premise. In this deployment model, customers run Employee Central, SuccessFactors Talent Solutions, and SuccessFactors Workforce Planning and Analytics in the cloud for a subset of employees and core HR with SuccessFactors Talent Management solutions for the remaining employees. SAP and SuccessFactors provide packaged integrations to enable easier and better integration between SAP ERP and the SuccessFactors HCM suite.

In this chapter, we also discussed how customers who need data and process integration across geographies on different core HR systems are good candidates to adopt the Side-By-Side HCM deployment model. There are multiple packaged integrations to connect Employee Central with SAP ERP, customized to address these different customer needs. In addition, we explored how HR business processes for events like hire, rehire, transfer, and terminate can be executed with same efficiency and ease of use as in a single system.

In the next chapter, we will take a look at SuccessFactors integration layers and open APIs that can be leveraged to integrate Employee Central and SuccessFactors Talent Management solutions with external systems for both data and process integrations.

PART III

SuccessFactors Integration Models

This chapter introduces SuccessFactors' integration layers and APIs. After reviewing this chapter, you will better understand SuccessFactors' logical integration architecture as well as the capabilities of its various APIs to integrate with SuccessFactors modules.

6   Integration Layers and APIs

In today's business world, companies use numerous applications that are not always from the same software provider. These applications are expected to interact with one another to increase productivity, reduce duplicate data entries, and provide an integrated experience to end users. The architecture of SuccessFactors products, from the early stages of their development, provide multiple mechanisms for integrating with third-party systems, both for data and process integrations (including real-time integrations).

Today, SuccessFactors products can be integrated with other systems to not only exchange data and implement a business process spanning across multiple systems but also extend and build new functionality that provides a seamless user interface (UI) and real-time data exchange with other systems.

In this chapter, we will discuss SuccessFactors' integration logical architecture, breaking down its various parts and looking at what roles are played in the integration process. Then, we will focus in on the importance of APIs in the various integration scenarios that occur.

6.1   SuccessFactors Integration Logical Layers

SuccessFactors products have been extended to work across multiple systems, providing a seamless UI and real-time data exchange. SuccessFactors owes this functionality to its innovative integration architecture and models.

Figure 6.1 illustrates the logical architecture to integrate with SuccessFactor products.

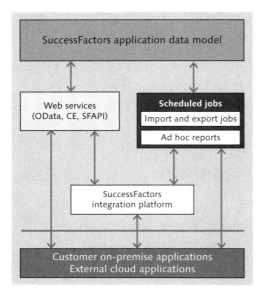

Figure 6.1 SuccessFactors Integration Logical Architecture

When integrating with SuccessFactors, the following four logic layers need to be considered:

- SuccessFactors data model (see Section 6.1.1)
- Data interfaces (see Section 6.1.2)
- SuccessFactors integration and extension platforms (see Section 6.1.3)
- Customer applications (both on-premise and in cloud systems, including SAP products; see Section 6.1.4)

Let's look at each of these layers now.

6.1.1 SuccessFactors Data Model

The SuccessFactors data model is flexible and configures to a customer's need. For example, in Employee Central you can define how the company's organization structure should look and what attributes need to be associated with the company, person, and employment data. All of this is done through configurations to the data model, allowing customers to define their own unique data models that fits specific and distinctive requirements. These configurations are upgrade compatible with each SuccessFactors release, providing seamless integration.

The following are the core data models in Employee Central:

- **Corporate data model**
  This model contains the data structures related to the company's organization, pay, and job structure.

- **Succession data model**
  This model contains the data structures related to the data of the people working in the company, like compensation and address.

- **Corporate data model (country specific)**
  This model contains country-specific corporate data, like location address information for each country in which the company has a presence.

- **Succession data model (country specific)**
  This model contains the international formats and fields, like national IDs and addresses.

These data models offer different purposes and customizations based on the needs of the customer.

6.1.2 Data Interfaces

SuccessFactors' core framework provides import and export jobs with specific predefined formats that can be used to extract data from or add data to different entities. These jobs are available through administration sections of the application for ad hoc runs and can be accessed if the user has specific permissions. They are also available to be scheduled as background jobs.

Ad hoc reports can also be configured with the fields that are needed and scheduled to export data to SFTP. There are options to encrypt data for data exchanges with SuccessFactors modules.

Web Service APIs

A web service API is the de facto standard for real-time integrations and is one of the most popular ways of interacting with SuccessFactors. Section 6.2 is dedicated to discussing the different types of APIs available in SuccessFactors.

6.1.3 SuccessFactors Integration Platform

The SuccessFactors integration platform can be used for data integrations with other systems to include transformations or customer-specific requirements.

SuccessFactors' products officially support SAP HANA Cloud Integration, SAP Process Integration (PI), and Dell Boomi AtomSphere platforms for data integrations. For building extensions to SuccessFactors products, SAP HANA Cloud Platform is the only option and requires the use of Java programming language for development.

> **Third-Party Applications and APIs**
>
> At the end of the day, SuccessFactors APIs are web services and can be invoked directly from third-party applications without the need for any middleware. Middleware, on the other hand, helps with transformation, business rules, notifications, and so on.

6.1.4   Customer Applications

Typically, SuccessFactors modules are integrated with a variety of applications, which can be on-premise applications such as SAP ERP and Microsoft Active Directory or third-party cloud applications such as benefits, time and attendance, payroll, and background screening vendors. Each of these types of applications can require a different integration pattern based on best practices. Typically, payroll integrations are complex, but a majority of the other integrations involve demographic data being passed from Employee Central to other third-party applications.

Now that we've looked at the architecture and integration layers of SuccessFactors, let's turn our attention to the web service APIs available.

6.2   SuccessFactors APIs

SuccessFactors has both SOAP-based and REST-based web services. There are three types of web services available today with SuccessFactors:

▸ **OData API**
This is the REST-based API and the ideal way to interface with SuccessFactors — especially Employee Central.

▸ **SFAPI**
This SOAP-based API is being used widely today to integrate SuccessFactors modules other than Employee Central.

▸ **Compound Employee API**
The CE API returns multiple SuccessFactors objects in a hierarchically structured

response XML file with the employee as the root node, and is a neat way to extract employee superset data.

The following sections look at these different APIs in further detail so that you can determine which API suits a specific scenario that you may encounter.

6.2.1 OData API

Open Data Protocol (OData) is a protocol for creating (POST), reading (GET), updating (PUT), and deleting (DELETE) data based on HTTP. In other words, OData offers CRUD (create, read, update, and delete) operations over HTTP.

OData is the web-equivalent of ODBC (Open Database Connectivity). It provides a uniform way to expose full-featured data APIs. It is an open protocol originally suggested by Microsoft and is now widely supported (MS, SAP, IBM, etc.). Many SAP products use OData as the default protocol for integrations with other systems.

Additional Information

For more details on OData, refer to *www.odata.org*.

The following sections discuss some of the critical components of SuccessFactors OData implementations and corresponding formats and examples to get you started.

OData Provisioning

OData is enabled by the support representatives on your instance. You should reach out to them in the standard way you interact with SuccessFactors support. The endpoint URLs for accessing OData APIs depend on which data center the instance is hosted on. Your SuccessFactors support representative will provide that data.

OData Authentication

OData APIs provide two types of authentication: HTTP-Basic authentication and OAuth authentication. In HTTP-Basic authentication, the client provides credentials, which are carried as plain text in the authorization header. OAuth is the authorization concept for OData services that offers constrained access without passing or storing credentials. We recommend OAuth authentication, because it is the more secure method.

HTTP-Basic Authentication

In HTTP-Basic authentication, the credentials are constructed in a certain way and are base encoded and passed in the authorization header.

The following format should be used to specify your credentials:

```
username@companyId:password
```

For example, if you have a company called ACEHR and the username/password is cgrant/pwd, then the string format is as follows:

```
cgrant@ACEHR:pwd
```

This string must be Base64 encoded. For example, the previous string encoded with Base64 should appear as follows:

```
Y2dyYW50QEFDRUhSOnB3ZA==
```

Next, you'll add this string into your HTTP header in the following format:

```
Authorization: Basic Y2dyYW50QEFDRUhSOnB3ZA==
```

OAuth 2.0 Authentication

OAuth 2.0 is an open authorization protocol that lets different applications share information with each other in a secure fashion. To enable OAuth 2.0, you have to go through the steps of granting permissions for the Role-Based Permissions (RBP) or user-based system and registering your OAuth client application.

> **Additional Information**
>
> For more information on the exact steps required, refer to the *SAP HCM Suite OData API User Guide* at *http://help.sap.com/saphelpiis_cloud4hr/en/successfactors_hcm_suite_odata_api_handbook_en.pdf*.

OData Metadata Document

The metadata document is a data structure that describes the capabilities of the API to your SuccessFactors instance. OData has a standard for the basic information that should be represented in the metadata document. It contains details of each of the entities that are accessible through the API, including the fields, names, labels, data types, and the relationships (associations) between the entities. The metadata document also lists the operations available in the API. SuccessFactors matches this standard and also adds additional information through an annotations-based approach.

The additional information, for example, includes localized labels for fields and behaviors to describe if the field is required when inserting or if the field is filterable.

The OData API metadata document can be accessed via *https://<hostname>/odata/v2/$metadata*. Make sure the credential is correctly set in the HTTP header and that you can access the OData metadata document via the preceding URL. This will return an XML serialization of the service, including the entity data model and the service operations descriptions. The metadata response supports only application or atom plus XML type. (You cannot get the metadata response in JSON, for example.)

The metadata document also describes the operations available in the API. The OData protocol specifies four basic database-style operations: insert, update, query, and delete. SuccessFactors also adds a fifth operation called *upsert*, which performs an insert or update operation.

The same metadata information is also available in the OData API Data Dictionary, which can be accessed within the SuccessFactors platform as long as the user has RBPs enabled for it. Figure 6.2 shows a snippet of the API Data Dictionary.

Admin Tools

Back to Admin Tools

OData API Data Dictionary
This page will list the data entities in your system that are available through the OData API and describe the fields in each entity.

Expand All   Contract All

OData API Entities

⊞ **AccrualCalculationBase**

⊟ **AlertMessage**
Supported Operations:Query, Insert, Merge, Replace, Upsert, Delete
Entity Name:AlertMessage
Fields:

Property Name	Label	Type	Picklist	Business Key	Nullable	Required	Insertable	Updatable	Upsertable	Selectable	Sortable	Filterable	MaxLength
alertDescription	alertDescription	string			true	false	true	true	true	true	true	true	255
alertHeader	alertHeader	string			true	false	true	true	true	true	true	true	255
createdBy	mdfSystemCreatedBy	string			true	false	true	false	false	true	true	true	255
createdDateTime	mdfSystemCreatedDate	datetimeoffset			true	false	false	false	false	true	true	true	
effectiveStatus	effectiveStatus	string			true	false	true	true	true	true	true	true	255
externalCode	externalCode	string		true	false	true	true	true	true	true	true	true	128
externalName	externalName	string			true	false	true	true	true	true	true	true	128
lastModifiedBy	mdfSystemLastModifi...	string			true	false	false	false	false	true	true	true	255

Figure 6.2 OData API Data Dictionary

193

In the future, SuccessFactors may add other custom operations. Typically, custom operations will perform specific business transactions, especially if a custom API is easier to manage versus a database-style approach against multiple entities. Regardless of which operations are used (create, read, update, delete, upsert, or even future custom operations), SuccessFactors will apply the appropriate business logic for each entity.

In other words, even though the operations appear to be database-centric, the API goes through the application business logic layer. The API does not go directly against the database, nor does it bypass the business logic layer. The entities in the API represent logical application objects that should be familiar to an application user. The entities do not represent the actual physical data storage implementation, which may be in a completely different structure. There should be no assumption of the underlying implementation details.

Speed Up Responses with a gzip Header

The metadata document can be quite large. You can reduce the response time of this operation by using gzip to compress the document in transit through HTTP, thereby saving bandwidth. To enable gzip, the client should issue the HTTP request with the header `Accept-Encoding:GZIP`. If the OData server gets this header, it will assume that the client expects a compressed stream, and responses will be a gzipped output stream to the client.

> **Client Application Code**
>
> It may sound obvious, but make sure your client application code supports gzip if you use this header.

OData Query Operations

The OData URI identifies resources defined in the data model that can be edited or published by simple HTTP messages using OData. The OData specification defines a set of recommended rules for constructing URIs to identify the data and metadata exposed by an OData server. Figure 6.3 displays the structure of the OData URI.

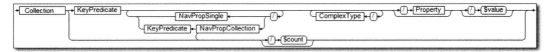

Figure 6.3 OData Query Format

This URI is used by different clients to interact with SuccessFactors data. It can be as simple as using a browser to display the results of the URI or can be as complex as using middleware to dynamically read the metadata and then act accordingly.

The following are important components of the OData URI:

- **Collection or EntitySet**
  This is the name of a collection or a custom service operation (which returns a collection of entries) exposed by the service.

- **KeyPredicate**
  This is a predicate that identifies the value(s) of the key properties of an entry. If the entry has a single key property, then the predicate may include only the value of the key property. If the key is made up of two or more properties, then its value must be stated using name/value pairs. More precisely, the syntax for a KeyPredicate is shown in Figure 6.4.

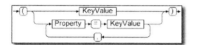

Figure 6.4 KeyPredicate Syntax

- **NavPropSingle**
  This is the name of a navigation property defined by the entry associated with the prior path segment. The navigation property must identify a single entity (that is, have a "to 1" relationship).

- **NavPropCollection**
- This is the same as NavPropSingle, except it must identify a collection of entries (that is, have a "too many" relationship).

- **ComplexType**
  This is the name of a declared or dynamic property of the entry or complex type associated with the prior path segment.

- **Property**
  This is the name of a declared or dynamic property of the entry or complex type associated with the prior path segment.

Let's now look at some examples based on the addressing rules stated previously:

- `https://<hostname>/odata/v2/User`

  - Identifies all user collections

- ▸ Is described by the entity set named `User` in the service metadata document
- ▸ `https://<hostname>/odata/v2/User('1')`
  - ▸ Identifies a single user entry with key value 1
  - ▸ Is described by the entity type named `User` in the service metadata document
- ▸ `https://<hostname>/odata/v2/User('1')/username`
  - ▸ Identifies the name property of the user entry with key value 1
  - ▸ Is described by the property named `Name` on the `User` entity type in the service metadata document
- ▸ `https://<hostname>/odata/v2/User('1')/proxy`
  - ▸ Identifies the collection of proxies associated with user entry with key value 1
  - ▸ Is described by the navigation property named proxy on the `User` entity type in the service metadata document
- ▸ `https://<hostname>/odata/v2/User('1')/proxy/$count`
  - ▸ Identifies the number of proxy entries associated with `User 1`
  - ▸ Is described by the navigation property named `proxy` on the `User` entity type in the service metadata document
- ▸ `https://<hostname>/odata/v2/User('1')/proxy('1')/hr/username`
  - ▸ Identifies the username of the `hr` for `proxy` 1, which is associated with `User 1`
  - ▸ Is described by the property named `username` on the `hr` entity type in the service metadata document

System Query Options

In some cases, you may want to refine the results of your query, which is where the system query options come in. These are very powerful mechanisms to help you get the data the way you want it. Table 6.1 lists the system query options supported.

Query Option	Brief Description
Orderby	Orders the result set with the values given in the clause. Ascending order by default.
Top	Picks the top N entries.
Skip	Skips the first N entries, and returns the remaining.

Table 6.1 OData Query Parameters

Query Option	Brief Description
Filter	Returns the subset of entries that satisfy the predicate expression.
Expand	Entries associated with the entry or collection of entries; must be represented inline.
Format	The media type that the response should conform to.
Select	Returns a subset of the properties.

Table 6.1 OData Query Parameters (Cont.)

For example, the following query is used to retrieve the user name and associated manager for the selected user. As in Table 6.1, you can see that the format is JSON, and the expand option helps retrieve the user's manager:

```
https://<hostname>/odata/v2/User?$format=json&$expand=manager&select=
userId,manager/userId
```

The query results are shown in Listing 6.1.

```
{
__metadata: {
uri: " https://<hostname>/odata/v2/User('01171917-1') "
type: "SFOData.User"
}
userId: "01171917-1"
manager: {
__metadata: {
uri: " https://<hostname>/odata/v2/User('01170004')"
type: "SFOData.User"
}
userId: "01170004"
}
}
```

Listing 6.1 Retreiving the User and Associated Manager

Troubleshooting OData Operations

Outside of logs that are available from the target system, troubleshooting OData operations with SuccessFactors modules can be accomplished in multiple ways. The following describes a few of these methods:

▸ **OData API audit logs**
The OData audit logs can be accessed by users who have the corresponding permissions granted through RBPs. The ellipsis (...) buttons under the HTTP column

provide the state of the HTTP headers for request and response. The buttons in the REST column provide the REST request and response data (see Figure 6.5).

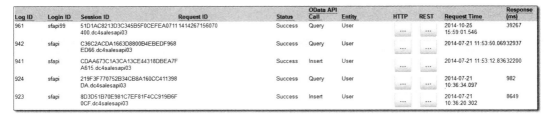

Log ID	Login ID	Session ID	Request ID	Status	OData API Call	Entity	HTTP	REST	Request Time	Response (ms)
961	sfapi99	51D1AC8213D3C345B5F0CEFEA0711 400.dc4salesapi03	1414267156070	Success	Query	User	...	...	2014-10-25 15:59:01.546	39267
942	sfapi	C36C2ACDA1663D8800B4EBEDF968 ED66.dc4salesapi03		Success	Query	User	...	...	2014-07-21 11:53:50.069	32937
941	sfapi	CDAA673C1A3CA13CE44318DBEA7F A615.dc4salesapi03		Success	Insert	User	...	...	2014-07-21 11:53:12.836	32200
924	sfapi	219F3F770752B34CB8A160CC411398 DA.dc4salesapi03		Success	Query	User	...	...	2014-07-21 10:36:34.097	982
923	sfapi	8D3D51B70E981C7EF81F4CC919B6F 0CF.dc4salesapi03		Success	Insert	User	...	...	2014-07-21 10:36:20.302	8649

Figure 6.5 OData Audit Logs in Admin Tools

▸ **OData API debug logs**
The debug logs for OData are accessible from Provisioning and will provide application-level logging information.

▸ **REST client**
By using REST client plug-ins with your Internet browser, you can invoke APIs for different scenarios and adjust your operation parameters accordingly (see Figure 6.6).

Figure 6.6 OData Query Modeling Using a REST Client

Now that we have discussed OData APIs, let's look at another important type of API.

6.2.2 SFAPI

SFAPI provides SOAP-based web services designed for importing and exporting data in and out of a SuccessFactors instance. It provides metadata operations for the entities in addition to generic CRUD operations.

In the case of Employee Central, SFAPI should only be used if there are no corresponding OData APIs available. In general, SuccessFactors is moving towards OData API but has committed to be backward compatible to SFAPI for quite some time.

> **Important!**
>
> Please note that SFAPI is the only and main option in some modules (such as SuccessFactors Recruiting) as of the time of writing (spring 2015).

SFObjects are the entities exposed by SFAPI. These objects are analogous to database tables, but in reality they are not directly related to tables underneath. Metadata operations are used to do things such as list SFObjects and fields within an entity. The CRUD operations enable you to access and manipulate the data within the objects.

SOAP provides the definition of the XML-based information, which can be used for exchanging structured and typed information between peers in a decentralized, distributed environment.

> **Additional Information**
>
> For more details on SOAP, refer to *www.w3.org*.

The following sections discuss some of the critical components of SuccessFactors SOAP (SFAPI) and corresponding formats and examples to get you started.

Provisioning SFAPI

Each user of the API must have an API login permission. An administrator of your SuccessFactors system can grant this permission. Provisioning SFAPI depends on the type of permission model implemented for your SuccessFactors instance. There are two types of permission models: user-based permissions and RBP. The permission setting in the UI is under MANAGE USERS • API LOGIN PERMISSION.

The following are instructions for each permission system:

▸ **User-based permission settings**
   This API login permission is granted via ADMIN TOOLS • MANAGE USERS • MANAGE API LOGIN PERMISSION.

▸ **RBP settings**
   This API login permission is granted via ADMIN TOOLS • MANAGE PERMISSION ROLES • CREATE NEW (see Figure 6.7).

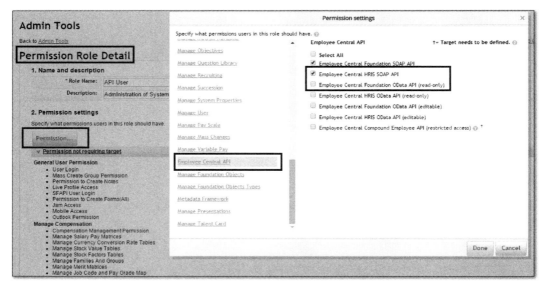

Figure 6.7 Role and Permission Settings

After creating an SFAPI role, assign API permissions to the newly created role, and assign the role to a group of users (see Figure 6.8).

Figure 6.8 Assign Role to Group Settings

Authentications

Authentication is established by the login operation by passing the proper credentials in the SFCredential object. This will return a session ID, which needs to be passed back for all subsequent HTTP requests invoking the API.

A successful login will return a session ID as an HTTP cookie. This cookie must be passed back to all subsequent HTTP requests that invoke API operations in order to authenticate.

The sessions will timeout after 10 minutes of inactivity. You can also manually invalidate a session by using the logout method.

SFAPI Operations

The SFAPI operations help get data out of SuccessFactors and put data into SuccessFactors. SFAPI is dynamic in the sense that you have to use the metadata operations to discover the schema and its data instead of using a static WSDL.

The five categories of SFAPI methods are as follows:

▶ Session Management (login/logout/isValidSession)

▶ Metadata Inspection (list/describe)

▶ Data Manipulation (insert/update/upsert/delete)

▶ Data Query (query/queryMore)

▶ Asynchronous Job (submitJob/getJobStatus/getJobResult/listJobs/cancelJob)

Let's look at the format of these categories more closely.

Session Management

Session Management contains the following operations:

▶ LoginResult login(SFCredential credential, List<SFParameters> params)
This operation involves the following variables:

   ▶ Includes boolean logout()

   ▶ Destroys the current API session

   ▶ Includes boolean isValidSession()

   ▶ Returns true if the current API session is still valid

   ▶ Includes String [] list()

This operation creates the SFAPI session shown in Listing 6.2.

```
<S:Envelope>
   <S:Header/>
   <S:Body>
      <login>
         <credential>
            <companyId>ACEHR</companyId>
            <username>cgrant</username>
            <password>pwd</password>
         </credential>
      </login>
   </S:Body> </S:Envelope>
```

Listing 6.2 LoginResult login(SFCredential credential, List<SFParameters> params)

It also lists the entities in your company instance, shown in Listing 6.3.

```
<S:Envelope>
   <S:Header/>
   <S:Body>
      <listSFObjects/>
   </S:Body> </S:Envelope>
```

Listing 6.3 Company Instance

▶ `DescribeResult describe(String type[], SFParameter params[])`
This returns metadata about the list of entities specified in the `type` parameter (both field and entity information). This method is deprecated, so use `describeEx`.

▶ `DescribeExResult describeEx(String type[], SFParameter params[])`
This is an extended version of the `describe` method; an example is shown in Listing 6.4.

```
<S:Envelope>
   <S:Body>
      <describeSFObjectsEx>
         <type>User</type>
      </describeSFObjectsEx>
   </S:Body> </S:Envelope>
```

Listing 6.4 DescribeExResult describeEx(String type[], SFParameter params[])

Data Manipulation

Data Manipulation contains the following operations:

▶ InsertResult insert(String type, SFObject[] objects, SFParameter[] processingParam)

This inserts the objects of the specified entity type. The operation will resume if one row has failed to insert, as shown in Listing 6.5.

```
<S:Envelope>
  <S:Body>
    <insert>
      <type>user</type>
      <sfobject>
        <type>user</type>
        <externalId>123</externalId>
        <firstName>John</firstName>
        <lastName>Doe</lastName>
        <managerExternalId  >NO_MANAGER</managerExternalId>
        <status>Active</status>
        <username>johndoe</username>
      </sfobject>
    </insert>
  </S:Body> </S:Envelope>
```

Listing 6.5 InsertResult insert(String type, SFObject[] objects, SFParameter[] processingParam)

▶ UpdateResult update(String type, SFObject[] objects, SFParameter[] processinParam)

This updates the objects of the specified entity type. The operation will resume if one row has failed to update, as shown in Listing 6.6.

```
<S:Envelope>
  <S:Body>
    <update>
      <type>user</type>
      <sfobject>
        <id>USR-johndoe</id>
        <type>user</type>
        <email>johndoe@successfactors.com</email>
        <status>active</status>
      </sfobject>
    </update>
  </S:Body> </S:Envelope>
```

Listing 6.6 UpdateResult update(String type, SFObject[] objects, SFParameter[] processinParam)

▶ UpsertResult upsert(String type, SFObject[] objects, SFParameter[] processingParam)

This inserts or updates the objects of the specified entity type. If the row doesn't exist, then perform the `insert` operation; if the row exists, then per-form the `update` operation. The operation will resume if one row has failed to upsert. Listing 6.7 shows an example.

```
<S:Envelope>
  <S:Body>
    <upsert>
      <type>user</type>
      <sfobject>
        <type>user</type>
        <email>johndoe@successfactors.com</email>
        <externalId>johndoe</externalId>
        <status>active</status>
      </sfobject>
    </upsert>
  </S:Body> </S:Envelope>
```

Listing 6.7 UpsertResult upsert(String type, SFObject[] objects, SFParameter[] processingParam)

In the example shown in Listing 6.7, `DeleteResult delete(String type, SFObject[] objects, SFParameter[] processingParam)` deletes the SFObjects specified by the type and the objects. The operation will resume if one row has failed to delete.

Data Query

The following are operations for Data Query:

▶ `QueryResult query(String queryString, SFParameter[] param)`
This queries the SuccessFactors platform with the given query string in SFQL (SuccessFactors Query Language). For a detailed grammar description, check the SFAPI reference guide. An example of this operation is shown in Listing 6.8.

```
<S:Envelope>
  <S:Body>
    <query>
      <queryString>SELECT city,externalId,firstName,lastName,salary,
zipCode
 FROM user </queryString>
      <param>
        <name>maxRows</name>
        <value>10</value>
      </param>
    </query>
  </S:Body></S:Envelope>
```

Listing 6.8 QueryResult query(String queryString, SFParameter[] param)

The response for the preceding query is shown in Listing 6.9.

```
<S:Envelope>
  <S:Header/>
  <S:Body>
    <queryResponse>
      <result>
        <sfobject>
          <id>USR-1</id>
          <type>User</type>
          <city>New York</city>
          <externalId>00016327</externalId>
          <firstName>Sam</firstName>
          <lastName>Fagan</lastName>
          <salary/>
          <zipCode>10110</zipCode>
        </sfobject>
        ...
        <numResults>800</numResults>
        <hasMore>true</hasMore>
        <querySessionId>2f8b0cb3-4044-4419-9f9d-ba2c0c0dc780</query-
SessionId>
      </result>
    </queryResponse>
  </S:Body></S:Envelope>
```

Listing 6.9 QueryResult query(String queryString, SFParameter[] param)Response

▶ `QueryResult queryMore(String querySessionId)`
The `queryMore` call is provided to support paging. It requires a `querySessionId` to identify the next page of results. The `querySessionId` is a parameter of the `QueryResult` object, obtained from a previous call to either the `query` or `queryMore` operation. An example of this operation is shown in Listing 6.10.

```
<S:Envelope>
  <S:Header/>
  <S:Body>
    <queryMore>
      <querySessionId>2f8b0cb3-4044-4419-9f9d-ba2c0c0dc780</
querySessionId>
    </queryMore>
  </S:Body> </S:Envelope>
```

Listing 6.10 QueryResult queryMore(String querySessionId)

Asynchronous Job

The following operations are available for Asynchronous Job:

- ► `TaskStatus submitQueryJob(String queryString, SFParameter[] param)`
  This submits the asynchronous query job to the SuccessFactors platform with the given query string in SFQL (SuccessFactors Query Language). `TaskStatus` includes `taskId`, which is used to identify a submitted job.

- ► `TaskStatus getJobStatus(String taskId)`
  This gets the execution status of the submitted asynchronous job.

- ► `DataHandler getJobResult(GetJobResult parameters)`
  This downloads the result of the submitted asynchronous query job.

- ► `TaskStatus[] listJobs()`
  This list all jobs that are running or waiting to run.

- ► `TaskStatus cancelJob(String taskId)`
  This downloads the result of the submitted asynchronous query job.

Thresholds and Limitations of SFAPI

There are a few thresholds and limitations to keep in mind when utilizing SFAPI, including the following:

- ► The `batchSize` parameter controls the number of rows that will be processed in a single `insert`/`update`/`upsert`/`delete` method. This number can be set to anything from 1 to 800, and the default value is 200.

- ► The `maxRows` parameter controls the number of rows returned by a single `Query`/`QueryMore` method. It can be set to any value between 1 and 800, and the default value is 200.

- ► A SOAP message cannot exceed 5MB, which is the limit when uploading binary attachments using SFAPI. The attachment storage configuration controls the total size of the storage for all attachments.

Troubleshooting SFAPI Operations

There are multiple ways to troubleshoot SFAPI operations. A few are described as follows:

- ► **API Audit log**
  This captures the last 10,000 API call payload details, allowing you to inspect the payload details for issues.

▸ **API Data Dictionary**
This gives access to all the SuccessFactors data entities and the corresponding field metadata in a readable format.

▸ **SOAP UI**
The SOAP UI tool can model SFAPI operations.

Now that we have gone through SFAPI in detail, let's talk about a specialized API created to take care of a common scenario.

6.2.3 Compound Employee API

The Compound Employee API for Employee Central is used to extract employee data out of Employee Central. One of the main focuses of this API is to query and replicate employee master data from Employee Central to SAP and the payroll and benefits systems. This API is based on SOAP protocol and uses the same login and logout operations discussed in Section 6.2.2.

Figure 6.9 displays the Compound Employee API XML schema.

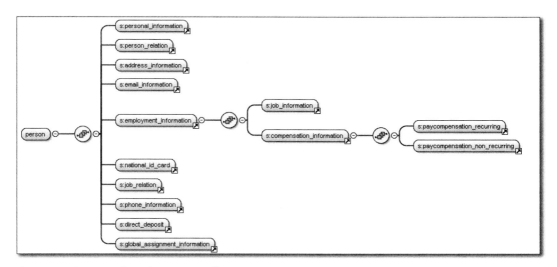

Figure 6.9 Compound Employee XML Schema

Some key features of this API are as follows:

▸ Returning all requested data of an employee in a single call provides a hierarchically structured response.

▶ Provides full employee historical information.

▶ Provides employee snapshot information for a given date.

▶ Provides employee changes only since a given date. This is the delta mode Compound Employee API.

▶ Results with changed segments indicate field-level changes.

▶ Results with changed segments indicate field-level changes along with other unchanged fields.

▶ Provides global assignment data.

Examples that demonstrate key features of the Compound Employee API are discussed ahead.

Full Historical Employee Details Query

The Full Historical Employee Details query extracts the complete historical data for all employees. This is used in integrations in which there is a need to send all employee data to another system. A good example is the Employee Central to SAP ERP packaged integration, in which this scenario is run (when you do not use filters; see Listing 6.11).

```
SELECT address_information,compensation_information,email_information,
employment_information,job_information,job_relation,
national_id_card,paycompensation_non_recurring,paycompensation_
recurring,person,Person_relation,personal_information,phone_
information FROM
CompoundEmployee
```
Listing 6.11 Full Historical Employee Details Query

A sample response XML for the preceding query is shown in Listing 6.12.

```
<S:Envelope>
   <S:Body>
      <queryResponse>
         <result>
            <sfobject>
               <id>137699</id>
               <type>CompoundEmployee</type>
               <person>
                  <logon_user_name>jDoe</logon_user_name>
                  <person_id_external>jDoe</person_id_external>
                  <personal_information>
```

```
                        <first_name>John</first_name>
                        <last_name>Doe</last_name>
                           ...
                  </personal_information>
                  <address_information>
                        ...
                  </address_information>
                  <employment_information>
                     ...
                     <job_information>
                        ...
                     </job_information>
                    <compensation_information>
                        ...
                     </compensation_information>
                     <job_relation>
                        ...
                     </job_relation>
                  </employment_information>
               </person>
            </sfobject>
            <numResults>1</numResults>
            <hasMore>false</hasMore>
         </result>
      </queryResponse>
   </S:Body>
</S:Envelope>
```

Listing 6.12 CompoundEmployee Query that Retrieves Historical Data

Snapshot Details Query

The Snapshot Details query extracts a snapshot of employee data at a specific time. This type of dataset is commonly used for demographic data synchronization with various third-party systems (see Listing 6.13).

```
<query>
<queryString>
SELECT
person, personal_information, address_information, email_
information, phone_information, employment_information, job_
information, compensation_information, paycompensation_
recurring, paycompensation_non_recurring, direct_deposit, national_id_
card, payment_information from CompoundEmployee where snapshot_date =
 to_date('10/09/12', 'DD/MM/YY') </queryString>
<param>
```

```
<name>queryMode</name>
<value>snapshot</value>
</param>
</query>
```
Listing 6.13 Snapshot Details Query

Changed Employee with Changed Segments Only Query

The Changed Employee with Changed Segments Only query results in only the changed fields in the changed segments, commonly called a *delta operation*. This scenario creates efficiency in third-party systems, because there are no redundant history records for the employee when nothing actually changed. This also takes away the need to perform a delta operation in the target system (see Listing 6.14).

```
<query>
<queryString>
SELECT address_information,compensation_information,email_
information,employment_information,job_information,job_
relation,national_id_card,paycompensation_non_
recurring,paycompensation_recurring,person,person_relation,personal_
information,phone_information FROM CompoundEmployee WHERE last_
modified_on > to_datetime('1970-01-01T00:00:00Z')
</queryString>
<param>
<name>queryMode</name>
<value>delta</value>
</param>
<param>
<name>resultOptions</name>
<value>changedSegmentsOnly</value>
</param>
</query>
```
Listing 6.14 Changed Employee with Changed Segments Only Query

A response XML is shown in Listing 6.15.

```
<S:Envelope>
  <S:Body>
    <queryResponse>
      <result>
        <sfobject>
          <id>137699</id>
          <type>CompoundEmployee</type>
          <person>
            <logon_user_name>jDoe</logon_user_name>
```

```
                <person_id_external>jDoe</person_id_external>
                ...
                <employment_information>
                    <action>NO CHANGE</action>
                    ...
                    <job_information>
                        <action>CHANGE</action>

                        <custom_string8>
                            ABC
                            <previous>XYZ<previous>

                    </job_information>
                    <job_event_information>
                        <action>INSERT</action>
                        ...
                    </job_event_information>
                </employment_information>
            </person>
        </sfobject>
        <numResults>1</numResults>
        <hasMore>false</hasMore>
    </result>
  </queryResponse>
  </S:Body>
</S:Envelope>
```

Listing 6.15 Response XML

Changed Employee with Changed Segments and Other Segments Details Query

This query is similar to the Changed Employee with Changed Segments query, except that it produces the changed segment with all fields instead of only the changed fields (see Listing 6.16).

```
<query>
<queryString>
SELECT address_information,compensation_information,email_
information,employment_information,job_information,job_
relation,national_id_card,paycompensation_non_
recurring,paycompensation_recurring,person,person_relation,personal_
information,phone_information FROM CompoundEmployee WHERE last_
modified_on > to_datetime('1970-01-01T00:00:00Z')
</queryString>
<param>
```

```
<name>queryMode</name>
<value>delta</value>
</param>
</query>
```
Listing 6.16 Changed Employee with Changed Segments and Other Segments Details Query

6.3 Summary

This chapter provided an overview of the integration architecture for Success-Factors and described the APIs based on SOAP (XML) protocol and OData, which is a REST-based framework. It also discussed how SOAP or OData APIs can be utilized, depending upon a client's needs and the middleware used in their landscape. SuccessFactors OData API enables the creation and consumption of REST APIs. Entities created using MDF in SuccessFactors architecture are automatically exposed as OData API objects. In the final section, we discussed the Compound Employee API, the most commonly used API for the master data replication of employee to third-party systems for integration between SAP on-premise systems.

In the next chapter, we will discuss another integration model, the standard integration templates. These come ready, out-of-the-box, and help accelerate the development of new custom integrations to various third-party systems with no existing packaged integrations.

In addition to building packaged integrations that connect Employee Central to specific cloud software providers, SAP product teams have also created standard templates based on commonly used patterns of integration.

7   Standard Integration Templates

A standard integration template is a process that can be adopted and extended by integration consultants to build integrations with different vendors as per their requirements. These template processes contain multiple standalone modules that are not connected with each other (i.e., each functionality is standalone and can be used independently). They provide all relevant data in HRXML or generic flat file formats. They are also completely configurable and are available on multiple supported middleware platforms but are not executable as is.

Additional Information

Up-to-date information on these templates is available at *http://help.sap.com/cloud4hr*.

Some key advantages of using standard integration templates include the following:

▶ **Reduced development costs**
Because templates have built-in extraction and transformation logic embedded in them, development of integrations typically adopts, extends, or modifies existing components to suit the integration requirements. This would reduce development time and hence the cost of building the integration.

▶ **Common design patterns**
Adopting templates will enforce common design patters across multiple integrations and across the entire customer base. This helps ease integration development and sustainability, because more developers are available in a market that is aware of the patterns and standards.

▶ **Template maintenance**
Templates are maintained by SAP product management and engineering teams, and new enhancements and defect fixes are introduced as part of the regular release cycles.

Adopting Enhancements

Even though new enhancements or bug fixes are incorporated into the templates with each release, integrations built with previous versions of the template do not automatically get these enhancements, because they represent copies of the template. Changes have to be analyzed and adopted into existing integrations.

In this chapter, we will discuss the basic design of standard integration templates and the various standard integration templates that are provided by SAP and SuccessFactors to build integrations with third-party services. The standard integration templates discussed in this chapter are available on the Dell Boomi AtomSphere middleware platform and will be available on SAP HCI in late 2015.

7.1 Design and Types

All templates that integrate with Employee Central share data with an external system and follow similar design patterns. The key differences among these templates are their mapping steps and file formats. The basic pattern is represented in Figure 7.1.

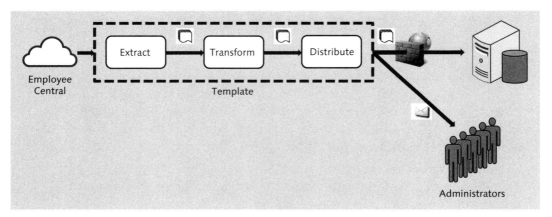

Figure 7.1 Standard Integration Templates Subcomponents

Looking at Figure 7.1, you can see the extract, transform, and distribute mapping steps. The following list provides further description of their functions:

▶ **Extract**

Each template provides multiple modules to extract data based on when the event is effective. The modules extract current, past, and future records, and employ the Compound Employee API (see Chapter 6, Section 6.2.3) to get the data, which outputs hierarchical XML. In addition, all the preceding modules support filter criteria based on pay group, employee class, employee type, location, company, country, business unit, and employee ID. There is also a module provided to generate denormalized XML from the hierarchical XML output. The templates also include code to merge data between multiple foundation objects and employee entities if they cannot be extracted as part of a single query.

▶ **Transform**

The transform step involves mapping between Employee Central entities and target formats. It also includes logic to handle global assignment and denormalized records, to format fields based on data type or business condition, to transform data to target system codes, and to exclude terminations based on pay periods and country-specific address fields mapped to common address attributes so data from different Employee Central HRIS fields appear in the same target address fields.

▶ **Distribute**

The distribute step includes generation of XML and/or flat files, encrypting and writing data to target SFTP servers, sending notifications on exceptions, and steps for debugging data or sending it via email where needed.

There are currently three different standard integration templates:

▶ Time management

▶ Benefits management

▶ Payroll management

Even though they are named based on their most likely use, you are free to use them for any integration to cut down on the development effort. In the following sections, we will discuss the standard templates for these three areas.

7.2   Time Management

Although SAP has partnered with Kronos and WorkForce Software for time and attendance management, customers use multiple time and attendance management providers in the cloud. To facilitate the integration of Employee Central with such time management providers, SAP provides a standard integration template. This standard template captures time management integration best practices. Using the standard template will reduce costs and implementation time for customers.

The standard template enables the replication of employee data with third-party time management providers. The template is designed to fetch all the employee data during the first replication and the changed data (delta data) in subsequent replications (see Figure 7.2).

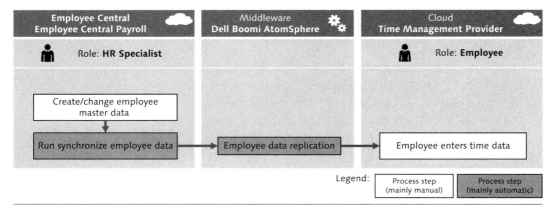

Figure 7.2 Standard Template for Employee Central Integration with Time Management Providers

Prerequisites

One prerequisite to keep in mind is that Dell Boomi AtomSphere integration middleware, which is licensed along with Employee Central, is required.

The following sections look at how to use the template to your advantage, the known assumptions and design boundaries to keep in mind during implementation, and the various data entries involved in the template.

7.2.1 Using the Time Management Integration Template

This template is provided as part of the process library in the Dell Boomi AtomSphere integration middleware. Customers need to install the time management template in their accounts as a process and build on or customize it to suit the needs of the specific time and attendance provider they use. The implementation steps are outlined in the integration guide *Standard Time Integration Template for Employee Central*. This document is available at *help.sap.com/cloud4hr*.

Dell Boomi AtomSphere Process Library

A process library is a collection of integration processes published in Dell Boomi Atom-Sphere for the purpose of sharing best practices. Customers install copies of processes in their accounts and use the installed processes as templates for processes tailored to their needs.

7.2.2 Known Assumptions and Design Boundaries

Separate mapping is required for fields that are country dependent (for example, ethnicity). Accommodating mapping for each country-specific field in the standard template is not feasible. Hence, some manual effort is required to adapt this process to a specific country. As a standard, this process has been adapted to work for the United States.

7.2.3 Time Management Entities

The time management template provides the same basic data as the benefits template but also includes concurrent employment information. It includes the following entities:

► Person information
► Home address
► Home and cell phone
► Work phone and business cell phone
► Work and personal email
► Manager and time approver information
► Employment information
► Job information
► Compensation information
► Recurring pay components (up to 15)
► Nonrecurring pay components (up to 15)
► Pay group information

7.3   Benefits Management

Although SAP has chosen Aon Hewitt and Benefitfocus as partners for benefits management, customers use multiple benefits management providers in the cloud. To facilitate the integration of Employee Central with such providers, SAP provides a standard integration template for benefits management. This standard template captures the benefits management integration best practices, reducing cost and implementation time for customers.

This standard template enables the replication of employee data with third-party benefits management providers. It is designed to fetch all the employee data during the first replication and the changed data (delta data) in subsequent replications. The process flow supported by this standard template is depicted in Figure 7.3.

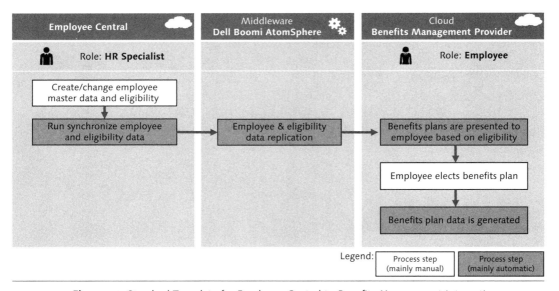

Figure 7.3 Standard Template for Employee Central to Benefits Management Integration

Prerequisites

As before, Dell Boomi AtomSphere integration middleware, which is licensed along with Employee Central, is required.

The following sections look at how to use the template to your advantage, the known assumptions and design boundaries to keep in mind during implementation, and the various data entries involved in the template.

7.3.1 Using the Benefits Management Integration Template

Standard benefits integration is a template process with a collection of stand-alone generic functionalities to replicate employee data and eligibility data from Employee Central to any third-party benefits management provider. Consultants can use it to build Employee Central integrations with any third-party benefits provider. This process is to be treated as a template with a collection of generic modules to build a provider-specific integration process. The implementation steps are outlined in the *Standard Benefits Integration Template for Employee Central* integration guide. This document is available at *help.sap.com/cloud4hr*.

7.3.2 Known Assumptions and Design Boundaries

This is not an out-of-box solution to integrate with any benefits provider. The process library is a collection of modules (standalone design patterns) that can be used to integrate Employee Central with benefits providers, with some modifications and manual mapping to achieve the provider-specific integration use case. The modules must be chosen based on the provider's requirements and built on with some custom development and provider-specific logic before it can be executed.

7.3.3 Benefits Entities

The benefits template includes basic demographic data for each employee, including global assignment information. It includes the following entities:

- Person information
- Personal information, including country-specific information
- Home address
- Home and cell phone
- Personal email
- Dependents' information

- Employment information
- Job information
- Annual and benefit salary
- Pay group information
- National ID information

7.4 Payroll Management

Although SAP has chosen ADP and NGA as partners for payroll, customers can use multiple payroll providers. To facilitate the integration of Employee Central with such providers, SAP provides a standard integration template for payroll. This standard template enables the replication of employee data with third-party payroll providers and is designed to fetch all the employee data during the first replication and the changed data (delta data) in subsequent replications.

This process is to be treated as a template with a collection of generic modules to build a provider-specific integration process (see Figure 7.4).

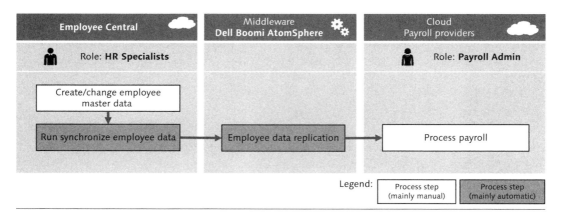

Figure 7.4 Standard Template for Employee Central to Payroll Integration

Prerequisites

To ensure a smooth integration, Dell Boomi AtomSphere integration middleware, licensed with Employee Central, is required.

The following sections look at how to use the template to your advantage, the known assumptions and design boundaries to keep in mind during implementation, and the various data entries involved in the template.

7.4.1 Using the Payroll Integration Template

Standard payroll integration is a template process with a collection of standalone generic functionalities to replicate employee data and eligibility data from Employee Central to any third-party payroll provider. Consultants can use it to build Employee Central integrations with any third-party payroll provider. The implementation steps are outlined in the *Standard Payroll Integration Template for Employee Central* integration guide, available at *help.sap.com/cloud4hr*.

7.4.2 Known Assumptions and Design Boundaries

Again, this is not an out-of-box solution to integrate with any payroll provider. The process library is a collection of modules (standalone design patterns) that can be used to integrate Employee Central with payroll providers, with some modifications and manual mapping to achieve the provider-specific integration use case. The modules must be chosen based on the provider's requirements and built on with some custom development and provider-specific logic before it can be executed.

7.4.3 Payroll Entities

Payroll integrations are typically the most complex and need a lot of data from Employee Central to be passed to payroll systems. The standard process cannot be consumed directly.

The payroll template includes the following entities:

- Person information
- Personal information, including country-specific information
- Home address
- Business, home, and cell phone
- Work and personal email
- Dependent information

- Employment information
- Job information
- Compensation information
- Recurring pay components (up to 15)
- Nonrecurring pay components (up to 15)
- Recurring deductions (up to 15)
- Nonrecurring deductions (up to 15)
- Direct deposit information
- National ID information
- Alternative cost distribution

Now that we've gone through the different types of standard integration templates available, let's shift our attention to the process of building integrations with these templates.

7.5 Building Integrations Using Standard Integration Templates

To provide a better understanding of how standard templates can be adopted to implement custom integrations, we will discuss adopting a standard payroll template to develop a custom payroll integration. Using similar steps and leveraging standard templates provided by SAP, you can build custom integrations that realize the benefits outlined at the beginning of the chapter.

7.5.1 Business Processes

Employee Central as the core HR system captures and records all employee lifecycle transactions. Employee master data, including payroll and other related information, needs to be transmitted periodically to a third-party payroll provider.

The standard payroll template is a collection of design patterns that can be used to integrate Employee Central with third-party payroll providers, with modifications to filter, transform, and map data to achieve the provider-specific integration use case. The template must be chosen based on the provider's data requirements and then modified to include specific logic based on the customer's and vendor's business needs. There could be scenarios in which a benefits template or a time and attendance template can be adopted to build employee demographics, because both of these templates include different types of information and one might suit better than the other for some customer implementations.

The payroll template is designed to fetch all the employee data during the first replication and changes in employee data in subsequent replications. The integration template is not available as an executable program. Customer-specific development or configuration will be needed to integrate independent templates into a comprehensive executable process.

In our scenario, Employee Central has been implemented, and we will be integrating a third-party payroll provider for a US-based employee population. Employees hired in Employee Central will need to be transferred to the provider via an interface; similarly, an employee's location changes or terminations need to be sent across. In addition to this information, an employee's personal address, employment, job info, national ID, dependents, and so on will also have to be transmitted to the payroll provider. Employee master data needs to be kept in sync on both systems via this interface.

Prerequisites

Most companies should have an agreement with their payroll provider and include the payroll provider in the implementation as a partner to provide access to environments, design the specification if it is not one of their standard ones, build or configure changes, and support testing the integration end to end. In the situation we have detailed here, it was decided that the vendor will accept a pipe-delimited file, which is PGP encrypted and posted to their SFTP server.

In addition, Dell Boomi AtomSphere integration will work as the middleware, licensed and procured through SuccessFactors.

Employee Central must have all required data elements configured. The following Employee Central data elements were configured and are to be sent to the payroll system as part of this implementation:

- Person information
- Personal information
- Address information
- Phone information
- Email information
- Employment information

- ▸ Job information
- ▸ Compensation information
- ▸ Pay component recurring
- ▸ Pay component nonrecurring
- ▸ National ID card information

One of the key tasks for the implementation team to keep in mind is enabling Dell Boomi AtomSphere. The basic steps that are needed for enabling Dell Boomi Atom-Sphere integrations are common for all integrations and are necessary for integrating Employee Central to external systems. These steps include the following:

- ▸ Enabling web services SFAPI
- ▸ Creating a SuccessFactors API user
- ▸ Creating a SuccessFactors API login exception

It will be assumed that you have already completed these steps and are ready to download the standard integration template within the company's Dell Boomi AtomSphere account (see Chapter 9, Section 9.1.2 for further details).

The remaining tasks for the implementation of integration template include the following:

- ▸ Identifying and mapping fields from the Employee Central specification to the payroll vendor specification
- ▸ Transformation of field values where necessary
- ▸ File and field formatting requirements
- ▸ Testing file outputs with the provider prior to production cutover

Let's now look at an overview of the high-level process flow for the payroll integration template, which includes the execution of these other tasks.

7.5.2   High-Level Payroll Template Process Flow

The replication of employee data from Employee Central to a payroll provider consists of the following steps:

1. Get the last execution date and time.

2. Extract data from Employee Central portlets.

3. Transform the Employee Central data.

4. Generate a flat file output.

5. Make the output file PGP encrypted.

6. Post the file to the assigned SFTP server location.

The process also incorporates subprocesses for sending email notifications upon process completion. The following sections go into greater detail about each step.

Get the Last Execution Date and Time

In this step, the Dell Boomi AtomSphere job extracts employee data from Employee Central as of the last execution date. LOCAL_LAST_EXECUTION_TIMESTAMP is a dynamic process property that is captured upon each successful run of the process. This property is persisted throughout the process and is updated when the property is left blank within the extension properties. This property is readied by the Compound Employee API to pull changes to employee data after the time stamp. For the first run of the interface, the property is updated to the date and time from which changes need to be pulled.

Figure 7.5 is a visual representation of the last execution date logic within the template.

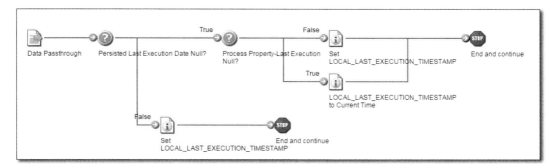

Figure 7.5 Dell Boomi AtomSphere Subprocess to Set Last Execution Timestamp

Extract Data from Employee Central Portlets

This is the main process of the implementation and is presented as four options provided as dynamic query filters for data extraction of employee data from Employee Central:

▸ Compound Employee Query Filter—Past+Current+Future Records

▸ Compound Employee Query Filter—Current Record

▸ Compound Employee Query Filter—Current+Future Records

▸ Compound Employee Query Filter—By Pay Calendar

Each of these variants can be used depending upon what kind of data the payroll vendor is requesting for the company workforce.

If the payroll vendor is requesting past, current, and future records, then the Compound Employee Query Filter—Past+Current+Future Records template/process should be enabled to retrieve data from Employee Central (see Figure 7.6).

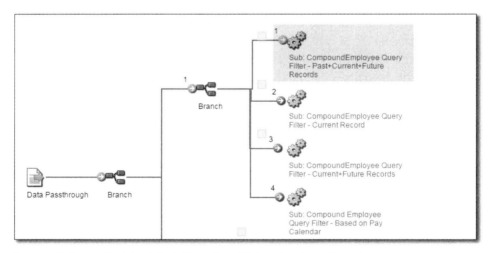

Figure 7.6 Process to Extract Past, Current, and Future Employee Records

If a payroll vendor is requesting only current records, then the Compound Employee Query Filter—Current Record template/process should be enabled to retrieve data from Employee Central (see Figure 7.7).

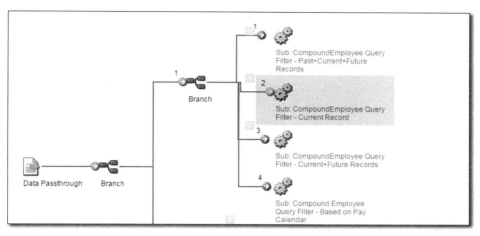

Figure 7.7 Process to Extract Current Employee Records

If a payroll vendor is requesting current and future records, then the Compound Employee Query Filter—Current+Future Records template/process should be enabled to retrieve data from Employee Central (see Figure 7.8).

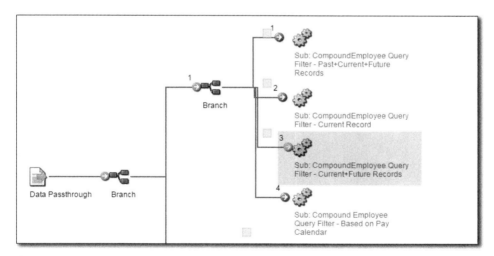

Figure 7.8 Process to Extract Current and Future Employee Records

If the payroll vendor is requesting records based on the pay calendar, then the Compound Employee Query Filter—By Pay Calendar template/process should be enabled to retrieve data from Employee Central (see Figure 7.9).

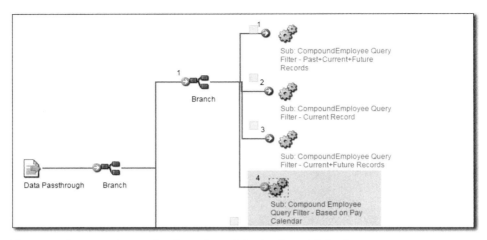

Figure 7.9 Process to Extract Employee Records by Pay Period/Calendar

The Compound Employee API extracts data in an XML format based upon the filter that has been implemented. Extracted data can be split into multiple record types as needed by payroll vendor. The interface template can extract data in CSV or XML format.

Transform the Employee Central Data

This step transforms the data extracted in the extraction process into a flat file output format. Each employee data extracted from Employee Central will be mapped to a payroll vendor-specific format (see Figure 7.10).

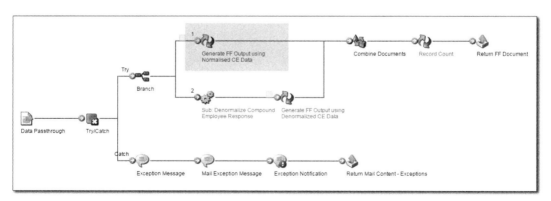

Figure 7.10 Map to Transform Employee Central Data to Target Format

An example of transforming data from Employee Central XML format to a payroll vendor-specific flat file format is shown in Figure 7.11.

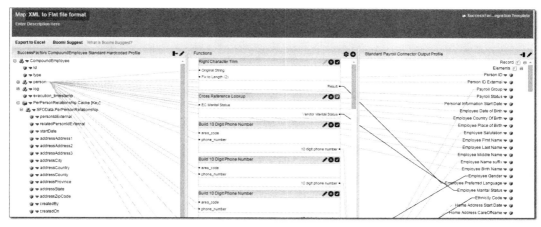

Figure 7.11 Transformation of Data from XML to Flat File Format

Generate a Flat File Output

This step maps the extracted and transformed data into a pipe-delimited flat file format or normalized XML format. Depending on the payroll vendor needs, the interface can select the appropriate subprocess (see Figure 7.12).

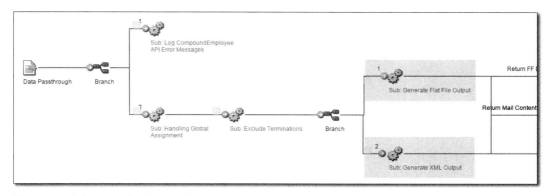

Figure 7.12 Subprocess for Output Format

Make the Output File PGP Encrypted

This subprocess encrypts the output file. The PGP keys can be provided either via an extension parameter or within the subprocess (see Figure 7.13).

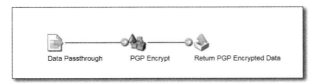

Figure 7.13 Subprocess for PGP Encryption

Post the File to the Assigned SFTP Server Location

This subprocess posts the encrypted file to the remote server location (see Figure 7.14).

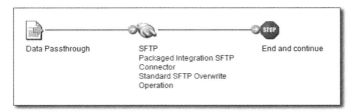

Figure 7.14 Subprocess to Post File to SFTP Server

7.6   Summary

In this chapter, we looked at the different types of standard integration templates available for building custom integrations with SuccessFactors. These template types for time management, benefits management, and payroll allow customers to utilize commonly used patterns of integration to save both time and money. Using the example of the standard payroll integration template, we walked through the high-level process of building an integration with one of these templates.

In the next chapter we will look at integrating talent solutions with third-party applications.

In this chapter, we will discuss how to integrate your instance of the SuccessFactors Talent Management suite with some of the leading cloud-based service providers. From there, we will move on to the standard data imports available in SuccessFactors that can be used to integrate with systems that do not have a packaged integration.

8   Integrating Talent Solutions with Third-Party Applications

SuccessFactors' market-leading talent modules are integrated not only within the suite but also with non-SAP systems to share data, execute end-to-end business processes, and provide an integrated user experience. SuccessFactors Talent Management applications make use of multiple third-party cloud applications for assessment verification, background checks, virtual learning, learning assessments, resume, and payroll.

Figure 8.1 illustrates different types of systems that integrate with SuccessFactors Talent Management suite.

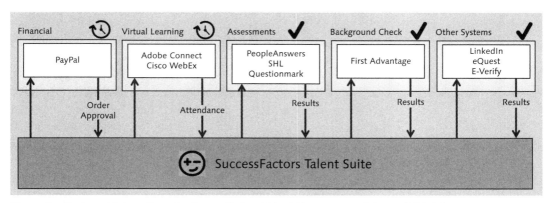

Figure 8.1 Packaged Integrations for SuccessFactors Talent Management Suite and Third-Party Applications

SAP provides packaged integrations to connect SuccessFactors Talent Management suite with the following:

▶ PeopleAnswers and SHL for pre-employment assessments (see Section 8.1.1)
▶ First Advantage for background check verification (see Section 8.1.2)
▶ eQuest for posting job requisitions to job boards (see Section 8.1.3)
▶ LinkedIn for creating candidate profiles (see Section 8.1.4)
▶ E-Verify for confirming employment eligibility
   (see Section 8.2, E-Verify Integration)
▶ PayPal Payflow Pro for payment processing (see Section 8.3.1)
▶ Virtual Learning System (VLS) for e-learning (see Section 8.3.2)
▶ Questionmark for learning assessments (see Section 8.3.3)

First, in Section 8.1, we detail the packaged integrations from SuccessFactors that connect SuccessFactors Recruiting with assessment verifications from PeopleAnswers and SHL, background checks from First Advantage, candidate profile information from LinkedIn, and job posting distribution data from eQuest. Section 8.2 analyzes packaged integrations that connect SuccessFactors Onboarding for employment verification through USCIS E-Verify. Section 8.3 describes packaged integrations by SuccessFactors Learning that integrate with virtual learning systems like Cisco WebEx and Adobe Connect, learning assessments through Questionmark, and the payment processor PayPal. Finally, in Section 8.4 we provide an overview of standard connectors available in the SuccessFactors Talent Management suite that enable data exchange with third-party applications.

8.1 Packaged Integrations for SuccessFactors Recruiting

In this section, we will look at how SuccessFactors integrations with PeopleAnswers, SHL, First Advantage, eQuest, and LinkedIn. PeopleAnswers and SHL assessment integrations use one of the middleware platforms supported by SAP and make use of event-based web services to trigger the integration in real-time. First Advantage, eQuest, and LinkedIn are built into the SuccessFactors Recruiting product and support real-time integration.

Other Third-Party Products

There are other third-party products that integrate with SuccessFactors Recruiting that are not covered in this section, such as LexisNexis and the Verifications Inc. background check. However, these will be depreciated due to acquisitions.

8.1.1   Assessment Vendor Integration

SuccessFactors Recruiting provides integrations to PeopleAnswers and SHL assessment solutions. The integrations for both providers use the same platform with similar configurations. PeopleAnswers and SHL are pre-employment assessment solutions that provide employers with a cloud-based solution to accurately match the right person with the right job. Assessment vendors receive candidate information along with the position applied for and assessment packages configured in the recruiting system to administer corresponding assessments.

Pre-employment assessments are used to screen job applicants and can include testing of cognitive abilities, knowledge, work skills, physical and motor abilities, personality, emotional intelligence, language proficiency, and even integrity. Employers use assessments to find the candidates most likely to succeed in the open positions and to screen out those who are unqualified, leading to additional company benefits, such as saving time and money in the selection process.

When a candidate applies for a job and if the requisition has assessments configured to be delivered immediately, the candidate will get the assessments link displayed after the job application is submitted. Otherwise, the candidate will be prompted to take the assessment by email when the application reaches the status associated with the assessment package.

The sequence of steps, actors, and systems involved in PeopleAnswers integration with SuccessFactors Recruiting is illustrated in Figure 8.2.

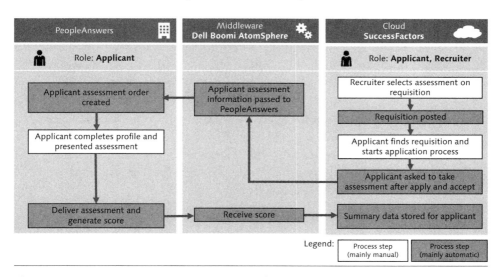

Figure 8.2 SuccessFactors Recruiting Integration with PeopleAnswers

The SHL integration with SuccessFactors Recruiting is illustrated in Figure 8.3.

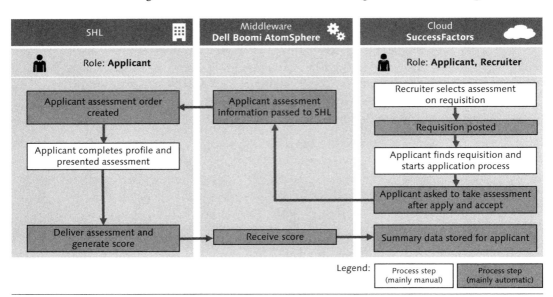

Figure 8.3 SuccessFactors Recruiting Integration with SHL

The integration is implemented with two web services. Both of these services will be hosted on the customer's Dell Boomi AtomSphere account:

▶ **Recruiting to PeopleAnswers or SHL— AssessmentOrder process**
This web service listens to requests from the SuccessFactors Recruiting API. When a request is received by this service, it will transform the data to the assessment vendor format and create an order by invoking the vendor's assessment order web service. The web service returns the order ID and unique assessment URL, which is updated on the job application entity in SuccessFactors.

▶ **PeopleAnswers or SHL to Recruiting— AssessmentOrderStatus process**
This web service is invoked by the assessment vendor and is supplied with the assessment score and result link. The recommendation and score, along with the detailed results link pointing to the providers' server, are updated in the corresponding standard fields in SuccessFactors.

Implementing Packaged Integrations

When you choose to implement packaged integrations for assessment vendors, the packaged integration content is directly available to install, configure, and run on the supported middleware you choose.

The following sections detail the process steps involved in this integration, as well as key considerations and benefits to keep in mind.

Integration Process Steps

The following steps describe the integration process to be undertaken:

1. Select Enable Assessment Integration (Requires Candidate Workbench), under Company Settings • Recruiting V2 Application, to access the assessment integration feature.

2. The Manage Assessment Vendors permission needs to be assigned to the Role-Based Permissions (RBP) user role—typically, an administrator that would configure assessment vendors in Recruiting.

3. Administrators with permission to manage assessment vendors can then import assessment vendor configurations. The vendor ID for PeopleAnswers and SHL are "PA" and "SHL", respectively.

4. Administrators should then upload assessment vendor packages using the SuccessFactors Provisioning Import/Export Assessment Vendor Packages option.

5. Configure assessment fields in a job requisition template with permissions to view and edit these fields set to be managed similarly to other job requisition fields. These fields will be shown in the job requisition page in the same order as they are configured in the template (see Figure 8.4).

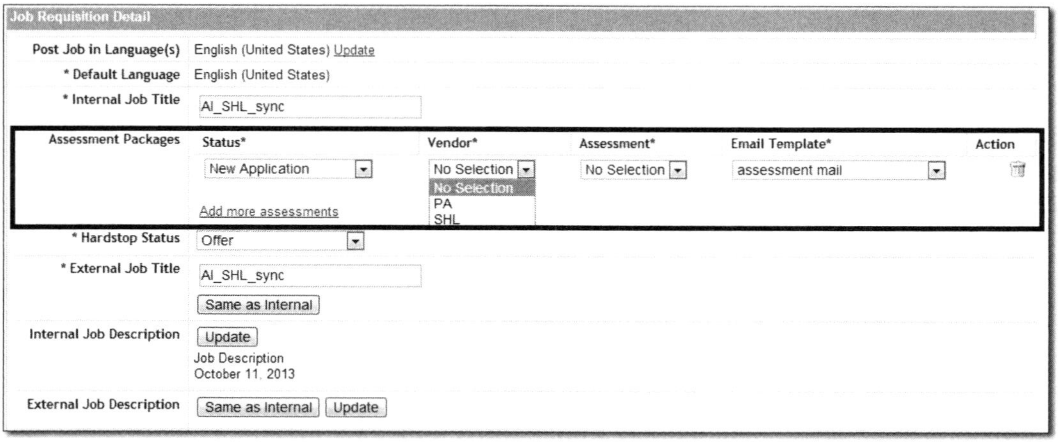

Figure 8.4 Setting Up Assessment for a Job Requisition

6. The SFAPI user needs to be set up in Admin Tools • Recruiting Permissions with the following options selected for each vendor (see the information on setting up an SFAPI user in Chapter 6):

   ▶ SFAPI Retrieve Assessment Order Permission

   ▶ SFAPI Update Assessment Report Permission

7. When a candidate applies for a job requisition that has assessment set up, an event is generated within SuccessFactors Recruiting and published to listening web services. The packaged integration's AssessmentOrder process receives the request and will process it as explained previously.

8. If the assessment is created immediately after the candidate applies, then the candidate will see a screen with assessment links (see Figure 8.5).

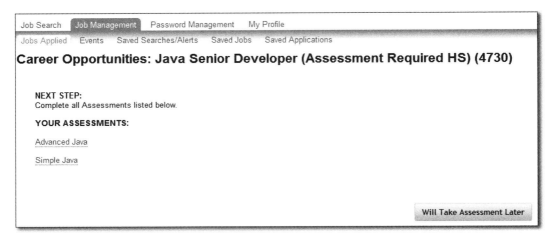

Figure 8.5 Candidate Assessments Screen

9. Once the candidate clicks on the assessment link, he or she is taken to the corresponding vendor's cloud application for assessment delivery.

10. Upon completion of the assessment, the vendor will send the results by sending data to the AssessmentOrderStatus process discussed previously.

11. The candidate summary page can be set up to display the assessment score, recommendation, and status of different assessments packages. All scores and recommendations for assessments will also be available in the assessment portlet in the applicant profile page (see Figure 8.6).

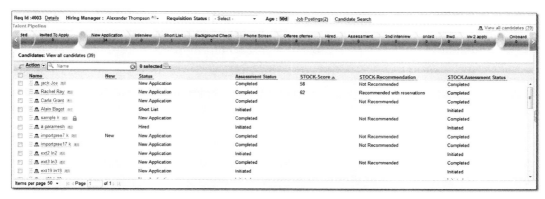

Figure 8.6 Applicant Profile Page with Assessment Score Results

12. There could be scenarios in which job applications can be processed even when assessment scores are not available until the application reaches certain steps in the recruiting workflow. This can be set up by choosing an option under the HARDSTOP STATUS dropdown field to the status value that should hold the application until the assessment results are available (see Figure 8.7).

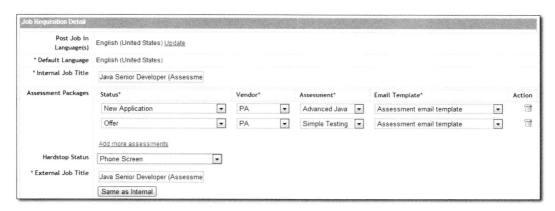

Figure 8.7 Setting Hardstop Status

Key Considerations and Benefits

With this integration, there are a number of key considerations and benefits, including the following:

▸ All data transmissions occur in real-time immediately after the candidate completes actions on either system.

▸ An email template can be created for assessment in the Admin Tools, and can be associated with a job requisition. This will enable a candidate to receive an email with the information configured in the template when assessment is initiated.

▸ Assessments can be created for candidates in one of two ways: The first is to have the assessment initiated immediately after the candidate submits the application. The second option is to create the assessment later in the recruiting process, usually after some initial application processing steps, and to send an email to the candidate with assessment links embedded in it.

▸ In situations where an error occurred while initiating assessment, an acknowledged assessment can be reinitiated from the applicant profile page by clicking on the INITIATE ASSESSMENT button.

▸ This integration ships with configurable settings for endpoint URLs and status code mappings.

▸ Using externalized settings and mappings enables customization through configuration.

▸ This integration can be deployed on multiple environments easily, and maintenance is seamless, with little to no custom code.

Prerequisites

The following prerequisites must be met to implement this integration:

▸ Appropriate licensing to use the assessment integration

▸ Dell Boomi AtomSphere or SAP HANA Cloud Integration middleware, procured through SAP

▸ A separate third-party contract with either PeopleAnswers or SHL for pre-employment assessments solution

8.1.2 First Advantage Integration

Employers may want to validate the claims of an applicant by initiating a background check. SuccessFactors Recruiting offers integration with the First Advantage Direct Advantage process.

When the recruiter or hiring manager initiates a background check request, the candidate invitation is initiated from SuccessFactors, and then First Advantage collects candidate data not prepopulated by SuccessFactors. The standard Direct Advantage functionality applies once the invitation is sent.

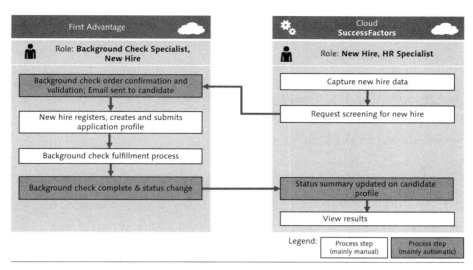

Figure 8.8 First Advantage Background Check: Direct Advantage

The following section describes the steps and interactions in both SuccessFactors and First Advantage for this integration and is illustrated in Figure 8.8.

Integration Process Steps

The following steps describe the integration process:

1. The candidate applies and progresses through the workflow in SuccessFactors. During this process, the candidate data are collected for the screening request.

2. The hiring manager or recruiter sends an invitation to the candidate via SuccessFactors.

3. First Advantage sends a request for additional information directly to the candidate's email.

4. The candidate provides consent, populates any missing information, and submits the application.

5. The customer also has the option of placing an instant order at this point or allowing a review by the recruiter.

6. Once the order is submitted, the request progresses through the fulfillment process.

7. First Advantage sends status updates to SuccessFactors as the request progresses through the screening order fulfillment process.

8. SuccessFactors displays the case level status and results for the request. In addition, a link in the application allows the user to access the detailed results in Enterprise Advantage.

The following section lays out the key considerations and benefits of using the First Advantage Direct Advantage process with SuccessFactors Recruiting.

Key Considerations and Benefits

When employing this integration, keep the following considerations and benefits in mind:

▶ Requires public records, education, and employment scope to be predefined and consistent per customer account.

▶ Requires the package to be defined in SuccessFactors and provided on the request.

▶ Data collected by First Advantage will not be sent back to update SuccessFactors but will reside in Enterprise Advantage.

▶ The candidate will be able to modify any of the data sent from SuccessFactors for the background check.

▶ Allows data to be reviewed and added by the candidate prior to submission.

▶ Allows signed consent forms and other forms to be provided directly from the candidate.

▶ For international searches, because the required data can vary by country, the requestor will be able to see any additional required information not provided by the source system.

▶ Minimal data can be sent from SuccessFactors, and First Advantage can reach out for any required missing information directly.

Prerequisites

First Advantage's Direct Advantage background check product is required.

8.1.3 eQuest Integration

SuccessFactors Recruiting integration with eQuest provides better board-to-board mapping accuracy and access to eQuest's continued feature innovations. It reduces the time to post jobs and enables the ability to easily add additional job boards, worldwide job board access, and detailed monthly transaction reports summarizing job posting usage.

As illustrated in Figure 8.9, after a job requisition is approved in SuccessFactors, it can be posted in one language per posting. Under the job board posting section, links are available to send the data to eQuest when the integration is enabled. In eQuest, the recruiter will have the ability to choose which job boards to post to and add specific information related to each board posting.

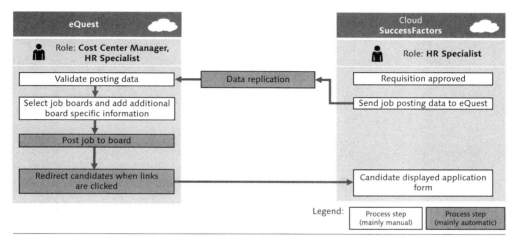

Figure 8.9 SuccessFactors Recruiting with eQuest Integration

The following sections provide a detailed step-by-step sequence of activities as part of eQuest integration as well as key considerations and benefits to keep in mind.

Integration Process Steps

The following steps describe the integration process:

1. The recruiter creates a job requisition in SuccessFactors Recruiting, providing all of the information required for posting to eQuest along with open position information. The recruiter then submits the requisition for approval.

2. The requisition progresses through the approval process, and the person with permission to post to job boards will see the ADD JOB BOARDS option appear.

3. After the job poster clicks on ADD JOB BOARDS, SuccessFactors Recruiting validates whether all data required by eQuest is provided, and the user is taken to eQuest.

4. Once in eQuest, the user will see all the boards his or her company has access to post to (see Figure 8.10).

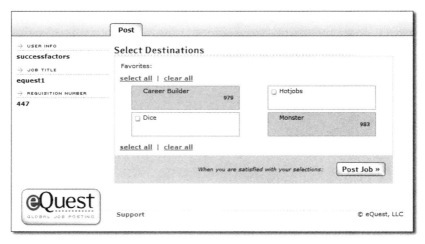

Figure 8.10 Posting to Job Boards in eQuest

5. The user clicks on the board to which the job needs to be posted and clicks on POST JOB. At this point, the information will be passed from eQuest to the individual job boards.

6. After the postings are submitted, the user is brought back to SuccessFactors and presented with the requisition's JOB POSTINGS page. The user should see the lower table populated with the job boards that were selected from eQuest (see Figure 8.11).

Figure 8.11 Job Postings with Job Board Information in SuccessFactors

Key Considerations and Benefits

When employing this integration, keep the following considerations and benefits in mind:

- The following information is required on the job requisition to post it to eQuest:
  - CLASSIFICATION TYPE
    - PERMANENT
    - CONTRACT
    - CONTRACT TO PERMANENT
    - INTERN
  - CLASSIFICATION TIME
    - FULL-TIME
    - PART-TIME
  - INDUSTRY
  - FUNCTION
  - CITY
  - STATE/PROVINCE
  - POSTAL CODE
  - COUNTRY
  - RECRUITER NAME
- If information is missing in the job requisition, then the user will be asked to provide the data while posting.
- You must request that the eQuest configuration and eQuest job board subscriptions are enable in SuccessFactors.
- We recommended that you use one eQuest login ID for all SuccessFactors jobs postings, which will enable multiple users to be able to post and edit the same job.
- Multiple eQuest logins can be used, in which case multiple user profiles for eQuest are required for the company's recruiters. This may be case if only some recruiters have access to post requisitions to certain job boards.
- The eQuest Advantage solution to purchase postings a la carte is not supported through this integration. SuccessFactors Marketing Central provides such features and is part of SuccessFactors Talent Management.

Prerequisites

A separate third-party license with eQuest is required.

8.1.4 LinkedIn Data Integration

When candidates apply for a job through SuccessFactors Recruiting, they can choose to apply either by entering their candidate profile data (typing the individual information into each field) or by using LinkedIn to populate certain data values on their candidate profiles.

> **External Users**
>
> This integration is initiated by external users that set up an account on your SuccessFactors instance. All other integrations discussed in this chapter send and receive data for users that have accounts on their own active SuccessFactors instances.

The LinkedIn integration can only be used as part of the application process; it is not possible to use LinkedIn to populate a candidate profile if the candidate is not presently applying for a job. This integration may only be initiated and authorized by candidates, not recruiting users.

In addition, this integration may only occur on a case-by-case basis, as depicted in Figure 8.12; the candidate's authorization may not be used to maintain a dynamic link to the LinkedIn data. LinkedIn only makes limited data available via integration, and not all available LinkedIn fields need to be mapped; customers may choose to use fewer fields than LinkedIn makes available.

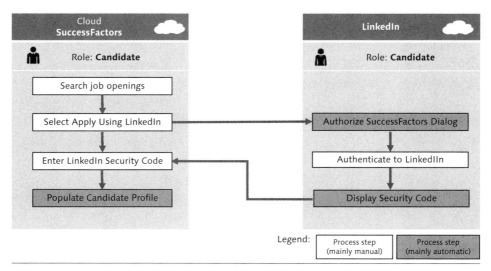

Figure 8.12 SuccessFactors Recruiting with LinkedIn Integration

The following sections provide a detailed step-by-step sequence of activities for the LinkedIn integration and key considerations and benefits to keep in mind.

Integration Process Steps

The following steps describe the integration process:

1. To begin, select the APPLY USING LINKEDIN option from the ACTION list of a job requisition or directly from a job requisition page (see Figure 8.13).

Figure 8.13 Apply Using LinkedIn from Search Page

2. On the next screen, enter the LINKEDIN SECURITY CODE to grant access to the LinkedIn account displayed in SuccessFactors (see Figure 8.14).

Figure 8.14 Enter LinkedIn Security Code in SuccessFactors

3. If you do not know or have the security code, click on GET A NEW SECURITY CODE, and a popup window will appear to provide account login so that you can obtain your security code. Popup blockers may interfere with LinkedIn's attempt to open a verification code window and may need to be manually disabled.

4. Once you authenticate your LinkedIn account, LinkedIn will display a security code.

5. Upon entering the code in the screen displayed in step 2, the candidate profile data will populate from LinkedIn, according to the standardized field mapping (see Figure 8.15).

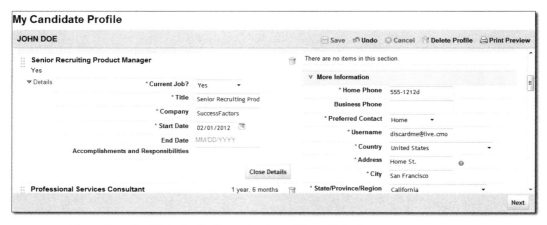

Figure 8.15 Candidate Profile Page after Import from LinkedIn

Key Considerations and Benefits

When employing this integration, keep the following considerations and benefits in mind:

▶ The standardized mapping supports only the following data structures:

  ▷ BASIC INFORMATION

    – FIRST NAME

    – LAST NAME

    – ADDRESS

    – DATE OF BIRTH

    – CELL PHONE

- ▸ WORK INFORMATION
  - – CURRENT TITLE
  - – CURRENT COMPANY
  - – EMPLOYER
  - – JOB TITLE
  - – PRESENT EMPLOYER
  - – EMPLOYMENT STATE DATE
  - – EMPLOYMENT END DATE
  - – JOB DESCRIPTION
- ▸ EDUCATION
  - – NAME OF SCHOOL
  - – DEGREE OBTAINED
  - – FIELD OF STUDY
  - – START DATE
  - – END DATE

- ▶ The candidate profile can be populated from LinkedIn during the application process and is not available just to synchronize data to the profile.

- ▶ Standard mapping between the candidate profile and LinkedIn data elements needs to be set up in Admin Tools. Standardized field mapping is necessary to define where the values from certain LinkedIn fields should be placed in the SuccessFactors Recruiting Management candidate profile. The values on the right are the values available from LinkedIn. The fields on the left are drop-down menus from which you can select fields you configured in the candidate profile XML. Some fields are limited to match types; for instance, you cannot map a field defined as text to a value that LinkedIn will send over as a date. Picklists in Recruiting cannot be mapped to LinkedIn fields.

Prerequisites

The following prerequisites must be met:
- ▶ Configure standardized mapping in Admin Tools
- ▶ The Provisioning setting ENHANCED JOB SEARCH UI must be enabled
- ▶ The Provisioning setting COMPLETE PROFILE BEFORE APPLICATION must be enabled

8.2 Packaged Integrations for SuccessFactors Onboarding

In this section, we will discuss the packaged integration between SuccessFactors Onboarding and a third-party system. As of the writing of this book (spring 2015), there is one standard integration that is offered through the USCIS E-Verify program. SuccessFactors Onboarding has functionality that can enable creating new forms, which can ultimately generate data through the standard export job, which can also be used to integrate most third-party systems.

E-Verify Integration

US law requires companies to employ only individuals who may legally work in the United States—either US citizens or foreign citizens who have the necessary authorization. E-Verify is an Internet-based system that compares information from an employee's Form I-9 (Employment Eligibility Verification) to data from US Department of Homeland Security (DHS) and Social Security Administration (SSA) records to confirm employment eligibility.

E-Verify process consists of the following four steps:

1. **Initial verification**
   The employee identification information is verified and sent to the DHS E-Verify program. An eligibility statement is returned providing confirmation or tentative nonconfirmation of an employee's eligibility to be employed.

2. **Secondary verification**
   Secondary verification is for employees who contest tentative nonconfirmations and provides final confirmation or nonconfirmation of the employee's employment eligibility within three federal government workdays from the initial inquiry date.

3. **Third verification**
   Additional processing of the employee's information occurs in cases in which the DHS tentative nonconformation is returned within 10 federal government workdays from the initial inquiry date.

4. **Signature**
   The employer representative and employee sign employment eligibility forms using the e-signature technology. This is the final step in the E-Verify process.

SuccessFactors Onboarding E-Verify process begins immediately after all I-9 documents are completed and electronically signed. The following process details how E-Verify works as implemented in the SuccessFactors Onboarding tool (see Figure 8.16).

The following sections provide a detailed step-by-step sequence of activities as part of E-Verify integration as well as key considerations and benefits to keep in mind.

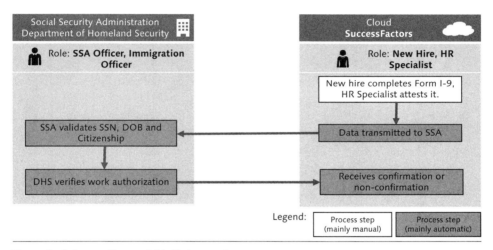

Figure 8.16 SuccessFactors E-Verify Integration

Integration Process Steps
The following steps describe the integration process:

1. After the Form I-9 is completed, new hire data is transmitted from SuccessFactors Onboarding to the Social Security Administration on behalf of the client. The start date of for E-Verify is determined based on the following criteria (see also Figure 8.17):

   ▶ If the E-Verify request create date is before the start date of the employee, then the hire date is the E-Verify create date.

   ▶ If the E-Verify create date is equal to or after the start date, then the E-Verify hire date is the start date.

2. SSA checks the validity of the following information (see Figure 8.17):

   ▶ Social Security Number

   ▶ Date of birth

   ▶ Citizenship

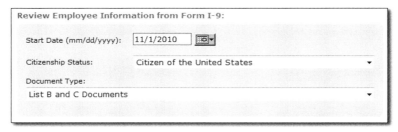

Figure 8.17 Review I-9 Form Data to Start E-Verify Process

3. SSA confirms the data then refers to DHS to verify work authorization according to the agency's immigration records.

4. After verification, DHS returns one of the following statements (see Figure 8.18):

   ▶ EMPLOYMENT AUTHORIZED

   ▶ SSA TENTATIVE NONCONFIRMATION

   ▶ DHS TENATIVE NONCONFIRMATION

   ▶ CASE INCOMPLETE

   ▶ PHOTO MATCHING REQUIRED

5. If work authorization is confirmed, then DHS will return EMPLOYMENT AUTHORIZED, which will be displayed in SuccessFactors Onboarding, as shown in Figure 8.18.

6. If neither agency can confirm work authorization, then the employer receives a TENTATIVE NONCONFIRMATION message.

7. Upon receiving this nonconfirmation, the employee and employer have the following options:

   ▶ The employee has eight days to contest or resolve.

   ▶ If the employee does not contest, then the employer can terminate without the employer being civilly liable for termination.

   ▶ If the employee contests, then the employer must sign the Notice of Non-confirmation.

▸ If the employee does not report to the SSA to resolve the nonconfirmation status and cannot resolve his or her status with the SSA or DHS, then employment can be terminated without the employer being civilly liable for termination.

▸ The employee can work during the eight-day period.

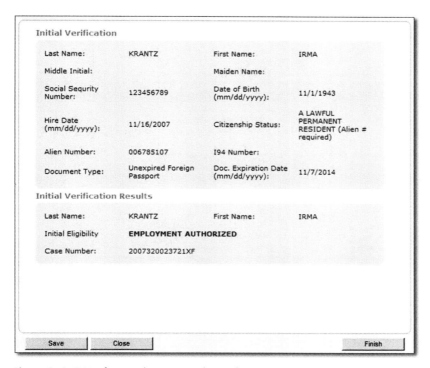

Figure 8.18 E-Verify—Employment Authorized

8. When the SSA or DHS TENTATIVE NONCONFIRMATION statement is returned, the new employee must be given an opportunity to contest or not contest the statement. The new employee must also acknowledge an understanding of the next steps associated with his or her decision and sign any notices and referral letters required (see Figure 8.19).

9. The SuccessFactors Onboarding remote employee process features updated language describing the reasons for the SSA tentative nonconfirmation that can be easily understood by both employers and employees and acted upon from different locations.

Figure 8.19 E-Verify—Tentative Nonconfirmation Screen

10. When PHOTO-MATCHING REQUIRED is returned, SuccessFactors Onboarding accommodates the automatic upload of the photo to the E-Verify program and assists with retaining a copy of the photo for your records.

Key Considerations and Benefits

When employing this integration, keep the following considerations and benefits in mind:

▶ The E-Verify process is not a substitute for pre-employment screenings and background checks and should not be used as such.

▶ A tentative nonconfirmation does not mean that the new hire is unauthorized to work, but rather that the data that was submitted cannot be confirmed. For example, the new hire may have a hyphen in his or her last name, but at the SSA there may be no hyphen on record.

▶ Photo-matching, as defined by the USCIS, is "an automatic part of the initial verification in E-Verify" that prompts employers to compare an employee's photo ID with a photo displayed on the E-Verify screen. This step helps employers ensure that the documents provided are valid.

> **User Interface**
>
> The UI provides wizards to guide the onboarding specialist through the E-Verify process. Only options that are relevant for each step are visible on the screen, along with helpful instructions pertaining to that step in the workflow.

- The photo-matching step occurs automatically when you perform a verification case for an employee who has presented a United States Passport or Passport Card, a Permanent Resident Card (Form I-551), or an Employment Authorization Document (Form I-766) as their Form I-9 documentation. When the employee presents any of these three documents and the Form I-9 information entered by the employer matches DHS records, the employee's photo will automatically display in SuccessFactors Onboarding on the E-Verify screen.

- According to the DHS, if an employer participates in the E-Verify program and the employee presents a document used as part of the Photo Screening tool as noted previously, then the employer must retain a photocopy of the document he or she presents when there is a photo nonmatch.

> **Prerequisites**
>
> SuccessFactors Onboarding E-Verify is required.

8.3   Packaged Integrations for SuccessFactors Learning

In this section, we will discuss the packaged integrations for SuccessFactors Learning. SuccessFactors Learning integrates with PayPal for enabling commerce functionality. It also integrates with Questionmark for learning assessments and with virtual learning systems such as Adobe Connect and Cisco WebEx to deliver training remotely. Each of these integrations are enabled with different configurations. This section will detail the required and more commonly used configurations.

> **Skillsoft**
>
> Skillsoft is not covered as a packaged integration, because it employs AICC or SCORM standards and is generic for all content that adopts these standards.

8.3.1 PayPal Payflow Pro Integration

A SuccessFactors Learning customer will train his or her customers, partners, and suppliers by providing curricula and courses available through resources outside the organization. External users pay for this training in multiple ways, including PO, chargebacks, credit card, and so on. When you connect SuccessFactors Learning to PayPal Payflow Pro, Payflow handles the financial transactions when users purchase courses from inside SuccessFactors Learning.

By allowing PayPal Payflow Pro to handle the transactions, you separate learning records from financial records: SuccessFactors does not store any credit card numbers unless you tell it to store the last four digits for auditing purposes. Even when you allow the last four digits to be saved in the database, SuccessFactors Learning encrypts the last four digits.

Because PayPal Payflow Pro handles both the information and the transaction, we recommend that you read the PayPal Payflow Pro documentation as a companion to the SuccessFactors documentation. PayPal publishes a *Payflow Developer's Guide* with the most current information about configuring the system. We recommend that you read the guide, particularly sections about testing the system. PayPal built a testing system that allows you to submit test transactions to Payflow without real credit card information. Figure 8.20 shows the steps and interactions between SuccessFactors Learning and PayPal Payflow Pro.

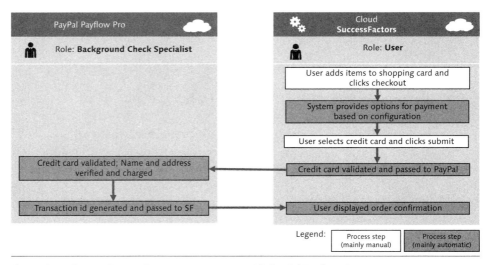

Figure 8.20 SuccessFactors Learning Integration with PayPal Payflow Pro

The following sections provide a detailed step-by-step sequence of activities as part of the integration, information on setting up and configuring your PayPal Payflow Pro account once you have established the integration, financial configuration steps to be taken within SuccessFactors Learning for PayPal, and finally key considerations to keep in mind when utilizing the integration.

Integration Process Steps

Perform the following process steps to successfully implement the integration between SuccessFactors Learning and PayPal:

1. Set up your PayPal Payflow Pro account before you configure the SuccessFactors Learning connection to the account.

2. Work with PayPal to set up your Payflow Pro payment gateway account. This account information is necessary for setting up SuccessFactors Learning to connect to Payflow.

3. Once PayPal account information is available, the following key configurations need to be configured for this integration to work:

   ▶ GATEWAY NAME
     The gateway that SuccessFactors Learning communicates with. The value is PAYPAL for PayPal Payflow Pro gateway.

   ▶ GATEWAY PASSWORD
     The password you set up when you created the Payflow Pro account. Contact PayPal support for your password.

   ▶ GATEWAY HOST ADDRESS AND PORT
     The host address and port number of the service that is hosting PayPal Payflow Pro.

   ▶ PARTNER NAME
     The ID provided to you by either PayPal or the reseller who created your account.

   ▶ VENDOR NAME
     The merchant login ID created with the PayPal account.

   ▶ USER NAME
     The username you created for the PayPal account.

   ▶ CURRENCY CODES
     The currency codes are the three-letter currency codes that the Payflow account accepts.

PayPal Payflow Pro Documentation

The Paypal Payflow Pro FAQ is available at *https://www.paypal.com/us/webapps/mpp/payflow-faq*, and API documentation is available at *https://developer.paypal.com/webapps/developer/docs*.

---

4. Set up the BOOTSTRAP-PAYMENT-GATEWAY in SuccessFactors Learning. The BOOTSTRAP-PAYMENT-GATEWAY file contains the network and logging settings of the PayPal Payflow Pro connection. It appears only to on-premise customers in SYSTEM ADMIN • CONFIGURATION • SYSTEM CONFIGURATION • BOOTSTRAP-PAYMENT-GATEWAY. For cloud learning, reach out to your SuccessFactors support representative for help. The key settings in this configuration are as follows:

   ▶ `hostAddress`
   The `hostAddress` property contains the URL of the host for the PayPal site hosting your Payflow Pro account. By default, SuccessFactors Learning goes to the test, or "pilot" site (*pilot-payflowpro.paypal.com*). Read more about the pilot site and find your live transaction site in the PayPal Payflow Pro documentation.

   ▶ `hostPort`
   The `hostPort` property contains the port that SuccessFactors uses and that PayPal Payflow Pro requires. The default is 443.

   ▶ `timeout`
   This is the number of seconds SuccessFactors Learning waits for a response before giving up.

5. Set up the financial configuration in SuccessFactors Learning. The financial configuration controls parts of SuccessFactors Learning commerce. It contains the PayPal Payflow Pro login settings and the settings to control the behavior of SuccessFactors Learning when a user provides payment information. This file appears to all customers in SYSTEM ADMIN • CONFIGURATION • SYSTEM CONFIGURATION • FINANCIAL. Some important configurations to be set are as follows:

   ▶ `financialTxApprovalRequired`
   If set to `true`, then the financial transactions will have to be approved by an administrator before the transactions can be extracted.

   ▶ `shoppingAccountTypeStudent`
   This property defines the default shopping account type for newly added

users. The shopping account type can be internal or external. A user's type matters, because external users can be excluded from some transactions.

▶ `shoppingAccountTypeOrganization`
Defines the default shopping account type for newly added organizations. The shopping account type can be internal or external. An organization's type matters, because users in external organizations can be excluded from some transactions

▶ `externalStudentPaymentMethodCreditCardEnabled`
When checking out at the shopping cart, this setting controls whether an external user (or user in an external organization) can use a credit card as a payment method.

▶ `creditCardAuthorizationEnabled`
Set `creditCardAuthorizationEnabled` to `true` to enable transactions through PayPal Payflow Pro.

▶ `creditCardSecurityCodeRequired`
Set `creditCardSecurityCodeRequired` to `true` to require users to enter their credit card security code (for example, the three digits on the back of a Visa card). Check PayPal Payflow Pro documentation and your PayPal Payflow Pro configuration before setting this property.

▶ `paymentGatewayCurrencies[USD]`
The `paymentGatewayCurrencies` sets the currencies accepted by PayPal Payflow Pro. By default, it is set to US Dollars (`USD`). For each currency you want to add, copy `paymentGatewayCurrencies[USD]` and change `USD` to the correct three-letter currency code, then set the property to `true`. To disable the currency while leaving its entry in the file, set it to `false`.

6. Next, the SuccessFactors Learning administrator needs to set up a catalog with prices and define payment methods, including credit card payment processor configuration. Although SuccessFactors Learning never stores full credit card numbers, you can decide how you want SuccessFactors Learning to handle the credit card at the moment the user enters the information and for auditing purposes. Your company might have a policy concerning these issues.

You have the following options when handling credit card information:

▶ You can mask the credit card numbers in the text box in which a user enters the numbers.

▶ You can store the last four digits, encrypted, for auditing purposes.

▸ You can validate the credit card number for simple errors before it is sent. For example, validation checks that Visa and MasterCard numbers are 16 digits.

▸ You can require the credit card security code.

▸ You can mask the security code when the user types it into text boxes.

▸ You can set how you want the system to handle the expiration year—that is, how many years into the future to show in the dropdown list.

After the successful completion of these steps, users will now be able to perform payment transactions for SuccessFactors Learning courses.

Users will be able to browse the catalogs they have access to and see the price of each item. Users can add items to a shopping cart and click on Checkout once they are done with selection. When a user clicks on Checkout, he or she is shown a shopping cart summary and address information. After confirmation, the user will see payment method options and, if credit card is selected, will be shown a screen to enter credit card details. Upon entering credit card information and clicking on Submit, connection with PayPal payment processor is established and order details (including price, address, and credit card information) are sent. Once PayPal successfully charges the credit card, a transaction ID and status is supplied to SuccessFactors Learning. The user is shown the order details and transaction status in SuccessFactors Learning.

Key Considerations and Benefits

When employing this integration, keep the following considerations and benefits in mind:

▸ Credit card information is not stored in SuccessFactors, but (based on the configuration) the last four digits of the credit card number can be stored for tracking purposes.

▸ The order ID is associated with the PayPal transaction ID in SuccessFactors Learning. This will enable tracking an order and its fulfillment details.

▸ User and organization shopping account types influence the payment options available in commerce functionality.

▸ The currency PayPal Payflow Pro accepts must have the matching currency code in SuccessFactors Learning.

The following prerequisites must be met to implement this integration:

► SuccessFactors Learning PayPal license

► PayPal Payflow Pro account

8.3.2 Virtual Learning Systems Integration

Virtual Learning Systems (VLS) enables e-learning over the web and mimics an in-person training delivery. VLS creates a classroom-type environment, allowing an instructor to deliver training through video, presentation, chatting, or phone. They enable discussions between participants through chat, phone, or a computer's speaker and microphone. Figure 8.21 details the interactions between SuccessFactors Learning and VLS, along with the steps performed in each system.

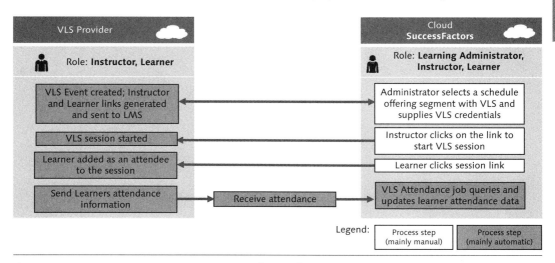

Figure 8.21 SuccessFactors Learning Integration with Virtual Learning Systems

SuccessFactors Learning VLS integration is designed to work when the user connects directly from SuccessFactors Learning to the listed virtual VLS classrooms. Therefore, users should always connect to virtual classrooms through SuccessFactors Learning. We recommend that you plan your use of the VLS server to match the options available to you through SuccessFactors Learning:

- ▶ CREATE USER
  Accounts need to be created for instructors on VLS.

- ▶ UPDATE USER
  Update instructor accounts on VLS.

- ▶ CREATE EVENT
  Create an online meeting or training session on VLS.

- ▶ UPDATE EVENT
  Update online meeting or training session on VLS.

- ▶ DELETE EVENT
  Remove online meeting or training session on VLS.

- ▶ ENROLL STUDENTS
  Register learners for a training session.

- ▶ WITHDRAW STUDENTS
  Remove learners from a training session.

- ▶ GET MEETING INFO
  Retrieve training session information from VLS.

- ▶ GET USER INFO
  Retrieve learner information from VLS.

- ▶ GET EVENTHOST URL
  Retrieve the URL for instructor to start training session.

- ▶ GET EVENTJOIN URL
  Retrieve the URL for learners to join the training session.

- ▶ GET HOST ATTENDANCE
  Retrieve the total duration of the session.

- ▶ GET STUDENT ATTENDANCE
  Retrieve the duration of attendance for each learner.

The following sections provide a detailed step-by-step sequence of activities for VLS integration and key considerations and benefits to keep in mind.

Integration Process Steps

The following steps describe the integration process:

1. The administrator should set up VLS configuration in SuccessFactors Learning, as documented in the *Virtual Meeting Rooms* guide available at *http://help.sap.com/cloud4hr*. Figure 8.22 shows the configuration screen.

2. When you sign up with a VLS vendor, the vendor should provide the following configuration information (if you already have a VLS provider, reach out to that provider for configuration information):

▸ XML API Address

▸ URL API Address

▸ Username

▸ Password

▸ Meeting Type

▸ Site Name

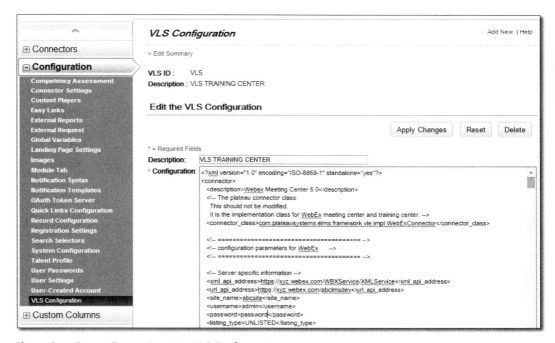

Figure 8.22 SuccessFactors Learning VLS Configuration

3. There may be additional configuration settings for your virtual learning server, but the settings in the previous step are the basic requirements for SuccessFactors VLS environment settings. SuccessFactors Learning can be configured with multiple VLS providers if your organization uses different ones based on different types of sessions.

4. VLS configuration is disabled by default. Therefore, you'll have to enable it. Go to System Admin • Configuration • System Configuration. From here, edit the LMS_ADMIN configuration page.

5. Find the `vleEnabled` setting, and change its value to `true`. Click on Apply Changes.

6. The SuccessFactors VLS connection configuration can be added or edited from SuccessFactors Learning Administration. To do so, log in to SuccessFactors Learning Administration, and then go to System Admin • Configuration • VLS Configuration.

7. Click on the Add New link, and then add a unique VLS ID, a description, and the XML configuration file provided by SuccessFactors in the Configuration box. Add a new VLS configuration for every VLS provider you want to connect to.

8. Click on Add.

9. Make provider-specific changes to the XML configuration, as described in the reference guide available at *http://help.sap.com/cloud4hr*.

<connector> and <connector_class>

Do not modify the `<connector>` and `<connector_class>` elements for any of these files. To edit the files, you should have an understanding of XML and technical knowledge of the VLS server to which you are integrating. The values you put in each of the XML elements are supplied by the vendor or the server you are integrating with.

Time zone mappings are contained in the VLS configuration files, in the `timezones` element. In almost every case, you can use the default time zone mappings. However, if participants in your meetings describe time zone issues, then you can check the map for their time zones to make sure that they are correct.

Set Up Instructors and Courses

Once the primary configurations for the integration are complete, the instructors that will deliver virtual courses should have their accounts set up with VLS credentials. VLS IDs can be created through SuccessFactors Learning, or existing ones can be associated with the instructor's account.

For an item's scheduled offerings, one or more segments can be set up as Virtual. When a segment is marked Virtual, the VLS server to be used should be selected from the dropdown; optionally, you can provide a password in case you want attendees to both access the meeting URL and enter a password to join (see Figure 8.23).

Once the session is created, the instructor is sent a VLS link that enables him or her to start the virtual meeting room. As users register and enroll in the course, emails with unique attendee URLs will be sent to them. The URLs include information to enable tracking for attendance. Users can attend the virtual sessions either by clicking on the URL or logging into SuccessFactors Learning and clicking on the launch link on the Learning Assignments dashboard. The link will be enabled prior to the session start based on VLS configuration.

Figure 8.23 Scheduled Offering with Virtual Segment

Data Synchronization with VLS

VLS synchronization is the process that transfers information from SuccessFactors Learning Administration to your VLS server. For example, if you add an instructor in SuccessFactors Learning Administration, then the instructor record is synchronized from SuccessFactors Learning Administration through VLS so that the instructor is recognized in both systems. The systems can be synchronized when you save the instructor record, or SuccessFactors Learning can synchronize changes in a batch.

▶ **To synchronize immediately**: Set the `sync` element in your VLS configuration XML file to `true`. By default, the `sync` element is set to `true`, because we recommend that you synchronize immediately unless you have a slow connection. As soon as you add, update, or delete a record that needs to be synchronized with VLS, SuccessFactors Learning Administration sends the information through VLS. This setting is recommended for most customers.

> ▶ **To synchronize at an interval**: Set the `sync` element to `false`, and then configure the synchronization frequency in System Admin • Configuration • Global Variables. When you synchronize at an interval, the synchronization process runs in the background at an interval. Any changes you make in SuccessFactors Learning do not appear immediately on the VLS server.

Once all the sessions in the scheduled offering are completed, the VLS Attendance Processing automatic process will run if enabled, retrieving information about the user and the duration for which he or she attended virtual sessions. If this duration meets or exceeds the attendance percentage that was set up, then the user is marked as having attended the course.

Key Considerations and Benefits

When employing this integration, keep the following considerations and benefits in mind:

- ▶ The course item should be classified as instructor-led or blended to be able to create scheduled offerings in SuccessFactors Learning.

- ▶ If you need to resend the email notifications to registered users, then you can send do so from the Scheduled Offering Segment screen.

- ▶ When a user drops and rejoins a virtual session, typically multiple attendance records are sent by VLS. All attendance records of a user are added to determine if they met the attendance percentage.

> **Prerequisites**
>
> The following prerequisites must be met to implement this integration:
> - ▶ SuccessFactors Learning VLS license
> - ▶ SuccessFactors Learning VLS configuration XML for your provider
> - ▶ VLS account with Cisco WebEx or Adobe Connect

8.3.3 Questionmark Integration

Questionmark is a provider of online assessment software for learning, certification, compliance, and channel expertise. The software allows you to create, deliver, and report on assessments.

After the assessments are authored in Questionmark, the SuccessFactors Learning administrator should copy the public URL for delivery of the assessment and configure a content object entity of type AICC or SCORM based on the specification provided by its author in SuccessFactors. The administrator should then associate the content object to a SuccessFactors Learning item and add it to one or more catalogs based on business need.

When the user launches the learning item, the SSO handshake is initiated between SuccessFactors and Questionmark, and the user is securely logged in and assessment information sent. Questionmark will display the assessment screens to the user. Upon completion of the assessment, the score is sent back and stored in SuccessFactors. The learning administrator can run Questionmark reports from SuccessFactors Learning. Figure 8.24 provides a sequence of events that would need to occur in each system for this integration to work and to return the score to SuccessFactors Learning.

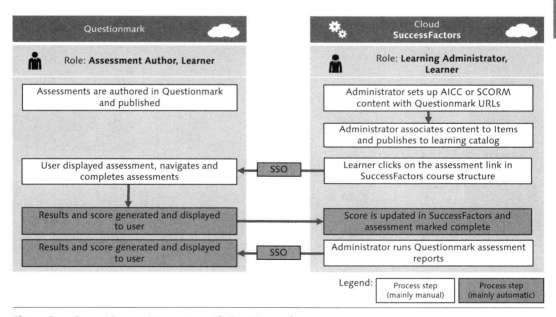

Figure 8.24 SuccessFactors Integration with Questionmark

The following sections provide a detailed step-by-step sequence of activities as part of Questionmark integration and key considerations and benefits to keep in mind.

Integration Process Steps

The following steps describe the integration process:

1. The following key configurations need to be set up for this integration to work:
   - ▸ `endPointAddress`: Questionmark SOAP end point URL
   - ▸ `apiClientID`: The client ID assigned by Questionmark
   - ▸ `apiChecksum`: Checksum value provided by Questionmark

2. Once the necessary configurations have been completed, the SuccessFactors Learning administrator should create a content object with the LAUNCH METHOD set as either AICC or SCORM, based on how the content was authored, and should also provide the Questionmark URL to launch for assessment delivery (see Figure 8.25).

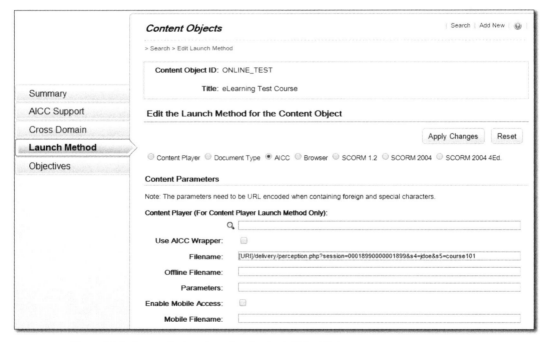

Figure 8.25 SuccessFactors Learning Content Object Setup

3. The administrator should then create an item and classify it as ONLINE ONLY, providing all relevant information, and associate the content object created in the previous step (see Figure 8.26).

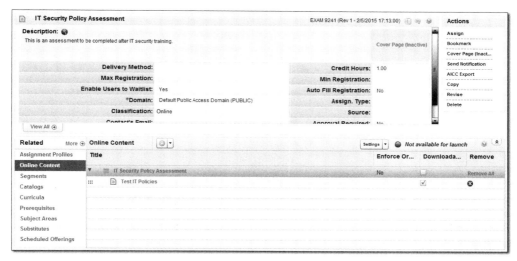

Figure 8.26 SuccessFactors Learning Online Item with Content

4. The item created in the previous step can be assigned to users as part of a curriculum or as a standalone course.

5. The item then appears on an assigned user's MY LEARNING ASSIGNMENTS screen. The user clicks on the assessment to launch it and then completes it (see Figure 8.27).

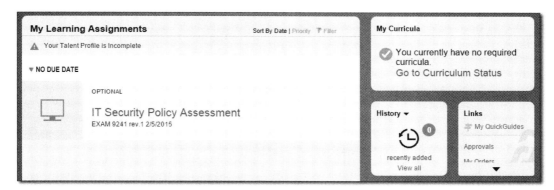

Figure 8.27 SuccessFactors My Learning Assignments Screen

The assessment results are simultaneously sent back to SuccessFactors Learning and recorded in the user's learning history. The same information is also available for the administrator in the USER ADMINISTRATION section.

Key Considerations and Benefits

When employing this integration, keep the following considerations and benefits in mind:

▸ The content object's file name should contain the full URL for the Questionmark assessment, including the domain name.

▸ When the score is available in SuccessFactors Learning, the success or failure based on the value specified can be determined in the MASTERY SCORE field.

▸ Refer to the SuccessFactors Learning help documentation for associating content to an item and enabling it to be available for users.

Prerequisites

A separate third-party contract with Questionmark for its learning assessments solution is required.

8.4   Standard Data Imports

Standard data imports are another way to integrate SuccessFactors with third-party vendors. The previous sections discussed the business process-based integrations. In this section, we will look at the data integrations.

Data is imported into SuccessFactors through standard import jobs. These data imports accept flat files (mostly in CSV format) and send out notifications when they complete processing data. This section discusses the high-level design and function of these standard import processes.

The next two sections look at the import process for the SuccessFactors HCM platform and data imports in SuccessFactors Learning.

8.4.1   SuccessFactors HCM Platform

The import process starts with the preparation of the file in SuccessFactors-defined format. The template files can be downloaded directly from the application in Admin Tools. The file format supported is a comma-delimited file. The first line contains the column technical name, and the second line includes the user-friendly column name. Figure 8.28 shows the steps performed by the import process to consume files and add data to the SuccessFactors platform.

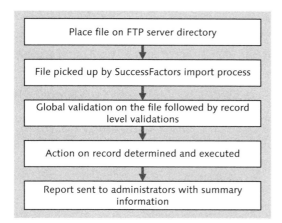

Figure 8.28 SuccessFactors HCM Import Process Internal Design

The data from the file is updated as is, but if specific data in SuccessFactors needs to be retained for a column, then `&&NO_OVERWRITE&&` needs to be specified in the file for the corresponding column. The file generated can be encrypted and is to be placed on the SuccessFactors-provided secure FTP server or the customer's FTP server. The file name can include the current date to not overwrite files that are still on the FTP server.

The file will be picked up at the scheduled time, decrypted, and validated for format and data consistency. Once these checks pass, the data in each row is validated against the data in the database, and actions that need to be taken on the record are determined and executed. Once all records are processed, an email is sent out to all users or groups specified at the time of scheduling the job. The email contains a summary of information, including counts of new and updated records, along with error counts and error messages.

8.4.2 SuccessFactors Learning

Data imports to SuccessFactors are also known as connectors. There are connectors for users, admins, organizations, domains, learning history, jobs, item domains, positions, scheduled offerings, and registration data. Connector workbooks defining the specifications are released along with product releases by SuccessFactors. Each of the following sections provide details on connector features.

File Format

SuccessFactors supports only the UTF-8 character set in the input file. Because many connectors have description fields that span multiple rows, it is recommended to use `!#!` as a row delimiter. The column delimiter is always a pipe (|) character. The connector will be set to the `header` method for processing the input file. This means that the order of the headers can vary, because the connector reads the header row and uses it to map data to the connector fields. All columns indicated in the header row must be supplied in the input file data. Two consecutive pipes indicate a null value.

Configuration Options

The SYSTEM ADMIN • CONFIGURATION • SYSTEM CONFIGURATION • CONNECTORS configuration menu contains both global settings applicable to all connectors and those that are specific to each connector. Properties starting with the `connector` prefix apply to all connectors. These can be overridden for a specific connector by adding a prefix to the property. If this needs to be changed only for a specific connector, then add a new property prefixing the property for that connector.

Example

The connector configuration ships with connector.pgp.enabled=false, indicating that file encryption is disabled. It can be enabled for a connector by adding a new property, `xyz.connector.pgp.enabled=true`, where `xyz` is the connector prefix.

Table 8.1 provides a list of connectors and their corresponding prefixes.

Connector Name	Connector Prefix
User Connector	user
Federal User Connector	federaluser
Organization Connector	organization
Domain Connector	domain
Item Connector	item
Learning History Connector	learninghistory
Schedule Offering Connector	scheduleoffering
Registration Connector	enrollment

Table 8.1 SuccessFactors Learning Connector Prefixes

Connector Name	Connector Prefix
Position Connector	position
Job Code Connector	jobposition

Table 8.1 SuccessFactors Learning Connector Prefixes (Cont.)

The default values for each of the connectors are specified in this configuration and can be altered to suit your needs. Connector input data to target database column mapping can be altered in this configuration, but it is not recommended.

Table 8.2 provides a listing of the different types of connectors and their particular uses.

Connector	Usage
User Connector	Add, update, or inactive users.
Federal User Connector	Add, update, or inactive users for customers that need to store PII data in SuccessFactors Learning.
Organization Connector	Add, update, and maintain organization hierarchy.
Domain Connector	Add, update, and maintain domain hierarchy.
Item Connector	▸ Add, update, revise, and inactive SuccessFactor Learning items and content objects. ▸ Maintain associations between items and content objects. ▸ SuccessFactors Learning item localization and competency mappings.
Learning History Connector	Add items based on training history for users.
Schedule Offering Connector	Add or update scheduled offerings.
Registration Connector	Enroll users for existing scheduled offerings.
Position Connector	Add or update positions.
Job Code Connector	Add or update job codes.
Curriculum Connector	▸ Add or update curricula. ▸ Maintain curricula parent/child relationships localization. ▸ Maintain item and requirement mappings to curricula.

Table 8.2 SuccessFactors Learning Connectors

Scheduling

A connector scheduler resembles WINDOWS SCHEDULER options, and each of the connector menus available at SYSTEM ADMIN • CONNECTORS displays the connector scheduler (see Figure 8.29).

Data Processing

Data from input files are loaded into staging tables. After comparing them with the target data, delta data is determined along with the type of operation that needs to be performed on each of the target records. Records determined as unchanged are ignored, and changed records are processed by the connector.

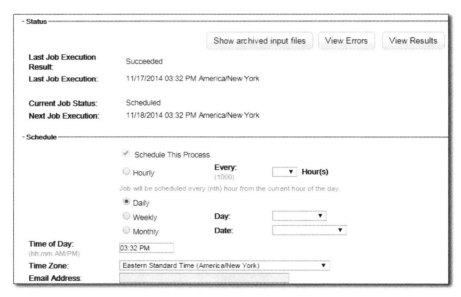

Figure 8.29 SuccessFactors Learning Connector—Schedule and Status

Reports and Error Logs

Once the connector completes processing all records, it generates two reports and emails them to the email address(es) specified on the scheduling screen. The summary report contains record counts for operations performed and aggregated information. The connector has the ability to archive processed files (see Figure 8.30).

Completed Connector Runs

Serial Number	Started	Finished	Completion Status	Processed	Exceptions	View Details	View Logs
1	06 Feb 2015 11:00 America/New York	06 Feb 2015 11:01 America/New York	WARN - NO RECORDS	0	0	⤓	View Logs
2	05 Feb 2015 11:00 America/New York	05 Feb 2015 11:01 America/New York	WARN - NO RECORDS	0	0	⤓	View Logs
3	04 Feb 2015 11:00 America/New York	04 Feb 2015 11:01 America/New York	WARN - NO RECORDS	0	0	⤓	View Logs
4	03 Feb 2015 11:00 America/New York	03 Feb 2015 11:01 America/New York	WARN - NO RECORDS	0	0	⤓	View Logs
5	02 Feb 2015 11:00 America/New York	02 Feb 2015 11:01 America/New York	WARN - NO RECORDS	0	0	⤓	View Logs
6	01 Feb 2015 11:00 America/New York	01 Feb 2015 11:01 America/New York	WARN - NO RECORDS	0	0	⤓	View Logs
7	31 Jan 2015 11:01 America/New York	31 Jan 2015 11:01 America/New York	WARN - NO RECORDS	0	0	⤓	View Logs
8	30 Jan 2015 11:00 America/New York	30 Jan 2015 11:01 America/New York	WARN - NO RECORDS	0	0	⤓	View Logs
9	29 Jan 2015 11:00 America/New York	29 Jan 2015 11:01 America/New York	WARN - NO RECORDS	0	0	⤓	View Logs
10	28 Jan 2015 11:01 America/New York	28 Jan 2015 11:02 America/New York	OK - SUCCESS	2	0	⤓	View Logs

Records per Page 10 ▼ (10 total records)

Figure 8.30 Connector Run Results with Report and Log Links

8.5 Summary

In this chapter, we discussed how to integrate SuccessFactors talent modules with third-party applications using delivered integrations. Some of these integrations do not require a middleware platform, whereas others (such as assessment integrations with SuccessFactors Recruiting) do need one. When middleware is needed, SuccessFactors and SAP deliver packaged integration content via both Dell Boomi AtomSphere and SAP HANA Cloud Integration. All of the integrations described in this chapter are with SuccessFactors partners that are in the cloud, with no further network configurations needed.

Moving on from business process-oriented integrations, we also touched on the various data imports and integrations involved with talent modules. A large number of SuccessFactors customers use flat file imports to add data to the talent suite. The data templates for standard imports to talent modules are available in Admin Tools.

The next chapter will showcase a few case studies for the Full Cloud HCM deployment model. This will provide real-world application to the concepts discussed throughout the book.

Moving your HR processes to the cloud is a process best handled by the Full Cloud HCM integrations. In this chapter, we will discuss the integration of Employee Central with SAP ERP, Employee Central Payroll and SAP Payroll, and third-party tools, such as Kronos Time Management.

9 Implementing the Full Cloud HCM Integrations

Full Cloud HCM integrations allow HR processes to be maintained in the cloud via Employee Central. Full Cloud HCM integrations with SAP ERP include standard integration solutions for cost center master data replication, employee data, and organizational replication using the Dell Boomi AtomSphere middleware tool. In addition, Employee Central can be integrated with third-party applications using Dell Boomi AtomSphere as the middleware with benefit vendors, payroll vendors, and Kronos Time Management for time processing.

Target Audience

The perfect candidates for Full Cloud HCM integrations are customers who are maintaining their core HR processes in the cloud within Employee Central. For more information, see Chapter 3.

The following sections provide detailed, step-by-step customer case studies that show how the standard integration scenarios can be implemented via standard integration templates to complete the integration between Employee Central and SAP ERP and third-party applications that use Dell Boomi AtomSphere for the following tasks:

▶ Employee Central integration with SAP ERP

▶ Employee Central integration with SAP Payroll or Employee Central Payroll

▶ Employee Central integration with Kronos Time Management

Let's begin by looking at the integration of Employee Central with SAP ERP.

9.1   Employee Central Integration to SAP ERP

The Employee Central to SAP ERP integration is tailored for customers using the Full Cloud HCM deployment model. Employee master data is managed in Employee Central in the cloud, but part of the employee record needs to be replicated back to SAP ERP to support other, non-HR processes. For example, if SAP ERP is used for procurement, then employee data may be required to determine approval structures in workflow processes.

Prerequisites

Prior to implementing Employee Central integration with SAP ERP, you will need to complete the following relevant configurations:

- Set up Employee Central with the latest version of SuccessFactors
- Set up Dell Boomi AtomSphere
- Have SFSF Employee Central Integration Add-on (PA_SE_IN 100 SP1 and ODTFINCC 600) deployed and configured in SAP. You must also have the following system minimum requirements:
  - SAP ERP 6.0 SPS 15 or higher
  - SAP ERP 6.0 SPS 08 EHP 2 or higher
  - SAP ERP 6.0 SPS 05 EHP 3 or higher
  - SAP ERP 6.0 SPS 05 EHP 4 or higher
  - SAP ERP 6.0/SAP NetWeaver 7.01 SPS 05 EHP 4 or higher
  - SAP ERP 6.0 SPS 06 EHP 5 or higher
  - SAP ERP 6.0 SPS 03 EHP 6 or higher
  - SAP ERP 6.0 on SAP HANA SPS 01 EHP 6 or higher
  - SAP ERP 6.0 ISS EHP 7 or higher
  - HR Renewal 1.0 SPS 03 or higher
- Have relevant access to SAP ERP with a sufficient authorization role for the configuration activities in SAP IMG, SALE, web service configuration, and background job scheduler, as well as access to the SuccessFactors Provisioning and Administration pages
- IT network configuration is required to enable communication through firewalls between Dell Boomi AtomSphere and SAP ERP

In a typical integration scenario, the cost center replication process is set to run first to replicate the cost center from SAP ERP to Employee Central for employee cost assignment purposes. Then, the employee master data, job information, and organizational structure information is replicated from Employee Central to SAP ERP. To link the employee master data with the job and organizational structure, organizational assignment information is replicated from Employee Central to SAP ERP.

We will use a case study example to demonstrate this process. A description of the parameters that this integration will entail is presented next, including the client scenario and an overview of the process steps.

9.1.1 Case Study Parameters

In this case study, we will focus on the Employee Central integration to SAP ERP. Specifically, we'll discuss the implementation steps necessary for both SAP ERP and SuccessFactors to implement the cost center, organizational, and employee data integration.

Client Scenario

ABC Global Services is headquartered in Dallas, Texas, and has operations sites across the United States—with over 5,000 employees in North America. The company currently uses SAP ERP to support its financials, sales and distribution, and materials management functions. ABC Global Services became increasingly interested in SuccessFactors because it is looking to lessen IT configuration support and have its system be more user maintained while providing a more positive user experience. Over time, ABC Global Services inspires to have modules to exchange and build on data—in hopes of bringing employees closer to their HR data.

At this point, ABC Global Services would like to implement the SuccessFactors Employee Central module for its core HR processes. ABC Global Service's existing IT footprint includes SAP ERP ECC 6.0 EHP 6.

To effectively integrate and transfer the cost center, organizational, and employee data, the team recognizes that the technical consultant will need to have a solid understanding of the basic settings of Employee Central integration with SAP ERP and the necessary Integration Add-ons and system requirements to make the integration successful. The biggest challenge will be to keep the systems and HR data in sync between SAP ERP and SuccessFactors.

With a successful integration, the benefits of moving to the cloud will include an easy and fast deployment of the Employee Central module and the ability to leverage standard Integration Add-ons delivered by SAP to ensure that the data is in sync between SuccessFactors and SAP ERP HCM. To ensure that the integration is successful, there are certain business requirements that will guarantee a smooth transfer of data. For example, there needs to be a single source of employee data from Employee Central.

To integrate and transfer data from SuccessFactors to SAP ERP using Dell Boomi AtomSphere middleware, execute the following steps:

1. Ensure that baseline integration configuration settings were made for SAP ERP and for the Employee Central integration by defining authorizations in SAP ERP to access the new integration transactions.

2. The middleware, installation, and configuration of Dell Boomi AtomSphere was set as an integration point between SAP ERP and SuccessFactors.

Process Overview

There are four main steps that are required to implement the Employee Central integration with SAP ERP:

▶ **Step 1: Basic setup**
In this step, we'll look at the basic system configuration necessary for integration with SuccessFactors to SAP ERP. This includes everything from creating a technical system user in SAP ERP to creating an RFC destination in SAP ERP (see Section 9.1.2).

▶ **Step 2: Employee Central configuration**
In this section step, we will look at setting up the configuration for Employee Central. This includes the data models, picklists, and Role-Based Permissions (RBP) enhancement configurations (see Section 9.1.3).

▶ **Step 3: SAP ERP configuration**
This section will cover the SAP ERP configuration setup steps, which involves tasks such as refining the default logic of a work schedule to organization structure, organizational assignment, and job classification replication (see Section 9.1.4).

▶ **Step 4: Middleware setup and web service activation**
This section discusses the necessary steps for configuring the Dell Boomi AtomSphere middleware, along with the SAP ERP web service activation and Application Link Enabling (ALE) distribution model for integrating cost center repli-

cation, employee data replication, and employee data replication confirmation scenarios between Employee Central and SAP ERP (see Section 9.1.5).

Let's begin with the basic setup process involved with this integration.

9.1.2 Step 1: Basic Setup

There is a baseline integration configuration that is required for setting up Employee Central in SAP ERP. This baseline system configuration covers settings for Employee Central, SAP ERP, and Dell Boomi AtomSphere middleware.

The basic setup is comprised of the following tasks:

▶ Creating a technical system user in SAP ERP

▶ Enabling web services for the SuccessFactors API

▶ Creating a SuccessFactors API user

▶ Configuring the SuccessFactors API user security

▶ Configuring the SuccessFactors API login exceptions

▶ Installing the integration pack in Dell Boomi AtomSphere

▶ Importing the SSL trusted CA certificate into SAP ERP

▶ Creating an RFC destination in SAP ERP

We'll begin by creating a technical user in SAP ERP.

Create a Technical System User in SAP ERP

To begin, we'll define the authorization for the communication of the Dell Boomi AtomSphere middleware with SAP ERP. To do this, you'll define the role by referring to standard roles `SAP_HR_PA_EC_EE_REPL` (which includes employee data replication access) and `SAP_HR_SFIOM_WEBSERVICES` (which includes organizational data replication access). You may use the standard roles as a template to define an authorization that suits your requirement.

Access Transaction PFCG to begin defining a role. Once you have defined the authorization, you can proceed to create a technical user by assigning the defined role. Access Transaction SU01 to begin creating a technical user, with SYSTEM designated as the USER TYPE.

Now, let's focus on enabling the web services for the SuccessFactors API.

279

Enable Web Services SuccessFactors API

In this task, you will want to activate the SuccessFactors web services API features.

To do so, log on to the SuccessFactors Provisioning page by accessing *https://<Instance URL>/provisioning_login* (the instance URL is provided by the Success-Factors team—for example, *https://performancemanager8.SuccessFactors.com/provisioning_login*).

Next, on the Provisioning page, go to COMPANY SETTINGS, then navigate to WEB SERVICES. Under WEB SERVICES, select the following features:

- SFAPI
- SFAPI AD HOC FEATURE
- EMPLOYEE CENTRAL SOAP API
- ODATA API
- EMPLOYEE CENTRAL ODATA API

Next, we'll talk about how to create a SuccessFactors API user.

Create a SuccessFactors API User

A SuccessFactors API user is required for the Dell Boomi AtomSphere middle-ware to integrate with Employee Central. The API user must first be created in the SuccessFactors provisioning tool. The same API user logon credential is then stored in the middleware credential setting of the Dell Boomi AtomSphere environment setup.

Log on to the SuccessFactors Provisioning site and choose COMPANY SETTINGS. Then, navigate to ADMIN USERNAME. Enter the following information:

- ADMIN USERNAME (we suggest using "SAP_API_USER")
- ADMIN PASSWORD (create a strong password)
- ADMIN FIRST NAME (Enter user's first name)
- ADMIN LAST NAME (Enter user's first name)
- ADMIN EMAIL (Enter user's email address)

Click on the CREATE ADMIN button to create the API user.

Now, let us turn our attention to the API user security.

Configure the SuccessFactors API User Security

In this step, you will grant security access to the API user created in the previous step. You will need to use RBP to assign permissions to the API User.

> **Role-Based Permissions**
>
> RBP will normally be created by your Employee Central functional consultant.

Proceed with the following steps:

1. Log on to the SuccessFactors instance URL as an admin—for example, *https:// performancemanager8.SuccessFactors.com.*

2. Create an RBP group and assign your API user to it. Navigate to ADMIN TOOLS • MANAGE EMPLOYEES • SET USER PERMISSIONS • MANAGE PERMISSION GROUPS (see Figure 9.1 and Figure 9.2).

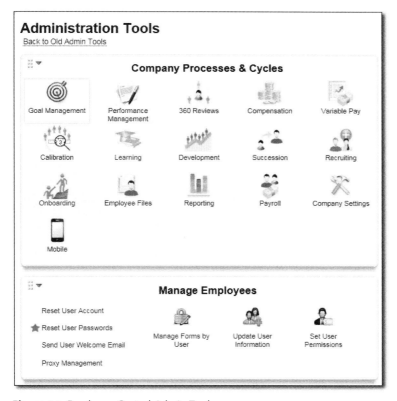

Figure 9.1 Employee Central Admin Tools

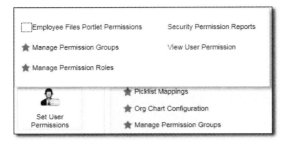

Figure 9.2 Employee Central Admin Tools—Set User Permissions

3. Create a permission group called SFAPI Users, and assign your SFAPI user to this group in the CHOOSE GROUP MEMBERS window (see Figure 9.3).

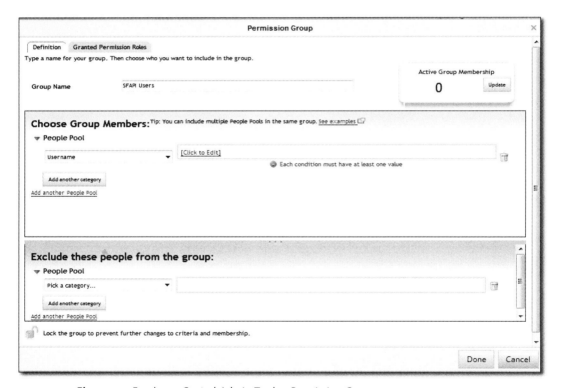

Figure 9.3 Employee Central Admin Tools—Permission Groups

4. Click on CREATE NEW. The DEFINITION tab will open. Type in a name for the PERMISSION GROUP—for example, "API Users".

5. Next, under Choose Group Members, first pick a Category—in this case, Username.

6. Select your user, for example SAP_API_USER. Click on Done to save the assignment of your user to a permission group.

7. Now, assign permissions to your API user. Navigate to Admin Tools • Manage Employees • Set User Permissions • Manage Permission Roles • Permission Role List.

8. Pick the API Users role from the Permission Role list in the Permission Role Detail window.

9. Click on the Permission Settings button to open a User Permissions window, which will contain a list of categories for permissions.

10. Make the minimum selections necessary for enabling the API user. Please work with an Employee Central functional consultant to determine any additional permissions needed. Select each category, and within the category select the settings shown in Figure 9.4.

Figure 9.4 Employee Central Admin Tools—Assigning Permissions to Roles

SuccessFactors API Login Exception

In this step, you will configure the API login exception for the API user that was just created. The purpose is to ensure that the password for the API user does not expire.

Log on to the SuccessFactors tenant as an admin user, then navigate to ADMIN TOOLS • COMPANY SETTINGS • PASSWORD & LOGIN POLICY SETTINGS • SET API LOGIN EXCEPTIONS. Then, add the following settings (see Figure 9.5):

- ▸ USERNAME
  sap_api_user

- ▸ MAXIMUM PASSWORD AGE (IN DAYS)
  - 1

- ▸ IP ADDRESS RESTRICTIONS
  Select designated external, EGRESS IP addresses, or the address range from which the API user is being accessed from. This can be used to ensure that the API user is only called from designated sources.

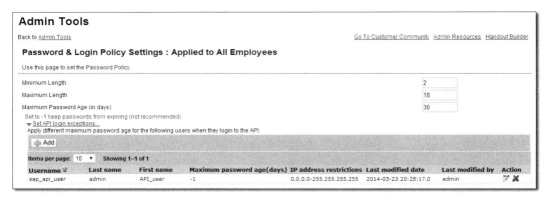

Figure 9.5 Set API Login Exceptions

Install the Integration Pack in Dell Boomi AtomSphere

Next, you will set up the preconfigured integration pack in Dell Boomi Atom-Sphere. This integration pack contains the required integration mapping between the Employee Central data fields and the corresponding fields of SAP ERP. Prior to the installation, you will have to create a separate Dell Boomi AtomSphere atom and environment for the integration pack to be able to deploy. Let's start by creating an atom. Proceed as follows:

1. Log on to the Dell Boomi AtomSphere system, and navigate to BUILD • CREATE COMPONENT • CREATE • ATOM. Under ATOM SETUP, select the IN THE CLOUD radio button, and choose ATOM CLOUD. Enter a name for your atom, and click on OK to create it (see Figure 9.6).

Figure 9.6 Atom Setup

2. Once the atom is created, you can proceed to create the environments. Go to MANAGE • ATOM MANAGEMENT. Click on the + (plus sign) icon (see Figure 9.7).

Figure 9.7 Add Environment

3. Under the ENVIRONMENTS properties, enter the environment name, and then click on SAVE. Once it is saved, the newly created environment will appear under ENVIRONMENTS on the left pane. Select the environment that was just created. Go to its properties, and then select the atom that was created earlier from the UNATTACHED ATOMS list and click on the << button to attach the atom to the environment. The atom will appear in the ATTACHED ATOMS list (see Figure 9.8).

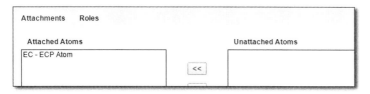

Figure 9.8 Attached Atoms

You have now successfully set up the required atom and environment and can now install the integration pack. You will install three integration packs as part of the Employee Central to SAP ERP integration:

► Employee master data replication scenario

► Cost center replication scenario

► Organizational management scenario

Proceed as follows:

1. Go to DEPLOY, and select INTEGRATION PACKS (see Figure 9.9).

Figure 9.9 Deploy and Select Integration Packs

2. Under INTEGRATION PACKS, click on the + icon to browse the integration packs catalog and look for the integration pack IFLOW EC TO EC PAYROLL EMPLOYEE REPLICATION V2.0. Click on VIEW AND INSTALL to complete the installation.

3. IFLOW EC TO EC PAYROLL EMPLOYEE REPLICATION V2.0 will now appear under INTEGRATION PACKS. You are ready to begin attaching an environment to the integration pack. Select the newly deployed integration pack, and attach the environment that was created earlier by choosing it from the UNATTACHED ENVIRONMENT list on the right side of the screen, then click on the << button to attach it. As a result, the environment will now appear under the ATTACHED ENVIRONMENTS list of the integration pack IFLOW EC TO EC PAYROLL EMPLOYEE REPLICATION V2.0 (see Figure 9.10).

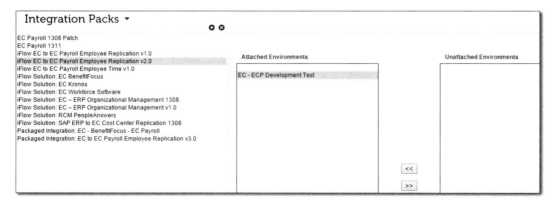

Figure 9.10 Integration Pack

4. Repeat the preceding steps to install the next integration packs: iFLOW SOLUTION SAP ERP TO EC COST CENTER REPLICATION 1308 and iFLOW SOLUTION: EC—ERP ORGANIZATIONAL MANAGEMENT v1.0.

SSL Trusted CA Certificate Import in SAP ERP

To enable the SSL connection between SAP ERP to the Dell Boomi AtomSphere middleware, first import the Dell Boomi AtomSphere SSL Trusted CA certificates into SAP ERP via Transaction STRUST.

Begin by downloading the SSL CA certificates from Dell Boomi AtomSphere. Then, proceed as follows:

1. Go to MANAGE • ENVIRONMENTS and select the atom that was created earlier. Under the ATOM PROPERTIES, open the SHARED WEB SERVER SETTINGS. Copy the base URL and paste it into the desired Internet browser (we recommend Google Chrome; see Figure 9.11).

Figure 9.11 Web Server Settings

2. Click on the SECURITY icon (a closed lock) next to the URL address box. Navigate to the CONNECTION tab, and click on the certificate information. A certificate dialog box will appear (see Figure 9.12).

> **HTTP Error 404**
>
> Please note that you may get HTTP error 404 when you access the URL; you may ignore the error and proceed to download the certificate.

Figure 9.12 URL Address Box

3. In the Certificate dialog box, navigate to Details • Copy to File to download the certificate to your local machine. Repeat the same steps to download all of the certificates listed in the certificate chain (see Figure 9.13).

Figure 9.13 Certificate Chain

4. After successfully downloading the certificates, import the certificates into SAP ERP via Transaction STRUST. Double-click on SSL System Client, and then choose Import Certificate in the lower-left corner of the UI.

Create an RFC Destination in SAP ERP

There is one more basic configuration that must be completed. This step involves creating an RFC destination in SAP ERP for connecting the Dell Boomi Atom-Sphere middleware. This connection will be used by the cost center replication scenario.

Follow these steps to proceed:

1. To begin, access Transaction SM59, and create an RFC destination with connection type G by entering the parameters shown in Table 9.1 (also see Figure 9.14).

Field	Parameter
TARGET HOST	Refer to the base URL of Dell Boomi AtomSphere (described earlier)
PATH PREFIX	/ws/simple/getODTF_CCTR01
SERVICE NO.	443

Table 9.1 RFC Destination Parameters

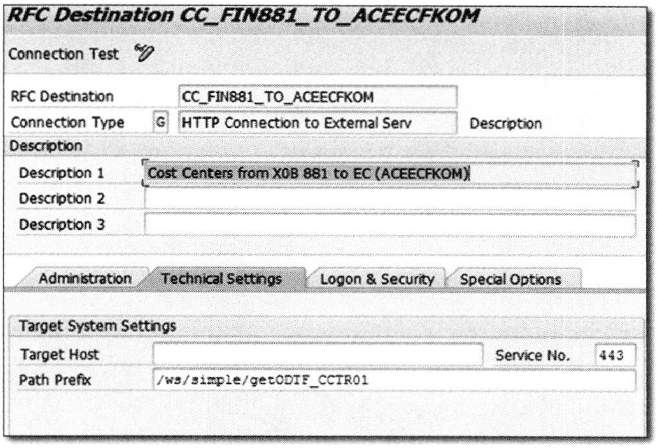

Figure 9.14 RFC Destination Technical Settings

Dell Boomi AtomSphere Username and Password

To obtain a Dell Boomi AtomSphere username and password, go to SHARED WEB SERVER SETTINGS • USER MANAGEMENT. Then, click on the GENERATE button to generate the password. Copy the username and password (see Figure 9.15).

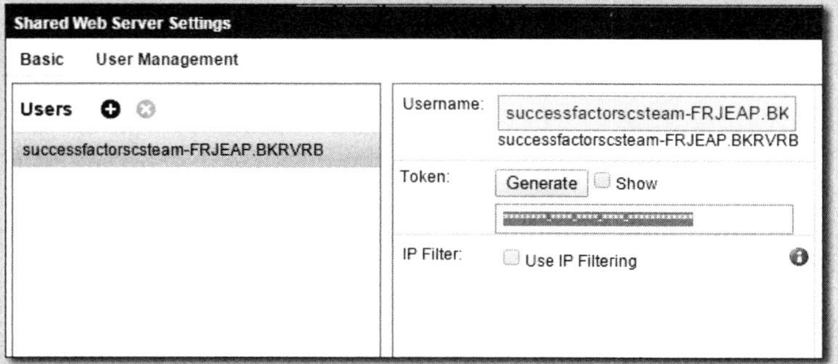

Figure 9.15 Shared Web Server Settings

2. Under the Logon & Security tab, choose Basic Authentication, and enter your Dell Boomi AtomSphere username and password (see Figure 9.16).

Figure 9.16 RFC Destination Logon and Security

9.1.3 Step 2: Employee Central Configuration

Now, let's turn our attention to the necessary Employee Central configuration steps required for setting up the Employee Central integration with SAP ERP.

This section covers the following tasks:

▶ Data model configuration
▶ Picklist configuration
▶ RBP enhancement configuration

Let's begin our discussion by defining the succession data model and corporate data model.

Data Model Configurations

There are two types of data models that need to be updated for this configuration: the *succession data model* and the *corporate data model*. The configuration steps for both data models are described in the next sections.

Succession Data Model Configuration

The succession data model governs the structure of the SuccessFactors system. It is accessible in the provisioning tool for each instance. This best practice data model contains all standard fields and background elements available to capture employee data.

In this step, you will update the required HRIS fields' attributes of the succession data model for the employee master data replication process. You will then export the succession data model for adjustment and import it back in the Provisioning tools.

Perform the following steps to proceed:

1. Log on to the SuccessFactors Provisioning page of your instance and navigate to Succession Management. From here, log on to *https://<server>.successfactors.com/provisioning_login* (see Figure 9.17).

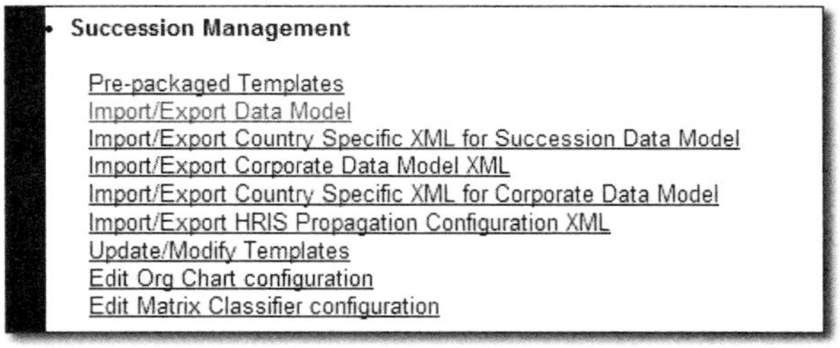

Figure 9.17 Provisioning—Succession Management

2. From this screen, click on the IMPORT/EXPORT DATA MODEL link, then select the EXPORT radio button.

3. Save the succession data model XML file to your local machine, and make the following adjustments:

   ▸ Open the XML file via the XML Editor tool, and edit the HRIS fields attribute based on the following information:

     – Visibility: "both"

     – Required: "true"

4. These changes are applicable to all required HRIS fields listed in Table 9.2.

Segment	Field Name	Employee Central Field ID
Personal Information	First Name	`first-name`
	Last Name	`last-name`
	Salutation	`salutation`
	Gender	`Gender`
	Nationality	`Nationality`
	Native Preferred Language	`native-preferred-lang`
Biographical Information	Date of Birth	`date-of-birth`
	Person ID	`person-id-external`
National ID Card	National Identification	`national-id`
	Country	`country`
Job Information	Company	`company`
	Location	`location`
	Cost center	`cost-center`
	Employee Class	`employee-class`
	Employment Type	`employment-type`
	Job classification	`jobCode`
	Time off Workschedule	`workschedule`
	Working Days Per Week	`workingDaysPerWeek`
Compensation Information	Pay Group	`pay-group`
Home Address Information (Country specific—US)	City	`City`
	State	`state`
	ZIP	`zip`

Table 9.2 HRIS Fields

5. The Employee Central HRIS fields in Table 9.3 may either be optional or required fields, based on your SAP ERP HCM setup.

	Salutation	Salutation
Personal Information Fields	Marital Status	`marital-status`
	Place of Birth	`place-of-birth`
	Birth Name	`Birth-Name`

Table 9.3 Personal Information Fields

▶ In the succession data model, ensure visibility is set to value "both" and required is set to "true", as seen in the following example for the first name:

```
<hris-field max-length="128" id="first-name" visibility="both" and
required="true"
```

6. Save the changes.

7. Go back to provisioning tool, and choose IMPORT/EXPORT SUCCESSION DATA MODEL, then select the IMPORT radio button.

8. Browse for and upload the updated XML.

Corporate Data Model Configuration

Continuing with the data model configuration, you will now update the corporate data model XML. The corporate data model update covers restricting the maximum length of the foundation field ID that can be handled by the API for employee master data replication and cost center replication processes.

In the SUCCESSION MANAGEMENT section of the SuccessFactors Provisioning page, perform the following steps:

1. Choose IMPORT/EXPORT CORPORATE DATA MODEL, then select the EXPORT radio button.

2. Save the corporate data model XML file to your local machine, and make the adjustments noted in the next step.

3. Open the XML file via the XML Editor tool, and edit the HRIS fields attribute based on the following information:

▶ MAX LENGTH OF ID: This refers to the maximum length handled by the API. Any field with a length set beyond the maximum length cannot be handled by the middleware and will end with an error.

▶ RECOMMENDATION LENGTH: This is based on the SAP ERP field length. Additional code mapping is required in SAP ERP if you are using fields with external code longer than the recommended characters. However, some fields require mandatory code mapping in SAP ERP. Refer to Section 9.1.4 for further details.

See Table 9.4 for the recommended field lengths for certain foundation objects.

Foundation Object	Max. Length of ID	Recommendation Length
COMPANY (LEGAL ENTITY)	20	<= 4
LOCATION	20	
COST CENTER	20	
JOB CLASSIFICATION	10	<= 2
PAY GROUP	4	<= 2
PAY COMPONENT	10	<= 4

Table 9.4 Corporate Data Model Recommended Length

4. Save the changes.

5. Go back to the SuccessFactors Provisioning page, and click on the IMPORT/EXPORT CORPORATE DATA MODEL link, then select the IMPORT radio button.

6. Browse for and upload the updated XML.

Let's now move on to configuring the picklists.

Picklist Configuration

In this step, you will define additional picklist information on an existing picklist template. You will have to add an external code for all picklists used for the employee master data replication scenario.

Prior to updating the picklist, there are some important points to consider:

▶ Make sure all codes are unique for their contexts; the external codes will be replicated and mapped to SAP ERP.

▶ External codes need to be in CAPITAL LETTERS and/or numbers.

▶ External codes that are longer than 10 characters are cut off during replication; only the first 10 characters are available for mapping in SAP ERP.

You are now ready to initiate the configuration. Perform the following steps:

1. To begin the picklist update, log on to Employee Central.

2. Go to ADMIN TOOLS • COMPANY SETTING • PICKLIST MANAGEMENT. Select EXPORT ALL PICKLISTS, and then click SUBMIT to save them to your local machine. Open the *picklist.csv* file, and update the external code for the relevant picklist (as listed in Table 9.5 for the Employee Central integration with SAP ERP).

Picklist	Remark
EMPLOYMENTTYPE	N/A
EMPLOYEECLASS	N/A
STATE_XXX	XXX represents the relevant ISO country code in the employee address—for example, STATE_USA
SALUTATION	Optional
ECMARITALSTATUS	Optional

Table 9.5 Picklists for Employee Central Integration with SAP ERP

As an example, we can update the external code for picklist employment type. Figure 9.18 illustrates what you need to do for each of the entries in the table.

^picklistId	Option	minVa	maxValu	valu	statu	external_co	parentO	en_US
employmentType	1061	-1	-1	-1	ACTIVE	RE	-1	RegularÊ
employmentType	1141	-1	-1	-1	ACTIVE	U0	-1	Hourly (U0)
employmentType	1062	-1	-1	-1	ACTIVE	U3	-1	Standard salary (u3)

Figure 9.18 Picklist External Code

Once the picklist is updated, go back to PICKLIST MANAGEMENT. Select IMPORT PICKLIST, and browse for the *picklist.csv* file. Click on SUBMIT to complete the upload.

Role-Based Permissions Enhancement Configuration

We have almost completed the configuration setup required in Employee Central. Now, let's start updating the RBP for a SuccessFactors API role.

Go to ADMIN TOOLS • SET USER PERMISSIONS • MANAGE PERMISSIONS ROLES. In the PERMISSION ROLE list, select the permission roles that correspond to the HR ADMINISTRATOR role, EMPLOYEE STANDARD role, and SUCCESSFACTOR API role, and update the user permissions accordingly (refer to Table 9.6).

Permission Role	User Permission	Permission	Checked
ADMINISTRATOR	EMPLOYEE DATA	PAYMENT INFORMATION	X
	EMPLOYEE CENTRAL EFFECTIVE DATE ENTITIES	JOB INFORMATION	All
		COMPENSATION	All
	EMPLOYEE VIEW	PAYROLL INFORMATION	X
	PAYROLL PERMISSIONS	PAYROLL ADMINISTRATION	X

Table 9.6 Permissions

Permission Role	User Permission	Permission	Checked
EMPLOYEE STANDARD	EMPLOYEE VIEW	PAYROLL	X
	PAYROLL PERMISSIONS	PAYROLL SELF SERVICE	X
SUCCESSFACTORS API	GENERAL USER PERMISSIONS	SFAPI USER LOGIN	X
	EMPLOYEE CENTRAL API	EMPLOYEE CENTRAL HRIS SOAP API	X
	MANAGER USER	EMPLOYEE EXPORT	X

Table 9.6 Permissions (Cont.)

Let's switch gears altogether now and discuss configuration setup for the SAP ERP side.

9.1.4 Step 3: SAP ERP Configuration

We will now discuss the necessary SAP ERP configurations steps required for setting up the Employee Central integration with SAP ERP.

The two main tasks we will cover are refining the default logic of the work schedule and refining the key mapping. Let's begin.

Refine Default Logic of Work Schedule

As a note, this is an optional step. Only execute this step if you have decided to use Employee Central Time Off for work schedule determination instead of the default SAP ERP system setting in which the work schedule is determined through table T508A's match with the employee's Employee Group (Employee Subgroup Grouping) and the Personnel Area (Personnel Subarea Grouping).

To disable default logic for work schedule determination, go to Transaction SM30. Maintain the entries as shown in Figure 9.19 in table/view V_T77S0, and save the entry.

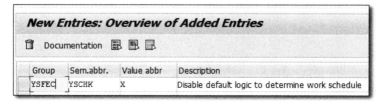

Figure 9.19 Disable Default Logic to Determine Work Schedule

Refine Mapping

In this configuration task, you will define the key mapping of the organization terms, mapping the code value list and wage type assignments to the infotype. These mappings are important for the integration to work, because they act as the functional translation key between Employee Central and SAP ERP.

Prior to maintaining the mappings, you must cross-check the picklist's external codes updated in the Employee Central configuration, as described in Section 9.1.3, because the Employee Central picklist external code will be replicated and mapped to the SAP ERP code within the same context.

To maintain the mapping, access the menu path SAP IMG • PERSONNEL MANAGEMENT • PERSONNEL ADMINISTRATION • INTERFACES AND INTEGRATION • INTEGRATION OF SAP ERP HR MASTER DATA AND SUCCESSFACTORS EMPLOYEE CENTRAL. From there, access the following areas:

▸ ASSIGNMENT OF CODE VALUES • DEFINE MAPPING CODE VALUE LISTS

▸ KEY MAPPING OF ORGANIZATIONAL TERMS • ASSIGN COMPANY CODE KEYS

▸ KEY MAPPING OF ORGANIZATIONAL TERMS • ASSIGN PLACE OF WORK KEYS

▸ INFOTYPE FILTERING • FILTER INFOTYPES

Let's take a closer look at each of the mapping activities and fill in the mapping according to your integration setup between Employee Central and SAP ERP. Let's begin by looking at the key mapping of organizational terms.

Key Mapping of Organizational Terms
The following list examines the key mapping of organizational terms between Employee Central and SAP ERP:

▸ **Company Code**
For the company code, maintain the mapping between the organization unit legal entity of Employee Central and the company code entity of SAP ERP. Click on ASSIGN COMPANY CODE KEYS from the INTEGRATION OF SAP ERP HR MASTER DATA AND SUCCESSFACTORS EMPLOYEE CENTRAL IMG menu path shown previously, and create a new entry, as indicated in Table 9.7. Then, save the entries that have been created.

Company ID	Company Code
<EC ID>—e.g., ECHCM01	<EC Payroll Code>—e.g., US01

Table 9.7 Company Code Mapping

► **Location**

The Employee Central location will be mapped to the SAP ERP Personnel Area and Personnel Subarea. Click on ASSIGN PLACE OF WORK KEYS from the IMG menu, and create a new entry as indicated in Table 9.8. Then, save the entries.

PermanentEstablishmentID	Personnel Area	Personnel Subarea
<EC ID>—e.g., US_NYC	<EC Payroll Code>—e.g., US01	<EC Payroll Code>—e.g., 0002

Table 9.8 Location Mapping

Mapping Code Value Lists

Under ASSIGNMENT CODE VALUE, click on the DEFINE MAPPING CODE VALUE LIST from the IMG menu, and create the following entries:

► **Salutation**

This is an optional step. Create a new mapping entry if you have a different salutation ID set up in Employee Central and SAP ERP. Then, create new entries as indicated in Table 9.9.

Field Name	Value
GDT NAME	FORM_OF_ADDRESS_CODE
CODE LIST ID	10120
LIST VERSION ID	<blank>
LIST AGENCY ID	310
GDT CODE VALUE	<EC ID>—e.g., MR
ERP KEY	<EC Payroll ID>—e.g., 1

Table 9.9 Salutation Mapping

► **Marital Status**

This is an optional step. Create a new mapping entry if you have a different marital status ID set up in Employee Central and SAP ERP. Create new entries as indicated in Table 9.10.

Field Name	Value
GDT Name	MARITAL_STATUS_CODE
Code List ID	10357
List Version ID	<blank>
List Agency ID	3055
GDT Code Value	<EC ID>—e.g., S
ERP Key	<EC Payroll ID>—e.g., 2

Table 9.10 Marital Status Mapping

▸ **Address Type**
Create a new mapping entry for address type set up in Employee Central and SAP ERP. Create new entries as indicated in Table 9.11.

Field Name	Value
GDT Name	ADDRESS_USAGE_CODE
Code List ID	10127
List Version ID	<blank>
List Agency ID	310
GDT Code Value	<EC ID>
ERP Key	<EC Payroll ID>

Table 9.11 Address Type mapping

In the system default settings, the mappings in Table 9.12 were set up.

GDT Code Value	ERP Kay
Business	5 (Mailing address)
Home	1 (Permanent residence)

Table 9.12 Address Type Mapping

▸ **Employee Class**
Create a new mapping entry for employee class set up in Employee Central and SAP ERP. Create new entries as indicated in Table 9.13.

Field Name	Value
GDT NAME	WORK_AGREEMENT_TYPE_CODE
CODE LIST ID	10091
LIST VERSION ID	<blank>
LIST AGENCY ID	310
GDT CODE VALUE	<EC ID>—e.g., A
ERP KEY	<EC Payroll ID>—e.g., 1

Table 9.13 Employee Class Mapping

▶ **Job Classification**
Create a new mapping entry for the job classification set up in Employee Central and SAP ERP. Create new entries as indicated in Table 9.14.

Field Name	Value
GDT NAME	JOB_ID
CODE LIST ID	91302 (for US)
LIST VERSION ID	<blank>
LIST AGENCY ID	310
GDT CODE VALUE	<EC ID>—e.g., *
ERP KEY	<EC Payroll ID>—e.g., 1

Table 9.14 Job Classification Mapping

▶ **Events**
Create a new mapping entry for event set up in Employee Central and SAP ERP. Create new entries as indicated in Table 9.15.

Field Name	Value
GDT NAME	PERSONNEL_EVENT_TYPE_CODE
CODE LIST ID	21201
LIST VERSION ID	<blank>
LIST AGENCY ID	310

Table 9.15 Event Type Code Mapping

Field Name	Value
GDT CODE VALUE	\<EC ID\>
ERP KEY	\<EC Payroll ID\>

Table 9.15 Event Type Code Mapping (Cont.)

The mappings in Table 9.16 are mapped by default.

GDT Code Value	SAP ERP Key
26	10
H	1
R	12
GA	1
EGA	10
5	2
SPP	1
1	1
2	2
3	10
16	2
15	2
4	10
9	12
Any other event code value defined in the event picklist	2

Table 9.16 Event Mapping

▶ **Event Reason**
Create a new mapping entry for event reason set up in Employee Central and SAP ERP. Create new entries as indicated in Table 9.17.

Field Name	Value
GDT NAME	PERSONNEL_EVENT_REASON_CODE
CODE LIST ID	10104

Table 9.17 Event Reason Mapping

Field Name	Value
LIST VERSION ID	<blank>
LIST AGENCY ID	310
GDT Code Value	<EC ID>
ERP Key	<EC Payroll ID>

Table 9.17 Event Reason Mapping (Cont.)

▶ **Work Schedule**

Create a new mapping entry for work schedule set up in Employee Central and SAP ERP. Create new entries as indicated in Table 9.18.

Field Name	Value
GDT NAME	WORK_SCHEDULE_RULE
CODE LIST ID	91810
LIST VERSION ID	<blank>
LIST AGENCY ID	310
GDT CODE VALUE	<EC ID>
ERP KEY	<EC Payroll ID>

Table 9.18 Work Schedule Rule Mapping

▶ **State**

Create a new mapping entry for state set up in Employee Central and SAP ERP. Create new entries as indicated in Table 9.19.

Field Name	Value
GDT NAME	REGION_CODE
CODE LIST ID	10660
LIST VERSION ID	<blank>
LIST AGENCY ID	310
GDT CODE VALUE	<EC ID>
ERP KEY	<EC Payroll ID>

Table 9.19 State Code Mapping

Key Mapping of Organization Structure Items

Here, you maintain the mappings between the department/division/business unit/job key setup in Employee Central and the organizational unit in SAP ERP. Go to Transaction SM30 to maintain the customizing table SFIOM_KMAP_OSI. Create new entries, as indicated in Table 9.20, and save the entries.

Type	Org. Structure Item ID	Org. unit
Department or Division or Business Unit or Job—e.g., DEPARTMENT	<EC Org Struc. ID>—e.g., FIN	<Org Unit Obj ID>—e.g., Finance

Table 9.20 Department Mapping

Infotype Mapping

Here, you will restrict the infotypes and subtypes being replicated in SAP ERP. If no entries are defined, then all infotypes will be replicated. If you define one country only, then that country will be replicated. All countries that require replication need to be specified.

Under INFOTYPE FILTERING, click on FILTER INFOTYPES from the IMG menu, and enter the fields as shown in Table 9.21.

Field Name	Value
COUNTRY GROUPING	<Country Code>
INFOTYPE	<Infotype>
SUBTYPE	<Subtype>

Table 9.21 Infotype Mapping

Suggested configuration values for replicating an employee mini master record into SAP ERP HCM are shown in Table 9.22.

Country Grouping	Infotype	Subtype
<Replicate for all relevant country groupings>	0000	
<Replicate for all relevant country groupings>	0001	

Table 9.22 Employee Mini Master Infotype Mapping

Country Grouping	Infotype	Subtype
<Replicate for all relevant country groupings>	0002	
<Replicate for all relevant country groupings>	0003	
<Replicate for all relevant country groupings>	0006	*
<Replicate for all relevant country groupings>	0007	
<Replicate for all relevant country groupings>	0041	
<Replicate for all relevant country groupings>	0105	*
<Replicate for all relevant country groupings>	0709	

Table 9.22 Employee Mini Master Infotype Mapping (Cont.)

Replication Employee Key Mapping Table

During the employee master data replication process, table PAOCFEC_EEKEY-MAP in SAP ERP is updated with the employee key mapping between Employee Central and SAP ERP for those employee master records that are successfully replicated. This employee key mapping table is updated to avoid any duplicate employee master record replication in SAP ERP.

To view table PAOCFEC_EEKEYMAP, use Transaction SE16.

You've now completed the Employee Central and SAP ERP configurations. Next, let's discuss the setup required for the middleware.

9.1.5   Step 4: Middleware Setup and Web Service Activation

This section describes the steps for configuring the Dell Boomi AtomSphere middleware. In addition, we will discuss the SAP ERP web service activation and ALE distribution model for integrating cost center replication, employee data replication, employee data replication confirmation, and organizational data replication scenarios between Employee Central and SAP ERP.

The basic setup steps are a prerequisite for configuring in this chapter. Therefore, make sure the basic setup is completed before you proceed (see Section 9.1.2).

The following activities are required to set up the middleware and web service activation:

▸ Cost center replication
▸ Employee data replication

- Employee data replication response

- Organization structure, organizational assignment, and job classification replication

Cost Center Replication

In this section, we will discuss the steps involved in setting up the cost center replication.

Perform the following steps:

1. Begin by defining the logical system. Go to interface IMG menu SALE • LOGICAL SYSTEMS • DEFINE LOGICAL SYSTEM. Create a new logical system that represents partner system Employee Central, as shown in Figure 9.20. Save the entry.

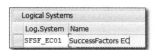

Figure 9.20 Logical System

2. Next, we'll create a distribution model. Go to Transaction BD64 to create the cost center distribution model view (see Figure 9.21).

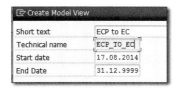

Figure 9.21 Distribution Model

3. Once the distribution model view is created, click on ADD MESSAGE TYPE, and enter the parameters shown in Table 9.23. Once the parameters have been entered, save the entries.

Field	Parameter
SENDER	<Logical System Name of SAP ERP>—e.g., RT7CLNT120

Table 9.23 Distribution Model Parameters

Field	Parameter
RECEIVER	\<Logical System Name of Employee Central\>—e.g., SFSF_EC01
MESSAGE TYPE	COST CENTER MESSAGE TYPE, ODTF_CCTR

Table 9.23 Distribution Model Parameters (Cont.)

4. The next task involves creating a port. Go to Transaction WE21 to create an XML HTTP port for connecting the Dell Boomi AtomSphere middleware. Enter the parameters shown in Table 9.24, and save the setting.

Field	Parameter
PORT	\< Port Name\>—e.g., BOOMI_HTTP
RFC DESTINATION	\<RFC destination created in basic setup\>
APPLICATION/X-SAP.IDOC	X
SOAP PROTOCOL	X

Table 9.24 Port Parameters

5. Now, create the partner profile. Go to Transaction WE20, and create a new partner type logical system. Enter the parameters provided in Table 9.25, and save.

Field	Parameter
PARTNER NO.	\<Logical System of Employee Central\>—e.g., SFSF_EC01
PARTNER TYPE	LS
TY (POSTPROCESSING: PERMITTED AGENT)	US
AGENT (POSTPROCESSING: PERMITTED AGENT)	\<userid\>

Table 9.25 Partner Profile Parameters

6. Once the new partner profile is saved, click on CREATE NEW OUTBOUND PARAMETER, and enter the parameters shown in Table 9.26. Once completed, save the entries.

Field	Parameter
MESSAGE TYPE	ODTF_CCTR
RECEIVER PORT	<Port created in previous steps>—e.g., BOOMI_HTTP
TRANSFER IDOC IMMED	X
BASIC TYPE	ODTF_CCTR01

Table 9.26 Outbound Parameter

7. Next, activate the change pointer for delta distribution. Go to Transaction BD61 and select the CHANGE POINTER ACTIVATED—GENERALLY checkbox. Go to Transaction BD50 and mark the checkbox as ACTIVE for message type ODTF_CCTR.

8. Once the change pointer has been activated for message type ODTF_CCTR, the cost center delta replication will be ready to handle program RBDMIDOC. In production system environment, it is advisable to schedule program RBDMIDOC to run in the background periodically according to your requirement.

9. Next, configure connection settings and process properties of iFLOW: ERP TO EC—COST CENTER 1308 in the Dell Boomi AtomSphere atom environment. Log on to Dell Boomi AtomSphere. Go to MANAGE, and select your environment that was created in the basic setup in Section 9.1.2. Under ENVIRONMENT PROPERTIES, click on ENVIRONMENT EXTENSIONS.

10. You will be prompted with the EXTENSIONS screen. Select iFLOW: ERP TO EC— COST CENTER 1308 from PROCESS FILTER. Under the CONNECTION settings, choose EC SFAPI CONNECTION and fill in the connection parameters as shown in Table 9.27.

Field	Parameter	Use Default
ENDPOINT	Other	Unchecked
OTHER ENDPOINT	<SFAPI URL>—e.g., https://api4.successfactors.com/sfapi/v1/soap	Unchecked
COMPANY ID	<SFSF EC Company ID>—e.g., ECHCM01	Unchecked
USERNAME	<SFAPI User>—e.g., SAP_API_USER	Unchecked
PASSWORD	<SFAPI Password>	Unchecked

Table 9.27 Employee Central and SFAPI Connection Parameters

11. Under PROCESS PROPERTIES, fill in USE_EXTERNAL_COST_CENTER with an X parameter, and have USE DEFAULT unchecked. The USE EXTERNAL COST CENTER flag is activated to replicate the external cost center code to Employee Central. This is useful if you do not want to maintain cost center mapping in SAP ERP, because the same cost center external code that is assigned to employee job information will be replicated from Employee Central to SAP ERP during the employee data replication process.

Now, let's discuss how to configure the web service for the employee data replication process in the SAP ERP system.

Employee Data Replication

This section will discuss the necessary steps for completing the employee data replication process.

First, configure the web service for the employee data replication process in SAP ERP. Proceed with the following steps:

1. Go to Transaction SOAMANAGER in SAP ERP. Choose SIMPLIFIED WEB SERVICE CONFIGURATION.

2. Under SEARCH SERVICE DEFINITION, enter search string "*employee*master*", and click on GO. Select EMPLOYEEMASTERDATAREPLICATIONR from the search result. Then, enter the parameters as shown in Table 9.28.

Field	Parameter
USERNAME/PASSWORD (BASIC)	X
X.509 CLIENT CERTIFICATE	Unchecked
SAP LOGON TICKET	Unchecked

Table 9.28 Simplified Web Service Configuration Parameters

3. From here, click on the SHOW DETAILS button. Copy the WSDL URL with WS policy into your local file. (This URL will be entered into the Dell Boomi AtomSphere atom environment connection setting later.) Next, copy the access URL into your local file.

Host Name
You might need to replace the actual host name with your SAP Web Dispatcher public host.

4. Next, configure connection settings and process properties of iFLOW: EC TO EC PAYROLL—EMPLOYEE REPLICATION v2.0 in the Dell Boomi AtomSphere atom environment. Go to MANAGE, and select the environment that was created in the basic setup (see Section 9.1.2). Under ENVIRONMENT PROPERTIES, click on ENVIRONMENT EXTENSIONS. You will then be prompted with the EXTENSIONS screen. From this screen, select iFLOW: EC TO EC PAYROLL—EMPLOYEE REPLICA-TION v2.0 from the PROCESS FILTER.

5. Under the CONNECTION settings, choose CONNECTION CON EC EMPLOYEE DATA v1.0, and enter the connection parameters shown in Table 9.29.

Field	Parameter	Use Default
ENDPOINT	Other	Unchecked
OTHER ENDPOINT	<SFAPI URL>—e.g., HTTPS://API4. SUCCESSFACTORS.COM/SFAPI/V1/SOAP	Unchecked
SFAPI ENDPOINT SUFFIX	/SFAPI/V1/SOAP	Unchecked
ENABLE SF ODATA ENTITY IMPORT	X	Unchecked
SF ODATA ENDPOINT SUFFIX	/ODATA/V2/	Unchecked
COMPANY ID	<SFSF EC Company ID>—e.g., ECHCM01	Unchecked
USERNAME	<SFAPI User>—e.g., SAP_API_USER	Unchecked
PASSWORD	<SFAPI Password>	Unchecked
DEFAULT BATCH SIZE	200	Unchecked
DEFAULT QUERY PAGE SIZE	200	Unchecked

Table 9.29 Employee Data Connection Parameters—Part 1

6. Once this is done, switch to CONNECTION CON EC PAYROLL EMPLOYEE DATA v1.0, and fill in the connection parameters shown in Table 9.30 (see also Figure 9.22).

Filling the WSDL and SOAP Endpoint URLs

For filling the WSDL URL and SOAP Endpoint URL, you might need to replace the actual host name copied from SAP ERP to your SAP Web Dispatcher public host if SAP Web Dispatcher is set up as the Internet gateway in your system landscape architecture.

Field	Parameter	Use Default
WSDL URL	WSDL URL with WS Policy copied from SOAMANAGER of EC Payroll	Unchecked
SOAP ENDPOINT URL	Access URL copied from SOAMANAGER of Employee Central Payroll	Unchecked
SECURITY TYPE	Basic	Unchecked
USER	System technical user of Employee Central Payroll created in basic setup step	Unchecked
PASSWORD	<System technical user password>	Unchecked
CLIENT SSL CERTIFICATE	<Empty>	Checked
TRUST SSL SERVER CERTIFICATE	<Empty>	Checked

Table 9.30 Employee Data Connection Parameters—Part 2

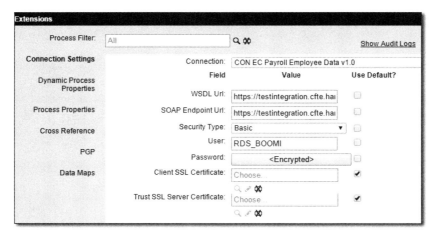

Figure 9.22 Connection Settings

7. Under PROCESS PROPERTIES, fill in the details shown in Table 9.31, and save the settings.

Field	Parameter	Use Default
ECERP_COMPANY	<Blank>	Checked
ECERP_COMPANY_TERRITORY_C	<Blank>	Checked
ECERP_EMPLOYEE_CLASS	<Blank>	Checked
ECERP_FULL_TRANSMISSION_ST	<Cutoff date>	Unchecked
ECERP_REPLICATION_TARGET_S	<Blank>	Checked
ECERP_EXTERNAL_COST_CENTER_ID_USAGE	X	Unchecked

Table 9.31 Employee Data Process Properties

8. The `ECERP_EXTERNAL_COST_CENTER_ID_USAGE` flag is activated to replicate the external cost center code in Employee Central. This is useful if you do not want to maintain cost center mapping in SAP ERP, because the same cost center external code that is assigned to EMPLOYEE JOB INFORMATION will be replicated from Employee Central to SAP ERP during the employee data replication process.

9. Use the `ECERP_FULL_TRANSMISSION_ST` flag to set a cutoff date for employee data transfer to SAP ERP.

Now, let's discuss how to configure the web service for employee data replication response process in the SAP ERP system.

Employee Data Replication Response

This section discusses the steps that must be undertaken to create an employee data replication response.

Perform the following steps:

1. First, configure the web service for the employee data replication response process in SAP ERP. Go to Transaction SOAMANAGER in SAP ERP. Click on WEB SERVICE CONFIGURATION. Under the SEARCH criteria, enter search string "*CO_PAOCF*" for OBJECT NAME, and click on GO. Select the consumer proxy CO_PAOCF_EC_EMPLOYEE_MASTER_DA from the search result (see Figure 9.23).

Figure 9.23 Web Service Configuration

2. Choose CREATE • MANUAL CONFIGURATION. Under LOGICAL PORT NAME, enter the logical port name and select the LOGICAL PORT IS DEFAULT checkbox.

3. Under CONSUMER SECURITY, select USER ID/PASSWORD from AUTHENTICATION settings. Enter the Dell Boomi AtomSphere username and password (see Figure 9.24). The Dell Boomi AtomSphere username and password were generated during the basic setup step (see Section 9.1.2).

Figure 9.24 Authentication Settings

4. Under HTTPS SETTINGS, enter the parameters shown in Table 9.32.

Field	Parameter
URL ACCESS PATH	*/ws/simple/getEmployeeMasterDataReplicationConfirmation_Out*
COMPUTER NAME OF ACCESS URL	Base URL of your Dell Boomi AtomSphere atom environment copied during basic setup
PORT NUMBER OF ACCESS URL	443
URL PROTOCOL INFORMATION	HTTPS

Table 9.32 Authentication Parameters—HTTPS Settings

Field	Parameter
NAME OF PROXY HOST	\<Enter proxy host if there is a proxy set up in your network infrastructure\>
PORT NUMBER OF PROXY HOST	\<Enter proxy port if there is a proxy set up in your network infrastructure\>

Table 9.32 Authentication Parameters—HTTPS Settings (Cont.)

5. Under SOAP PROTOCOL, enter the parameters from Table 9.33. Choose FINISH to save the settings.

Field	Parameter
RM PROTOCOL	WS-RM 2005/02
MESSAGE ID PROTOCOL	WS-A Message ID
DATA TRANSFER SCOPE	Enhanced Data Transfer
TRANSFER PROTOCOL	Transfer via SOAP Header

Table 9.33 SOAP Protocol Parameters

6. Once you have finished configuring web service settings in Transaction SOAManager, the next step is to enable the master data replication response in table/view V_T77S0. Go to Transaction SM30 to maintain table/view V_T77S0. Create a new entry, and enter the parameters shown in Table 9.34. Save the entry.

Field	Parameter
GROUP	YSFEC
SEM. ABBR	YRESP
VALUE ABBR.	X
DESCRIPTION	Trigger master data replication response message

Table 9.34 Authentication Parameters—Master Data Replication Response

7. Now, you'll move to Dell Boomi AtomSphere to configure connection settings and process properties of iFLOW: EC TO EC PAYROLL—EMPLOYEE CONFIRMATION v2.0. Select MANAGE, and select the environment you created in the basic setup (see Section 9.1.2). Under ENVIRONMENT PROPERTIES, click on ENVIRONMENT EXTENSIONS.

8. You will be prompted with the EXTENSIONS screen. Select IFLOW: EC TO EC PAY-ROLL—EMPLOYEE CONFIRMATION v2.0 from the PROCESS FILTER. Under the CONNECTION settings, choose CONNECTION EC EMPLOYEE DATA v1.0.2, and enter the connection parameters shown in Table 9.35.

Field	Parameter	Use Default
ENDPOINT	Other	Unchecked
OTHER ENDPOINT	<SFAPI URL>—e.g., *https://api4.* *successfactors.com/sfapi/v1/soap*	Unchecked
SFAPI ENDPOINT SUFFIX	/SFAPI/V1/SOAP	Unchecked
ENABLE SF ODATA ENTITY IMPORT	X	Unchecked
SF ODATA ENDPOINT SUFFIX	/ODATA/V2/	Unchecked
COMPANY ID	<SFSF EC Company ID>—e.g., ECHCM01	Unchecked
USERNAME	<SFAPI User>—e.g., SAP_API_USER	Unchecked
PASSWORD	<SFAPI Password>	Unchecked
DEFAULT BATCH SIZE	200	Unchecked
DEFAULT QUERY PAGE SIZE	200	Unchecked

Table 9.35 Connection Parameters of iFlow: EC to EC Payroll—Employee Confirmation v2.0

9. Under PROCESS PROPERTIES, from ECERP_LOG_CURRENT_DATA, check the USE DEFAULT field, and leave the PARAMETER field blank. Save your settings.

Now, let's discuss how to configure the web service for the organizational structure, organizational assignment, and job classification replication process, which is only applicable for the Employee Central integration with SAP ERP.

Organizational Structure, Organizational Assignment, and Job Classification Replications

This section will discuss the steps involved in completing the organizational structure, organizational assignment, and job classification replications.

Perform the following steps:

1. First, configure the web service for organizational structure, organizational assignment, and job classification replication in SAP ERP. Go to Transaction SOAMANAGER in SAP ERP. Click on SIMPLIFIED WEB SERVICE CONFIGURATION.

2. Under Search Service Definition, enter search string "*ORGSTRUCTURE-REPLREQUEST*", and click on Go. Select ORGSTRUCTUREREPLREQUEST from the search results. Then, enter the parameters shown in Table 9.36.

Field	Parameter	
Username/Password (Basic)	X	
X.509 Client Certificate	Unchecked	
SAP Logon Ticket	Unchecked	

Table 9.36 Web Service Configuration Parameters

3. Click on the Show Details button. Copy the WSDL URL with WS policy into your local file. (This URL will be entered into the Dell Boomi AtomSphere atom environment connection settings later.) Copy the access URL into your local file.

4. Repeat the web service steps for the following web service definitions:
   - JOBREPLICATIONREQUEST
   - EMPLOYEEORGASSIGNMREPLREQUEST

5. Next, configure connection settings and process properties of iFlow Solution: EC—ERP Organizational Management v1.0 in the Dell Boomi AtomSphere atom environment. Go to Manage, and select the environment that you created in the basic setup (see Section 9.1.2). Under Environment Properties, click on Environment Extensions.

6. You will be prompted with the Extensions screen. From this screen, select iFlow: EC to EC Payroll—Employee Replication v2.0 from Process Filter.

7. Under the Connection settings, for the connections CON EC OrgStructure-Item Replication and CON EC to ERP Job Code, enter the connection parameters shown in Table 9.37.

Field	Parameter	Use Default
Endpoint	Other	Unchecked
Other Endpoint	<SFAPI URL>—e.g., *https://api4.successfactors.com/sfapi/v1/soap*	Unchecked
SFAPI Endpoint Suffix	*/sfapi/v1/soap*	Unchecked

Table 9.37 Connection Parameters for the Organizational Management iFlow—Part 1

Field	Parameter	Use Default
ENABLE SF ODATA ENTITY IMPORT	X	Unchecked
SF ODATA ENDPOINT SUFFIX	/odata/v2/	Unchecked
COMPANY ID	<SFSF EC Company ID>—e.g., ECHCM01	Unchecked
USERNAME	<SFAPI User>— e.g., SAP_API_USER	Unchecked
PASSWORD	<SFAPI Password>	Unchecked
DEFAULT BATCH SIZE	200	Unchecked
DEFAULT QUERY PAGE SIZE	200	Unchecked
DEFAULT ASYNC QUERY TIMEOUT TIME		Checked
DEFAULT SLEEP/WAIT TIME		Checked
DEFAULT SLEEP/WAIT TIME		Checked
HTTP/WEB SERVICE TIMEOUT		Checked

Table 9.37 Connection Parameters for the Organizational Management iFlow—Part 1 (Cont.)

8. Once this is done for the connections CON ERP JOB REPLICATION REQUEST IN, CON ORGANIZATIONAL STRUCTURE REPLICATION REQUEST_IN, and CON_EC TO ERP REPLICATION OF EMPLOYEE ORGANIZATIONAL ASSIGNMENT DATA, enter the connection parameters shown in Table 9.38.

WSDL and SOAP Endpoint URL

For filling the WSDL URL and SOAP Endpoint URL, you might need to replace the actual host name copied from SAP ERP with your SAP Web Dispatcher public host if SAP Web Dispatcher is set up as the Internet gateway in your system landscape architecture.

Field	Parameter	Use Default
WSDL URL	WSDL URL with WS Policy copied from SOAMANAGER of Employee Central Payroll	Unchecked
SOAP ENDPOINT URL	Access URL copied from SOAMANAGER of Employee Central Payroll	Unchecked
SECURITY TYPE	Basic	Unchecked

Table 9.38 Connection Parameters for the Organizational Management iFlow—Part 2

Field	Parameter	Use Default
USER	System technical user of EC Payroll that created in the basic setup step	Unchecked
PASSWORD	<System Technical User Password>	Unchecked
CLIENT SSL CERTIFICATE	<empty>	Checked
TRUST SSL SERVER CERTIFICATE	<empty>	Checked

Table 9.38 Connection Parameters for the Organizational Management iFlow—Part 2 (Cont.)

9. Under PROCESS PROPERTIES, select EC EMPL ORG ASSIGN PROCESS PROPERTIES, and enter the parameters shown in Table 9.39.

Field	Parameter	Use Default
ECERPORG_COMPANY	<blank>	Checked
ECERP_FULL_TRANSMISSION	<cutoff date>	Unchecked
ECERPORG_TRANSFER_DEPARTMENT_ASSIGNMENT	<blank>	Checked
ECERPORG_USE_EXTERNAL_COST_CENTER_ID	X	Unchecked
ECERPORG_INITIAL_LOAD	<blank>	Checked
ECERPORG_READ_MANAGER_COMPANY	<blank>	Checked
ECERPORG_REPLICATE_JOB_ASS	X	Unchecked
ECERPORG_REPLICATE_INACTIVE_JOB_INFO	<blank>	Checked

Table 9.39 Process Properties Parameters

10. Use the `ECERP_FULL_TRANSMISSION` flag to set a cutoff date for organizational assignment replication process. The `ECERPORG_USE_EXTERNAL_COST_CENTER_ID` flag is activated to replicate the external cost center code to Employee Central. This is useful if you do not want to maintain cost center mapping in SAP ERP, because the same cost center external code that is assigned to employee job information will be replicated from Employee Central to SAP ERP during the organizational assignment replication process.

11. Use the `ECERPORG_REPLICATE_JOB_ASS` flag to replicate job assignment during the organizational assignment replication process.

12. Under PROCESS PROPERTIES, select EC ORGSTRUCTUREITEM REPLICATION PROCESS PROPERTIES and enter the parameters shown in Table 9.40.

Field	Parameter	Use Default
ECERPOS_FULL_TRANSMISSION_START_DATE	<cutoff date>	Unchecked
ECERPOS_REPLICATE_BU	<blank>	Checked
ECERPOS_INITIAL_LOAD	<blank>	Checked
ECERPOS_REPLICATE_DIV	<blank>	Checked
ECERPOS_REPLICATE_DEP	<blank>	Checked

Table 9.40 OrgStructureItem Process Properties Parameters

13. Use the ECERPOS_FULL_TRANSMISSION_START_DATE flag to set a cutoff date for the organizational structure replication process. Under PROCESS PROPERTIES, select EC TO ERP JOB REPLICATION PROCESS PROPERTIES, and fill in the parameters shown in Table 9.41.

Field	Parameter	Use Default
ECERPJOB_FULL_TRANSMISSION_START_DATE	<cutoff date>	Unchecked
ECERPJOB_INITIAL_LOAD	<blank>	Checked

Table 9.41 Job Replication Process Properties Parameters

14. Use the ECERPJOB_FULL_TRANSMISSION_START_DATE flag to set a cutoff date for the job replication process. Save the settings.

This completes the Dell Boomi AtomSphere integration middleware configuration setup. You can now execute the cost center data, employee data, and organizational data replication integration scenarios. This case study detailed the necessary configuration and technical steps required to implement the Employee Central integration with SAP ERP using the Full Cloud HCM deployment model.

9.2   Employee Central to Payroll Integration

The Employee Central to SAP Payroll on-premise or Employee Central Payroll integration allows customers to manage their employee master data in the cloud or have the payroll run in-house. Because the data is maintained in two different systems (Employee Central and either SAP Payroll or Employee Central Payroll), the integration brings the two systems in sync by integrating cost center replication and employee master data replication processes.

Prerequisites

Prior to implementing Employee Central integration with SAP Payroll on-premise or Employee Central Payroll, you will need to complete the following relevant configurations:

- ▶ Employee Central has been set up in the latest version of SuccessFactors
- ▶ Dell Boomi AtomSphere has been set up
- ▶ Have SFSF Employee Central Integration Add-On (PA_SE_IN 100 SP1 and ODTFINCC 600) deployed and configured in SAP
- ▶ The following system minimum requirements:
  - ▶ SAP ERP 6.0 SPS 15 or higher
  - ▶ SAP ERP 6.0 SPS 08 EHP 2 or higher
  - ▶ SAP ERP 6.0 SPS 05 EHP 3 or higher
  - ▶ SAP ERP 6.0 SPS 05 EHP 4 or higher
  - ▶ SAP ERP 6.0/SAP NetWeaver 7.01 SPS 05 EHP 4 or higher
  - ▶ SAP ERP 6.0 SPS 06 EHP 5 or higher
  - ▶ SAP ERP 6.0 SPS 03 EHP 6 or higher
  - ▶ SAP ERP 6.0 on SAP HANA SPS 01 EHP 6 or higher
  - ▶ SAP ERP 6.0 ISS EHP 7 or higher
  - ▶ HR Renewal 1.0 SPS 03 or higher
- ▶ Have relevant access to SAP Payroll/Employee Central Payroll with a sufficient authorization role for the configuration activities in SAP IMG, SALE, web service configuration, and background job scheduler, as well as access to SuccessFactors Provisioning and Administration pages
- ▶ IT network configuration is required to enable communication through firewalls between Dell Boomi AtomSphere and SAP Payroll/Employee Central Payroll

In a typical integration scenario, the cost center replication process is set to run first to replicate the cost center from Employee Central Payroll to Employee Central for employee cost assignment purposes. The employee master data, together with the cost center assignment, is then replicated from Employee Central to Employee Central Payroll for payroll processing purposes. The Employee Central Payroll system is not the truth source of the cost center. The cost center is always distributed from the finance source system; it's transferred from the finance system to Employee Central Payroll prior to any replication process run.

We will use a case study example to demonstrate this process; a description of the parameters that this integration will entail is presented next, including the client scenario and an overview of the process steps.

9.2.1 Case Study Parameters

This case study focuses on how a customer who desires to implement Employee Central will integrate and transfer employee data from Employee Central to on-premise SAP Payroll or cloud-based Employee Central Payroll, using Dell Boomi AtomSphere as the integration middleware. Also, the case study covers the cost center integration between SAP Payroll on-premise or Employee Central Payroll with Employee Central.

Specifically, we'll discuss the implementation steps necessary for both Success-Factors and SAP Payroll or Employee Central Payroll to implement the employee data integration. We'll use a client scenario to demonstrate our case. A snapshot of our client is presented next.

Client Scenario

ABC Global Services has just implemented Employee Central and has selected Employee Central Payroll to run its payroll operations.

Important Integration Notice

Please note that for this client scenario, ABC Global Services is implementing the Employee Central integration with Employee Central Payroll. However, the technical activities to set up the integration with SAP Payroll and Employee Central Payroll are the same, so throughout this case study both on-premise SAP Payroll and cloud payroll in Employee Central Payroll are being referred to.

At this point, ABC Global Services would like to implement the SuccessFactors Employee Central integrations with Employee Central Payroll to ensure data consistency between the two systems. To effectively integrate and transfer the cost center, organizational, and employee data, the team recognizes that the technical consultant will need to have a solid understanding of the basic settings of the Employee Central integration with Employee Central Payroll, as well as the necessary Integration Add-ons and system requirements to make the integration successful. The biggest challenge will be to keep the systems and HR data in sync between SuccessFactors and Employee Central Payroll.

To ensure that the integration is successful, there are certain business requirements that will guarantee a smooth transfer of data. For example, there needs to be a single source of employee data from Employee Central and a single source of cost center data.

To integrate and transfer data from Employee Central using Dell Boomi Atom-Sphere middleware, the following steps must be executed:

1. Prior to implementing Employee Central integration with SAP Payroll/Employee Central Payroll using Dell Boomi AtomSphere as the integration middleware, ensure that SAP Payroll/Employee Central Payroll has the latest Integration Add-on deployed and configured. Also ensure that you have relevant access to SAP Payroll/Employee Central Payroll with a sufficient authorization role for all configuration activities.

2. Ensure that baseline integration configuration settings were made for SAP Payroll/Employee Central Payroll as well as for Employee Central integration by defining authorizations in SAP Payroll/Employee Central Payroll to access the new integration transactions.

3. For setting the middleware, ensure that the installation and configuration of Dell Boomi AtomSphere was set as an integration point between SuccessFactors and SAP Payroll/Employee Central Payroll.

Process Overview

There are four main steps required to implement the SuccessFactors Employee Central integration with SAP Payroll/Employee Central Payroll:

▶ **Step 1: Basic setup**
In this step, we'll look at the basic system configuration necessary for integration with Employee Central to SAP Payroll and Employee Central Payroll. This includes everything from creating a technical system user in SAP ERP to creating an RFC destination in SAP ERP (see Section 9.2.2).

▶ **Step 2: SuccessFactors configuration**
This section discuss the SuccessFactors configuration setup necessary for the integration with Employee Central Payroll and SAP Payroll on-premise. This step also includes an EMPLOYEE FILES tab configuration specific to the integration of Employee Central Payroll and SAP Payroll (see Section 9.2.3).

▶ **Step 3: SAP Payroll and Employee Central Payroll configuration**
This step revolves around the specific configuration tasks that must be completed within SAP Payroll and Employee Central Payroll. Remember, these steps are the same whether integrating SAP Payroll or Employee Central Payroll, unless specified otherwise (see Section 9.2.4).

▶ **Step 4: Middleware setup and web service activation**
This step involves setting up the Dell Boomi AtomSphere middleware and activating the web service for Employee Central Payroll and SAP Payroll. Similar to the integration of Employee Central with SAP ERP, this step also involves cost center replication, employee data replication, and employee data replication response (see Section 9.2.5).

Let's begin by looking at the basic setup involved with this integration.

9.2.2 Step 1: Basic Setup

There is a baseline integration configuration that is required for integrating Employee Central and SAP Payroll/Employee Central Payroll. This baseline system configuration covers settings in Employee Central, SAP Payroll/Employee Central Payroll, and Dell Boomi AtomSphere middleware.

The basic setup for this integration is comprised of the following tasks:

▶ Creating a technical system user in SAP ERP

▶ Enabling the web services SuccessFactors API

▶ Creating a SuccessFactors API user

▶ Configuring the SuccessFactors API user security

▶ Configuring the SuccessFactors API login exception

▶ Installing the integration pack in Dell Boomi AtomSphere

▶ Importing the SSL trusted CA certificate in SAP ERP

▶ Creating an RFC destination in SAP ERP

We'll begin by creating an SAP Payroll/Employee Central Payroll technical user as our first task.

Create a Technical System User in SAP Payroll/Employee Central Payroll

First, define the authorization for the communication of the Dell Boomi AtomSphere middleware with SAP Payroll/Employee Central Payroll. To do this, you'll define the role by referring to standard role SAP_HR_PA_EC_EE_REPL, which comprises the authorizations that a user needs to run the employee data replication process in SAP Payroll/Employee Central Payroll system. You may use it as a template to define an authorization that suits your requirements. Access Transaction PFCG to begin defining a role.

Once you have defined the authorization, you can create a technical user by assigning the role defined previously. Then, access Transaction SU01 to begin creating a technical user, with SYSTEM as the USER TYPE.

Enable Web Services SuccessFactors API

In this step, you will activate SuccessFactors Talent Solutions web services API features.

For the detailed steps, refer to Section 9.1.2, Enable Web Services SuccessFactors API.

Create a SuccessFactors API User

A SuccessFactors API user is required for Dell Boomi AtomSphere middleware to integrate with Employee Central. An API user must first be created in the SuccessFactors provisioning tool. The same API user logon credential is then stored in the middleware credentials setting of the Dell Boomi AtomSphere environment setup.

For the detailed steps, refer to Section 9.1.2, Create a SuccessFactors API User.

Configure the SuccessFactors API User Security

In this step, you will configure the security RBP and group for the API user created in the previous step. For detailed steps, refer to Section 9.1.2, Configure the SuccessFactors API User Security.

SuccessFactors API Login Exception

In this step, you will configure the API login exception for the API user that was just created. The purpose is to ensure that the password for the API user does not expire.

For the detailed steps, refer to Section 9.1.2, SuccessFactors API Login Exception.

Install the Integration Pack in Dell Boomi AtomSphere

Next, you will setup the preconfigured integration pack in Dell Boomi AtomSphere. This integration pack contains the required integration mapping between the Employee Central data fields and the corresponding fields of SAP Payroll/Employee Central Payroll. Prior to the installation, you will have to create a separate Dell Boomi AtomSphere atom and environment for the integration pack to be able to deploy. For the detailed steps, refer to Section 9.1.2, Install the Integration Pack in Dell Boomi AtomSphere.

Two integration packs are part of the Employee Central to SAP Payroll/Employee Central Payroll integration installation. The first installation is for the employee master data replication scenario and the second installation is for the cost center replication scenario.

The integration packs that should be downloaded for the Employee Central to Employee Central Payroll integrations are as follows:

▶ iFlow EC to EC Payroll Employee Replication v2

▶ iFlow Solution: SAP ERP to EC Cost Center Replication 1308

SSL Trusted CA Certificate Import in SAP Payroll/Employee Central Payroll

In this section you will enable the SSL connection between SAP Payroll/Employee Central Payroll to Dell Boomi AtomSphere middleware. Dell Boomi AtomSphere SSL trusted CA certificates must be imported into SAP Payroll/Employee Central Payroll via Transaction STRUST.

For the detailed steps, refer to Section 9.1.2, SSL Trusted CA Certificate Import in SAP ERP.

Create RFC Destination in SAP Payroll/Employee Central Payroll

One last basic setting that must be completed is to create an RFC destination in SAP Payroll/Employee Central Payroll for connecting Dell Boomi AtomSphere middleware. This connection will be used by the cost center replication scenario. For detailed steps, refer to Section 9.1.2, Create an RFC Destination in SAP ERP.

Now that the basic setup has been completed, let's turn our attention to the Employee Central configuration.

9.2.3 Step 2: Employee Central Configuration

Now, let's discuss the necessary Employee Central configuration steps required for setting up the Employee Central integration with SAP Payroll/Employee Central Payroll.

This section covers the following tasks:

- Data model configuration
- Picklist configuration
- Employee Central Payroll-related configuration:
  - EMPLOYEE FILES tab configuration
  - Payroll configuration
  - Creating payment methods
- RBP enhancement configuration

Let's begin our discussion by defining the succession data model and corporate data model.

Data Model Configurations

There are two data models to be updated: the succession data model and the corporate data model.

For the detailed steps, refer to Section 9.1.3, Data Model Configurations.

Picklist Configuration

In this step, you will define additional picklist information on the existing picklist template. You will have to add external codes for all picklists that are used for the employee master data replication scenario.

For the detailed steps, refer to Section 9.1.3, Picklist Configuration. Prior to updating the picklist, there are some important notes to consider:

- Make sure all codes are unique for their contexts; the external codes will be replicated and mapped to SAP Payroll/Employee Central Payroll.
- External codes need to be in CAPITAL LETTERS and/or numbers.
- External codes that are longer than 10 characters are cut off during replication, and only first 10 characters are available for mapping in the SAP Payroll/ Employee Central Payroll.

To begin the picklist update, log on to Employee Central. Then, perform the following steps:

1. Go to Admin Tools • Company Setting • Picklist Management. Select Export All Picklists and Submit to save them to your local machine. Open the *picklist.csv* file and update the external code for the relevant picklist, as listed in Table 9.42.

Picklist	Remark
PayScaleType	N/A
PayScaleArea	N/A
Employment-Type	N/A
Employee-Class	N/A
ProcessType	Direct Deposit, using values B = bonus, E = expenses, P = payroll
State_XXX	XXX represents the relevant ISO country code in the employee address—e.g., STATE_USA
AccountType	SG = Savings, 03 = Checking
Salutation	Optional
ecMaritalStatus	Optional

Table 9.42 Picklist—External Code

For example, you can update the external code for a picklist pay scale type, as shown in Figure 9.25.

^picklistId	Option	minVal	maxVal	value	status	external_cod	parent(	en_US
1 pay-scale-area	1041	-1	-1	-1	ACTIVE	Z1		572 East Region
2 pay-scale-area	1042	-1	-1	-1	ACTIVE	Z2		572 West Region
3 pay-scale-type	1043	-1	-1	-1	ACTIVE	Z3		572 Salaried Exempt
4 pay-scale-type	1044	-1	-1	-1	ACTIVE	Z4		572 Salaried Non-Exempt
5 pay-scale-type	1045	-1	-1	-1	ACTIVE	Z5		572 Hourly

Figure 9.25 Picklist—External Code

2. Once the picklist is updated, go back to Picklist Management. Select Import Picklist, and browse for the *picklist.csv* file. Click on Submit to complete the upload.

Let's move on to the next step, which will focus specifically on the Employee Central Payroll-related configuration that must happen if you choose this payroll method over the on-premise SAP Payroll option.

Employee Central Payroll-Related Configuration

Next, we will concentrate on the Employee Central Payroll-related configuration. This is separate from the configuration and setup of SAP Payroll and should only be employed if you plan on implementing Employee Central Payroll. We will enable payroll information in the EMPLOYEE FILE tab and set up the Employee Central Payroll system-related information in the Employee Central and Employee Central Payroll payment method setup.

Employee Files Tab Configuration

In this step, you enable the payroll information to appear in the EMPLOYEE FILE tab. Go to ADMIN TOOL • EMPLOYEE FILE • CONFIGURE EMPLOYEE FILES. Select the PAYROLL checkbox, and save.

Set Up Payroll Configuration

To set up the payroll configuration for Employee Central Payroll, go to ADMIN TOOLS • PAYROLL • PAYROLL CONFIGURATION. Under CREATE NEW, select DEFAULT PORTLETS (see Figure 9.26), then select the countries that are in scope for payroll, and save. In this case, set up the payroll configuration for the United States.

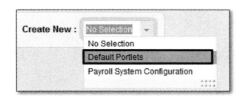

Figure 9.26 Default Portlets

Once the configuration is created, you'll need to further configure the payroll settings. From the same page, choose SEARCH, and search for "payroll system configuration". Choose the corresponding countries that are in scope for payroll, then select TAKE ACTION • MAKE CORRECTION. Finally, enter the details shown in Table 9.43, and save the changes (see also Figure 9.27).

Field	Parameter
PAYROLL SYSTEM URL	ECP SYSTEM URL
PAYROLL SYSTEM URL	ECP SYSTEM CLIENT ID
ENABLE ACCESS TO BSI eFORMSFACTORY (United States only)	YES

Table 9.43 Payroll System Parameters

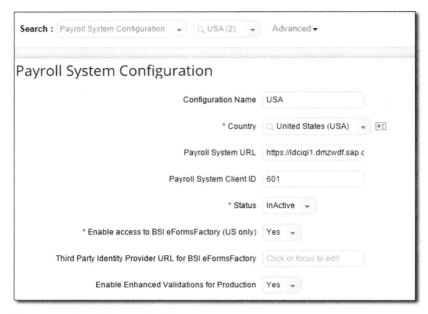

Figure 9.27 Payroll System Configuration

Let's now move on to creating a payment method.

Create Payment Method

In this configuration step, you will create a new payment method for payroll. Go to ADMIN TOOLS • EMPLOYEE FILE • MANAGE DATA. Under CREATE NEW, select PAYMENT METHOD. To create payment methods, enter the details from Table 9.44, and save the changes.

ExternalCode	ExternalName	BankTransfer
05	BANK TRANSFER	YES
06	CHECK	No
09	CASH	No

Table 9.44 Payment Method Details

Let's now move on to configuring RBPs.

Role-Based Permissions Enhancement Configurations

You have almost completed the payroll-related configuration in Employee Central. Now, we have to update the RBPs for the HR Administrator role, Employee Standard role, and SFAPI role to add additional roles for accessing payroll-related processes.

Go to ADMIN TOOLS • SET USER PERMISSIONS • MANAGE PERMISSIONS ROLES. In the PERMISSION ROLE list, select the permission roles that corresponds to the HR ADMINISTRATOR role, EMPLOYEE STANDARD role, and SFAPI role, and update their user permissions accordingly by referring to Table 9.45.

Permission Role	User Permission	Permission	Checked
ADMINISTRATOR	EMPLOYEE DATA	PAYMENT INFORMATION	X
	EMPLOYEE CENTRAL EFFECTIVE DATE ENTITIES	JOB INFORMATION	All
		COMPENSATION	All
	EMPLOYEE VIEW	PAYROLL INFORMATION	X
	PAYROLL PERMISSIONS	PAYROLL ADMINISTRATION	X
EMPLOYEE STANDARD ROLE	EMPLOYEE VIEW	PAYROLL	X
	PAYROLL PERMISSIONS	PAYROLL SELF SERVICE	X
SFAPI	GENERAL USER PERMISSIONS	SFAPI USER LOGIN	X
	EMPLOYEE CENTRAL API	EMPLOYEE CENTRAL HRIS SOAP API	X
	MANAGER USER	EMPLOYEE EXPORT	X

Table 9.45 SFAPI Permissions

9.2.4 Step 3: SAP Payroll/Employee Central Payroll Configurations

Now, let's proceed to the necessary SAP Payroll/Employee Central Payroll configuration steps required for setting up the Employee Central integration.

We will cover two main activities in this section, which include refining the default logic of the work schedule and refining mapping.

Refine Default Logic of Work Schedule

This is an optional step. Only execute this step if you decide to use Employee Central Time Off for work schedule determination. This would replace the use of the default settings in Employee Central Payroll or the on-premise SAP Payroll system, in which the work schedule is determined through table T508A match with an employee's Employee Group (Employee Subgroup Grouping) and the Personnel Area (Personnel Subarea Grouping).

For the detailed steps to disable the default logic for work schedule determination, refer to Section 9.1.4, Refine Default Logic of Work Schedule.

Refine Mapping

In this configuration activity, you will define the key mappings of organizational terms, mapping code value lists, and wage type assignments to an infotype. These mappings act as the functional translation keys between Employee Central and SAP Payroll/Employee Central Payroll. Prior to maintaining the mappings, you need to cross-check the picklist external codes updated in the Employee Central configuration setup, because the Employee Central picklist external codes will be replicated and mapped to the SAP Payroll/Employee Central Payroll code within the same context.

Let's take a closer look at each mapping activity and fill in the mappings according to your integration setup between Employee Central and SAP Payroll/Employee Central Payroll system.

Mapping activities for the following fields are covered in Section 9.1.4, Refining Mapping: company code, location, salutation, marital status, address type, employee class, job classification, events, event reason, work schedule, state, department, division, business unit, and infotype mappings.

Additional key mappings required for integration with SAP Payroll/Employee Central Payroll are as follows:

- **Pay Group**
  Create a new mapping entry for pay group setup in Employee Central and SAP ERP. Create new entries as shown in Table 9.46.

Field Name	Value
GDT Name	PAYROLL_GROUP_CODE
Code List ID	37002 (for United States)

Table 9.46 Pay Group Mapping

Field Name	Value
LIST VERSION ID	\<blank\>
LIST AGENCY ID	310
GDT CODE VALUE	\<EC ID\>
ERP KEY	\<EC Payroll ID\>

Table 9.46 Pay Group Mapping (Cont.)

▸ **Payment Method**
Create a new mapping entry for payment method setup in Employee Central and SAP ERP. Create new entries as shown in Table 9.47.

Field Name	Value
GDT NAME	PAYMENT_FORM_CODE
CODE LIST ID	91402 (for United States)
LIST VERSION ID	\<blank\>
LIST AGENCY ID	310
GDT CODE VALUE	\<EC ID\>
ERP KEY	\<EC Payroll ID\>

Table 9.47 Payment Method Mapping

▸ **Pay Scale Area and Pay Scale Type**
Create a new mapping entry for payment scale area and type setup in Employee Central and SAP ERP. Create new entries as shown in Table 9.48.

Field Name	Value
GDT NAME	PAY_SCALE_AREA_CODE
CODE LIST ID	91402 (for United States)
LIST VERSION ID	\<blank\>
LIST AGENCY ID	310
GDT CODE VALUE	\<EC ID\>
ERP KEY	\<EC Payroll ID\>

Table 9.48 Pay Scale Area and Type Mapping

▶ **Pay Component Recurring/Nonrecurring**
Create a new mapping entry for pay component setup in Employee Central and SAP ERP. Create new entries as shown in Table 9.49.

Field Name	Value
GDT NAME	COMPENSATION_COMPONENT_TYPE_ID
CODE LIST ID	91202 (for United States)
LIST VERSION ID	<blank>
LIST AGENCY ID	310
GDT CODE VALUE	<EC ID>
ERP KEY	<EC Payroll ID>

Table 9.49 Pay Component Mapping

▶ **Assigning Wage Types to Infotypes**
Under WAGE TYPE PROCESSING, click on ASSIGNING WAGE TYPES TO INFOTYPE from the IMG menu, and create entries as shown in Table 9.50.

Country Group	Wage Type	Infotype
<Country Grouping> e.g., 01	<EC Payroll Code>—e.g., /510	<EC Payroll Code>—e.g., 0008

Table 9.50 Wage Types to Infotypes Mapping

Replication Employee Key Mapping Table

During the employee master data replication process, table PAOCFEC_EEKEY-MAP is updated with employee key mapping between Employee Central and SAP Payroll/Employee Central Payroll for those employee master records that are successfully replicated. This employee key mapping table is updated to avoid any duplicate employee master record replication in the SAP Payroll/Employee Central Payroll systems. This same table is useful to keep your employee master records in sync within your system landscape if you plan to replicate the same employee master record set from Employee Central to your SAP Finance system. You can transfer this table from SAP Payroll/Employee Central Payroll to your SAP Finance system to avoid having any existing employee created with a different personnel number in the SAP Finance system. To view table PAOCFEC_EEKEYMAP, use Transaction SE16.

Now that we've completed the SAP Payroll/Employee Central Payroll configurations, let's discuss the setup required for the middleware.

9.2.5 Step 4: Middleware Setup and Web Service Activation

This section describes the necessary steps for configuring Dell Boomi AtomSphere middleware, SAP Payroll/Employee Central Payroll web service activation, and configuring the ALE distribution model for integrating cost center replication, employee data replication, and employee data replication confirmation scenarios between Employee Central and SAP Payroll/Employee Central Payroll.

See Section 9.2.2 for the basic setup that needs to be completed prior to this configuration. We will walk through the configuration based on each integration scenario.

The following tasks are required to set up the middleware and web service activation:

▸ Cost center replication
▸ Employee data replication
▸ Employee data replication response

Let's start with the cost center replication, then employee data replication, followed by the employee data replication confirmation scenario.

Cost Center Replication

This step covers the cost center distribution in SAP Payroll/Employee Central Payroll system. This process is similar to steps we've already taken in this chapter. Therefore, for the detailed steps of this process, please refer to Section 9.1.5, Cost Center Replication.

Employee Data Replication

This step covers the configuration of the web service for the employee data replication process in SAP Payroll/Employee Central Payroll system. This process is similar to steps we've already taken in this chapter. Therefore, for detailed steps of this process, please refer to Section 9.1.5, Employee Data Replication.

Employee Data Replication Response

This step covers the configuration of the web service for the employee data replication response process in SAP Payroll/Employee Central Payroll. This process is similar to steps we've already taken in this chapter. Therefore, for the detailed steps of this process, please refer to Section 9.1.5, Employee Data Replication Response.

In this case study, along with the ABC Global Services example provided, we detailed the necessary configuration and technical steps required to implement the Employee Central integration with SAP Payroll on-premise or Employee Central Payroll using the Full Cloud HCM deployment model. The goal of this case study was to highlight the necessary steps that you can follow to implement Employee Central integration with payroll, be it on-premise SAP Payroll or Employee Central Payroll in the cloud.

In the next section, we will discuss how to integrate Employee Central with a third-party system: Kronos Time Management.

9.3 Employee Central to Kronos Time Management

Kronos Workforce Central software provides complete automation for workforce management functions and processes around time and attendance, scheduling, absence management, human resources, payroll, hiring, and labor analytics. Kronos Workforce Central receives information from employee administration (core HR) systems such as Employee Central and uses that information for time and attendance management purposes. SAP provides a packaged implementation product built on the Dell Boomi AtomSphere platform to support the integration of employee master data from Employee Central to Kronos Time Management.

Kronos Time Management is a time, attendance, and labor management solution. Kronos Time Management also provides companies with a cloud-based solution to manage their employees' and contractors' time- and labor-related information. Kronos Time Management sends periodic updates to employee administration and payroll systems that require time data for legal reporting and payroll processing.

Employee data is extracted from Employee Central and sent to Kronos Time Management periodically. When the integration middleware extracts the data, it maps and reformats the employee data to a Kronos format, then sends the employee data to Kronos Time Management, which then accepts the data and populates necessary systems.

Employees enter time- and attendance-related data in Kronos Time Management, which then makes such time data available. This data is captured by the integration middleware technology, Dell Boomi AtomSphere, and provided to Employee Central Payroll, which uses the information for payroll purposes.

In this section, we will cover the implementation steps needed in integrating Employee Central with Kronos Time Management using standard best practices. Figure 9.28 displays this integration via middleware in action.

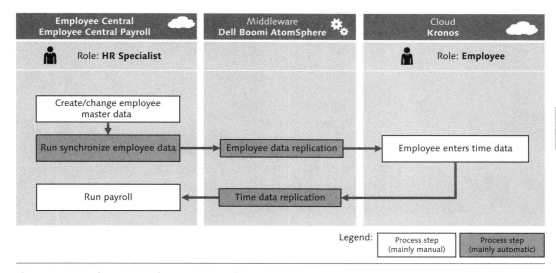

Figure 9.28 Employee Central Integration with Kronos Time Management

Prerequisites

Prior to the Employee Central integration with Kronos Time Management, you will need to ensure that the following relevant configurations and customizations have been completed:

▶ Obtain licensing to use Kronos Time Management

▶ Configure Kronos Time Management to build an employee master table and subsequent time management configuration to record and evaluate time data

▶ Obtain Dell Boomi AtomSphere integration middleware, licensed along with Employee Central

▶ Complete necessary configurations for Employee Central

The following key pieces of Employee Central master data configuration will need to be completed by the configuration team prior to commencement of the integration project:

▶ Personal information

▶ Employment information

▶ Job information

▶ Email information

▶ Phone information

▶ Pay component recurring

This information is needed by the Kronos Workforce Central system in order to allow time data entry and evaluate time. Employee master data tables within Kronos Time Management will need to be configured to receive and process this data from Employee Central.

SAP and Kronos have partnered to deliver packaged integration content that will integrate data between Employee Central core HR and Kronos Time Management. The delivered integration content consists of three integration options, which can be implemented independently of one another:

▶ **Employee Central to Kronos Time Management employee data replication**
This is used to replicate employee master data relevant for time management.

▶ **Kronos to Employee Central Payroll**
This is used to transfer evaluated time data from Kronos Time Management to SAP infotypes via an IDoc.

▶ **User Interface Integration via Single Sign- On**
This allows users to seamlessly access Kronos Time Management from within Employee Central.

This case study will focus on the Employee Central to Kronos Time Management integration using the standard integration template. Ahead is a description of the parameters that this integration will entail, including the client scenario and an overview of the process steps.

9.3.1 Case Study Parameters

This case study focuses on how a customer can integrate its current Employee Central system with Kronos Time Management to manage its employees' and contractors' time- and labor-related information using Dell Boomi AtomSphere as the integration middleware.

Specifically, we'll discuss the prerequisites and steps necessary to implement the Employee Central to Kronos Time Management packaged integrations and the HR master data replication process that will help keep the company's data in sync between both systems.

We'll use a client scenario to demonstrate our case. A snapshot of our client is presented next.

Client Scenario

ABC Global Services is headquartered in Dallas, Texas, and has operations sites across the United States — with over 5,000 employees in North America. The company currently uses SAP ERP to support its financials, sales and distribution, and materials management functions and uses Employee Central as its core HR system.

ABC Global Services has implemented the Kronos Workforce Central Time and Attendance, Workforce Scheduling, and Absence Management, and parts of the Labor Analytics modules, for most of its North American manufacturing locations. Kronos Workforce Central requires employee master data from Employee Central, and employees hired in Employee Central will need to be transferred to Kronos Time Management; similarly, employees transferred or terminated will have to be transmitted to Kronos Time Management. Therefore, it is imperative that the employee master data is kept in sync in both systems.

At this point, ABC Global Services would like to integrate its current core HR system, Employee Central, with Kronos Time Management, using the Dell Boomi AtomSphere cloud integration platform, which requires a knowledgeable Dell Boomi AtomSphere integration resource in order to implement and customize the packaged integrations.

Now, let's discuss how you can achieve a successful integration between Employee Central and Kronos Time Management, using Dell Boomi AtomSphere as your integration middleware. We'll begin with an overview of the process.

Process Overview

In order to properly set up the Kronos Time Management packaged integration, the following steps must be taken:

- **Step 1: SuccessFactors configuration**
  In this section, we will discuss the basic configuration steps required for setting up the employee data integration between Employee Central and the third-party Kronos Time Management system. This involves such steps as enabling web services for SuccessFactors API, creating a SuccessFactors API user, and more (see Section 9.3.2).

- **Step 2: Employee replication process setup for Employee Central to Kronos Time Management integration**
  In this section, we'll look at an overview of the employee replication process for the integration of Employee Central with Kronos (see Section 9.3.3).

- **Step 3: Customize and deploy the Employee Central to Kronos Time Management packaged integrations**
  In this section, we will discuss the key steps that need to be taken in order to customize and deploy the Employee Central to Kronos Time Management packaged integrations. Some of these steps include configuring the connections settings, field mapping review and setup, reviewing map functions, reviewing cross-reference tables, and more (see Section 9.3.4).

Let's begin by looking at the basic configuration of this integration.

9.3.2 Step 1: SuccessFactors Configuration

The following activities describe the necessary SuccessFactors configuration steps required for setting up the employee data integration with Employee Central and other third-party systems, like Kronos Time Management.

The basic configuration for this integration is comprised of the following tasks:

- Enabling web services SuccessFactors API
- Creating a SuccessFactors API User
- Configuring the SuccessFactors API user security
- Configuring SuccessFactors API login exceptions
- Downloading the packaged content for Employee Central to Kronos Time Management integration

Settings Configuration

These settings should be completed by the Employee Central functional consultant.

We'll begin by enabling the web services SuccessFactors API.

Enable Web Services SuccessFactors API

In this step, you will activate Employee Central web services and SuccessFactors API features needed for implementing integrations to and from Employee Central. For the detailed steps, refer to Section 9.1.2, Enable Web Services SuccessFactors API.

Next, we'll talk about how to create a SuccessFactors API user and assign RBP.

Create a SuccessFactors API User

A SuccessFactors API user is required for Dell Boomi AtomSphere middleware to integrate with Employee Central. The API user must first be created in the SuccessFactors provisioning tool. The same API user logon credential is then stored in the middleware credentials setting of the Dell Boomi Atomsphere environment setup. For the detailed steps, refer to Section 9.1.2, Create a SuccessFactors API User.

Now, let's focus on setting up the API user security.

Configure the SuccessFactors API User Security

In this step, you will configure the security RBP and group for the API user created in the previous step. For the detailed steps, refer to Section 9.1.2, Configure the SuccessFactors API User Security.

The following key permissions should be selected by checking the related checkboxes in order to set up integration access for the API user:

- GENERAL USER PERMISSION
    - USER LOGIN
    - LIVE PROFILE ACCESS
    - SFAPI USER LOGIN
- MANAGE SYSTEM PROPERTIES
    - PICKLIST MANAGEMENT AND PICKLISTS MAPPINGS SET UP
- REPORTS PERMISSION
- AD HOC REPORT BUILDER STANDARD REPORTS BIN

- ▶ ENABLE AD HOC CROSS DOMAIN REPORTS
- ▶ ENABLE AD HOC MULTI DATA SET REPORTS
- ▶ MANAGE INTEGRATION TOOLS
  - ▶ ACCESS TO SFAPI AUDIT LOG
  - ▶ ACCESS TO SFAPI METERING DETAILS
  - ▶ ACCESS TO SFAPI DATA DICTIONARY
  - ▶ ACCESS TO EVENT NOTIFICATION SUBSCRIPTION
  - ▶ ACCESS TO EVENT NOTIFICATION AUDIT LOG
  - ▶ ADMIN ACCESS TO ODATA API
  - ▶ MANAGE OAUTH2 CLIENT APPLICATIONS
  - ▶ ACCESS TO ODATA API AUDIT LOG
  - ▶ ACCESS TO ODATA API METADATA REFRESH AND EXPORT
- ▶ EMPLOYEE CENTRAL API
  - ▶ EMPLOYEE CENTRAL FOUNDATION SOAP API
  - ▶ EMPLOYEE CENTRAL HRIS SOAP API
  - ▶ EMPLOYEE CENTRAL FOUNDATION ODATA API (READ-ONLY)
  - ▶ EMPLOYEE CENTRAL HRIS ODATA API (READ-ONLY)
  - ▶ EMPLOYEE CENTRAL FOUNDATION ODATA API (EDITABLE)
  - ▶ EMPLOYEE CENTRAL HRIS ODATA API (EDITABLE)
- ▶ METADATA FRAMEWORK
  - ▶ CONFIGURE OBJECT DEFINITIONS
  - ▶ READ/WRITE PERMISSION ON METADATA FRAMEWORK
  - ▶ IMPORT PERMISSION ON METADATA FRAMEWORK
  - ▶ MANAGE DATA
  - ▶ CONFIGURE BUSINESS RULES
  - ▶ MANAGE CONFIGURATION UI
  - ▶ MANAGE POSITIONS
  - ▶ MANAGE SEQUENCE

You have successfully completed the steps for setting up API user security. Now, let's turn our attention to the API login exception.

SuccessFactors API Login Exception

In this step, you will configure the API login exception for the API user just created. The purpose is to ensure that the password for the API user does not expire. For the detailed steps, refer to Section 9.1.2, SuccessFactors API Login Exception.

Download the Packaged Content

SuccessFactors delivers standard packaged integration content for integrating Employee Central with Kronos Time Management. This content is available via the Business Process Library available to all customers. The standard integration package content can be used as a starting point from which customers and/or partners can further extend.

Integration Note
The following steps should be performed by an experienced integration resource consultant, trained and certified in Dell Boomi AtomSphere.

The content can be downloaded by performing the following steps:

1. Log on to your Dell Boomi AtomSphere account (as seen in Figure 9.29) with your credentials (email address) via the correct URL (e.g., *https://platform.boomi.com*).

Figure 9.29 Dell Boomi AtomSphere Login Screen

2. Upon logging in, click on the BUILD tab, as shown in Figure 9.30.

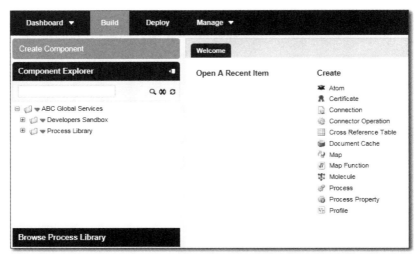

Figure 9.30 Dell Boomi AtomSphere Dashboard Build Tab

3. Create a folder to house the standard Kronos Time Management packaged integrations. Click on the root folder (ABC GLOBAL SERVICES), and select CREATE NEW FOLDER. Name the new folder "Packaged Integrations Content" (see Figure 9.31).

Figure 9.31 Dell Boomi AtomSphere New Folder Creation

4. Click on OK to save the new folder under the root folder. You will now see the new folder under COMPONENT EXPLORER (see Figure 9.32).

5. You are now ready to import the Kronos Time Management packaged integration into your new folder. Click on BROWSE PROCESS LIBRARY.

Browse Process Library

The BROWSE PROCESS LIBRARY option needs to be enabled by SuccessFactors Operations as part of your company account settings. Please work with your SuccessFactors Operations support team to enable this option if it is not available within your account.

Figure 9.32 Dell Boomi AtomSphere Component Explorer Folder Directory

6. Scroll down through the list of available packaged integrations to the option PACKAGED INTEGRATION: EC TO KRONOS WORKFORCE CENTRAL—EMPLOYEE (*see* Figure 9.33).

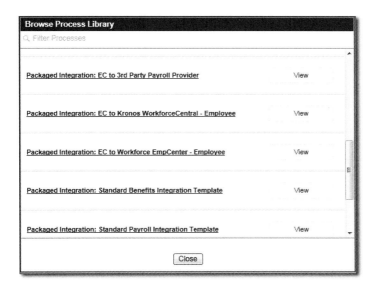

Figure 9.33 Dell Boomi AtomSphere Process Library

7. Click on VIEW next to your selected packaged integration. Click on the INSTALL button.

8. Choose a destination folder: PACKAGED INTEGRATIONS CONTENT. You can rename the integration to a name of your choice—for example, "Employee Central to Kronos North America", to identify that this integration is for the

North American installations of ABC Global Services. For purposes of this case study we will retain the default name (see Figure 9.34).

Figure 9.34 Dell Boomi AtomSphere Process Installation

9. Click on COMPLETE INSTALLATION. You will see a message indicating that the installation was successful (see Figure 9.35).

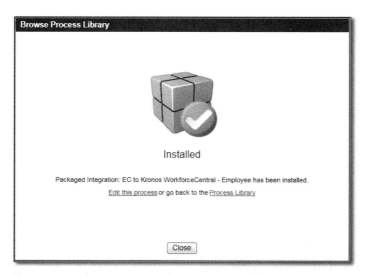

Figure 9.35 Dell Boomi AtomSphere Process Installation Success Message

10. Close the window. Click the REFRESH icon within the COMPONENT EXPLORER to finish installing the packaged integration (see Figure 9.36).

Figure 9.36 Dell Boomi AtomSphere Component Explorer Packaged Integration Content

The Kronos Time Management integration package content has now been successfully downloaded into the ABC Global Services account within the Dell Boomi AtomSphere integration middleware tool. The standard content is delivered as a template that can be customized to suit your company's specific requirements. Mapping tables and logic are normally customer-specific, and this package can be customized as needed while using the delivered content as a guideline. You are now ready to customize the packaged integration to suit your specific requirements.

Now, let's move on to the employee data replication integration process between Employee Central and Kronos Time Management.

9.3.3   Step 2: Overview of the Employee Data Replication Process

The replication of employee data from Employee Central to Kronos Time Management is comprised of the following steps:

1. The interface is scheduled to run, typically on a daily basis. The interface extracts employee data from Employee Central as of the previous run.

2. The extracted data is mapped to and conforms to a WSDL (Web Services Description Language) published by Kronos.

345

3. Dell Boomi AtomSphere calls the web service and sends the employee data to Kronos Time Management.

4. Once data is received, employee import processing occurs within Kronos Time Management.

This job runs on a daily basis and extracts changes only from the last successful run date and time, which is stored within the Dell Boomi AtomSphere process as a variable. The Dell Boomi AtomSphere process calls the compound employee API to extract employee data from Employee Central in the form of a hierarchically structured XML response.

The compound employee API extracts data from the following Employee Central portlets:

- Personal information
- Employment information
- Job information
- Email information
- Phone information
- Pay component recurring

The data received within the XML is then mapped and transformed into Kronos fields using map functions and cross-reference tables as part of the processing steps within Dell Boomi AtomSphere. It is then presented in a CSV file format as prescribed by Kronos.

The process is designed to output two files: *Person_import.txt* and *Costcenter_ import.txt*.

The output file format for the *Person_import.txt* file has been detailed in a field mapping Table 9.51 which captures the source Employee Central fields and maps them to target fields in Kronos Time Managment; any data transformation requirements are also captured within the mapping table.

In this case study for ABC Global Services, we will focus on the employee data replication file (Person_import.txt), because cost centers will be directly sent over from SAP ERP to Kronos Time Management via a feed from SAP ERP. Hence, we will customize the implementation by disabling the process to generate a cost center file from Employee Central to Kronos Time Management via this integration.

The overall process starts with the extraction of employee data from Employee Central followed by field mapping and data translations that produce an output file in the required format. This is depicted in the process flow diagram in Figure 9.37. The main process is split into many subprocesses that are required in order to complete the integration. The main subprocesses include the following:

▸ Identification of the last successful run date and time and persisting the last successful run date/time throughout the process

▸ Deciding whether a cost center file is needed and subsequent processing or ending of the subprocess for the cost center file

▸ Compounding an employee query to extract employee data and subsequent processing to produce the output file in the prescribed format

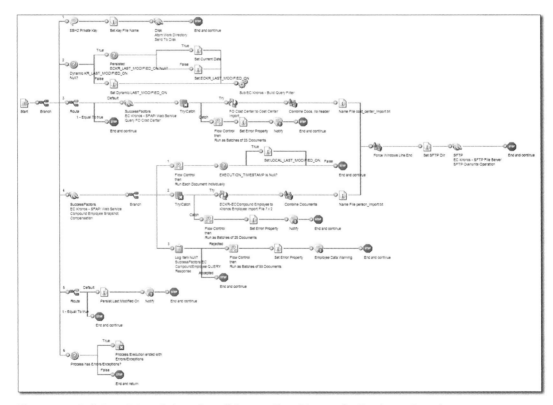

Figure 9.37 Dell Boomi AtomSphere Overall Process Flow Diagram for Employee Central to Kronos Time Management Integration

The steps needed to customize the integration process for the current case study are discussed in the following sections.

9.3.4   Step 3: Customize and Deploy the Packaged Integration

In the previous sections, we have seen the process of downloading a prepackaged implementation and the prerequisites required to enable the integration with Kronos Time Management. In this section, we will review some configuration steps and customization opportunities for our implementation of this integration.

The steps will broadly consist of the following:

- Configuring the connections settings
- Reviewing field mappings and setup
- Reviewing map functions
- Reviewing cross-reference tables
- Specifying process properties
- Setting up the Dell Boomi AtomSphere environment and atom
- Deploy the process
- Executing the process

The current version of the Employee Central to Kronos Time Management packaged integration is delivered for the United States, but it can be used for any country with minor adjustments as needed. The integration is designed to run for one country at a time. Another limitation of this integration is that it is not built to support future-dated transactions. Therefore, if future-dated transactions need to be sent across, then additional coding or customization will be needed.

We will now go over each of the steps to enable and customize this integration.

Configure the Connection Settings

In this step, you will configure the parameters for the SuccessFactors API via the following steps:

1. In Dell Boomi AtomSphere, open the BUILD tab.

2. Within the COMPONENT EXPLORER, navigate to the PACKAGED INTEGRATION CONTENT folder. Open the CONNECTORS folder, then follow the menu path SUCCESS-

FACTORS • CONNECTIONS • EC KRONOS SFAPI WEB SERVICES (see Figure 9.38). Add the following settings for the Employee Central to Kronos Time Management SuccessFactors API web service connections:

▸ ENDPOINT: The endpoints of the API–SuccessFactors data center

▸ COMPANY ID: The company ID of the Employee Central instance

▸ USERNAME: The SuccessFactors API username (the SuccessFactors API user used to query data from Employee Central was configured in a previous step for example SAP_API_USER)

▸ PASSWORD: The SuccessFactors API user password

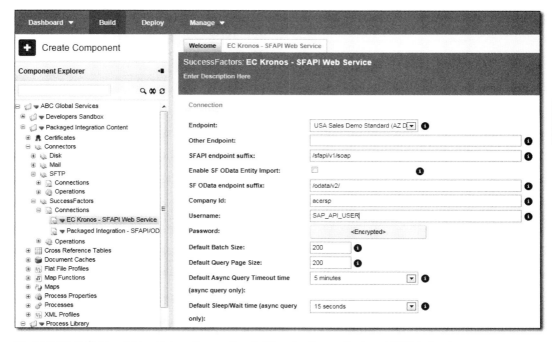

Figure 9.38 Dell Boomi AtomSphere Connection Settings for SuccessFactors API Web Services

3. Next, configure the Kronos Time Management SFTP settings. Click on the BUILD tab. Within the COMPONENT EXPLORER, navigate to the PACKAGED INTEGRATION CONTENT folder. From here, open the CONNECTORS folder, and follow the menu path SFTP • CONNECTIONS • EC KRONOS SFTP FILE SERVER (see Figure 9.39). Then, add the following settings for the Employee Central to Kronos Time Management SFTP File Server connection:

▶ HOST: Kronos Time Management SFTP file IP address

▶ PORT: Kronos Time Management SFTP server port

▶ USER NAME: Username to access Kronos Time Management

▶ PASSWORD: Password for the user entered in USER

Figure 9.39 Dell Boomi AtomSphere Connection Settings—SFTP File Server

Next, we will review field mapping settings delivered with the packaged integration.

Field Mapping Review and Setup

Fields are mapped within Dell Boomi AtomSphere using field maps, as shown in Figure 9.40.

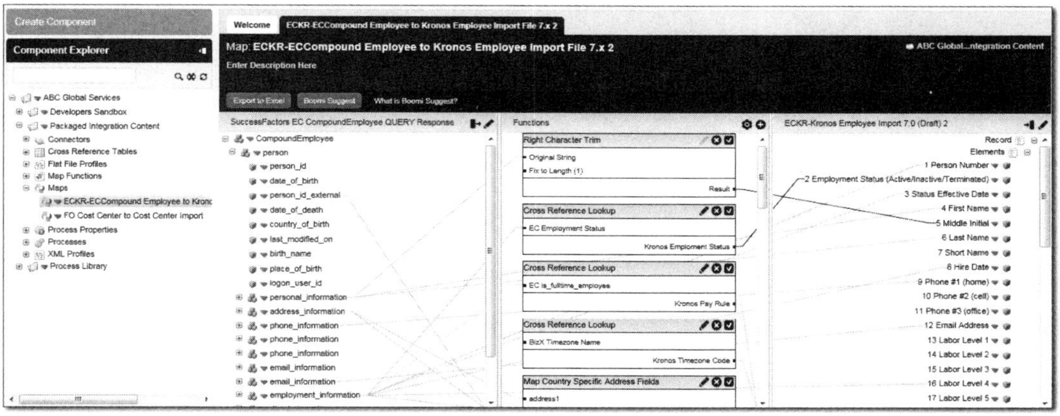

Figure 9.40 Dell Boomi AtomSphere Field Maps

The delivered field mapping setup adapted for ABC Global Services' requirements is shown in Table 9.51. The following setup was employed:

▶ The first column, SFSF Employee Central Fields, indicates source fields from Employee Central.

▶ The second column refers to Required versus Optional or Constant values for the target system.

▶ The third column, Mapping/Transformation Required, further defines if mapping or transformation is required.

▶ The fourth column, Kronos Field, refers to mapping target fields of Kronos Time Management.

▶ The fifth column is a Description of the field or a transformation rule.

SFSF Employee Central Fields	Required/ Optional/ Constant	Mapping/ Transforma-tion Required	Kronos Field	Description
PERSON ID	R	N	PERSON NUMBER	Employee ID.
EMPLOYMENT STATUS	R	Y	EMPLOYMENT STATUS	Active, inactive, terminated, etc.

Table 9.51 Field Mapping

SFSF Employee Central Fields	Required/ Optional/ Constant	Mapping/ Transformation Required	Kronos Field	Description
EFFECTIVE START DATE	O	N	STATUS EFFECTIVE DATE	Effective as of the date from the latest record from the job portlet.
FIRST NAME	R	N	FIRST NAME	First name.
MIDDLE NAME	O	Y	MIDDLE INITIAL	Middle initial, not middle name; send only the first character.
LAST NAME	R	N	LAST NAME	Last name.
PREFERRED NAME	O	N	SHORT NAME	A nickname by which the person wants to be known.
ORIGINAL HIRE DATE	R	N	HIRE DATE	The date when the person was hired.
PHONE NUMBER	O	N	PHONE 1 (Cell)	Send PHONE NUMBER field along with PHONE TYPE field = CELL—e.g., 9776172920.
PHONE NUMBER	O	Y	PHONE 2 (Home)	Send PHONE number field along with PHONE TYPE field = HOME—e.g., 9700678698.
PHONE NUMBER	O	Y	PHONE 3 (Office)	Send PHONE NUMBER field along with PHONE TYPE field = BUSINESS—e.g., 9036172920.
EMAIL ADDRESS	O	Y	EMAIL ADDRESS	Send work email if present; otherwise, send personal. If neither exists, send blank.
COST CENTER	R	N	LABOR LEVEL 4	The name of the labor level entry to which the labor account belongs. This is the cost center in Employee Central.
START DATE	R	N	PRIMARY LABOR ACCOUNT EFFECTIVE DATE	The date on which the employee started working in the cost center.

Table 9.51 Field Mapping (Cont.)

SFSF Employee Central Fields	Required/ Optional/ Constant	Mapping/ Transformation Required	Kronos Field	Description
TIME ZONE	R	Y	TIME ZONE	Get the employee's work location and go to FO work location. Get the time zone from there.
PAY COMPONENT VALUE	O	N	BASE WAGE RATE	Pay component value when component equals base pay.
START DATE	O	N	BASE WAGE RATE EFFECTIVE DATE	DD/MM/YYYY. Effective as of date from the last record from the pay component portlet.
IS FULLTIME EMPLOYEE	R	Y	PAY RULE	Full time or part time employee.
START DATE	R	N	PAY RULE EFFECTIVE DATE	Start date of pay rule.
MANAGER ID	O	N	REPORTS TO	Manager ID from job information.
PAYROLL ID	O	N	BADGE NUMBER	If no payroll ID, send blank.
CITY	O	N	HOME ADDRESS CITY	Home city of the employee.
COUNTRY	O	N	HOME ADDRESS COUNTRY	Home country of the employee.
POSTCODE	O	N	HOME ADDRESS ZIP CODE	Home address zip code of the employee
STATE	O	N	HOME ADDRESS STATE	Home address state of the employee.
ADDRESS 1	O	N	HOME ADDRESS STREET	Home address street of the employee.

Table 9.51 Field Mapping (Cont.)

SFSF Employee Central Fields	Required/ Optional/ Constant	Mapping/ Transforma- tion Required	Kronos Field	Description
ADDRESS TYPE	O	Y	CATEGORY OF ADDRESS	Category of address (for example, home).
CUSTOM STRING 1	O	N	CUSTOM STRING 1	The custom field for Work-force Central Custom string 1. Custom fields can be used for a customer specific instance / configuration of Kronos Workforce Central
CUSTOM STRING 2	O	N	CUSTOM STRING 2	The custom field for Work-force Central Custom string 2.
CUSTOM STRING 3	O	N	CUSTOM STRING 3	The custom field for Work-force Central Custom string 3.
CUSTOM STRING 4	O	N	CUSTOM STRING 4	The custom field for Work-force Central Custom string 4.
CUSTOM STRING 5	O	N	CUSTOM STRING 5	The custom field for Work-force Central Custom string 5.
CUSTOM STRING 6	O	N	CUSTOM STRING 6	The custom field for Work-force Central Custom string 6.
CUSTOM STRING 7	O	N	CUSTOM STRING 7	The custom field for Work-force Central Custom string 7.
CUSTOM STRING 8	O	N	CUSTOM STRING 8	The custom field for Work-force Central Custom string 8.
CUSTOM STRING 9	O	N	CUSTOM STRING 9	The custom field for Work-force Central Custom string 9.
CUSTOM STRING 10	O	N	CUSTOM STRING 10	The custom field for Workforce Central Custom string 10.

Table 9.51 Field Mapping (Cont.)

Next, we will review map functions, which capture the logic required for field value transformations.

Map Functions

Map functions are used to capture any translation or transformation logic requirements. In Table 9.51, some fields have been defined as those that require transformation. Transformations can be accomplished by using a map function or a cross-reference table.

Map functions have been defined for MIDDLE INITIAL. Employee Central captures the middle name as a field value. We will use a right-justified trim function on the field value to remove all characters except the first one. In this way, the first character of the MIDDLE NAME field of Employee Central is mapped to the MIDDLE INITIAL field in Kronos Workforce Central.

This is an example of a map function that is relevant for ABC Global Services' configuration. Map functions can be created for any field, depending upon source and target field configuration and customer-specific requirements.

Another method of data transformation is the use of translations or cross-reference tables.

Cross-Reference Tables

Cross-reference tables have been defined to transform the following Employee Central fields into the corresponding values in Kronos Workforce Central:

▶ EMPLOYMENT STATUS
The cross-reference table for mapping EMPLOYMENT STATUS values in Employee Central to those in Kronos Time Management is shown in Figure 9.41.

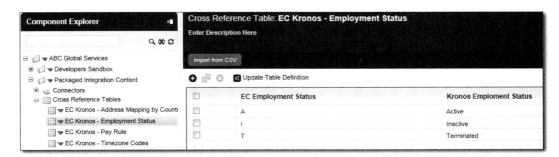

Figure 9.41 Dell Boomi AtomSphere Cross-Reference Tables—Employment Status

▶ Pay Rule

The cross-reference table for mapping pay rules in Kronos Time Management to full- or part-time status values in Employee Central is shown in Figure 9.42.

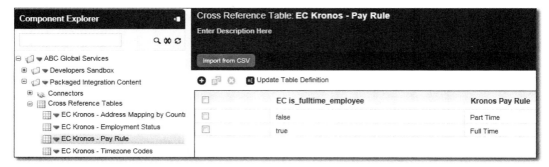

Figure 9.42 Dell Boomi AtomSphere Cross-Reference Tables—Pay Rules

▶ Timezone Codes

The cross-reference table for mapping timezone codes is shown in Table 9.43.

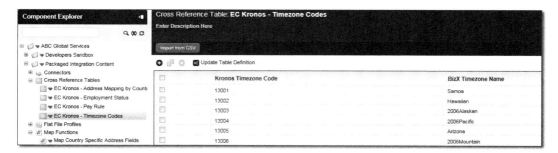

Figure 9.43 Dell Boomi AtomSphere Cross-Reference Tables—Time Zone Codes

▶ Address Mapping by Country

Address fields tend to change with each country. The cross-reference table for address field formats for each country's values in Employee Central is shown in Figure 9.44.

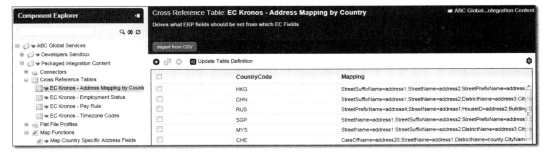

Figure 9.44 Dell Boomi AtomSphere Cross-Reference Tables—Country Address Field Mapping

Additional field maps or map functions can be defined in a similar way.

Now, let's move on to setting the process properties needed for the integration.

Specify Process Properties

Process properties can be found as an option within the COMPONENT EXPLORER. Process properties are used to specify processing parameters or conditions. The Employee Central packaged integration comes delivered with two process properties that allow you to define data filters and general settings for the integration:

▶ EMPLOYEE FILTER CRITERIA
The EMPLOYEE FILTER CRITERIA allows selecting the type of employee to be sent across to Kronos Time Management. Each criteria can be selected, and the values relevant for selection can be specified in this step (see Figure 9.45).

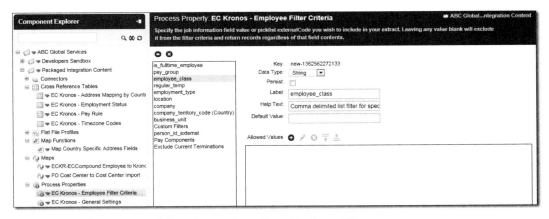

Figure 9.45 Dell Boomi AtomSphere Process Properties—Employee Filters

357

▶ GENERAL SETTINGS

GENERAL SETTINGS allows you to define settings such as the Kronos SFTP Directory and whether the cost center file is required to be generated. In this case, choose not to generate the cost center extract as part of this integration.

As shown Figure 9.46, select the AVOID GENERATION OF COST CENTER FILE option in order to restrict your processing and output to the single person file.

Figure 9.46 Dell Boomi AtomSphere Process Properties—General Settings

As you can see from the preceding examples, map functions and cross-reference tables can be configured or built for any field within the map. You can also use process properties to set employee filters or to specify SFTP locations or processing parameters for each interface run.

You will now deploy your enhanced integration in order to test it.

Set Up the Dell Boomi AtomSphere Environment and Atom

Upon completion of the initial development of the integration, you will need to deploy the integration to an atom that is connected to an Employee Central instance from which data will need to be extracted.

The deployment process will consist of first creating an environment for the implementation and then attaching an atom to it; this will be a one-time activity for each environment and is generally performed by the Dell Boomi AtomSphere administrator.

Perform the following steps:

1. Environments and atoms are managed from within the MANAGE tab in Dell Boomi AtomSphere; click on MANAGE, and access the ATOM MANAGEMENT functionality (see Figure 9.47).

Figure 9.47 Dell Boomi AtomSphere Atom Management

2. Environments can be added by clicking on the ADD ENVIRONMENT (+) button and specifying properties for the environment (see Figure 9.48).

Figure 9.48 Dell Boomi AtomSphere—Creating an Environment

3. Atoms are typically created by the Dell Boomi AtomSphere administrator; these atoms will then be attached to an environment. In this example, the atom for ABC Global Services has been created (see Figure 9.49).

4. Attach the atom to your environment by moving it from the UNATTACHED ATOMS section on the right to the ATTACHED ATOMS section on the left via the << button (see Figure 9.50).

Figure 9.49 Dell Boomi AtomSphere—Set Atom Properties

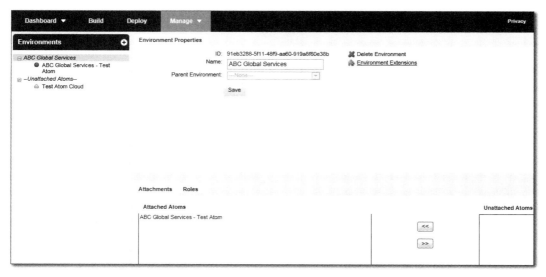

Figure 9.50 Dell Boomi AtomSphere—Set Environment Properties

5. Assign roles to the atom by selecting the ROLES tab and moving the required roles from the right to the left using the << button. For this example, select the STANDARD USER role (see Figure 9.51).

Figure 9.51 Dell Boomi AtomSphere—Set Environment Properties, Assign Roles

You are now ready to deploy the Kronos Time Management packaged integration to your atom.

Deploy the Process Integration

Next, you will deploy the process integration. Perform the following steps:

1. Click on the DEPLOY tab on the header, and then select the main process. It is sufficient to select the main process; all subprocesses within the main process are automatically deployed as part of the deployment of the main process (see Figure 9.52).

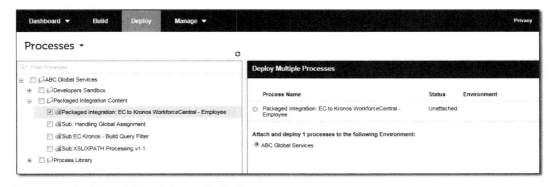

Figure 9.52 Dell Boomi AtomSphere—Deploy Process

2. Enter comments to indicate the version of the deployment and key changes made to the process via this deployment (see Figure 9.53).

Process
Each process may undergo multiple deployments during the testing and bug resolution phases.

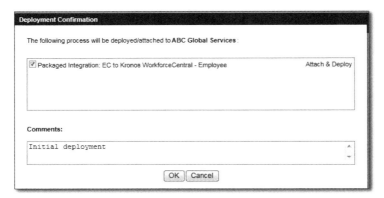

Figure 9.53 Dell Boomi AtomSphere—Deploy Process Confirmation

3. Upon the successful completion of the deployment step, the deployed process will appear in the DEPLOYED PROCESSES window at the right side of the pane.

4. Check the environment extensions to identify the source and target systems for the environment. From the MANAGE tab, click on your environment, and then select the ENVIRONMENT EXTENSIONS option on the right (see Figure 9.54).

Figure 9.54 Dell Boomi AtomSphere—Deploy Process, Environment Properties

The ENVIRONMENT EXTENSIONS option allows you to customize or adapt process-specific properties for each deployed environment and enables you to apply variations per environment.

Please note that the settings made here pertain to the deployment within this environment only. The settings here allow you to point to specific environments or SFTP servers, or to test with specific employee filter criteria. They settings are generic and default in nature, whereas settings made within extensions when a process is deployed to a specific environment affect and influence that deployment or process runs within that environment only.

Options available for each environment include the following:

▶ Connection settings

▶ Dynamic process properties

▶ Process properties

▶ Cross-reference tables

▶ PGP

▶ Data maps

We will now go over each extension to review the options available.

Connection Settings

Here, you set the endpoints for each of the connections available. The endpoint for EC KRONOS—SFAPI WEB SERVICE (under CONNECTION) is set to point to the Employee Central instance from which data will be extracted. You can specify the SuccessFactors API user and password setting as well (see Figure 9.55).

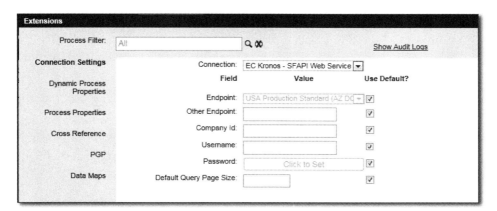

Figure 9.55 Dell Boomi AtomSphere—Deploy Process, Extensions, Connection Settings, SuccessFactors API Web Service Endpoints

The end point for EMPLOYEE CENTRAL KRONOS—SFTP FILE SERVER (under CONNECTION) is set to point to the Kronos Time Management file server to which the data files will be sent. You can specify the server user ID and password as well (see Figure 9.56).

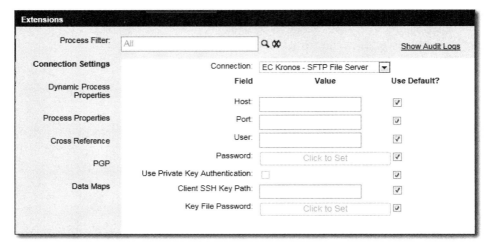

Figure 9.56 Dell Boomi AtomSphere—Deploy Process, Extensions, Connection Settings, File Server

Dynamic Process Properties

Here, you will set the properties that will vary dynamically for each run of the interface. The property to be set is KR_LAST_MODIFIED ON.

This property will be set manually for the first run to a date such as 01/01/1900. The first run of the interface is expected to set the baseline in the Kronos Time Management system and will include all historical records.

Subsequently, after the first run is complete and the baseline established within Kronos Time Management, you will return to this setting to remove the data entered here. Leaving this setting blank will allow the system to dynamically populate the last successful run after each run of the interface (see Figure 9.57).

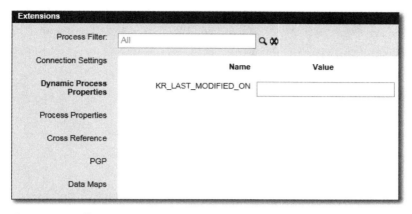

Figure 9.57 Dell Boomi AtomSphere—Deploy Process, Extensions, Dynamic Process Properties

Process Properties

In PROCESS PROPERTIES, you can enter values for the following:

▶ GENERAL SETTINGS

Within the GENERAL SETTINGS, specify the SFTP directory and SFTP certificates and identify if you will be passing cost center information to Kronos Time Management via this interface. In this case, you will not be sending cost center information to Kronos Time Management and hence will select the AVOID GENERATION OF COST CENTER FILE checkbox (see Figure 9.58).

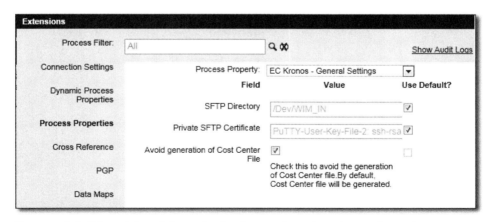

Figure 9.58 Dell Boomi AtomSphere—Deploy Process, Extensions, Process Properties

365

▶ EMPLOYEE FILTER CRITERIA

EMPLOYEE FILTER CRITERIA allows you to define filters to extract employee data. The following options are available to filter employees as part of the delivered package:

▶ PAY_GROUP

▶ EMPLOYEE_CLASS

▶ LOCATION

▶ COMPANY

▶ COMPANY_TERRITORY_CODE (COUNTRY)

In this case, set the COUNTRY filter to the USA, and leave the other filters blank (see Figure 9.59).

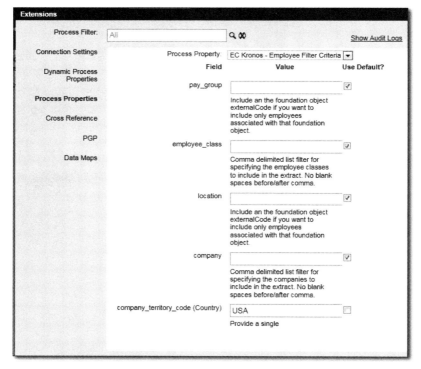

Figure 9.59 Dell Boomi AtomSphere—Deploy Process, Extensions, Process Properties, Filter Criteria

► CROSS REFERENCE

This property allows you to override the cross-reference table values set within the process for this environment. This setting will only be needed if a cross-reference table value is different for this environment, which could possibly occur if configurations have been updated in development or testing but not made it to production (see Figure 9.60).

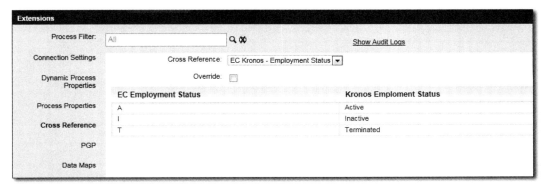

Figure 9.60 Dell Boomi AtomSphere — Deploy Process, Extensions, Cross-Reference Tables

When selected, the OVERRIDE checkbox indicates that the values specified here must be referenced by the interface.

► PGP

The PGP setting allows you to specify the PGP keys needed for cases of data encryption cases (see Figure 9.61).

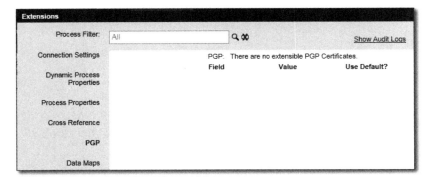

Figure 9.61 Dell Boomi AtomSphere — Deploy Process, Extensions, PGP Key Settings

367

▶ DATA MAPS

The DATA MAPS extension allows you to specify a different mapping than what exists within the main process. This property would normally not be set here (see Figure 9.62).

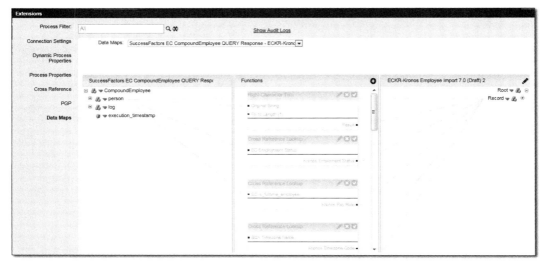

Figure 9.62 Dell Boomi AtomSphere—Deploy Process, Extensions, Data Maps

You have now specified all the properties and filter criteria for your integration and are ready to execute this interface for testing.

Execute the Process

You have completed your development and deployed the integration to your test atom. You have updated the extensions and identified the source and target systems. You have also updated the properties to identify employee data filters to be applied.

Now, you're ready to execute the interface. Navigate to the MANAGE tab and select your atom. Then, go to the DEPLOYED PROCESSES section, right-click on your process, and select the EXECUTE PROCESS option (see Figure 9.63).

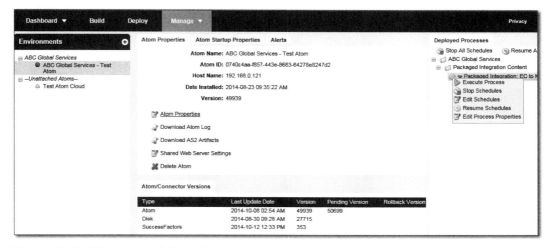

Figure 9.63 Dell Boomi AtomSphere—Process Execution

This action will trigger the execution of the process within Dell Boomi Atom-Sphere. The API will extract data out of the source Employee Central instance, apply filters that have been set within the properties, map and transform the data, and then produce an output file, which is posted to the Kronos SFTP server, as specified within the environment extensions. You then review the output files and error logs to monitor fields that are required and test for field mapping and mapping logic.

Then, continue to test multiple runs for various scenarios, and execute a complete end-to-end system test in which data from Employee Central updates Kronos Wokforce Central and time evaluation is executed within Kronos Time Managment.

In this case study, we discussed the Employee Central integration with Kronos Time Management, using the Dell Boomi AtomSphere cloud integration platform. The goal of this case study was to highlight the necessary steps that need to be followed to implement the Employee Central integrations with Kronos Time Management by downloading and adapting the SAP-delivered packaged integration.

9.4   Summary

This chapter detailed the necessary configuration and technical steps required to implement the Full Cloud HCM packaged integrations. In our first case study, we looked at the Employee Central to SAP ERP integration. Then, we looked at integrating Employee Central with payroll and the similar steps involved in integrating SAP Payroll and Employee Central Payroll with Employee Central while also identifying where the processes diverged. Finally, we looked at the integration of Employee Central with third-party applications, using the example of Kronos Time Management to guide us.

The next chapter will showcase a few case studies for the Talent Hybrid deployment model using concepts discussed in Chapter 8 and APIs from Chapter 6. Talent Hybrid deployments can be implemented by exporting data into files from SAP ERP HCM in the format needed by SuccessFactors Talent Management modules and scheduling imports discussed in this chapter. Data can also be exchanged to support business processes through a middleware platform. The case studies in the next chapter use the latter mechanism for implementing Talent Hybrid packaged integrations.

In this chapter, we will look at individual case studies for implementing the Talent Hybrid integrations. Through step-by-step instructions and practical application, you will be able to grasp these implementation processes.

10 Implementing the Talent Hybrid Integrations

Once the Talent Hybrid deployment model is implemented, you can integrate individual SuccessFactors modules. SuccessFactors Talent Management solutions in the cloud can be integrated easily with SAP ERP HCM with the standard integration solutions for employee data, compensation, and recruiting processes using the SAP Process Integration (SAP PI) middleware tool. In addition, a single point of entry for the end users can be established by achieving Single Sign-On (SSO) between SAP ERP HCM and SuccessFactors.

Target Audience

The perfect candidates for the Talent Hybrid deployment model are existing SAP customers who utilize the SAP ERP HCM module to maintain core HR processes, such as organizational management and personnel administration, in their on-premise landscapes. For more information, see Chapter 4.

The following sections provide detailed, step-by-step case studies based on SAP best practices of how the standard process integration scenarios can be implemented to complete the integration between SAP ERP HCM and SuccessFactors using SAP PI for the following tasks:

- Implementation steps necessary to configure SAP PI to support particular integration scenarios (see Section 10.1)
- Employee data integration (see Section 10.2)
- Compensation process integration (see Section 10.3)

▶ Recruiting process integration (see Section 10.4)

▶ User authentication integration (see Section 10.5)

By following the integration steps that are provided within each of the cases studies, you will be guided through how to integrate and transfer data from SAP ERP HCM to SuccessFactors Talent Management Solutions, using SAP PI on-premise as the integration middleware.

Let's first begin by discussing the SAP PI integration steps involved.

10.1 Integration of SAP Process Integration

To begin the different integration scenarios of employee data, compensation, and recruiting, you'll first need to implement SAP PI to support these integrations. This section provides a case study that discusses the integration steps involved in implementing SAP PI.

> **Prerequisites**
>
> Prior to implementing SAP PI, you will need to check for and implement, if required, the following configurations:
>
> ▶ Have SAP PI 7.0 (at a minimum) or above running in your system landscape environment.
>
> ▶ Have the AXIS framework component deployed. The Integration Add-on solution in SAP PI uses the AXIS framework in the SOAP adapter for communicating with the SuccessFactors web services API. The AXIS framework component is not in the SAP PI standard installation. Refer to SAP Note 1039369 (FAQ XI Axis Adapter) for the component deployment guide.

Let's begin by looking at the case study parameters and client involved.

10.1.1 Case Study Parameters

This case study focuses on how a customer, who plans to set up SuccessFactors Talent Management Solutions to integrate with an existing SAP ERP HCM system, will implement SAP PI on-premise as the integration middleware. Specifically, we'll discuss the system requirements and implementation steps necessary to set up SAP PI. We'll use a client scenario to demonstrate our case to begin and then will look at the steps involved in the integration.

Client Scenario

MedTron Inc. is headquartered in Los Angeles, California, and has manufacturing sites across the United States and Canada—with over 3,000 employees in North America. Their presales team successfully sold the technical capabilities of integrating SuccessFactors Talent Management Solutions with SAP ERP HCM, using SAP PI as the integration middleware.

At this point, MedTron would like to implement SAP PI as the integration software for the following benefits:

▶ Automatic updating of HR data between two different systems to reduce data entry and errors

▶ Stable middleware-based data exchange with standard web services usage

▶ Secure data transfer with standardized security protocols

Once the SAP PI middleware is set up, MedTron will be able to implement the Talent Hybrid integration between SAP ERP HCM and SuccessFactors. The implementation of SAP PI is a prerequisite to enable employee data integration, compensation process integration, and recruiting process integration. MedTron will begin with the Performance Management module. In the future, the Talent Management Roadmap, which includes SuccessFactors Compensation, will be implemented in phase 2, followed by the Succession Planning module implementation in phase 3, and finally the Recruiting module in the phase 4 implementation work.

MedTron's existing IT footprint includes SAP ERP HCM ECC 6.0 EHP 6. MedTron currently runs Organizational Management (OM) and PA (Personnel Administration) in SAP. In addition, they also use SAP PI version 7.4 Java stack.

Process Overview

To set up the SAP PI middleware, follow these steps:

▶ **Step 1: Basic setup**
In this step, you'll look at the basic system configuration necessary for integration with SuccessFactors, with settings covered in both SAP PI and SAP ERP HCM (see Section 10.1.2).

▶ **Step 2: SAP ERP HCM integration setup**
This step covers the settings for the middleware you need to implement for SAP ERP HCM (see Section 10.1.3).

▶ **Step 3: SAP PI Integration Directory configuration**
This step describes the set up and configuration of the SAP PI Integration Directory. This will be used in relation to the different integration scenarios discussed later in the chapter (see Section 10.1.4).

▶ **Step 4: Creating communication channels**
In this step, you will create the integration channels shared by the employee data, compensation data, and recruiting data transfer (see Section 10.1.5).

▶ **Step 5: Creating the integration scenarios**
This step will help you create the integration scenarios for three of your integrations: employee data, compensation, and recruiting (see Section 10.1.6).

> **Important**
>
> Some Integration Add-on support package releases require specific versions of SAP PI to be installed, so you will need to check this in the release.

The following sections detail each of the processes in the preceding list.

10.1.2 Step 1: Basic Setup

This section describes the system configuration that is needed for SAP SuccessFactors integration, regardless of the scenario (such as employee data, compensation process, and recruiting process integration; see Section 10.1.6). The system configuration covers settings in SAP ERP HCM and SAP PI.

You will need knowledge of SAP Basis and SAP PI administration to perform the following system configuration tasks.

SAP PI Enterprise Services Repository Design Content Deployment

The following steps explain how to download and import objects for the SAP PI Enterprise Services Repository. In this step, the design object is delivered by SAP as part of the SuccessFactors Integration Add-on.

To download the design content, follow these steps:

1. Find the ESR content on the SAP Service Marketplace. Navigate to *http://service.sap.com/swdc*, and then go to SAP SOFTWARE DOWNLOAD CENTER • SUPPORT PACKAGES AND PATCHES • BROWSE OUR DOWNLOAD CATALOG • SAP CONTENT • ESR CONTENT (XI CONTENT).

2. Select XI CONTENT SFIHCM01 for implementing the Integration Add-on 1.0, which enables the employee data and compensation data integration scenarios. Or, select both XI CONTENT SFIHCM01 and XI CONTENT SFIHCM02 for implementing Integration Add-on 2.0 to enable the recruiting data integration scenario.

3. Click on the #DATABASE INDEPENDENT link to select the Integration Add-on support package level. Determine the desired support package level to use, and then download the XI content as a ZIP file.

4. Unzip the file. You should see a TPZ file in the unzipped folder.

Now that you have downloaded the content, you will want to import it. Complete the following steps to import the design content:

1. Open the SAP PI landing page by accessing the following URL: http://*<pi_hostname>:<pi_http_port>/dir*.

2. Open the Enterprise Services Builder tool within the Enterprise Service Repository by clicking on the ENTERPRISE SERVICES BUILDER link.

3. Navigate to the top menu, and click TOOLS • IMPORT DESIGN OBJECTS in the Enterprise Services Repository.

4. Select CLIENT as the import source.

5. Select the XI content TPZ file downloaded in the earlier step, then click IMPORT. Select IMPORT again when a warning message appears.

6. Once imported successfully, the new software component SFIHCM01 600 or both SFIHCM01 600 and SFIHCM02 600 should appear in the Enterprise Services Repository design objects list.

This completes your first task of step 1, downloading and importing objects for the SAP PI Enterprise Service Repository.

Now, let's move on to the next task in this step, which covers setting up the RFC destinations to connect SAP ERP HCM and SAP PI.

Set Up Connectivity between SAP ERP HCM and SAP PI

In the following steps, you will set up the RFC destinations in SAP ERP HCM to connect with SAP PI. The SuccessFactors Integration Add-on uses an ABAP proxy runtime interface for exchanging messages between SAP ERP HCM and the SAP PI integration server. Note that there are multiple subtasks needed to set up connectivity between SAP ERP HCM and SAP PI.

Proceed as follows:

1. Set up the HTTP destination from the SAP ERP HCM system to the SAP PI Integration Engine or Adapter Engine, depending on what type of installation you used for the SAP PI system.

2. Create an RFC destination type H to connect SAP ERP HCM to the SAP PI dual-stack system (ABAP and Java), or create an RFC destination type G to connect SAP ERP HCM to SAP PI AEX (Java single-stack system), or the Advanced Adapter Engine of SAP PI (7.11 or above). Access Transaction SM59, and perform the following substeps:

   ▶ Highlight connection type H (HTTP CONNECTIONS TO ABAP SYSTEM) or type G (HTTP CONNECTIONS TO EXTERNAL SERVER), and click on CREATE. Enter a description with the suggested name of "XI_Integration_Engine_<SID>" for type H or "XI_ADAPTER_ENGINE_<SID>" for type G.

   ▶ Maintain the following information on the TECHNICAL SETTINGS tab:

     – TARGET HOST: <Host name of SAP PI>

     – SERVICE NO.: <Port of SAP PI>

     – PATH PREFIX: */sap/xi/engine?type=entry* for connection type H for connecting the Integration Engine or */XISOAPAdapter/MessageServlet?ximessage=true* for connection type G for connecting the Advanced Adapter Engine.

   ▶ Maintain the following information on the LOGON AND SECURITY tab:

     – CLIENT: <Client number of SAP PI>

     – USER: PIAPPL<SID>

     – PASSWORD: <Password>

3. Save you entries, and test the connection by clicking on the CONNECTION TEST button. If the connection is successful, then you should be able to see HTTP response status 500 for the Integration Engine connection or HTTP response

status 200 for the Advanced Adapter Engine connection (see Figure 10.1 and Figure 10.2).

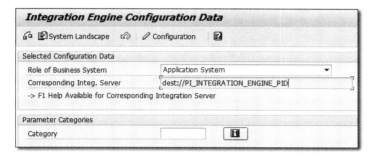

Figure 10.1 HTTP Connection—Integration Engine

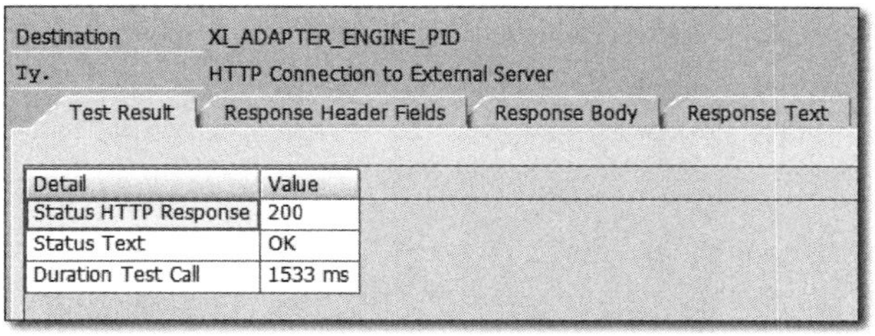

Figure 10.2 HTTP Connection—Adapter Engine

4. Set up the TCP/IP connection from SAP ERP HCM to the SAP PI system. The SAPSLDAPI connection is used by ABAP SLD API to read system landscape information from the SAP PI System Landscape Directory (SLD).

SAP PI AEX (Java Single Stack) Step

The following are optional steps for connecting SAP PI AEX (Java single stack):

1. Access Transaction SM59. Highlight connection type T (TCP/IP CONNECTION), and click on CREATE. Enter the RFC destination name "SAPSLDAPI".

2. Maintain the following information on the TECHNICAL SETTINGS tab:

   ▶ ACTIVATION TYPE: Select registered server program

   ▶ PROGRAM ID OF REGISTERED SERVER PROGRAM: SAPSLDAPI_<SID>

   ▶ GATEWAY HOST: <Gateway host name of SAP PI>

   ▶ GATEWAY SERVICE: <Gateway service of SAP PI>

3. Save your entries, and test the connection by clicking on the CONNECTION TEST button. If the connection is successful, then you won't be able to view any error messages in the test result.

5. Set up the TCP/IP connection from SAP ERP HCM to the SAP PI system. The LCRSAPRFC connection is used by ABAP SLD API to read system landscape information from the SAP PI SLD.

SAP PI AEX (Java Single Stack) Step

The following are optional steps for connecting to SAP PI AEX (Java single stack):

1. Access Transaction SM59. Highlight connection type T (TCP/IP CONNECTION), and click on CREATE. Enter the RFC destination name "LCRSAPRFC".

2. Maintain the following information on technical settings tab:
   ▶ ACTIVATION TYPE: Select registered server program
   ▶ PROGRAM ID OF REGISTERED SERVER PROGRAM: SAPSLDAPI_<SID>
   ▶ GATEWAY HOST: <Gateway host name of SAP PI>
   ▶ GATEWAY SERVICE: <Gateway service of SAP PI>

3. Save your entries, and test the connection by clicking on the CONNECTION TEST BUTTON. If the connection is successful, then you should be able to view the test result with HTTP response status 200 for the Advanced Adapter Engine connection.

6. Set up the HTTP connection from SAP ERP HCM to the SAP PI system. The SAP_PROXY_ESR connection is used to access the Enterprise Service Repository content of SAP PI. This is a mandatory step for connecting SAP PI AEX (Java single stack), and an optional step for those who use an SAP PI dual-stack system. Perform the following substeps:

   ▶ Access Transaction SM59.

   ▶ Highlight connection type G (HTTP CONNECTIONS TO EXTERNAL SERVER) and click on CREATE. Enter the RFC destination name "SAP_PROXY_ESR".

   ▶ Maintain the following information on the TECHNICAL SETTINGS tab:

      – TARGET HOST: <Host name of SAP PI>

      – SERVER NO.: <Port of SAP PI>

      – PATH PREFIX: */rep*; for connection type H for connecting the integration engine

- ▶ Maintain the following information on the LOGON AND SECURITY tab:
  - – USER: PIAPPL<SID>
  - – PASSWORD: <Password>
- ▶ Save your entries, and test the connection by clicking on the CONNECTION TEST button. If the connection is successful, you should not see any error messages in the test result.

You have just finished completing the multiple subtasks needed to set up connectivity between SAP ERP HCM and SAP PI.

Now, let's discuss the next task of this step, which is to define SLD access and register the SAP ERP HCM technical and business systems.

Integrating SAP ERP HCM into the SAP PI SLD

After you have completed setting up the RFC destinations, you are ready to further define the SLD access data and register the SAP ERP HCM technical system and business system in the SLD of SAP PI. Just like in the previous section, there are multiple subtasks required to integrate SAP ERP HCM into the SAP PI SLD. To access the SLD server, perform the following steps:

1. Access Transaction SLDAPICUST, switch to CHANGE mode, and create a new entry with the following information:
   - ▶ Select ACCESS TO SLD SERVER USING RFC or ACCESS TO SLD SERVER USING HTTP at your preference to configure the connection parameters:
     - – ALIAS NAME: <SID of SAP PI> e.g.: PID
     - – PRIM.: Select the checkbox
     - – HOST NAME: <Host name of SAP PI>
     - – PORT: <Port of SAP PI>
     - – USER: PIAPPL<SID>
     - – PASSWORD: <Password>
   - ▶ Save the entry.
2. Highlight the entry, and click TEST SLD CONNECTION. If the SLD connection is successful, you should able to see CONNECTION TO SLD WORKS CORRECTLY in the test results (see Figure 10.3).

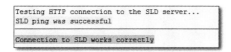

Testing HTTP connection to the SLD server...
SLD ping was successful

Connection to SLD works correctly

Figure 10.3 Confirmation Message

Next, we will register the SAP ERP HCM system in SLD. Perform the following steps:

1. Access Transaction RZ70, and maintain the following fields:

   ▸ GATEWAY HOST: <Gateway host name of SAP PI>

   ▸ GATEWAY SERVICE: <Gateway service of SAP PI>

2. Click on START SLD DATA COLLECTION AND JOB SCHEDULING, or press F5 .

3. To check the registration result, go to the SAP PI landing page at *http://<pi_host-name>:<pi_http_port>/dir*, then click on the SYSTEM LANDSCAPE DIRECTORY link and log on to the SLD. Click on TECHNICAL SYSTEM, then enter the SLD of the SAP ERP HCM system in the search filter. If the registration in the SLD was successful, then the technical system name of SAP ERP HCM should appear in the result table. If the technical system is not displayed in the SLD, then there was an issue during the registration of the SAP ERP HCM system in the SLD or during the maintenance of the SLD access data. Recheck these steps again to ensure that everything was performed as described here.

System Landscape Directory

If you want to send data to the SLD on a regular basis, choose SCHEDULED JOB by pressing F7 .

4. Next, select the SAP ERP HCM system name, then navigate to the BUSINESS SYSTEMS tab at bottom of the page. Check whether all of the available business system clients from SAP ERP HCM are displayed in the table. If the business systems are not displayed in the SLD, then you need to add the business systems manually.

5. On the same page, click on the ADD NEW BUSINESS SYSTEM button to begin the business system wizard. Add the following entries:

   ▸ SYSTEM: <technical system name of SAP ERP HCM system>

   ▸ CLIENT: <Choose the client you want to use as business system>

   ▸ URL: <blank>

6. Click on NEXT to proceed to the next step. Enter the name you want to give to your business system (e.g., EC6CLNT120), then click on NEXT again.

7. In the last step of the wizard, make the following entries:

   ▸ BUSINESS SYSTEM ROLE: <Choose APPLICATION SYSTEM from the list>

   ▸ RELATED INTEGRATION SERVER: <Choose the SAP PI system connecting to the SAP ERP HCM system>

8. Click on FINISH.

9. Check the SLD data access connection by accessing Transaction SLDCHECK. If the SLD connection is successful, then you should see the list of business systems that you registered in the SLD, including your newly registered SAP ERP HCM business system (see Figure 10.4).

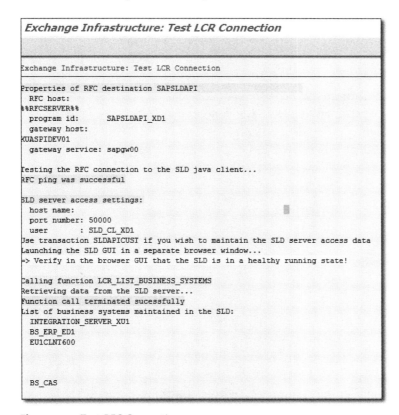

Figure 10.4 Test RFC Connection

You have now finished completing the multiple subtasks needed to integrate SAP ERP HCM into the SAP PI SLD.

Now, let's discuss the next task of this step, which is to configure and activate the local integration engine.

Configure and Activate Local Integration Engine

Now, you will connect the SAP ERP HCM business system with the local integration engine to the SAP PI Integration Engine or AEX (Advanced Adapter Engine). You will use the HTTP destination that you created in the Set Up Connectivity between SAP ERP HCM and SAP PI section. Access Transaction SXMB_ADM in SAP ERP HCM, and complete the following steps (see Figure 10.5):

1. Go to the CONFIGURATION section of the Integration Engine by opening the directory configuration. Double-click on the INTEGRATION ENGINE CONFIGURATION activity.

2. Choose EDIT • CHANGE GLOBAL CONFIGURATION DATA.

3. Select the APPLICATION SYSTEM option from the ROLE OF BUSINESS SYSTEM field. In the CORRESPONDING INTEG. SERVER field, enter *dest://<name of HTTP destination>*; here, *<name of HTTP destination>* refers to the HTTP destination in the Integration Engine or Advanced Adapter Engine that was previously created.

4. Save the entry.

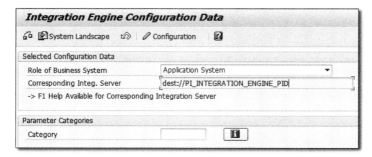

Figure 10.5 Integration Engine Configuration

You now know how to connect the SAP ERP HCM business system with the local integration engine to the SAP PI Integration Engine or AEX. Next, you will deploy SuccessFactors SSL certificates.

Deploy SuccessFactors SSL Certificates

Now, you will download the tenant certificate from the tenant API URL, then import it into the SAP PI Administration tool. The SuccessFactors Integration Add-on uses SSL connectivity for connecting SAP PI to the SuccessFactors tenant URL. In order to establish a secure SSL connectivity, the SuccessFactors tenant certificate needs to be downloaded. Note that there are multiple subtasks needed to deploy SuccessFactors SSL certificates.

Download the SuccessFactors tenant SSL certificates in the following steps:

1. Access the SuccessFactors tenant API URL in your Internet browser.
   Please contact your SuccessFactors consultant to obtain the SuccessFactors API endpoint URL.

Browser

The Google Chrome browser is used in our download example. You are able to use other browsers for the certificate download, but the procedures may be different from those described in this section.

2. Click on the LOCK button, then on CONNECTION • CERTIFICATE INFORMATION to view the certificate information (see Figure 10.6).

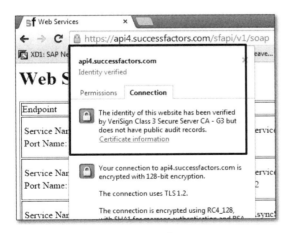

Figure 10.6 Connection to Certificate

3. Navigate to the DETAILS tab, and click on COPY TO FILE… (see Figure 10.7) to open the Certificate Export wizard.

Figure 10.7 Access Certificate Wizard

4. Select BASE 64 ENCODED X.509 format, and click on the NEXT button to save the certificate to a location as a CER file (see Figure 10.8 and Figure 10.9).

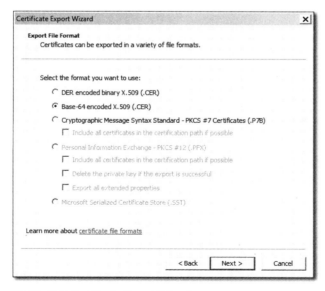

Figure 10.8 Certificate Export Wizard

Figure 10.9 Saving Certificate

After downloading the certificates, you will need to import them. Perform the following steps:

1. Access the SAP NetWeaver Administration of SAP PI via the following URL: *<Hostname>:<PI Http port>/nwa*.

2. Navigate to the CONFIGURATION tab, then to SECURITY • CERTIFICATES AND KEYS.

3. In the KEY STORAGE VIEWS table (KEYSTORE VIEWS in SAP PI 7.11), select the TRUSTEDCAs view name. Choose IMPORT ENTRY from the VIEW ENTRY DETAILS tab of TRUSTEDCAs. In the IMPORT ENTRY dialog box, select X.509 CERTIFICATE, and BROWSE to the location of the CER files downloaded in the previous section. Click on IMPORT. Rename the imported key to "*.successfactors.com" in the VIEW ENTRY DETAILS tab (see Figure 10.10).

Figure 10.10 Importing Certificates

This completes the step for downloading the tenant certificate from the tenant API URL and importing it into the SAP PI Administration tool. The next step covers checking the network firewall port.

Check Network Firewall Port 443 Connection

Some organizations block outgoing network port 443 by using a firewall due to network security concerns. To ensure that the SAP PI server is able to make an outgoing connection to the SuccessFactors tenant URL, check with your network security team whether port 443 is open for the SAP PI server to connect to the SuccessFactors tenant URL.

This concludes the checking of the network firewall port and all the steps required for basic setup of SAP PI. The next section will cover the steps for setting up the SAP ERP HCM integration.

10.1.3   Step 2: SAP ERP HCM Integration Setup

This section covers the settings for middleware that need to be implemented in SAP ERP HCM. You will need to set up API credentials and define the number of records for each package sent to SuccessFactors via SAP PI. There are the two tasks associated with this step: storing credentials for integration scenarios and the defining package size for data transfer.

In the SAP ERP HCM to SuccessFactors integration run, SAP ERP HCM sends API credentials to SAP PI. The same API credentials are mapped to the HTTPS header by SAP PI then forwarded to the SuccessFactors tenant URL for logon purposes. Let's begin.

Store Credentials for Integration Scenarios

In this step, you will enter API credentials for each integration scenario. Before completing this step, you will need to have logon information at hand, including company ID and the API user ID and password set up in SuccessFactors. Perform the following steps for each integration scenario:

1. To maintain the API logon credentials for employee data transfer, compensation data transfer, and recruiting data transfer, you will repeat this process three times. First, go to the IMG and access PERSONNEL MANAGEMENT • INTEGRA-

TION ADD-ON FOR SAP ERP HCM AND SUCCESSFACTORS BIZX • BASIC SETTINGS • SETTINGS FOR MIDDLEWARE.

2. For the employee data transfer step, click on STORE CREDENTIALS FOR TRANSFERRING EMPLOYEE DATA TO SECURE STORAGE. For the compensation data transfer step, click on STORE CREDENTIALS FOR TRANSFERRING COMPENSATION DATA TO SECURE STORAGE. For the recruiting data transfer step, click on STORE CREDENTIALS FOR TRANSFERRING RECRUITING DATA TO SECURE STORAGE.

3. For employee data, compensation, and recruiting data: enter the COMPANY ID, for example (acexbc), used by MedTron in SuccessFactors, the USER ID, for example (SAP_API_USER), of the SAP API user, and each related PASSWORD.

This completes all the subtasks needed to enter API credentials for each integration scenario. Next, you will enter the data transfer package size for each scenario you need to complete.

Define Package Size for Data Transfer

In this task, you will specify the number of records for each package sent to SuccessFactors via SAP PI. Proceed as follows:

1. To define the package size for transferring employee data, go to the IMG and access PERSONNEL MANAGEMENT • INTEGRATION ADD-ON FOR SAP ERP HCM AND SUCCESSFACTORS BIZX • BASIC SETTINGS • SETTINGS FOR MIDDLEWARE • DEFINE PACKAGE SIZE FOR TRANSFERRING EMPLOYEE DATA.

2. Enter a value of 200 to define a standard package size.

3. Repeat the same steps to define the package size for transferring compensation data, but instead click on DEFINE PACKAGE SIZE FOR TRANSFERRING COMPENSATION DATA at the end of the menu path.

4. Repeat the same steps to define the package size for transferring recruiting data, but instead click on DEFINE PACKAGE SIZE FOR RECRUITING DATA at the end of the menu path.

This concludes the set up for the SAP ERP HCM integration. You are now done with step 2. The next section will discuss the SAP PI Integration Directory configuration.

10.1.4 Step 3: SAP PI Integration Directory Configuration

This section describes the tasks required for setting up the SAP PI Integration Directory for the employee data, compensation data, and recruiting data integration scenarios.

For these tasks, you will need to access the INTEGRATION BUILDER link to start the Integration Directory from the SAP PI landing page: *<Hostname>:<PI HTTP port>/dir*.

Create a Communication Component and Assign a Business System

In this task, you will be creating a business component for SuccessFactors and assigning the SAP ERP HCM business system from the SLD in the SAP PI Integration Directory.

SAP ERP HCM Business System

If the SAP ERP HCM business system has been assigned in the Integration Directory, then you do not need to assign the SAP ERP HCM business system.

Make sure the necessary software components XI content SFIHCM01 600 and SFIHCM02 600 of the Integration Add-on are included as installed software in the SLD. Create the new product, and assign the SFIHCM01 600 and SFIHCM02 600 software components so that service interfaces can be used in the Integration Directory configuration. Begin by assigning the SAP ERP HCM business system:

1. Go to the top menu, and click on ENVIRONMENT • CLEAR SLD DATA CACHE to get updated information from the SLD. Then, also in the top menu, choose TOOLS • ASSIGN BUSINESS SYSTEM (see Figure 10.11).

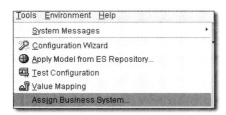

Figure 10.11 Assign Business System

2. Click on CONTINUE twice from the dialog box.

3. Select the corresponding SAP ERP HCM business system, and click on FINISH.

4. A summary appears. Close the dialog box, and save the entry. You should see the SAP ERP HCM business system appear under the Business System category.

Next, you'll want to create the SuccessFactors business component. To do so, perform the following steps:

1. Go to the Objects view, then right-click on Communication Component Without Party, and choose New Business Component.

2. In the dialog popup box, choose SuccessFactors as the Communication Component.

3. Click on Create, and then save the entry. You should see the SuccessFactors business component appear under the Business Component category (see Figure 10.12).

Figure 10.12 Check SuccessFactors Business Component

4. Open the SuccessFactors business component, and switch to Change mode. Add the following inbound interfaces on the Receiver tab, based on your Integration Add-on requirements (see Table 10.1, Table 10.2, and Table 10.3):

▸ Integration Add-on : 1.0

▸ Namespace: *http://sap.com/xi/SFIHCM01*

▸ Software Component Version: SFIHCM01 600

No.	Interface Name
1	SFSFCompensationManagementUpsertRequestConfirmation_In
2	SFSFQueryHandlingCancelJobQueryResponse_In
3	SFSFQueryHandlingGetJobResultEmbeddedQueryResponse_In
4	SFSFQueryHandlingGetJobStatusQueryResponse_In
5	SFSFQueryHandlingSubmitJobQueryResponse_In
6	SFSFSessionHandlingLoginQueryResult_In

Table 10.1 Integration Add-On 1.0

No.	Interface Name
7	SFSFSessionHandlingLogoutQueryResult_In
8	SFSFAPIDictionaryDescribeSFObjectsExResult_In
9	SFSFAPIDictionaryListSFObjectsResult_In
10	SFSFUserUpsertRequestConfirmation_In

Table 10.1 Integration Add-On 1.0 (Cont.)

- ▶ INTEGRATION ADD-ON: 2.0
- ▶ NAMESPACE: *http://sap.com/xi/SFIHCM02*
- ▶ SOFTWARE COMPONENT VERSION: SFIHCM02 600

No.	Interface Name
1	SFSFJobApplicationStatusUpdateRequestConfirmation_In
2	SFSFGenericUpsertRequestConfirmation_In
3	SFSFGenericUpdateRequestConfirmation_In
4	SFSFCandidateUserIdUpdateRequestConfirmation_In

Table 10.2 Integration Add-On 2.0

- ▶ INTEGRATION ADD-ON: 3.0
- ▶ NAMESPACE: *http://sap.com/xi/SFIHCM02*
- ▶ SOFTWARE COMPONENT VERSION: SFIHCM03 600

No.	Interface Name
1	SFSFGenericDeleteRequestConfirmation_In
2	SFSFGenericInsertRequestConfirmation_In
3	SFSFUserQueryRequest_In

Table 10.3 Integration Add-On 3.0

Note
If you are implementing the Integration Add-on 2.0, then the interface objects from both Integration Add-ons 1.0 and 2.0 need to be added.

This concludes step 3. Now, let's turn our attention to step 4, creating a communication channel.

10.1.5   Step 4: Create Communication Channel

This section covers the tasks required to create the SOAP sender and receiver communication channels for integration. In this step, you will be creating three communication channels, which are shared by the employee data, compensation data, and recruiting data transfers. The SuccessFactors Integration Add-on uses ABAP Proxy technology to integrate SAP ERP HCM with SAP PI. The web service SOAP protocol is used to integrate SAP PI with SuccessFactors. Let's begin.

Create a SOAP Sender Communication Channel

In this step, you will be creating a SOAP sender communication channel that is assigned to the SAP ERP HCM business system. This SOAP sender communication channel is then configured to receive proxy runtime requests from the SAP ERP HCM system for all data transfer scenarios.

To receive proxy runtime requests, the SOAP sender communication channel configuration is different depending on the SAP PI system installation. Dual stack or Java single stack can be used, or you can use the integration configuration method (classical configuration or AE integrated configuration).

To begin, you will need to check and then select the SAP ERP HCM business system in the OBJECT view, as follows:

1. Right-click on the communication channel, and choose NEW.

2. Choose SOAPSENDER for COMMUNICATION CHANNEL, and click on CREATE. For classical configuration (SAP PI dual-stack system), enter the field values seen in Figure 10.13 in the PARAMETERS and GENERAL tabs.

3. For the ADVANCED tab, in the ADAPTER-SPECIFIC MESSAGE ATTRIBUTES section, deselect SET ADAPTER-SPECIFIC MESSAGE ATTRIBUTES. Then, for the ADAPTER STATUS, set STATUS to ACTIVE.

4. For AAE integrated configuration (SAP PI Java single-stack system or SAP PI dual-stack system 7.1 or above), enter the field values seen in Figure 10.14 for the PARAMETERS and GENERAL tabs.

5. For the ADVANCED tab, in the ADAPTER-SPECIFIC MESSAGE ATTRIBUTES section, deselect SET ADAPTER-SPECIFIC MESSAGE ATTRIBUTES. Then, for the ADAPTER STATUS, set STATUS to ACTIVE.

6. Next, under the ACKNOWLEDGEMENTS HANDLING tab, HTTP DESTINATION (FROM NWA) should be UNFILLED.

Figure 10.13 SOAP Sender Parameters — Classic Configuration

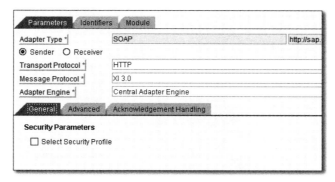

Figure 10.14 SOAP Sender Parameters — Integrated Configuration

This completes the task of creating of a SOAP sender communication channel. Next, you will create the SOAP receiver communication channel.

Create SOAP Receiver Communication Channel (for Logon Request)

In this step, you will create a SOAP receiver communication channel that is assigned to the SuccessFactors business component. This SOAP receiver communication channel is then configured to send API logon requests to the SuccessFactors tenant for all data transfer scenarios.

The SOAP receiver communication channel configuration for logon operations is different depending on the Integration Add-on support package releases. To begin, check for and select the SuccessFactors business component in the OBJECT view, as follows:

1. Right-click on the COMMUNICATION CHANNEL, and select NEW.

2. Choose SOAPRECEIVER or SOAPAXISRECEIVERLOGON for the COMMUNICATION CHANNEL, and click on CREATE.

3. Enter the parameters based on the Integration Add-on release. For Integration Add-on 1.0 (SP 4.0) and Integration Add-on 2.0 (SP 2.0), enter the field values shown in Figure 10.15 for the PARAMETERS and GENERAL tabs.

Figure 10.15 SOAP Receiver Parameters

▶ For the ADVANCED tab, in the ADAPTER-SPECIFIC MESSAGE ATTRIBUTES section, select both USE ADAPTER-SPECIFIC MESSAGE ATTRIBUTES and VARIABLE TRANSPORT BINDING. Then, in the VARIABLE HEADER (XHEADERNAME1), enter TServerLocation.

▶ Next, for the AUTHENTICATION KEYS section, unselect VIEW AUTHENTICATION KEYS. Set ADAPTER STATUS to ACTIVE.

4. For the Integration Add-on 1.0 (SP 6.0) or Integration Add-on 2.0 (SP 2.0), enter the field values seen in Figure 10.16 under the PARAMETERS tab. The handling of HTTP cookies has been enhanced in this Integration Add-on support package release. Hence, the SOAP AXIS protocol is used in the enhancement.

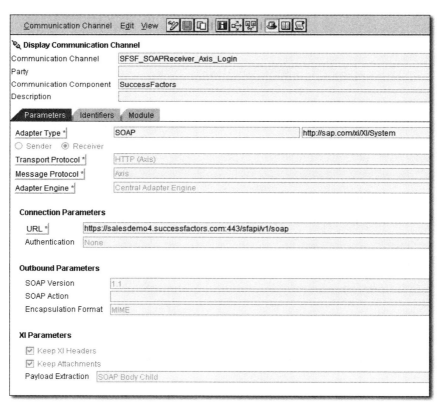

Figure 10.16 SOAP Receiver Parameters

5. Enter the values seen in Table 10.4 under the PROCESSING SEQUENCE section of the MODULE tab when creating the communication channel.

Processing Sequence			
No.	**Module Name**	**Type**	**Mod. Key**
1	AF_Adapters/axis/AFAdapterBean	Local Enterprise Bean	afreq
2	AF_Adapters/axis/HandlerBean	Local Enterprise Bean	xireq
3	AF_Adapters/axis/HandlerBean	Local Enterprise Bean	dcreq
4	AF_Adapters/axis/HandlerBean	Local Enterprise Bean	rem
5	AF_Adapters/axis/HandlerBean	Local Enterprise Bean	prop
6	AF_Adapters/axis/HandlerBean	Local Enterprise Bean	trp
7	AF_Adapters/axis/HandlerBean	Local Enterprise Bean	dcres
8	AF_Adapters/axis/HandlerBean	Local Enterprise Bean	dcres2
9	AF_Adapters/axis/HandlerBean	Local Enterprise Bean	xires
10	AF_Adapters/axis/AFAdapterBean	Local Enterprise Bean	afres
Module Configuration			
Mod. Key	**Parameter Name**	**Parameter Value**	
dcreq	handler.type	java:com.sap.aii.axis.xi. XI30DynamicConfigurationHandler	
dcres	handler.type	java:com.sap.aii.axis.xi. XI30DynamicConfigurationHandler	
dcres	key.a	read http://sap.com/xi/ System/HTTP SetCookie	
dcres	location.a	header	
dcres	value.b	Set-Cookie	
dcres2	key.a	write http://sap.com/xi/ System/HTTP Cookie2	
dcres2	location.a	header	
dcres2	value.b	Set-Cookie2	
prop	handle.type	java:com.sap.aii.axis.soap. HeaderRemovalHandler	
prop	key.1	set axis.transport.version	
prop	value.1	1.1	

Table 10.4 SOAP Module Configuration

Module Configuration		
Mod. Key	**Parameter Name**	**Parameter Value**
rem	handler.type	java:com.sap.aii.axis.soap.HeaderRemovalHandler
rem	namespace	http://sap.com/xi/XI/Message/30
trp	handler.type	java:com.sap.aii.adapter.axis.ra.transport.http.HTTPSender
trp	http.proxyHost	
trp	http.proxyPort	
trp	module.pivot	TRUE
xireq	handler.type	java:com.sap.aii.axis.xi.XI30OutboundHandler
xires	handler.type	java:com.sap.aii.axis.xi.XI30OutboundHandler

Table 10.4 SOAP Module Configuration (Cont.)

This concludes the task of creating a SOAP receiver communication channel. Next, you will create the SOAP AXIS receiver communication channel, which is used for query, upsert, and logout requests.

Create the SOAP AXIS Receiver Communication Channel

In this task, you will create the SOAP AXIS receiver communication channel that is assigned to the SuccessFactors business component. This SOAP AXIS receiver communication channel is then configured to send query, upsert, and logout requests to the SuccessFactors tenant for all of the data transfer scenarios.

To begin, check for and select the SuccessFactors business component in the OBJECT view. Now, perform the following steps:

1. Right-click on the communication channel, and choose NEW.

2. Choose SOAPAxisReceiver for the COMMUNICATION CHANNEL field, and click on CREATE.

3. Enter the fields as seen in Figure 10.17 under the PARAMETERS tab.

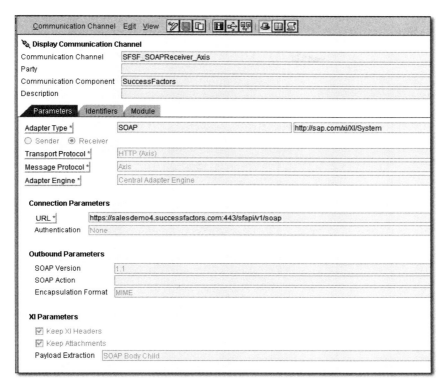

Figure 10.17 SOAP AXIS Receiver Parameters

4. Enter the details provided in Table 10.5 under the PROCESSING SEQUENCE section of the MODULE tab when creating the communication channel.

No.	Module Name	Type	Mod. Key
Processing Sequence			
1	AF_Adapters/axis/AFAdapterBean	Local Enterprise Bean	afreq
2	AF_Adapters/axis/HandlerBean	Local Enterprise Bean	xireq
3	AF_Adapters/axis/HandlerBean	Local Enterprise Bean	dcreq
4	AF_Adapters/axis/HandlerBean	Local Enterprise Bean	rem
5	AF_Adapters/axis/HandlerBean	Local Enterprise Bean	trp
6	AF_Adapters/axis/HandlerBean	Local Enterprise Bean	xires
7	AF_Adapters/axis/AFAdapterBean	Local Enterprise Bean	afres

Table 10.5 SOAP Axis Receiver Module

Module Configuration		
Mod. Key	**Parameter Name**	**Parameter Value**
dcreq	handler.type	java:com.sap.aii.axis.xi.XI30DynamicConfigurationHandler
dcreq	key.a	write http://sap.com/xi/System/HTTP SetCookie
dcreq	location.a	header
dcreq	value.b	Cookie
rem	handler.type	java:com.sap.aii.axis.soap.HeaderRemovalHandler
rem	namespace	http://sap.com/xi/XI/Message/30
trp	handler.type	java:com.sap.aii.adapter.axis.ra.transport.http.HTTPSender
trp	http.proxyHost	\<proxy host if necessary\>
trp	http.proxyPort	\<proxy port if necessary\>
trp	module.pivot	TRUE
xireq	handler.type	java:com.sap.aii.axis.xi.XI30OutboundHandler
xires	handler.type	java:com.sap.aii.axis.xi.XI30OutboundHandler

Table 10.5 SOAP Axis Receiver Module (Cont.)

This concludes the final creation of communication channels for the integration in step 4. In step 5, you'll create the integration scenarios for the employee data, compensation, and recruiting scenarios.

10.1.6 Step 5: Create Integration Scenarios

This section covers the integration scenario configuration for basic employee data, compensation, and recruiting, which are set up using the SAP PI Integration Directory. At a minimum, the basic employee data transfer scenario must be configured for the SAP to SuccessFactors integration. The basic employee data transfer scenario acts as a baseline for the compensation and recruiting scenarios.

Pre-configuration Check

Before you begin configuration in the SAP PI Integration Directory, make sure that the XI content SFIHCM01 and SFIHCM02 are deployed as described in the SAP PI Enterprise Services Repository Design Content Deployment section.

The first task associated with this step addresses how to complete the employee data scenario.

Create the Employee Data Scenario

Configure the employee data integration scenario based on the standard Enterprise Service Repository objects delivered by SAP as part of the Integration Add-on 1.0 (XI content SFIHCM01).

You have a choice between using integrated configuration or the SAP PI Integration Directory classic configuration for setting up the employee data scenario, depending on your SAP PI installation and your implementation strategy. There are three service interfaces delivered for the employee data transfer. Each of interface must be configured in the SAP PI Integration Directory as shown in Table 10.6.

Interface No.	SAP_ERP (Sender Action)	Sender Channel	Receiver Channel	SuccessFactors (Receiver Action)
1	SFSFSessionHandlingLoginQueryResult_Out	<SOAPSender>	<SOAPReceiver> or <SOAPAxisReceiver_login>	SFSFSessionHandlingLoginQueryResult_In
2	SFSFUserUpsertRequestConfirmation_Out	<SOAPSender>	<SOAPAxisReceiver>	SFSFUserUpsertRequestConfirmation_In
3	SFSFSessionHandlingLogoutQueryResult_Out	<SOAPSender>	<SOAPAxisReceiver>	SFSFSessionHandlingLogoutQueryResult_In

Table 10.6 Interfaces to Configure for the SAP PI Integration Directory

The following steps cover the integration configuration method (option 1):

1. Right-click on CONFIGURATION SCENARIO in the object tree, and click on NEW to create a new configuration scenario. In the CREATE OBJECT view, enter the data shown in Figure 10.18, and then click on CREATE.

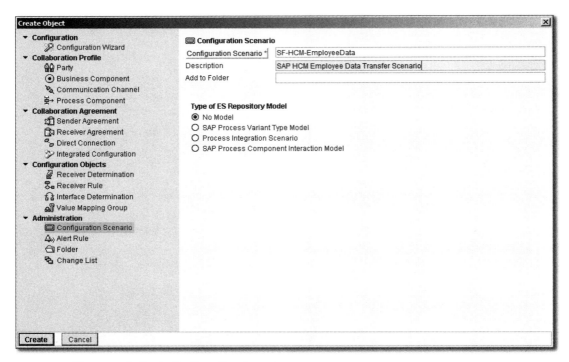

Figure 10.18 Create Configuration Scenario

2. In the EDIT CONFIGURATION SCENARIO screen, navigate to the OBJECT tab (see Figure 10.19), and choose CREATE OBJECT to create the first interface operation, SFSFSessionHandlingLoginQueryResult_Out.

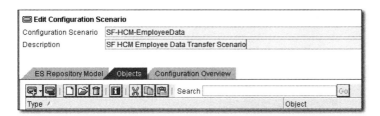

Figure 10.19 Create Object

3. Next, select INTEGRATED CONFIGURATION, in the dropdown menu and enter the following data, and then click on CREATE:

► COMMUNICATION PARTY: <blank>

► COMMUNICATION COMPONENT: <SAP ERP HCM system>

► INTERFACE: SFSFSessionHandlingLoginQueryResult_Out

► NAMESPACE: http://sap.com/xi/SFIHCM01

4. On the next screen, enter the data as displayed in Table 10.7.

Inbound Processing Tab	Field Value
COMMUNICATION CHANNEL	SOAPSENDER
SCHEMA VALIDATION	No validation
Receiver Tab	**Field Value**
CONDITION	blank
COMMUNICATION PARTY	blank
COMMUNICATION COMPONENT	SUCCESSFACTORS
Receiver Interfaces Tab	**Field Values**
CONDITION	blank
OPERATION MAPPING	SFSFSESSIONHANDLINGLOGINQUERYRESULT_OUT_TO_ SFSFSESSIONHANDLINGLOGINQUERYRESULT_IN
NAME	SFSFSESSIONHANDLINGLOGINQUERYRESULT_IN
NAMESPACE	HTTP://SAP.COM/XI/SFIHCM01
SOFTWARE COMPONENT VERSION	SFIHCM01 600
Outbound Processing Tab	**Field Values**
COMMUNICATION CHANNEL	SOAPRECEIVER or SOAPAXISRECEIVERLOGIN
SCHEMA VALIDATION	No validation (in PI7.30 and above)

Table 10.7 Specify SOAP Communication Channel

You have now successfully completed the first option.

Outbound Processing

Under the OUTBOUND PROCESSING tab, use communication channel SOAPRECEIVER if you are implementing Integration Add-on 1.0 SP 4.0; otherwise, use communication channel SOAPAXISRECEIVERLOGIN.

If your version of SAP PI does not support integrated configuration, then configuration can be done via the Integration Directory classic configuration method. The following steps cover the classic configuration method (option 2):

1. Create a new configuration scenario, as described in step 1 of option 1. Next, look at the steps ahead for creating the sender agreement, receiver determination, interface determination, and receiver agreement.

2. In the EDIT CONFIGURATION SCENARIO screen, navigate to the OBJECT tab, and choose CREATE OBJECT to create the sender agreement operation SFSFSessionHandlingLoginQueryResult_Out.

3. Select SENDER AGREEMENT, and enter the data as shown in Figure 10.20.

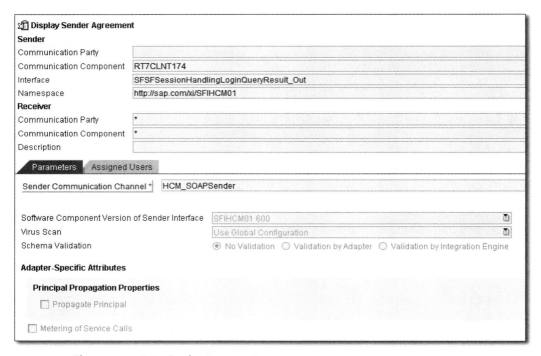

Figure 10.20 Enter Sender Agreement

4. Click on CREATE and then on SAVE.

5. Return to the EDIT CONFIGURATION SCENARIO screen, and navigate once again to the OBJECT tab. Click on CREATE OBJECT to create the receiver determination operation, SFSFSessionHandlingLoginQueryResult_Out.

6. Select the RECEIVER DETERMINATION, and enter the data as shown in Figure 10.21.

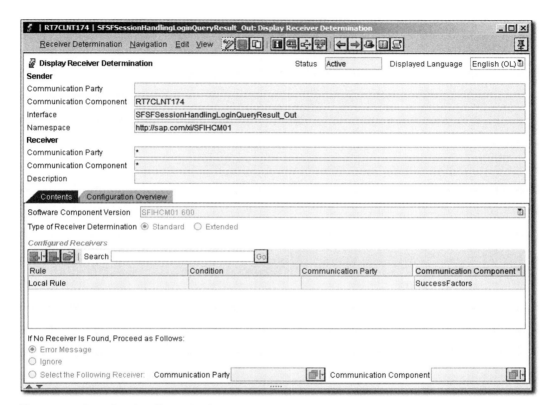

Figure 10.21 Enter Receiver Determination

7. Click on CREATE and then on SAVE.

8. Return to the EDIT CONFIGURATION SCENARIO screen, then navigate to the OBJECT tab, and choose CREATE OBJECT to create the interface determination operation, SFSFSessionHandlingLoginQueryResult_Out.

9. Select INTERFACE DETERMINATION, and enter the data as shown in Figure 10.22.

10. Click on CREATE and then on SAVE.

11. Return to the EDIT CONFIGURATION SCENARIO screen, and navigate to the OBJECT tab. Click on CREATE OBJECT to create the receiver agreement operation, SFSFSessionHandlingLoginQueryResult_In.

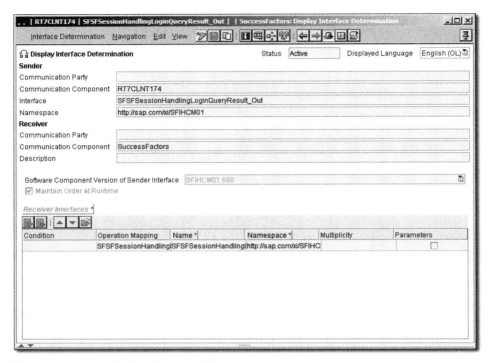

Figure 10.22 Enter Interface Determination

12. Select RECEIVER AGREEMENT, and enter the data as shown in Figure 10.23.

Receiver Communication Channel

In the RECEIVER COMMUNICATION CHANNEL field, choose communication channel SOAPRECEIVER if you are implementing Integration Add-on 1.0 SP 6.0; otherwise, use communication channel SOAPAXISRECEIVERLOGIN.

13. Click on CREATE and then on SAVE.

14. Repeat the integrated configuration method (option 1) or the classic configuration method (option 2) for the sender agreement, receiver determination, interface determination, and receiver agreement configuration steps for your other interfaces, as shown in Table 10.8, for the remaining employee data transfer interfaces. Choose the communication channel SOAPAXISRECEIVER and the corresponding operations mapping for each interface in the RECEIVER INTERFACE tab.

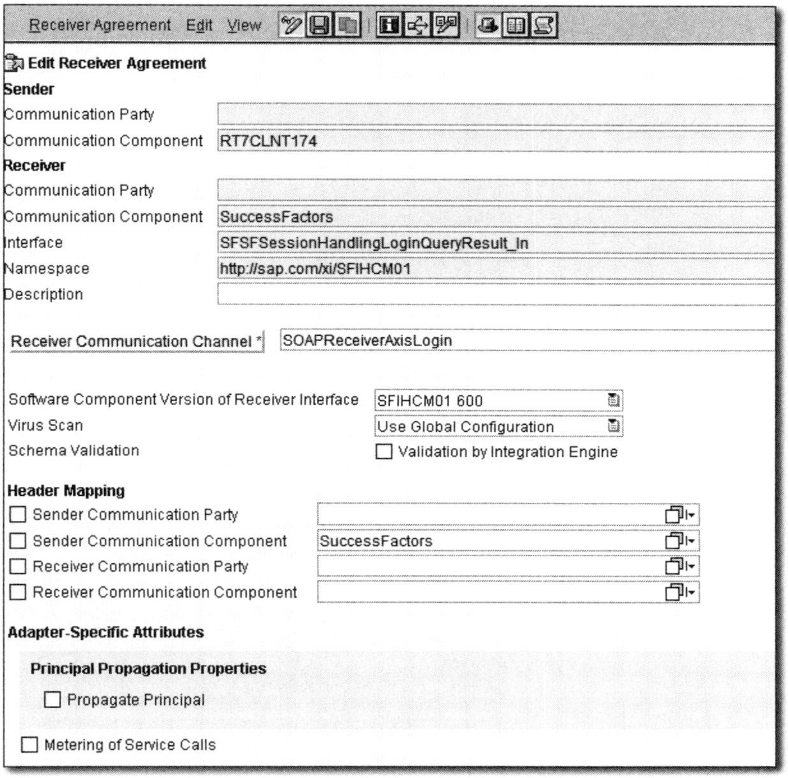

Figure 10.23 Enter Receiver Agreement

Interface No.	SAP_ERP (Sender Action)	Sender Channel	Receiver Channel	SuccessFactors (Receiver Action)
2	SFSFUserUp-sertRequestCon-firmation_Out	<SOAPSender>	<SOAPAxisRe-ceiver>	SFSFUserUp-sertRequestCon-firmation_In
3	SFSFSessionHan-dlingLogoutQue-ryResult_Out	<SOAPSender>	<SOAPAxisRe-ceiver>	SFSFSessionHan-dlingLogoutQue-ryResult_In

Table 10.8 Remaining Employee Data Scenario Interface List to Configure

This concludes the tasks required to set up the employee data scenario in the SAP PI Integration Directory. We will cover the compensation data scenario next.

Create Compensation Data Scenario

This section covers the configuration of the compensation data integration scenario, based on the SAP standard Enterprise Service Repository objects delivered by SAP as part of Integration Add-on 1.0 (XI content SFIHCM01).

You can either use the SAP PI Integration Directory classic configuration or the integrated configuration for setting up the compensation data scenario, depending on your SAP PI installation and your system requirements. There are nine service interfaces delivered for the compensation data transfer, each of which must be configured in the SAP Integration Directory. The employee data scenario is the baseline for the compensation data scenario, so ensure that you have completed the employee data scenario configuration. Perform the following steps:

1. Right-click on CONFIGURATION SCENARIO in the object tree, and click on NEW to create a new configuration scenario.

2. In the CREATE OBJECT view, enter the data seen in Figure 10.24, then click on CREATE.

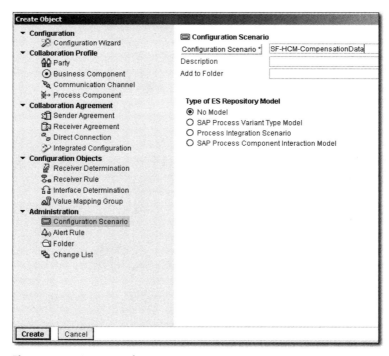

Figure 10.24 Create Configuration Scenario—Compensation Data

3. For the remainder of the configuration steps, refer to the employee data scenario configuration section (Section 10.2). Repeat the option 1 (integrated configuration method) step. Otherwise, repeat the option 2 (classic configuration method) sender agreement, receiver determination, interface determination, and receiver agreement steps, for every compensation data scenario interface described in Table 10.9.

4. Use the communication channel `SOAPReceiver` or `SOAPAxisReceiver_login` for the first interface and `SOAPAxisReceiver` for subsequent interfaces. Assign corresponding operations mappings for each interface in the RECEIVER INTERFACE tab. Refer to Table 10.9 for the steps to be entered.

Interface No.	SAP_ERP (Sender Action)	Sender Channel	Receiver Channel	SuccessFactors (Receiver Action)
1	SFSFSessionHandlingLoginQueryResult_Out	\<SOAPSender\>	\<SOAPReceiver\> or \<SOAPAxisReceiver_login\>	SFSFSessionHandlingLoginQueryResult_In
2	SFSFQueryHandlingSubmitJobQueryResponse_Out	\<SOAPSender\>	\<SOAPAxisReceiver\>	SFSFQueryHandlingSubmitJobQueryResponse_In
3	SFSFQueryHandlingGetJobStatusQueryResponse_Out	\<SOAPSender\>	\<SOAPAxisReceiver\>	SFSFQueryHandlingGetJobStatusQueryResponse_In
4	SFSFQueryHandlingGetJobResultEmbeddedQueryResponse_Out	\<SOAPSender\>	\<SOAPAxisReceiver\>	SFSFQueryHandlingGetJobResultEmbeddedQueryResponse_In
5	SFSFQueryHandlingCancelJobQueryResponse_Out	\<SOAPSender\>	\<SOAPAxisReceiver\>	SFSFQueryHandlingCancelJobQueryResponse_In
6	SFSFCompensationManagementUpsertRequestConfirmation_Out	\<SOAPSender\>	\<SOAPAxisReceiver\>	SFSFCompensationManagementUpsertRequestConfirmation_In

Table 10.9 Remaining Compensation Data Scenario Interfaces to Configure

Interface No.	SAP_ERP (Sender Action)	Sender Channel	Receiver Channel	SuccessFactors (Receiver Action)
7	SFSFAPIDic-tionaryDe-scribeSFOb-jectsExRe-sult_Out	\<SOAPSender>	\<SOAPAxisRe-ceiver>	SFSFAPIDic-tionaryDes-cribeSFOb-jectsExRe-sult_In
8	SFSFAPIDictio-naryListSFOb-jectsResult_Out	\<SOAPSender>	\<SOAPAxisRe-ceiver>	SFSFAPIDictio-naryListSFOb-jectsResult_In
9	SFSFSessionHan-dlingLogoutQue-ryResult_Out	\<SOAPSender>	\<SOAPAxisRe-ceiver>	SFSFSessionHan-dlingLogoutQue-ryResult_In

Table 10.9 Remaining Compensation Data Scenario Interfaces to Configure (Cont.)

This concludes the tasks required to set up the compensation data scenario in the SAP PI Integration Directory. Next, we will cover the recruiting data scenario.

Create Recruiting Data Scenario

In this step, you will configure the recruiting data integration scenario, based on the standard Enterprise Service Repository objects delivered by SAP as part of Integration Add-on 2.0 (XI content SFIHCM02).

You can choose to either use the SAP PI Integration Directory classic configuration or the integrated configuration to set up the recruiting data scenario, depending on your SAP PI installation and your system requirements. There are 11 service interfaces delivered for the recruiting data transfer, each of which must be configured in the SAP PI Integration Directory. The employee data scenario is the baseline for the recruiting data scenario, so ensure that you have completed the employee data scenario configuration.

Proceed as follows:

1. Right-click on CONFIGURATION SCENARIO in the object tree, and click on NEW to create a new configuration scenario.

2. In the CREATE OBJECT view, enter the data as shown in Figure 10.25, then click on CREATE.

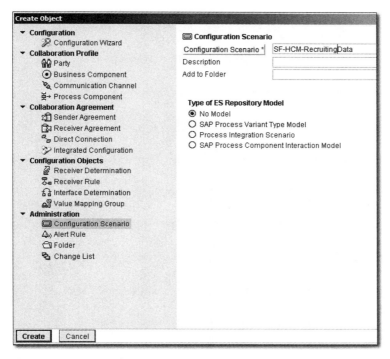

Figure 10.25 Create Object—Recruiting Data

3. To continue configuration, refer to the Create the Employee Data Scenario section. Repeat the integrated configuration method steps. Otherwise, repeat the classic configuration method for every recruiting data scenario interface, as described in Table 10.10.

Interface No	SAP_ERP (Sender Action)	Sender Channel	Receiver Channel	SuccessFactors (Receiver Action)
1	SFSFSessionHan-dlingLoginQue-ryResult_Out	\<SOAPSender\>	\<SOAPRe-ceiver\> or \<SOAPAxisRe-ceiver_login\>	SFSFSessionHan-dlingLoginQue-ryResult_In
2	SFSFQueryHan-dlingSub-mitJobQueryRe-sponse_Out	\<SOAPSender\>	\<SOAPAxisRe-ceiver\>	SFSFQueryHan-dlingSub-mitJobQueryRe-sponse_In

Table 10.10 Remaining Recruiting Data Scenario Interfaces to Configure

Interface No	SAP_ERP (Sender Action)	Sender Channel	Receiver Channel	SuccessFactors (Receiver Action)
3	SFSFQueryHan-dlingGetJobSta-tusQueryRe-sponse_Out	<SOAPSender>	<SOAPAxisRe-ceiver>	SFSFQueryHan-dlingGetJobSta-tusQueryRe-sponse_In
4	SFSFQueryHan-dlingGetJobRe-sultEmbed-dedQueryRe-sponse_Out	<SOAPSender>	<SOAPAxisRe-ceiver>	SFSFQueryHan-dlingGetJobRe-sultEmbed-dedQueryRe-sponse_In
5	SFSFJobApplica-tionStatusUp-dateRequestCon-firmation_Out	<SOAPSender>	<SOAPAxisRe-ceiver>	SFSFJobApplica-tionStatusUp-dateRequestCon-firmation_In
6	SFSFAPIDictio-naryListSFOb-jectsResult_Out	<SOAPSender>	<SOAPAxisRe-ceiver>	SFSFAPIDictio-naryListSFOb-jectsResult_In
7	SFSFAPIDic-tionaryDe-scribeSFOb-jectsExRe-sult_Out	<SOAPSender>	<SOAPAxisRe-ceiver>	SFSFAPIDic-tionaryDe-scribeSFOb-jectsExRe-sult_In
8	SFSFSessionHan-dlingLogoutQue-ryResult_Out	<SOAPSender>	<SOAPAxisRe-ceiver>	SFSFSessionHan-dlingLogoutQue-ryResult_In
9	SFSFGenericUp-sertRequestCon-firmation_Out	<SOAPSender>	<SOAPAxisRe-ceiver>	SFSFGenericUp-sertRequestCon-firmation_In
10	SFSFCandi-dateUserIdUp-dateRequestCon-firmation_Out	<SOAPSender>	<SOAPAxisRe-ceiver>	SFSFCandi-dateUserIdUp-dateRequestCon-firmation_In
11	SFSFGenericUp-sertRequestCon-firmation_Out	<SOAPSender>	<SOAPAxisRe-ceiver>	SFSFGenericUp-sertRequestCon-firmation_In

Table 10.10 Remaining Recruiting Data Scenario Interfaces to Configure (Cont.)

4. Use the communication channel `SOAPReceiver` or `SOAPAxisReceiver_login` for the first interface and `SOAPAxisReceiver` for subsequent interfaces. Assign the corresponding operations mappings for each interface in the RECEIVER INTERFACE tab. Refer to Table 10.10 for the steps to be entered.

This concludes the configuration of integration scenarios setup in the SAP PI Integration Directory and the SAP PI integration case study. We covered the steps involved in implementing the middleware between SAP ERP HCM and SuccessFactors. Once the SAP PI middleware is set up, MedTron will be able to implement the remaining Talent Hybrid integration scenarios. Remember, the implementation of SAP PI is a prerequisite to enable the employee data, compensation process, and recruiting process integrations.

10.2 Employee Data Integration

In this section, we will discuss the employee data integration scenario, using a case study as our guide for application. Specifically, we'll look at the implementation steps necessary for both SAP ERP and SuccessFactors to implement the employee data integration.

Prerequisites

Prior to implementing the SuccessFactors employee data integration with SAP ERP HCM, you will need to complete the following relevant configurations:

▶ Have both the SAP ERP HCM and SAP PI systems with the latest Integration Add-on deployed and configured.

▶ Have the following system minimum requirements prior to implementing the latest Integration Add-on:

  ▶ SAP ERP Human Capital Management (SAP ERP HCM), SAP ERP 6.0 SPS 15 or higher

  ▶ SAP HANA Cloud Integration or one of the following versions or higher of SAP Process Integration:

    – SAP PI 7.1 EHP1 SP 08 (minimum requirement for dual-stack deployment)

    – SAP PI 7.3 SP 05 (minimum requirement for Java-only deployment)

    – SAP PI 7.31 SP 04 (minimum requirement for Java-only deployment)

    – SAP PI 7.4 SP 04

  ▶ SuccessFactors Talent Solutions 1402

> ▶ Have relevant access to SAP ERP HCM, with a sufficient authorization role for the configuration activities in SAP IMG, ABAP development, and background job scheduler, as well as access to the SuccessFactors Provisioning and Administration page.
>
> ▶ Have your IT network configured to enable communication through firewalls between SuccessFactors Talent Management and SAP PI.

First, we will look at the parameters of our case study, including the client scenario. Then, we will cover what the process for this integration will entail and the steps we can expect to go through to complete the case study.

10.2.1 Case Study Parameters

This case study focuses on the employee data integration using best practices and how a customer that desires to implement SuccessFactors Talent Management Solutions will integrate and transfer its employee data from SAP ERP HCM to SuccessFactors Talent Management Solutions, using SAP PI on-premise as the integration middleware.

Client Scenario

MedTron has become increasingly interested in SuccessFactors, because it is looking to lessen IT configuration support and have its system be more user maintained while providing a more positive user experience. Over time, MedTron wishes to have modules to exchange and build on data—in hopes of bringing employees closer to their HR data.

At this point, MedTron would like to implement the SuccessFactors Talent Management Solutions—beginning with the Performance Management module. In the future, the Talent Management Roadmap, which includes Compensation, will be implemented in phase 2, followed by the Succession Planning module implementation in phase 3 and the SuccessFactors Recruiting module in the phase 4 implementation work.

MedTron's existing IT footprint includes SAP ERP HCM ECC 6.0 EHP 6. MedTron currently runs OM and PA in SAP. In addition, MedTron also uses SAP PI version 7.4 Java stack.

To effectively integrate and transfer the employee data, the team recognizes that the technical consultant will need to have a solid understanding of the basic settings of the Talent Hybrid integration with SAP ERP HCM and the necessary

Integration Add-ons and system requirements to make the integration successful. The biggest challenge will be to keep the systems and HCM data in sync between SAP ERP HCM and SuccessFactors.

With a successful integration, the benefits of moving to the cloud will include an easy and fast deployment of SuccessFactors Talent Management Solutions, as well as the ability to leverage standard Integration Add-ons delivered by SAP to ensure that the data is in sync between SuccessFactors and SAP ERP HCM. To ensure that the integration is successful, there are certain business requirements needed to guarantee a smooth transfer of data.

For example, there needs to be a single source of employee data from SAP ERP HCM. In addition, the employee profile and user data need to be created from SAP ERP HCM data (the USER ID field is the SAP Central Person [CP]). Finally, there must be a change of mapping of location to the SAP address infotype (IT0006).

To integrate and transfer employee data from SAP ERP HCM to SuccessFactors Talent Management Solutions using SAP PI middleware, the following steps must be executed:

1. Ensure that baseline integration configuration settings were made for SAP ERP HCM and for SuccessFactors employee data integration by defining authorizations in SAP ERP HCM to access the new integration transactions.
2. For setting the middleware, set the installation and configuration of SAP PI as an integration point between SAP ERP HCM and SuccessFactors Talent Management Solutions.

Process Overview

SAP ERP HCM on-premise and SuccessFactors Talent Management Solutions in the cloud serve as two different systems; therefore, integrating SAP ERP HCM with SuccessFactors Talent Management Solutions enables data consistency between two systems as part of Talent Management.

There are four main steps that are required to integrate and transfer employee data from SAP ERP HCM to SuccessFactors Talent Management Solutions. These are as follows:

▶ **Step 1: Basic setup**
   In this step, you will need to complete the baseline integration configuration necessary for implementation. This includes defining authorizations in SAP

ERP HCM, settings for middleware, and creating an SAP PI employee data scenario (see Section 10.2.2).

▶ **Step 2: SAP ERP HCM configuration**
The next step entails setting up the SAP ERP HCM configuration, which has a variety of tasks that need to be performed, from defining name formats for fields to enhancing employee data extraction with BAdI implementations (see Section 10.2.3).

▶ **Step 3: SuccessFactors configuration**
The SuccessFactors configuration steps for employee data integration include everything from activating the SuccessFactors APIs to the creation of the API user (see Section 10.2.4).

▶ **Step 4: SAP PI middleware setup**
For step 4, you will need to set up the SAP PI middleware. Therefore, refer to Section 10.1 for a detailed description.

In this section, we'll highlight the necessary information for customers using the Talent Hybrid deployment model to run SAP ERP HCM for Personnel Administration and Organization Management, as well as benefits, time, and payroll and SuccessFactors Talent Management Solutions. The employee data integration scenario must be in place prior to implementing the other integration scenarios for compensation and recruiting.

The following basic implementation steps help to kick start the integration efforts for employee data integration. Let's begin with the fundamentals that will allow these two systems to talk with one another.

10.2.2 Step 1: Basic Setup

There is a baseline integration configuration that is required along with an SAP ERP HCM configuration for setting up SuccessFactors employee data integration. This baseline system configuration covers settings from SAP ERP HCM and SAP PI. To complete the basic setup, you'll need to perform the following tasks:

▶ Define authorizations in SAP ERP HCM

▶ Set up middleware

▶ Create an SAP PI employee data scenario

Let's begin.

Define Authorization in SAP ERP HCM

To begin our basic setup, first we'll need to define the authorization for the Integration Add-on for SAP ERP HCM and SuccessFactors Talent Solutions. To do this, you'll define the role SAP_HR_SFI_EMPL_DATA_REPL, which comprises the authorizations that a user needs to run the following reports for extracting employee data to SuccessFactors Talent Solutions:

► **RH_SFI_TRIGGER_EMPL_DATA_REPL**
  Extract employee data for SuccessFactors

► **RH_SFI_SYNCHRONIZE_EMPL_DATA**
  Sync employee data with SuccessFactors

► **RH_SFI_WITHDRAW_VARIANT**
  Discontinue data extraction for a group of employees

The role SAP_HR_SFI_EMPL_DATA_REPL is assigned to a composite role, SAP_HR_SFI_C2, which contains other authorization roles that a user needs for compensation and recruiting data transfer as part of the Integration Add-on. You may use it as a template to define authorizations that suit your requirements. Access Transaction PFCG to define roles. Copy the template role SAP_HR_SFI_EMPL_DATA_REPL to a customer role and edit it according to your requirement.

You have now defined authorizations in SAP ERP HCM. The next step in completing the basic setup for configuring the baseline integration is to setup the middleware. Let's discuss this now.

Set Up the Middleware

To set the middleware, configure SuccessFactors API user logon information, and define the package size for transferring employee data in the SAP ERP HCM system. In this step, specify the number of employees for whom data will be transferred each time the web services for transferring employee data from SAP ERP to SuccessFactors Talent Solutions is called.

Additional Information

For more information, refer to the Define Package Size for Data Transfer section (in Section 10.1.3).

The last step in completing the basic setup for configuring baseline integration is to create SAP PI employee data.

Create SAP PI Employee Data Scenario

The SuccessFactors Integration Add-on uses SAP PI as an integration point between SAP ERP HCM and SuccessFactors Talent Solutions. You'll need to make sure that the necessary SAP PI configuration is created for setting up the employee data integration.

> **Additional Information**
>
> For more information on how to configure SAP PI, refer to Section 9.1.

Now that the basic setup has been completed, let's turn our attention to the SAP ERP HCM configuration setup.

10.2.3   Step 2: SAP ERP HCM Configuration

The following activities describe SAP ERP HCM basic configuration steps that are required for setting up employee data integrations to SuccessFactors Talent Solutions:

▶ Defining name format for the FIRSTNAME and LASTNAME fields

▶ Creating a report variant for employee data extraction

▶ Specifying allowed variants for delta extraction

▶ Running extraction of employee data and organization data

▶ Discontinuing data extraction for group employees

▶ Enhancing employee data extraction with BAdI implementation

Let's first define the name format for the FIRSTNAME and LASTNAME fields. Then, we'll discuss the configuration steps.

Define Name Format for the FIRSTNAME and LASTNAME Fields

In this step, you will define the name format for the FIRSTNAME and LASTNAME fields that are used for employee data extract. These are mandatory fields in SuccessFactors Talent Solutions.

When defining the name format fields, be sure to specify which SAP ERP HCM employee FIRSTNAME and LASTNAME fields are to be used or mapped to the

SuccessFactors Talent Solutions FIRSTNAME and LASTNAME fields. The formatted name setting here will affect SuccessFactors Talent Solutions in several ways, such as displaying the employee name on the UI, name search, and sorting behavior.

It is important to define the name format before you run any employee data extraction to SuccessFactors Talent Solutions to avoid any inconsistency of name formatting stored in SuccessFactors Talent Solutions. Keep the following points in mind:

▸ If the format for the FIRSTNAME and LASTNAME fields has already been defined as part of the existing SAP ERP HCM implementation, then this configuration step is not needed.

▸ If no specific name format is defined, then the extract program will default to use of PA0002-VORNA and PA0002-NACHN fields. To define a name format specific for the integration, use following name formats:

  ▹ FIRSTNAME: -71

  ▹ LASTNAME: -72

Next, perform the following steps:

1. Access Transaction SPRO, then navigate to IMG • Personnel Management • Integration Add-on for SAP ERP HCM and SuccessFactors BizX • Integration Scenario for Employee Data • Define Name Format for Fields FIRSTNAME and LASTNAME.

2. Choose New Entries, and add the entries shown in Figure 10.26.

Ctry Grouping	10				
HR Name Format with Infotype Views					
Format	Prefix	Name	Seq.	Field name	Conv
71	0002	0	1	VORNA	
71	0002	0	2	MIDNM	
72	0002	0	1	NACHN	

Figure 10.26 HR Name Format with Infotype Views

Now, let's discuss the configuration of SAP ERP HCM to create the report variant for employee data extraction.

Create Report Variant for Employee Data Extraction

In this step, you will create an employee data extraction report variant that must be saved with selection parameters and fields mapping required for the integration of SuccessFactors Talent Solutions.

The extraction report used here is called the Employee Data Sync with Success-Factors (with delta and inactive logic) report.

The report variant is important and must be created prior to any employee extraction run, because the variant must be specified during executing the extraction report. Only those variants assigned in ALLOWED VARIANTS FOR DELTA EXTRACTION will be available in report selection. You will perform this step right after report variant creation. The transaction code and report name are as follows:

- **Transaction code**
  HRSFI_SYNCH_EMP_DATA

- **Report name**
  RH_SFI_SYNCHRONIZE_EMPL_DAT

This report extracts changes to employee data. During the initial run for an employee, a full record is extracted. The initial run includes full records for all employees that satisfy the report criteria. If the full employee population is large, then segmenting into multiple batches through variants may be required. During each subsequent run, the report extracts only the employees for whom data has changed compared with the last run of the report.

The report also ensures that employees who are no longer contained in the selection area receive the status INACTIVE (for example, if the employees have switched to another enterprise area, in which there is no integration with SuccessFactors Talent Solutions).

Let's take a closer look at setting up the SYNC EMPLOYEE DATA WITH SUCCESSFAC-TORS (WITH DELTA AND INACTIVE LOGIC) report. You'll need to access Transaction HRSFI_SYNCH_EMP_DATA and perform the following three main steps:

- Setup report PERIOD and SELECTION CRITERIA for employee extraction

- Setup report DEFAULT SETTINGS

- Setup report FIELDS MAPPING

Let's begin with setting up the report PERIOD and SELECTION CRITERIA:

1. To begin setting up the report PERIOD and SELECTION CRITERIA, first select the desired REPORTING PERIOD by specifying TODAY or any key date or period for which the employee data is to be extracted. The default is set as TODAY (see Figure 10.27).

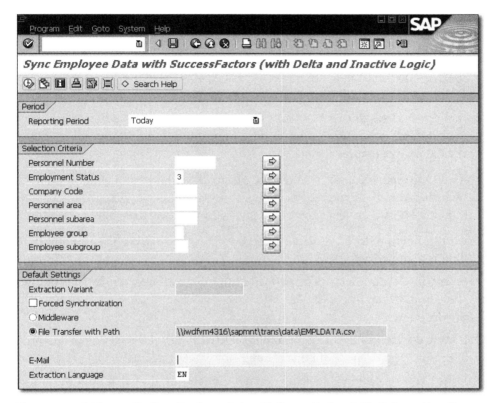

Figure 10.27 Setting up the Sync Employee Data with SuccessFactors (with Delta and Inactive Logic) Report Variant

2. Next, set the selection criteria and set EMPLOYMENT STATUS to 3. This means that the report selects only employees for whom the employment status is ACTIVE.

3. During the initial employee data extract, you cannot extract employee data with a status other than ACTIVE to SuccessFactors Talent Solutions; it will only process existing employee data with the status changed from ACTIVE to INACTIVE for subsequent employee data transfer.

To set up the DEFAULT SETTINGS, specify default settings for employee data integration behavior (see Figure 10.27). Proceed as follows:

1. First, choose the MIDDLEWARE option for employee extraction to SuccessFactors Talent Solutions through SAP PI.

2. Enter an email address. This is default email that the extraction report uses when it cannot determine the employee's email address using the EMAIL field.

3. Choose an EXTRACTION LANGUAGE. To avoid any data inconsistencies, transfer to SuccessFactors Talent Solutions. Do not change the extraction language after you have initiated the first employee data extract run.

4. Activate the LOG ERROR MESSAGES field only. Do not activate the field FORCED SYNCHRONIZATION, which should only be used for manual extraction repeat runs in case of employee data correction.

To setup the reports for FIELD MAPPING, specify the employee data selection fields to be included in the extraction transfer as well as fields mapping from SAP standard fields or BAdI enhancement implementation. Proceed as follows:

1. Go through the list of available selection fields, and select the checkbox if the field is mandatory for extraction.

2. In every selection field, you can further define field mapping by selecting the choices of STANDARD FIELD MAPPING, OWN IMPLEMENTATION, or EXCLUDE from the dropdown box.

3. If the OWN IMPLEMENTATION option is selected for a field, then you must implement that particular BAdI enhancement for data selection.

4. If the EXCLUDE option is selected for an optional field, then that field will not be included in the employee data transfer to SuccessFactors Talent Solutions.

Refer to the Enhancement of Employee Data Extraction with BAdI Implementation section for additional information regarding BAdI enhancements.

Field Mapping Setup

Table 10.11 is an example report field mapping setup for the MedTron organization based on its employee data requirements. The first column, SFSF FIELDS, indicates target mapping fields of SuccessFactors Talent Solutions. The second column refers to the mapping source field option of SAP ERP HCM. The third column, REQUIRED, further defines if mapping is mandatory. For fields with the option OWN IMPLEMENTATION set, the data will be mapped based on BAdI implementation instead of standard mapping.

SFSF Fields	SAP Field Option	Required	Description
STATUS	IT0000-STAT2	Yes	Standard mapping, employment status
USER ID	CENTRAL PERSON ID	Yes	Standard mapping, Central Person ID
USER NAME	USER ID	Yes	Standard mapping, SAP user ID
FIRST NAME	FORMATTED NAME	Yes	Standard mapping, formatted first name
LAST NAME	FORMATTED NAME	Yes	Standard mapping, formatted last name
MIDDLE NAME	EXCLUDE	No	No mapping, exclude from extraction
GENDER	IT0002	Yes	Standard mapping, gender from Infotype 0002
EMAIL	IT0105 SUBTYPE 0010	Yes	Standard mapping, email from Infotype 0105
MANAGER	MANAGER POSITION	Yes	Standard mapping, manager determination based on B012 relationship
HUMAN RESOURCE	IT0001 PERSADMIN	Yes	Standard mapping, HR master administration from Infotype 0001
DEPARTMENT	IT0001 ORGUNIT	Yes	Standard mapping, Org. Unit from Infotype 0001
JOB CODE	EXCLUDE	No	No mapping, exclude from extraction
DIVISION	IT0001 COMPANY CODE	Yes	Standard mapping, company code from Infotype 0001
LOCATION	IT0001 PERSONNEL AREA	Yes	Standard mapping, personnel area from Infotype 0001
TIME ZONE	USER DATA	Yes	Standard mapping, employee user time profile

Table 10.11 Field Mapping

SFSF Fields	SAP Field Option	Required	Description
HIRE DATE	INITIAL HIREDATE	No	No mapping, exclude from extraction
EMPLOYEE ID	PERSONNEL NUMBER	No	Standard mapping, employee personnel number
TITLE	EXCLUDE	No	No mapping, exclude from extraction
BUSINESS PHONE	EXCLUDE	No	No mapping, exclude from extraction
FAX	EXCLUDE	No	No mapping, exclude from extraction
ADDRESS 1	OWN IMPLEMENTATION	No	BAdI enhancement, address 1 determined based on custom logic
ADDRESS 2	OWN IMPLEMENTATION	No	BADI enhancement, address 2 determined based on custom logic
CITY	OWN IMPLEMENTATION	No	BADI enhancement, city determined based on custom logic
STATE	OWN IMPLEMENTATION	No	BADI enhancement, state determined based on custom logic
ZIP	OWN IMPLEMENTATION	No	BADI enhancement, ZIP determined based on custom logic
COUNTRY	OWN IMPLEMENTATION	No	BADI enhancement, country determined based on custom logic

Table 10.11 Field Mapping (Cont.)

This is how the employee data sync program in the SAP ERP HCM system will look. Once the field mapping is done, perform the following steps:

1. Save the settings into a variant using the SAVE button.

2. Give the variant a meaningful name and description (e.g., "US_CAD" as name and "US and Canada employees" as description).

3. Save the variant again.

This section described how to create a report variant for employee data extraction. Now, let's turn our attention to understanding how to specify allowed variants for delta extraction.

Specify Allowed Variants for Delta Extraction

Once you have created the report variants for employee data extraction, the next step is to further define which extraction variants will be available for use in the report Sync Employee Data process (RH_SFI_SYNCHRONIZE_EMPL_DATA). Only those variants identified in this configuration will be available for selection by the user or to be run in the scheduled job.

Proceed as follows:

1. Access Transaction SPRO, and go to the IMG menu. Then, navigate to PERSONNEL MANAGEMENT • INTEGRATION ADD-ON FOR SAP ERP HCM AND SUCCESSFACTORS BIZX • INTEGRATION SCENARIO FOR EMPLOYEE DATA • SPECIFY ALLOWED VARIANTS FOR DELTA EXTRACTION.

2. On the next screen, click on NEW ENTRIES, and select the appropriate one or more variants that are permissible for use in the program SYNC EMPLOYEE DATA WITH SFSF (RH_SFI_SYNCHRONIZE_EMPL_DATA; see Figure 10.28). Save your entries.

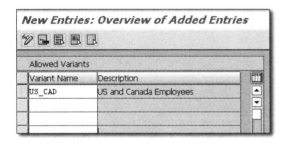

Figure 10.28 Specifying Allowed Variants for Delta Extraction—New Entries (Overview of Added Entries)

Now, let's discuss how to run an extraction of employee and organizational data.

Run Extraction of Employee and Organizational Data

For this task, we will run an extraction of the employee and organizational data. To run this extraction, schedule a background job for the report Sync Employee Data with SuccessFactors (RH_SFI_SYNCHRONIZE_EMPL_DATA) to extract employee data and transfer to SuccessFactors Talent Solutions regularly. Perform the following steps:

1. Access Transaction SM36, and define the job name, job class, and, if necessary, execution server and spool recipient. Click on START CONDITION, then click on DATE/TIME to schedule the periodic job (see Figure 10.29).

2. Enter the execution start date and time. Select the PERIODIC JOB checkbox, then choose PERIOD VALUES, and select the frequency (e.g., monthly, weekly, or daily). Choose STEP to specify the program to be executed in the background job (see Figure 10.30).

3. Enter report name RH_SFI_SYNCHRONIZE_EMPL_DATA and the desired variant. Then, click on SAVE.

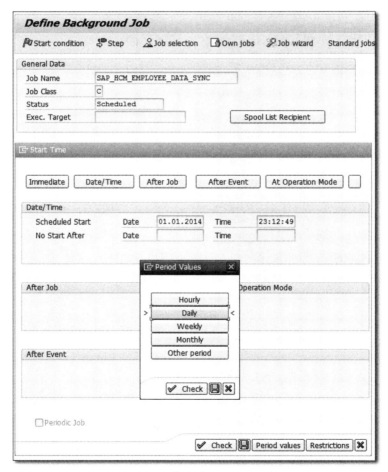

Figure 10.29 Running Extraction of Employee Data and Organization Data—Define Background Job

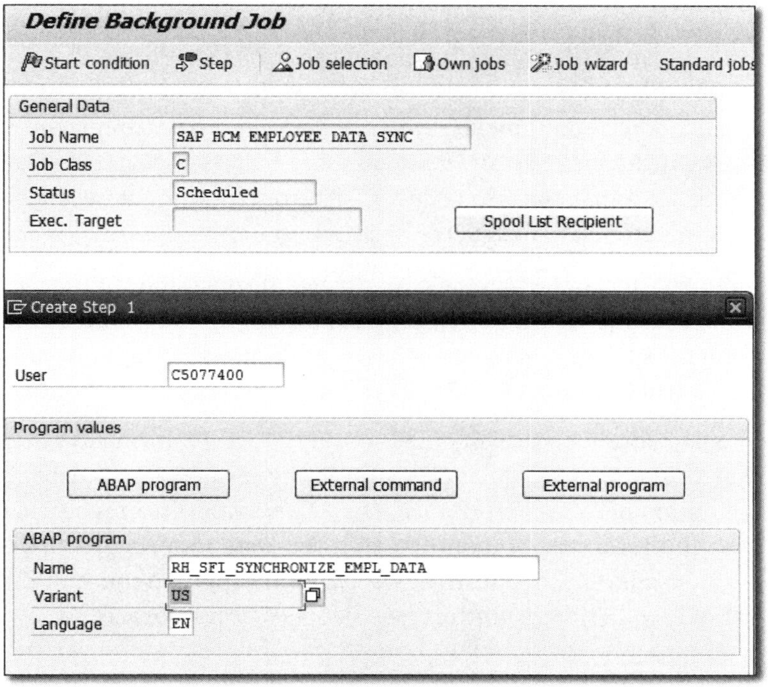

Figure 10.30 Define Background Job—Create Step

Discontinue Data Extraction for Group of Employees

In addition to the report Sync Employee Data with SuccessFactors (RH_SFI_SYN-CHRONIZE_EMPL_DATA), there is a report to stop existing employee data synchronization between SAP ERP HCM and SuccessFactors Talent Solutions. This report uses the variant created from the report Sync Employee Data and set group of the previous transferred employees' status to INACTIVE in SuccessFactors Talent Solutions, depending on the variant selection. This report is useful if you want to exclude a group of employees which you have previously transferred data to SuccessFactors Talent Solutions, from data transfer in future.

In a case in which employee data transfer exclusion is needed, schedule and run report RH_SFI_WITHDRAW_VARIANT with a report variant from the Sync Employee Data with SuccessFactors report (RH_SFI_SYNCHRONIZE_EMPL_DATA).

Enhancement of Employee Data Extraction with BAdI Implementation

In a case in which standard SAP table fields mapping options for the Sync Employee Data with SuccessFactors report (RH_SFI_SYNCHRONIZE_EMPL_DATA) does not meet your requirements, enhance the report extraction process by implementing BAdI: Replication of Employee Data (HRSFI_B_EMPL_DATA_REPLICATION) with customer-specific code for data retrieval for all available fields in the Sync Employee Data with SuccessFactors report.

The use of customer-specific extraction logic is activated through the OWN IMPLEMENTING option in each field of the report together with the BAdI implementation described here. Let's take a closer look at BAdI: Replication of Employee Data for our example scenario (see Table 10.12).

The requirement is to map SuccessFactors field ADDRESS 1 with information from Infotype 0006, but no standard SAP table fields for Infotype 0006 are available in the field mapping option of the report. Hence, OWN IMPLEMENTATION is selected here together with the BAdI: Replication of Employee Data implementation to supply Infotype 0006 address information via customer-specific codes. Table 10.12 details the field requirements for Infotype 0006 address information.

Fields	Field Option	Required	Description
ADDRESS 1	OWN IMPLEMENTATION	No	BAdI enhancement, address 1 is determined based on custom logic
ADDRESS 2	OWN IMPLEMENTATION	No	BAdI enhancement, address 2 is determined based on custom logic
CITY	OWN IMPLEMENTATION	No	BAdI enhancement, city is determined based on custom logic
STATE	OWN IMPLEMENTATION	No	BAdI enhancement, state is determined based on custom logic
ZIP	OWN IMPLEMENTATION	No	BAdI enhancement, ZIP is determined based on custom logic
COUNTRY	OWN IMPLEMENTATION	No	BAdI enhancement, country is determined based on custom logic

Table 10.12 Infotype 0006 Field Requirements

Next, perform the following steps:

1. Access Transaction SPRO, and open the IMG menu. Navigate to PERSONNEL MANAGEMENT • INTEGRATION ADD-ON FOR SAP ERP HCM AND SUCCESSFACTORS

BIZX • INTEGRATION SCENARIO FOR EMPLOYEE DATA • BUSINESS ADD-INS (BADIS) • BADI: REPLICATION OF EMPLOYEE DATA.

2. Create an implementation by clicking the CREATE icon on the BADI IMPLEMENTATION window.

3. Close the subsequent popup information message. In the second window, define the ENHANCEMENT IMPLEMENTATION and SHORT TEXT fields as shown in Figure 10.31.

4. On the next screen, define the BAdI implementation as follows:

   ► BADI IMPLEMENTATION: HRSFI_INTY0006_ADDRESS1

   ► IMPLEMENTATION CLASS: ZCL_HRSFI_INTY0006_ADDRESS1

5. Click on the green checkmark button, which will create all relevant BAdI objects. In the implementation class of HRSFI_INTY0006_ADDRESS1, double-click on method IF_HRSFI_EMPL_DATA_REPLICATION~GET_ADDR1 to implement the customer-specific source code.

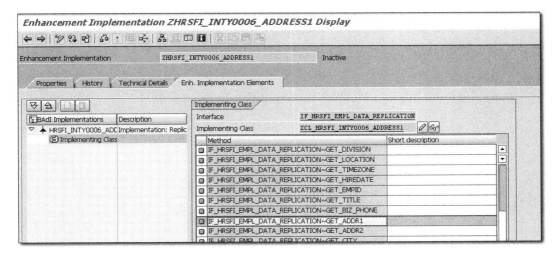

Figure 10.31 Customer-Specific Source Code

6. Add the customer-specific code to retrieve address information from Infotype 0006 based on the personnel number (import parameter lv_pernr) to supply to the method in CLASS BUILDER. The Infotype 0006 address is then passed to export parameter rv_value, the result of this method (see Figure 10.32).

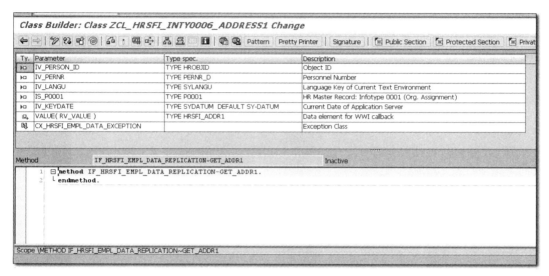

Figure 10.32 Class Builder

7. Once done, save your changes and repeat for the remaining fields that require customer-specific code for data extraction.

Now, let's switch gears to learn about the SuccessFactors side of the integration. We'll begin by discussing the SuccessFactors API configuration.

10.2.4 Step 3: SuccessFactors Configuration

The following activities describe the necessary SuccessFactors configuration steps required for setting up employee data integration from SAP ER HCM to SuccessFactors Talent Management Solutions. It covers the activation of the SuccessFactors APIs, succession data model configurations, creation of the API user, and security set up.

To set up the configuration in SuccessFactors, perform the following steps:

▶ Enable SuccessFactors web services API

▶ Establish SuccessFactors succession data model configuration

▶ Create a SuccessFactors API user

▶ Set up a SuccessFactors API user security

▶ Create a SuccessFactors API login exception

Enable Web Services SuccessFactors API

In this step, you will activate SuccessFactors Talent Solutions web services API features.

To begin, log on to SuccessFactors' Provisioning page via *https://<Instance URL>/ provisioning_login.* The instance URL is provided by the SuccessFactors team; for example, it could look like *https://performancemanager8.successfactors.com/provisioning_login.*

In the provisioning tool, go to COMPANY SETTINGS, then navigate to WEB SERVICES. Under WEB SERVICES, select the following features (see Figure 10.33):

▸ SFAPI

▸ SFAPI AD HOC FEATURE

Figure 10.33 Activating SuccessFactors Talent Solutions Web Services API Features

From the same screen, select the ENABLE SFAPI WEBSERVICES checkbox, and then save your changes (see Figure 10.34).

Figure 10.34 Enabling SuccessFactors API Web Services

Next, we'll discuss the SuccessFactors succession data model configuration.

SuccessFactors Succession Data Model Configuration

The succession data model governs the structure of the SuccessFactors system and is accessible in the provisioning tool for each instance. The best practice data model contains all standard fields and background elements available capture employee data.

In this step, you will import the succession *data model.xml* file in the SuccessFactors provisioning tools. Perform the following steps to proceed:

1. Log on to the provisioning tool for your instance, and then navigate to SUCCESSION MANAGEMENT (see Figure 10.35).

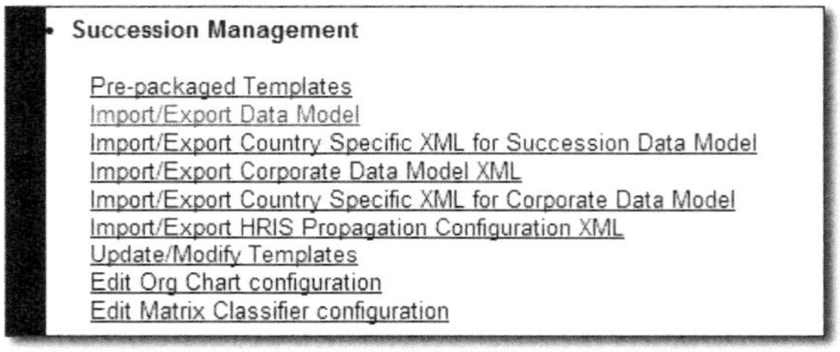

Succession Management

Pre-packaged Templates
Import/Export Data Model
Import/Export Country Specific XML for Succession Data Model
Import/Export Corporate Data Model XML
Import/Export Country Specific XML for Corporate Data Model
Import/Export HRIS Propagation Configuration XML
Update/Modify Templates
Edit Org Chart configuration
Edit Matrix Classifier configuration

Figure 10.35 Importing Succession Data Model XML File in SuccessFactors Provisioning Tool

2. Click on IMPORT/EXPORT DATA MODEL, then select the IMPORT radio button.

3. Browse for and upload the succession data model XML file. (Contact your SuccessFactors team for the template file.) The message TEMPLATES HAVE BEEN UPLOADED AND SAVED will appear, showing that the process was successful.

Next, we'll talk about how to create a SuccessFactors API user.

Create SuccessFactors API User

A SuccessFactors API user is required for SAP ERP HCM to integrate with SuccessFactors Talent Solutions through SAP PI. The API user must first be created in the SuccessFactors provisioning tool. The same API user logon credential is then stored in the middleware credential settings of SAP ERP HCM.

Log on to the SuccessFactors provisioning tool, and choose COMPANY SETTINGS. Then, navigate to ADMIN USERNAME, and enter the following information:

▸ ADMIN USERNAME
We suggest using "SAP_API_USER".

- ADMIN PASSWORD
  Create a strong password.

- ADMIN FIRST NAME
  Provide the appropriate admin user's first name.

- ADMIN LAST NAME
  Provide the appropriate admin user's last name.

- ADMIN EMAIL
  Provide the appropriate admin user's email address.

Select CREATE ADMIN to create the API user. Once the API user is created, pass the API user name and password together with the tenant company ID (where the API user was created) to store the API user credentials in SAP ERP HCM. Now, let's focus on setting up the API user security.

SuccessFactors API User Security Setup

In this step, you will grant security access to the API user created in the previous substep.

1. Log on to the SuccessFactors instance URL as an admin.

2. Navigate to ADMIN TOOLS • SET USER PERMISSIONS • SF API LOGIN PERMISSION • MANAGE SFAPI LOGIN PERMISSION.

3. Select the API user that created previously, then select the SELECT ALL checkbox.

4. Select GRANT PERMISSIONS button. Then, navigate to ADMIN TOOLS • SET USER PERMISSIONS • DEFAULT USER PERMISSIONS.

5. Under REPORT PERMISSIONS, select REPORTS PERMISSION. Next, under SFAPI RETRIEVE JOB APPLICANT PERMISSION, select SFAPI RETRIEVE JOB APPLICANT PERMISSION.

6. Then, under RUN REPORTS, select RUN ALL REPORTS • RUN RECRUITING V2 REPORT • RUN RECRUITING V2 SECURED REPORT • RUN EMPLOYEE PROFILE REPORT • RUN COMPENSATION PLANNING REPORT.

7. From here, click on the SAVE SETTING button, then navigate to ADMIN TOOLS • RECRUITING • RECRUITING PERMISSIONS.

8. Select the MANAGE RECRUITING PERMISSIONS THROUGH INDIVIDUAL USERS option, and then click on the SEARCH USERS button.

9. Select the SAP API user created from the process, and grant permission for all SuccessFactors API functionalities.

You have now completed the steps for setting up API user security. Now let's turn our attention to the API login exception.

SuccessFactors API Login Exception

In this step, you will configure the API login exception for the API created previously. The purpose is to ensure that the password for the API user does not expire.

Log on to the SuccessFactors tenant as an admin, then navigate to ADMIN TOOLS • COMPANY SETTINGS • PASSWORD AND LOGIN POLICY SETTINGS • SET API LOGIN EXCEPTIONS.

Now, add the following settings (see Figure 10.36):

▸ USERNAME
sap_api_user

▸ MAXIMUM PASSWORD AGE (DAYS)
- 1 days

▸ IP ADDRESS RESTRICTIONS
Designated external or EGRESS IP addresses or address range from which the API user is being accessed from (can be used to ensure that the API user is only called from designated sources)

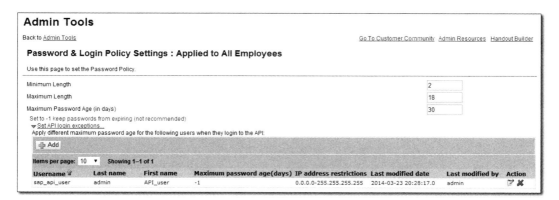

Figure 10.36 Configure the API Login Exception for an API User

Test the System Prior to Production Cutover

After the basic settings and configurations in SAP ERP HCM, SuccessFactors, and SAP PI have been setup, you will need to test the system prior to cutting over in your production system.

In this case study, we detailed the configuration steps required for implementing the SuccessFactors employee data integration within SAP ERP HCM using the Talent Hybrid integration deployment model. By successfully completing these steps, you will be able to run the employee data between SAP ERP HCM and SuccessFactors.

10.3 Compensation Process Integration

In this section, we'll cover the implementation steps required in both SAP ERP and SuccessFactors to implement the compensation integration. We'll use a client scenario to demonstrate the integration steps. The details for our client are provided ahead.

> **Prerequisites**
>
> Refer to Section 10.2 for a list of the prerequisites required prior to beginning the configuration of the compensation process integration scenario.

10.3.1 Case Study Parameters

This case study illustrates how a customer who wants to implement SuccessFactors Talent Management Solutions will integrate and transfer their compensation data between SAP ERP HCM and SuccessFactors Talent Management Solutions, using SAP PI on-premise as the integration middleware.

Client Scenario

Our presales team at MedTron Inc. successfully sold the technical capabilities of integrating and transferring employee data between SAP ERP HCM and SuccessFactors Talent Management Solutions, using SAP PI as the integration middleware. Because SAP PI is already implemented for employee data integration, the compensation integration will continue to use this middleware.

Building on the implementation of SAP PI and employee data integration, MedTron is interested in the pay-for-performance, end-to-end process offered in this solution. They want to continue using SAP ERP HCM for their payroll processing but want to use SuccessFactors for their compensation planning. The end-to-end integration of the pay-for-performance process ensures that the salary-related data is transferred from SAP ERP HCM to SuccessFactors. When the manager has granted a salary change or lump sum payment, the changed data is transferred from SuccessFactors back to SAP ERP HCM for payroll processing. MedTron has already implemented the Performance Management module, and the Talent Management roadmap includes compensation as part of phase 3. The succession planning module implementation is part of phase 3, with the final Recruiting module in the phase 4 implementation work.

MedTron's existing IT footprint includes SAP ERP HCM ECC 6.0 EHP 6. MedTron currently runs OM, PA, and SAP Payroll in SAP. In addition, MedTron also uses SAP PI version 7.4 Java stack.

To effectively integrate and transfer compensation data, the team recognizes that the technical consultant will need to have a solid understanding of the basic settings of SuccessFactors Talent Solutions integration with SAP ERP HCM and the necessary Integration Add-ons and system requirements needed to make the integration successful. The implementation of compensation planning in SuccessFactors will allow managers to award merit payments, bonuses, lump sum payments, and pay adjustments. This includes an approval process and, after completion, the transfer of relevant data to SAP ERP HCM.

With a successful integration, the benefits of moving to the cloud will include an easy and fast deployment of SuccessFactors Talent Management Solutions and the ability to leverage standard Integration Add-ons delivered by SAP to ensure that the data is in sync between SuccessFactors and SAP ERP HCM. To ensure that the integration is successful, there are certain business requirements needed to guarantee a smooth transfer of data. SuccessFactors employee profile integration with SAP ERP HCM must be implemented, and employees must be available for compensation planning. Refer to Section 10.2, which covers employee data integration.

To transfer compensation data between SAP ERP HCM and SuccessFactors Talent Management Solutions, using SAP PI as the middleware, the following steps must be executed:

1. Ensure that integration configuration settings have been made for SAP ERP HCM and for SAP SuccessFactors compensation data integration by defining authorizations in SAP ERP HCM to access the new integration transactions.

2. For setting the middleware, the installation and configuration of SAP PI was set as an integration point between SAP ERP HCM and SuccessFactors Talent Solutions.

Metadata Transfer

The metadata transfer report will need to be run once SuccessFactors configuration is completed in order to complete the field mappings for the importing of the compensation data.

The SuccessFactors configuration must be completed before the metadata transfer to SAP can be performed. This task transfers objects from SuccessFactors to SAP ERP, which enables the import and activation of compensation data.

Now, let's discuss how you can achieve a successful integration between SAP ERP HCM and the SuccessFactors Compensation module, using SAP PI on-premise as your integration middleware. We'll begin with an overview of the process.

Process Overview

SAP ERP HCM on-premise and SuccessFactors Talent Management Solutions in the cloud serve as two different systems; therefore, integrating SAP ERP HCM with SuccessFactors Compensation enables data consistency between the two systems.

In this section, we'll highlight the necessary information for customers using the Talent Hybrid deployment model to run SAP ERP HCM for Personnel Administration and Organization Management as well as benefits, time, and payroll and SuccessFactors for their compensation planning. The employee's compensation data will be exported from SAP ERP HCM to SuccessFactors, where it will be used for the compensation planning process. Once the manager has awarded the salary increase or lump sum bonus, the data will be imported back into SAP ERP HCM, where it will be activated as an ongoing amount (salary) or a one-off payment (lump sum).

There are four main steps that are required in setting up the compensation process integration between SAP ERP HCM and SuccessFactors Talent Management Solutions:

▶ **Step 1: Basic setup**
There are basic integration configuration steps that must be performed in order to begin this process. This includes tasks such as defining authorization in SAP ERP HCM, setting middleware, and creating a compensation data scenario from SAP PI (see Section 10.3.2).

▶ **Step 2: SAP ERP HCM configuration**
In this step, you will perform the SAP ERP HCM basic configuration for setting up compensation data transfer between SAP ERP HCM and SuccessFactors Talent Management Solutions (see Section 10.3.3).

▶ **Step 3: SuccessFactors configuration**
This step describes the SuccessFactors configuration process for setting up the compensation data integration between SAP ERP HCM and SuccessFactors Talent Management (see Section 10.3.4).

▶ **Step 4: SAP PI middleware setup**
For step 4, you will need to set up the SAP PI middleware. Therefore, refer to Section 10.1 for a detailed description.

The following section offers basic implementation steps that help to kick start the integration efforts for the compensation process integration.

10.3.2   Step 1: Basic Setup

There is some basic integration configuration required, along with SAP ERP HCM configuration for setting up SuccessFactors compensation process integration. This basic system configuration covers settings from SAP ERP HCM and SAP PI. To complete the basic setup, you'll need to perform the following tasks:

▶ Define authorizations in SAP ERP HCM

▶ Set up the middleware

▶ Create an SAP PI compensation data scenario

Define an Authorization in SAP ERP HCM

First, you'll need to define the authorization for the Integration Add-on for SAP ERP HCM and SuccessFactors Talent Management Solutions. To do this, define the role `SAP_HR_SFI_COMP_DATA_REPL`, which contains the authorizations that a user needs to run the report for extracting compensation data to SuccessFactors Talent Solutions. The report for extracting compensation data to SuccessFactors Talent Management Solutions is RH_SFI_SYNCH_COMP_DATA (Extraction of Compensation Data for SuccessFactors).

The role SAP_HR_SFI_COMP_DATA_IMPORT contains the authorizations that a user needs to run the reports for extracting and updating compensation data from SuccessFactors. The reports for extracting compensation data to SuccessFactors Talent Solutions include the following:

▶ **RH_SFI_IMPORT_COMP_DATA**
Import compensation data to SAP ERP

▶ **RH_SFI_ACTIVATE_COMP_DATA**
Activate compensation data in SAP ERP

The roles are assigned to composite role SAP_HR_SFI_C2, which contains other authorization roles that a user needs for data transfer as part of the Integration Add-on. The roles SAP_HR_SFI_COMP_DATA_REPL and SAP_HR_SFI_COMP_DATA_IMPORT include the infotypes for which the user will need access. However, no default values are defined for the personnel area, the employee group, or the employee subgroup, for example.

Therefore, in any customer-specific roles, values for the fields of authorization objects P_ORGIN, P_ORGINCON, and PLOG, will need to be specified according to the client's requirements.

In addition, the following infotype authorizations for customer-specific versions of the role SAP_HR_SFI_COMP_DATA_IMPORT for the authorization objects P_ORGIN and P_ORGINCON will need to be specified:

▶ Read authorization for Infotype 0001 (Organizational Assignment)

▶ Read and write authorization for Infotypes 0008 (Basic Pay) and 0015 (Additional Payments)

The delivered roles can be used as a template to define further authorizations should MedTron decide that it has additional security requirements. Access to Transaction PFCG is required to define additional roles.

The next step in completing the basic setup is to configure the middleware.

Set Up the Middleware

To set up the middleware, configure the SuccessFactors API user logon information, and define the package size for transferring compensation data in SAP ERP HCM. Specify the number of employees for whom data is to be transferred each time the web services for transferring compensation data from SAP ERP to SuccessFactors Talent Management Solutions are called.

> **Additional Information**
>
> For more information, refer to the Define Package Size for Data Transfer section in Section 10.1.3.

Create the SAP PI Compensation Data Scenario

The latest SAP SuccessFactors Integration Add-on uses SAP PI as an integration point between SAP ERP HCM and SuccessFactors Talent Management Solutions. You'll need to make sure the necessary SAP PI configuration is created for setting up compensation data integration.

> **Additional Information**
>
> For more information on how to configure SAP PI, refer to Section 10.1 for a detailed description.

Now that the basic setup has been completed, let's turn our attention to the SAP ERP HCM configuration setup.

10.3.3   Step 2: SAP ERP HCM Configuration

The following activities describe the SAP ERP HCM basic configuration steps that are required for setting up the compensation data transfer between SAP ERP HCM and SuccessFactors Talent Management Solutions:

▶ Defining fields for extracting compensation data from SAP ERP HCM
▶ Defining fields for importing compensation data from SuccessFactors
▶ Importing metadata from SuccessFactors
▶ Enhancing the transfer of compensation data with BAdI implementation

Let's begin by defining the fields for extracting compensation data from SAP ERP HCM.

Define Fields for Extracting Compensation Data from SAP ERP HCM

In this step, you will map the fields required for extracting data to the compensation planning process in SuccessFactors. The RH_SFI_SYNCH_COMP_DATA report is used to transfer the data from the SAP ERP HCM system to SuccessFactors.

Fields are mapped by defining field sets that provide the required data to the SuccessFactors system. A *field set* is used to define a group of fields that are extracted together. A field set must be specified as a runtime parameter in the extraction program RH_SFI_SYNCH_COMP_DATA.

This step can be accessed from the DISPLAY IMG screen. Navigate to PERSONNEL MANAGEMENT • INTEGRATION ADD-ON FOR SAP ERP HCM AND SUCCESSFACTORS TALENT SOLUTIONS • INTEGRATION SCENARIO FOR COMPENSATION DATA • DATA TRANSFER FROM SAP ERP TO SUCCESSFACTORS BIZX • DEFINE FIELDS FOR EXTRACTING COMPENSATION DATA.

In order to map the SAP fields to SuccessFactors Talent Management, the user will need to create the field set and double-click on the FIELD ASSIGNMENTS folder under the DIALOG STRUCTURE (see Figure 10.37).

Next, create new entries on the VIEW FIELD ASSIGNMENTS screen to map the following fields:

▸ SFSF FIELD ID
SuccessFactors field name.

▸ DATA EXTRACTION FOR EXP.
BAdIs set up to map to SAP ERP HCM fields.

▸ REQUIRED
Select YES if the fields are required and should be checked during data import.

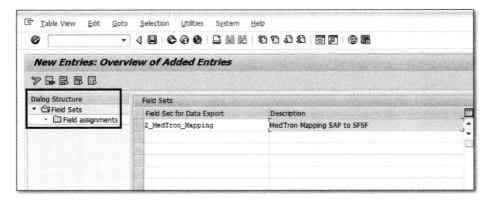

Figure 10.37 Creating the Field Set for Data Export

Figure 10.38 shows a mapping for the salary fields for current salary and local currency.

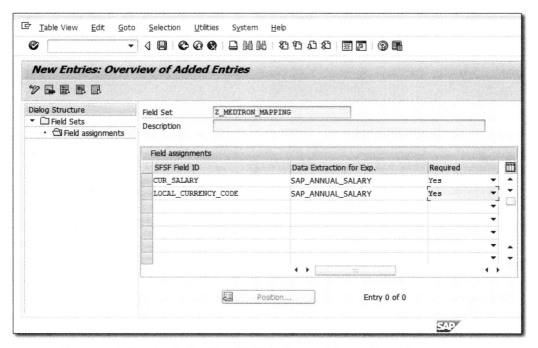

Figure 10.38 Mapping for the Salary Fields for Current Salary and Local Currency

> **Note**
>
> The fields defined in this step must correspond to the SuccessFactors field names. Only use those field names listed in the input help of the SFSF FIELD ID.

Define Fields for Importing Compensation Data from SuccessFactors

In this step, you will map the fields required for importing data from SuccessFactors. The RH_SFI_IMPORT_COMP_DATA report transfers the data from SuccessFactors to the SAP ERP system. Then, the data is activated using the RH_SFI_ACTIVATE_COMP_DATA report.

> **SuccessFactors Configuration**
>
> The SuccessFactors configuration *must* be completed prior to performing this step, and the metadata must be transferred.

Fields are mapped by defining field sets that provide the required data to the SAP ERP system.

> **Ad Hoc Report**
>
> The ad hoc report must be enabled for use with the API user that SAP PI will use to access the SuccessFactors system.

This step can be accessed from the DISPLAY IMG screen. Navigate to PERSONNEL MANAGEMENT • INTEGRATION ADD-ON FOR SAP ERP HCM AND SUCCESSFACTORS BIZX • INTEGRATION SCENARIO FOR COMPENSATION DATA • DATA TRANSFER FROM SUCCESSFACTORS BIZX TO SAP ERP • DEFINE FIELDS FOR IMPORTING COMPENSATION DATA.

In order to map the SuccessFactors fields to SAP ERP HCM fields, the user will need to create the field mappings, then double-click on the FIELD DEFINITIONS folder under the DIALOG STRUCTURE (see Figure 10.39).

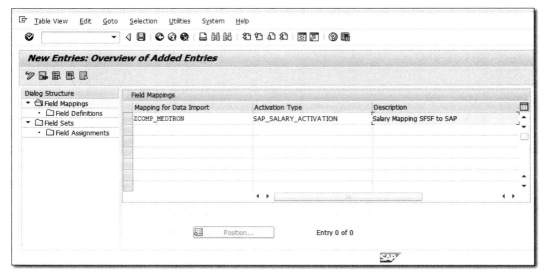

Figure 10.39 Mapping SuccessFactors Fields to SAP Fields

Create new entries on the VIEW FIELD MAPPINGS screen for the following fields:

- ▸ MAPPING FOR DATA IMPORT
  Enter a name for the import.

- ▸ ACTIVATION TYPE
  Select either a bonus or salary activation type for the mapping.

- ▸ DESCRIPTION
  Enter a description for the import.

Create new entries on the VIEW FIELD DEFINITIONS screen to map the following:

- ▸ INTERNAL FIELD ID
  Enter the SAP ERP HCM field name.

- ▸ FIELD TYPE
  Specify if the field is imported from SuccessFactors or determined via a BAdI, or enter the SuccessFactors field name.

- ▸ SFSF FIELD ID
  Specify the SuccessFactors field name.

▶ REQUIRED
Select YES if the fields are required and should be checked during data import.

▶ DATA ELEMENT
Enter the SAP ERP HCM technical field name.

▶ DESCRIPTION
Enter your own description of the field.

Figure 10.40 displays entries mapping the ANNUAL SALARY, CURRENCY, DATE, REASON, and WAGE TYPE fields between SAP ERP HCM and SuccessFactors.

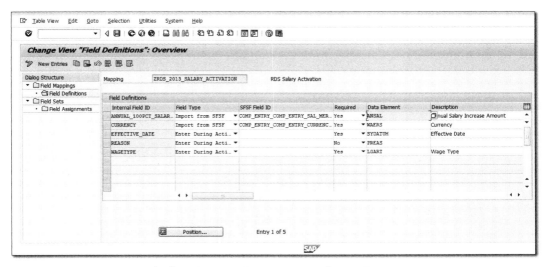

Figure 10.40 Mapping Annual Salary, Currency, Date, Reason, and Wage Type

---

Fields

The fields defined in this step must correspond to the SuccessFactors field names. Only use those field names listed in the input help of the field SFSF FIELD ID.

Next, create new entries on the VIEW FIELD SETS screen (see Figure 10.41):

▶ FIELD SET FOR DATA IMPORT
Enter a name for the import of the salary information (e.g., "ZMEDTRON_SALARY").

▶ DESCRIPTION
Enter a description for the import (e.g., "Salary Import").

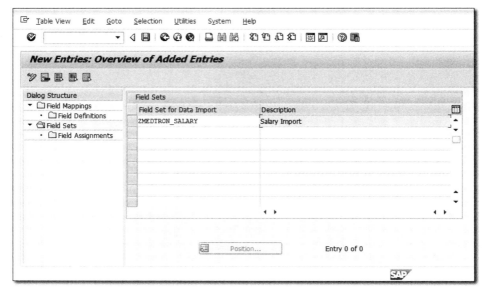

Figure 10.41 Creating New Entries on the View Field Sets Screen

Create the following new entries on the VIEW FIELD ASSIGNMENTS screen:

▶ MAPPING FOR DATA IMPORT
Select the field mapping previously created.

▶ DESCRIPTION
Enter the description as per the field mapping description.

Import Metadata from SuccessFactors

In this step, the user will execute the report Importing Metadata from SuccessFactors BizX (Transaction RH_SFI_SYNCH_METADATA) in order to extract the metadata from SuccessFactors HCM into SAP ERP HCM. This data will then be transferred and used as input help, dropdown values in the integration programs, and configuration for the compensation processes.

This step can be accessed from the DISPLAY IMG screen. Navigate to PERSONNEL MANAGEMENT • INTEGRATION ADD-ON FOR SAP ERP HCM AND SUCCESSFACTORS BIZX • BASIC SETTINGS • IMPORTING METADATA FROM SUCCESSFACTORS BIZX.

On the initial screen, select the checkboxes under the SYNCHRONIZATION SETTINGS FOR COMPENSATION section (see Figure 10.42). This will enable the group IDs and ad hoc reports to be selected when importing and activating compensation data.

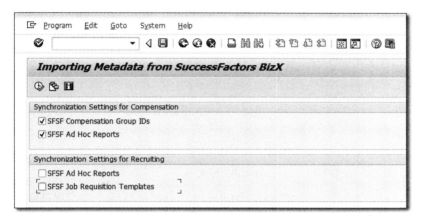

Figure 10.42 Importing Metadata from SuccessFactors BizX

Once your selections have been saved, the report will need to be scheduled in the follow-on systems (e.g., the test or productive system) as a regular background job to regularly update the metadata.

SuccessFactors Configuration

The SuccessFactors configuration must be completed prior to performing this step. To execute the report, you must have the proper security role to access the SAP Reference IMG.

Each SuccessFactors instance will generate a different SuccessFactors ad hoc report and compensation group IDs. In addition, this step cannot be transported from SAP and therefore must be executed in each customer SAP project system.

Enhance Transfer of Compensation Data with BAdI Implementation

There are two standard BAdI implementations available when you activate compensation data received from SuccessFactors: salary activations and bonus activations.

During the activation process, the data is moved from the internal tables to the SAP ERP HCM infotypes. Salary activations impact Infotype 0008 (Basic Pay), and bonus activations impact Infotype 0015 (Additional Payments).

This step can be accessed from the DISPLAY IMG screen. Navigate to PERSONNEL MANAGEMENT • INTEGRATION ADD-ON FOR SAP ERP HCM AND SUCCESSFACTORS BIZX INTEGRATION SCENARIO FOR COMPENSATION DATA • DATA TRANSFER FROM SUCCESSFACTORS BIZX TO SAP ERP • BADI: ACTIVATION OF COMPENSATION DATA IMPORTED FROM SFSF.

On the implementations for BAdI definition HRSI_B_COMP_DATA_ACTIVATION, activate HRSFI_COMP_BONUS_ACTIVATION and HRSFI_COMP_SALARY_ACTIVATION. Then, click on the green checkmark.

Now, let's switch gears to learn about the SuccessFactors side of the integration. We'll begin by discussing the SuccessFactors API configuration.

10.3.4 Step 3: SuccessFactors Configuration

The following activities describe the necessary SuccessFactors configuration steps required for setting up the compensation data integration from SAP ERP HCM to SuccessFactors Talent Management Solutions. It covers the activation of the SuccessFactors APIs, compensation template configurations, ad hoc report definitions, the creation of and API user, and security setup.

To setup the configuration in SuccessFactors, perform the following tasks:

▶ Configure the compensation template

▶ Update compensation forms with staging table data

▶ Enable the web services SuccessFactors API

▶ Create SuccessFactors API user permissions

▶ Enable use of the Ad Hoc Report Builder

▶ Create ad hoc reporting definitions and share reports with the API user

Configure the Compensation Template

In this step, the user will log in to the SuccessFactors Provisioning tool to edit the XML of an existing compensation template or to upload a new template. A compensation template XML defines the fields and functions for the template. We will be adding a group ID to the XML in this step, which will identify the specific compensation plan used in SuccessFactors and enable it to be referenced in SAP ERP HCM when running the import program. This step can be accessed from the SuccessFactors Provisioning client home page (from there, click on COMPANY • FORM TEMPLATE ADMINISTRATION).

On the COMPANIES screen, you will select the existing compensation template used for the current year. Scroll down to the bottom of XML code on the EDIT COMPENSATION TEMPLATE screen.

Add a `<comp-group>` tag entry to specify a desired compensation group ID near the very end of the XML file (see Figure 10.43). The ID attribute value should be a value that can be easily identified in further processing.

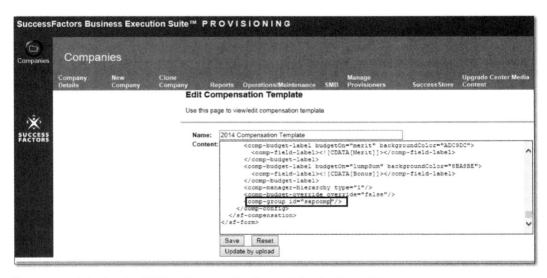

Figure 10.43 Selecting the Existing Compensation Template for the Current Year

Once you have updated the group ID, save the code by clicking on SAVE.

Update Compensation Forms with Staging Table Data

Next, we'll schedule a nightly job to update compensation forms. In this step, you will setup a scheduled nightly job to update the compensation forms with the data that will be imported into the compensation staging tables through the API.

The nightly update job can be setup in the SuccessFactors Provisioning client home page (click on COMPANY • MANAGING JOB SCHEDULER • MANAGE SCHEDULED JOBS).

On the CREATE NEW JOB screen, enter a name for the job, the owner, and the compensation template and job parameters. Once all details have been entered, click on SAVE.

Next, we'll enable the SuccessFactors API for web services.

Enable Web Services SuccessFactors API

In this step, you will activate SuccessFactors Talent Solutions web services API features. This process follows the same steps as those covered in Section 10.2.4, so refer back to that section for further details.

Next, we'll cover creating SuccessFactors API user permissions for Compensation.

Create SuccessFactors API User Permissions

As part of the basic setup for integration, the API user will have already been created. In this step, the user will setup and grant permissions for the API user to gain access to compensation objects and the API login. This step can be accessed from the Admin Tools, under MANAGE EMPLOYEES • SET USER PERMISSIONS • SELECT MANAGE PERMISSION ROLES.

> **Note**
>
> This step is only applicable if Role-Based Permissions (RBP) are being used. If this is the case, then an admin user with access to Admin Tools and specifically the RBP tasks needs to complete this step.

From the PERMISSION ROLE LIST, the user will need to specify the permission role by typing in the ROLE NAME or by searching through the list and clicking on the PERMISSION ROLE NAME (e.g., sap_api_user). Under PERMISSION ROLE DETAIL, click on the PERMISSION button to make the following settings for the API LOGIN PRIVILEGES and COMPENSATION PERMISSIONS (see Figure 10.44):

- API LOGIN PRIVILEGES
  Make the selection under GENERAL USER PERMISSION only if you are using RBP.
- SFAPI USER LOGIN
  Specify the SFAPI user login previously created e.g. "SAP_API_USER".

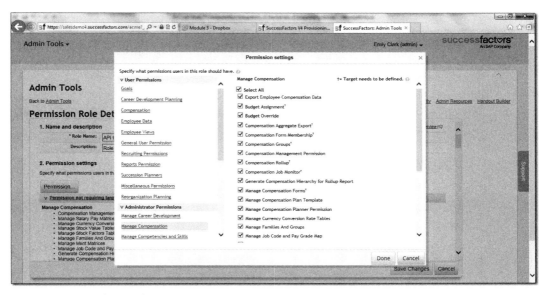

Figure 10.44 Specifying Role-Based Permissions

For non-Role-Based Permissions, complete the settings in the ADMIN TOOLS •
MANAGE API LOGIN PERMISSION section. If RBP is active and turned on, then MAN-
AGE API LOGIN PERMISSIONS will not appear under the ADMIN TOOLS.

> **API Login**
>
> Prevent the API user from being able to log in to the application UI by removing user
> login permission from the Admin Tools. When setting up the API and resolving errors,
> it's useful to have access to the API data dictionary and API audit log. This access can be
> granted in the Manager Integration tools permissions. Please note that in the API audit
> log the full payload data (including sensitive data) can be visible; therefore, this access
> should only be granted to the appropriate users.

Under the same PERMISSION SETTINGS screen, under MANAGE COMPENSATION (in
the USER PERMISSIONS section), select the SELECT ALL checkbox, and click on DONE
(see Figure 10.45).

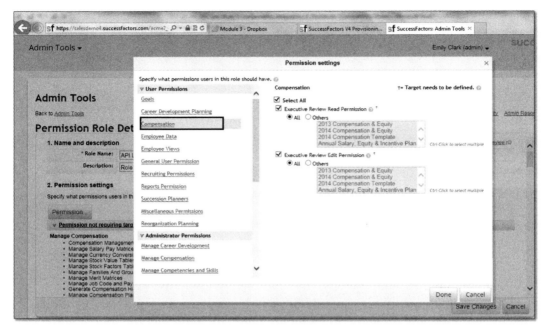

Figure 10.45 Setting Permissions

Finally, save your changes on the PERMISSION ROLE DETAIL screen.

Next, we'll look at the ad hoc report.

Enable Use of Ad Hoc Report Builder

This step turns on the Ad Hoc Report Builder feature and the Compensation Planning subdomain schemas in SuccessFactors Provisioning. This setting must be enabled in each SuccessFactors instance that will be used in the integration scenario (i.e., test and production).

This step can be accessed from the Provisioning client home page (go to COMPANY • COMPANY SETTINGS). Then, scroll down to the AD HOC REPORT BUILDER section and select the COMPENSATION PLANNING option (see Figure 10.46). Click on SAVE FEATURE to save the setting.

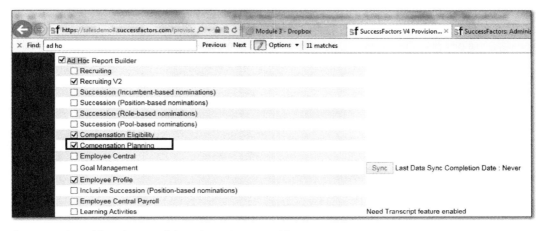

Figure 10.46 Enabling the Use of the Ad Hoc Report Builder

Create Ad Hoc Reporting Definition and Share Reports with API User

This step creates the ad hoc report used to integrate with SAP ERP HCM. Once the ad hoc report is created, an entity name is generated, which is referenced in SAP ERP HCM. This step can be accessed from the main page, under HOME • REPORTS • AD HOC REPORTS.

On the AD HOC REPORTS screen, select CREATE NEW REPORT, and select SINGLE DOMAIN REPORT as the REPORT TYPE and COMPENSATION PLANNING as the REPORT DEFINITION TYPE (see Figure 10.47).

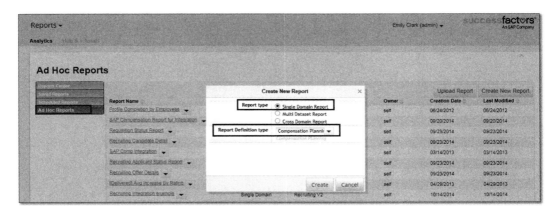

Figure 10.47 Creating a New Ad Hoc Report

From here, click on CREATE, and give the report a name and description in the REPORT NAME and DESCRIPTION fields.

Then, click on DATA SETS, to select the template used for the report. Next, select the compensation template you are using in your system from the dropdown list, and click on OK. The dropdown list appears when you click on SELECT TEMPLATE (see Figure 10.48).

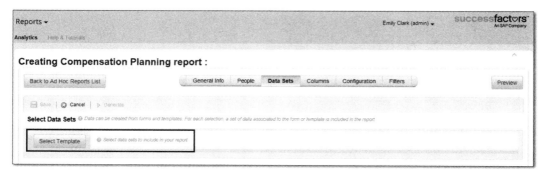

Figure 10.48 Creating a Compensation Report

Next, click on COLUMNS, and select the following fields to include in the ad hoc report (see Figure 10.49):

► FORM TEMPLATE ID
► FORM TEMPLATE NAME
► USER ID
► FIRST NAME
► LAST NAME
► COMP PLAN OWNER
► COMP PLAN ID
► COMP PLAN NAME
► MERIT
► BONUS
► LOCAL CURRENCY CODE

Ensure that basic details such as the USER ID and name are included as well as the compensation planning values you want to import to SAP ERP HCM. When you have finished selecting the fields, click on DONE.

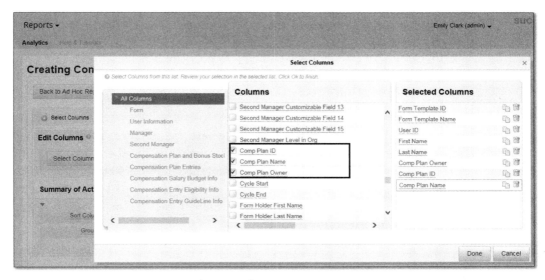

Figure 10.49 Ensuring Compensation Planning Values

The next step is to generate the report and check the output to make sure the results look correct. On the GENERAL INFO tab, click on GENERATE, and download the CSV file for further checking. Save the report once you are satisfied that all the required columns have been added.

Once the report has been saved, you need to share it with the API user. Search for the report in the list on the AD HOC REPORTS screen. Click on the down arrow and select the SHARE option.

On the SHARE COMPENSATION REPORT FOR INTEGRATION screen, search for the API user and select its checkbox under SEARCH RESULTS (see Figure 10.50).

Figure 10.50 Search for API User and Select Under the Search Results

453

Once selected, the user will appear on the right-hand box, in the SELECTED section. Click on SHARE.

Now that you have created the ad hoc report and shared it with the API user, you need to find the entity name in the API Data Dictionary. To access the API Data Dictionary, go to ADMIN TOOLS • COMPANY SETTINGS • SFAPI DATA DICTIONARY (see Figure 10.51).

Search for "AdhocReport_xxxx" entities, where "xxxx" represents the unique number for the report (there could be several unique numbers, depending on how many reports have been created). Expand the report detail by clicking on the plus sign (+) until you find the one that you created. Note the ad hoc report entity identified with the unique number. This value will be used in SAP ERP HCM to link to the correct report during integration.

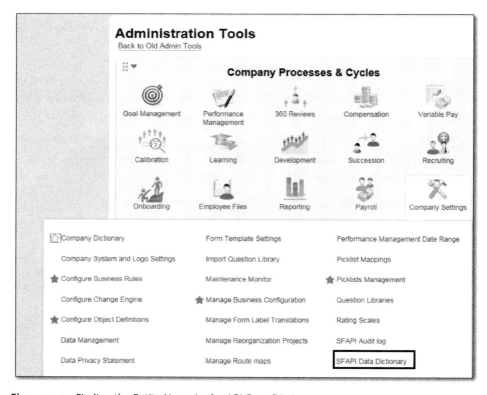

Figure 10.51 Finding the Entity Name in the API Data Dictionary

> **Metadata Transfer Report**
>
> The list displayed in the API Data Dictionary is sorted alphabetically, so the most recently created report should appear at the bottom of the list. This value, along with the compensation group ID, is required for the transfer of metadata step. The metadata transfer report will need to be run in SAP ERP HCM once the SuccessFactors configuration is completed. This is required in order to complete the field mapping configurations for importing compensation data. This is covered in the Import Metadata from SuccessFactors section.

In this section, via the MedTron example, we provided the detailed configuration and technical steps required to implement the SuccessFactors Compensation integration with SAP ERP HCM using the Talent Hybrid integration deployment model. On successful completion of the configuration steps, you will be able to run the compensation integration programs between SAP ERP HCM and SuccessFactors. Compensation data in SAP ERP HCM will be exported to SuccessFactors, where managers will be able to complete the compensation planning process by awarding a merit increase or bonuses to their employees. The updated pay values will be imported to SAP ERP HCM from the SuccessFactors Compensation module, where the salary increase or one-off payment will be further processed in SAP Payroll.

10.4 Recruiting Process Integration

In this section, we'll discuss the implementation steps necessary for both SAP ERP HCM and SuccessFactors to implement the recruiting process integration. We'll use a client scenario to demonstrate our case. A snapshot of our client is presented ahead.

> **Prerequisites**
>
> Refer to Section 10.2.1 for a list of the system prerequisites required prior to beginning the configuration of the recruiting process integration scenario.
>
> In addition, you will need to ensure that the following relevant configurations and customizations have been completed:
>
> ▶ Ensure that you have installed the latest SAP SuccessFactors Integration Add-on, which can be downloaded from SAP Service Marketplace and implemented in the SAP development landscape (refer to SAP Note 1841471 for more information).
>
> ▶ The integration middleware must also be configured (i.e., SAP PI integration or SAP HANA Cloud integration; refer to Section 10.1).

> ▶ After the middleware is configured, software and security requirements will need to be applied to grant a user access to the SAP IMG and to the new recruiting programs.
>
> ▶ To enable SuccessFactors recruiting integration with SAP ERP HCM, you must also implement SuccessFactors employee profile integration with SAP ERP HCM (refer to section Section 10.2 for more information).
>
> ▶ You will need access to the SuccessFactors Provisioning client and administration access (Admin Tools) to the SuccessFactors tenant.

10.4.1 Case Study Parameters

This case study focuses on how a customer who desires to implement SuccessFactors Talent Management Solutions will integrate and transfer their recruiting data from SAP ERP HCM to SuccessFactors Talent Management Solutions using SAP PI on-premise as the integration middleware. Let's look at our client scenario and process overview.

Client Scenario

MedTron has successfully implemented the employee and compensation process integrations as part of their Talent Hybrid integration deployment model so far. Medtron's focus is to implement SuccessFactors Recruiting next as well as integrating the recruiting data between SAP and SuccessFactors using the standard recruiting process integration using SAP PI.

Currently, MedTron uses OM and PA in SAP to manage its employee data. MedTron runs SAP ERP HCM ECC 6.0 EHP 6. In addition, the company has been advised to use SAP PI version 7.4 Java stack as its middleware.

The biggest concern for MedTron is keeping the systems and the HCM data in sync between SAP ERP HCM and SuccessFactors. This thought has been keeping the IT Vice President up at night. Therefore, the SuccessFactors consultant spent quality time assuring the client that the dual systems will have a seamless and successful implementation with leveraging SAP's standard recruiting process integrations.

Over the course of 14 months, this project was successfully sold based on the modularity of the solution that allows the client to grow with the system over time. In addition, the simplicity for the end user made this decision much easier.

In fact, the benefits of easy, fast deployment of recruiting functionality in the cloud, along with the ability to leverage standard Integration Add-ons delivered by SAP to ensure that the data is in sync between SAP ERP HCM and SuccessFactors, gave the VP of IT peace of mind and the comfort of knowing that this migration and the management of data involved will be successful.

The business requirements for MedTron's Talent Hybrid deployment model will rely on the following details:

▶ Vacancies will be maintained in SAP OM, utilizing Infotype 1007, where the job requisition will be triggered.

▶ There will be no custom development required.

Process Overview

The following four main steps are required to setup the recruiting process integration from SAP ERP HCM to SuccessFactors Talent Management Solutions:

▶ **Step 1: Basic setup**
There are basic integration configuration steps that must be performed in order to begin this process. This includes tasks such as importing metadata from SuccessFactors and activating the vacancy Infotype 1007 in SAP ERP HCM (see Section 10.4.2).

▶ **Step 2: SAP ERP HCM configuration**
In this step, you will apply the recruiting basic configuration and customizations in SAP ERP HCM. The tasks involved in this step range from activating additional functions to choosing an option for deriving the SuccessFactors HCM user ID from SAP ERP HCM (see Section 10.4.3).

▶ **Step 3: SuccessFactors configuration**
This step provides the configuration activities that take place in the SuccessFactors Talent Management Solutions Tenant and Provisioning client to support recruiting integration between SAP ERP HCM and SuccessFactors in the cloud (see Section 10.4.4).

▶ **Step 4: SAP PI middleware setup**
For step 4, you will need to setup the SAP PI middleware. Therefore, refer to Section 10.1 for a detailed description.

The integration specified here is tailored to those customers using the Talent Hybrid deployment approach to run the following systems:

- SAP ERP HCM on-premise for:
  - Personnel Administration (PA)
  - Organizational Management (OM)
  - Benefits, time, and payroll (PY)
- SuccessFactors for Talent Management Suite in the cloud, which includes Recruiting

Because both systems are used to process recruiting data, and in order to avoid disparate processes, it is imperative that the processes are integrated as tightly as possible from one system to another.

The process overview can also be divided into two main scenarios:

- **Job requisition creation scenario**
  - The Job Requisition process can be triggered from the SAP OM module.
  - When a new position is created in the SAP OM module, the SuccessFactors job requisition ID is assigned to the position, and it subsequently triggers the creation of a job requisition in SuccessFactors Recruiting.
  - The requisition will have the same job requisition ID assigned in SAP OM Infotype 1107 (SFSF Job Requisition).
  - These data objects are necessary for the recruiting process and can be transferred to — and stored in — SuccessFactors Talent Management Solutions.
  - The data is then stored as requisition data to support the recruiting process with information such as job description, responsible manager, position title, location, and country.
- **Candidate selection process scenario**
  - The candidate selection process allows users to conduct searches and find a qualified candidate for a specific requisition.
  - At this point, the candidate's data is transferred back to SAP ERP to be hired directly into the new position that was created in the SAP OM module.
  - The candidate is therefore hired into the SAP PA module as an employee.

> **Consultant Note**
>
> Some customers do not use the SAP OM module and thus would not use a new position to trigger a job requisition in SuccessFactors.
>
> However, they may need other entities in the job requisition—such as personnel area/ subarea, employee group/subgroup, cost center, or country—that are required when a candidate has been selected to be hired.
>
> Customers using SAP OM and the position object will have personnel structure data maintained in SAP OM and therefore only need the position to identify the area to which the candidate needs to be assigned.
>
> In addition, it is very likely that customers have customer-specific infotypes or custom infotype fields in SAP ERP HCM that they also want to see in the SuccessFactors recruiting system. Some customers may have different views on the data required for the recruiting process.
>
> You should be mindful that the goal for the recruiting integration should be to consider only those data or infotype fields that are absolutely required for the integration process for hiring a new employee or for rehiring employees. Other information that customers may collect with the SuccessFactors Recruiting system can also be transferred, but it differs from customer to customer.
>
> A second goal is to make the integration interface as flexible as possible. Customers can then extend the number of fields they wish to transfer from SuccessFactors HCM to SAP ERP HCM. As before, let's begin with the basic setup.

10.4.2 Step 1: Basic Setup

The basic setup for the recruiting process integration is comprised of two important steps:

- Importing metadata from SuccessFactors
- Activating the Vacancy infotype (1007) in SAP ERP HCM

We will begin our discussion by looking at the first of these two important tasks.

Import Metadata from SuccessFactors

To import metadata from SuccessFactors, the user will execute the report Importing Metadata from SuccessFactors HCM (Transaction RH_SFI_SYNCH_META-DATA), which is needed to extract the metadata from SuccessFactors Recruiting into SAP ERP HCM.

This data will then be transferred and used as follows:

▸ For input help

▸ To provide dropdown values in the integration programs

▸ In configuration for the recruiting processes

This step can be accessed via the SAP IMG menu path PERSONNEL MANAGEMENT • INTEGRATION ADD-ON FOR SAP ERP HCM AND SUCCESSFACTORS BIZX • IMPORTING METADATA FROM SUCCESSFACTORS BIZX. Then, on the initial screen, make the selection for the SYNCHRONIZATION SETTINGS FOR RECRUITING, which includes checkbox selections for SFSF ad hoc reports and SFSF job requisition templates, described ahead (see Figure 10.52):

▸ SFSF AD HOC REPORTS
When the selection is made, this setting will extract and store the following information into SAP tables:

  ▸ Ad hoc report IDs and descriptions (table T77SFI_SFO: SFSF Objects)

  ▸ Ad hoc technical names and labels of the fields that the relevant ad hoc report contains (table T77SFI_SFO_FLDS: SFSF Object Fields)

▸ SFSF JOB REQUISITIONS TEMPLATES
When the selection is made, this setting will extract and store the following information into SAP tables:

  ▸ Job requisition template IDs and descriptions (table T77SFI_SFO: SFSF Objects)

  ▸ Job requisition technical names and labels of the fields that the relevant job requisition template contains (table T77SFI_SFO_FLDS: SFSF Object Fields)

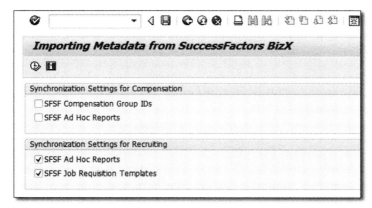

Figure 10.52 Sync Settings for Recruiting

Once your selections have been saved, the report will then need to be scheduled in the follow-on systems (e.g., test or productive systems) as a regular background job to update the metadata and continually keep it current.

> **Consultant Note**
>
> Before we begin the first step, preliminary actions must first take place. Prior to importing any metadata, the following SuccessFactors configuration scenarios must be completed:
>
> ▶ To execute the report, you must have the proper security role to access the SAP reference IMG.
>
> ▶ Each SuccessFactors instance will generate a different SFSF ad hoc report and job requisition template ID.
>
> ▶ In addition, this step cannot be transported from SAP and therefore must be executed in each customer SAP project system.

Activate the Vacancy Infotype

For our case study, MedTron Inc. plans to use the Vacancy infotype (1007). Thus, we will activate Infotype 1007 in SAP ERP HCM. The Vacancy infotype can be activated in SAP table T77S0 or by following the SAP IMG menu path PERSONNEL MANAGEMENT • ORGANIZATIONAL MANAGEMENT • INFOTYPE SETTINGS • ACTIVATE/DEACTIVATE "VACANCY" INFOTYPE.

Once you arrive on the VACANCY EDITING screen, the value abbreviation must be entered for the SYNCHRONIZATION SETTINGS FOR RECRUITING.

Placing a "1" in the VALUE ABBR. FOR GROUP PPVAC. SEM ABBR—PPVAC field indicates that an unfilled position is only considered vacant if it has Infotype 1007, thus making the vacancy infotype ACTIVE.

When the staffing status is updated on the Vacancy infotype, the corresponding SFSF Requisition (Infotype 1107) will automatically be updated. The SFSF Requisition infotype is used by the recruiting integration programs.

By leaving VALUE ABBR. GROUP PPVAC—PPVAC blank, VACANCY MANAGEMENT is DEACTIVATED, and the Vacancy infotype is not used.

In this instance, the SFSF Requisition infotype will need to be updated directly.

> **Note**
>
> For MedTron, the Vacancy infotype is activated. PPVAC is set to a value of "1".

Now that the basic setup has been completed, let's turn our attention to the SAP ERP HCM configuration setup.

10.4.3 Step 2: SAP ERP HCM Configuration

Here, you will need to apply the recruiting basic configuration and customizations in SAP ERP HCM, required for the recruiting integration from SAP ERP HCM to SuccessFactors.

The recruiting basic configuration for SAP consists of the following 16 tasks:

- Activate additional functions
- Assign SuccessFactors HCM objects to field sets
- Map SuccessFactors HCM fields and SAP ERP fields to each other
- Check field sets for required fields and correct
- Implement BAdIs for transfer of job requisitions (SAP to SFSF)
- Define values of job requisition status used in SFSF
- Specify handling of existing vacancies during data transfer
- Display Infotype SFSF job requisition in OM applications
- Correct status of job requisitions in SAP
- Implement BAdI for transfer of job applications (SuccessFactors to SAP)
- Change application status values used in SuccessFactors HCM
- Define additional display fields
- Define names of SuccessFactors HCM fields
- Change print form used for PDF overview
- Choose option for deriving SuccessFactors HCM user ID from SAP ERP
- Enter ID of candidate template from SuccessFactors HCM

Let's begin with the first step.

Activate Additional Functions

In this step, the user will activate two switches. The first is for transferring the SAP personnel number to SuccessFactors HCM, and the second is for triggering the creation of job requisitions in SuccessFactors HCM from SAP ERP HCM.

This step can be accessed using the SAP IMG menu path PERSONNEL MANAGE-MENT • INTEGRATION ADD-ON FOR SAP ERP HCM AND SUCCESSFACTORS BIZX • INTE-GRATION SCENARIO FOR RECRUITING DATA • ACTIVATE ADDITIONAL FUNCTIONS.

Let's now discuss how to activate the first switch, which transfers the SAP person-nel number to SuccessFactors.

On the ACTIVATION SWITCHES screen, set the parameter values for the following functions (see Figure 10.53):

▶ CANDIDATE_UPDATE_ACTIVE = "X"
By setting the parameter value to "X", this defines that you want to transfer the SAP personnel number back to SuccessFactors HCM after transferring and accepting a candidate into SAP ERP HCM as a new employee.

When the personnel number transfers to SuccessFactors HCM, it becomes the user ID and is stored in the candidate object table in SuccessFactors HCM.

This establishes a connection between the data of the external candidate, who applied via SuccessFactors HCM and that of the new employee who has been hired in SAP ERP Personnel Administration.

To activate the second switch, we need to trigger the creation of job requisi-tions in SuccessFactors HCM from SAP ERP HCM.

▶ JOB_REQUISITION_INTEGR_ACTIVE = "X"
By setting the parameter value to "X", you can define whether you want to transfer information about vacant positions from SAP ERP HCM to SuccessFac-tors HCM so that corresponding job requisitions can be created or changed there.

For this case study, the activation switches for the candidate update and job requisition are activated and set to a parameter value of "1".

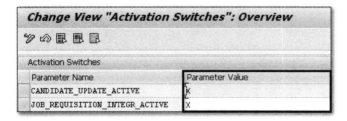

Figure 10.53 Activation Switches—Setting the Parameter

Vacancy Information

The default setting is that the creation of job requisitions in SuccessFactors HCM is not triggered from SAP ERP HCM.

If you want to transfer information about vacant positions from the SAP ERP HCM system to SuccessFactors HCM and want to create corresponding job requisitions in SuccessFactors HCM, then set the value of the parameter JOB_REQUISITION_INTEGR_ACTIVE to "X".

For migrating existing vacancies, see the Specify Handling of Existing Vacancies during Data Transfer section.

Now, let's discuss the next task, assigning SuccessFactors HCM objects to field sets.

Assign SuccessFactors HCM Objects to Field Sets

In this step, the user will assign SuccessFactors objects that are transferred from SuccessFactors via the IMPORTING METADATA from the SuccessFactors ad hoc report to existing field sets that map single SuccessFactors fields to SAP ERP fields.

The step can be accessed using the SAP IMG menu path PERSONNEL MANAGEMENT • INTEGRATION ADD-ON FOR SAP ERP HCM AND SUCCESSFACTORS BIZX • INTEGRATION SCENARIO FOR RECRUITING DATA • ASSIGN SUCCESSFACTORS BIZX OBJECTS TO FIELD SETS.

On the ASSIGNMENT OF SFSF OBJECTS TO FIELDS SETS screen, you'll need to set the parameter values for the following functions:

▶ FIELD SET
This field is used as a grouping, which maps individual SuccessFactors HCM fields to SAP ERP fields.

▶ FIELD SET DESCRIPTION
This field is used to describe the field set.

▶ SFSF OBJECT ID
This field is the SuccessFactors object ID, which is the recruiting ad hoc report technical name or the job requisition template ID that contains the fields you wish to import into SAP ERP HCM. The dropdown configurable values are filled during the importing of the metadata in the basic settings configuration.

▶ SFSF OBJECT TYPE

This field specifies the type of SuccessFactors object (e.g., the ad hoc report or the job requisition template).

▶ SFSF OBJECT DESCRIPTION

This field describes the SuccessFactors object.

For MedTron, the standard SAP_DEMO_01 field set is used and assigned to the correct SuccessFactors recruiting ad hoc report (see Figure 10.54).

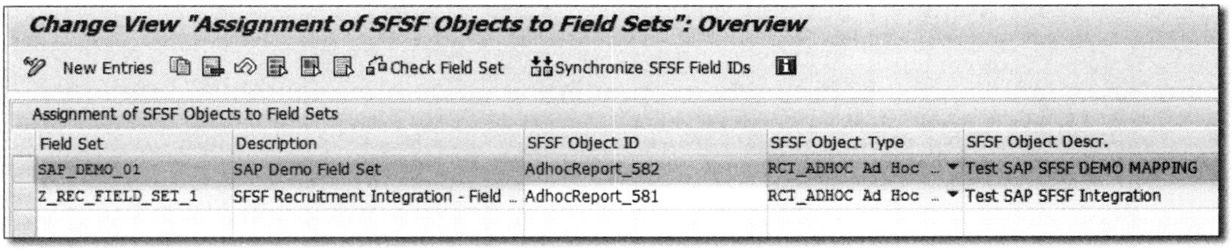

Field Set	Description	SFSF Object ID	SFSF Object Type	SFSF Object Descr.
SAP_DEMO_01	SAP Demo Field Set	AdhocReport_582	RCT_ADHOC Ad Hoc ... ▼	Test SAP SFSF DEMO MAPPING
Z_REC_FIELD_SET_1	SFSF Recruitment Integration - Field ...	AdhocReport_581	RCT_ADHOC Ad Hoc ... ▼	Test SAP SFSF Integration

Figure 10.54 Assignment of SFSF Objects to Field Sets

SuccessFactors Recruiting Ad Hoc

In order for the correct SuccessFactors Recruiting ad hoc report to be selected, the report must be created in SuccessFactors, and the import metadata step (discussed under the Section 10.4.2) must be executed.

This completes the SAP ERP HCM configuration setup. Now, let's discuss checking field sets for required fields and how to correct them.

Map SuccessFactors HCM Fields and SAP ERP HCM Fields to Each Other

In this step, the user will define and map the SuccessFactors fields and SAP fields to each other in the fields and mapping dialog structure. It is the mapping that is required to transfer job requisition data from SAP ERP HCM to SuccessFactors HCM and applications from SuccessFactors Recruiting to SAP ERP HCM. Prior to setting this up, you must have used the IMPORT METADATA from SuccessFactors HCM ad-hoc report to transfer the objects that you want to assign the SAP fields to. Once the data objects have been transferred, you may move forward with this activity to create the field set FS_01 and define the field mappings as desired, then transport the field set to the follow-on systems.

The step can be accessed using the SAP IMG menu path Personnel Manage-ment • Integration Add-on for SAP ERP HCM and SuccessFactors BizX • Inte-gration Scenario for Recruiting Data • Map SuccessFactors BizX Fields and SAP ERP Fields to Each Other.

In order to map the SFSF fields to SAP fields, the user will need to highlight the field set and double-click on the Fields and Mapping folder under the dialog structure.

To create a new entry to map, set the following fields (see Figure 10.55):

▶ SFSF Field ID
This is the SuccessFactors field name.

▶ Mapping Mode
The SuccessFactors fields can be:

▶ T: Mapped via Table,

▶ B: Mapped via BAdI (this can be mapped via custom BAdI logic: BAdI — Map-ping of SAP ERP infotype fields to SFSF fields), or

▶ N: Not Mapped (display only).

▶ Country Dependent
Select this checkbox if you have specified a separate field mapping for each country.

▶ Required
Select this checkbox if the fields are required and should be checked during data import. If a required field is missing, then the job application is sent back to SuccessFactors with an error.

▶ Field Description
This field is used to describe the SFSF Field ID.

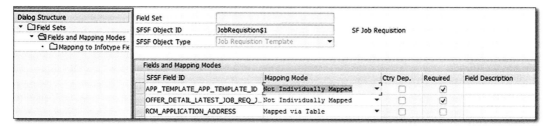

Figure 10.55 Mapping the Fields and Mapping Modes

Once the fields and mapping modes have been defined, double-click on the MAP-PING TO INFOTYPE FIELDS dialog structure to create a new entry that will include the SuccessFactors fields that you have set as MAPPED VIA TABLE in the previous step. Here, you will define the following details (see Figure 10.56):

▶ COUNTRY GROUPING
This field defines the country that the mapping is applicable for. This is only required if you have set the field as country dependent and require separate mappings for different countries. In this example, we are using CTRY GROUPING value "99 Other Countries".

▶ INFOTYPE
This is the SAP infotype to which the SFSF field is mapped. In this example, we are mapping the SFSF field ID RCM_APPLICATION_ADDRESS to the ADDRESS INFOTYPE (0006).

▶ SUBTYPE
This field is the SAP subtype to which the SFSF field is mapped. In this example, we are mapping subtype 1.

▶ FIELD NAME
This is the SAP field name to which the SFSF field is mapped. In this example, we entered the technical field name STRAS (Address Line) that the SFSF ID should be mapped to.

▶ IT RECORD NO.
This is the SAP infotype record number to which the SFSF field is mapped. This is used to differentiate between records that have the same key.

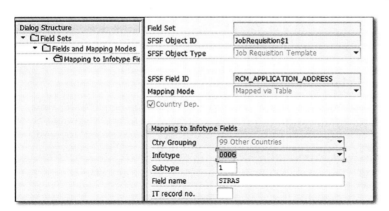

Figure 10.56 Mapping to Infotype Fields

Now, let's discuss checking field sets for required fields and correcting.

Check Field Sets for Required Fields and Correct

Once the SuccessFactors fields are mapped to the SAP ERP HCM fields, the user can run a validation program to check if the fields marked as REQUIRED are mapped correctly and do not contain errors.

This step can be accessed using the SAP IMG menu path PERSONNEL MANAGEMENT • INTEGRATION ADD-ON FOR SAP ERP HCM AND SUCCESSFACTORS BIZX • INTEGRATION SCENARIO FOR RECRUITING DATA • CHECK FIELD SETS FOR REQUIRED FIELDS AND CORRECT.

On the INSERT AND CHECK REQUIRED FIELDS IN FIELD SETS screen, execute the report for the SFSF object type in test mode. Then, deselect TEST RUN when you are ready for the productive run (see Figure 10.57).

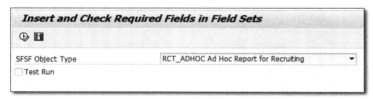

Figure 10.57 Insert and Check Required Fields in Field Sets

> **Note**
>
> If the configured fields or indicators are missing and they are required in SAP, then the report will add these fields automatically. If the REQUIRED indicator is not set for fields that the SAP ERP HCM system requires, then this report sets this indicator.

BAdIs for Transfer of Job Requisitions

SAP provides three BAdIs that support the data transfer of job requisition data for recruiting integration from SAP ERP HCM to SuccessFactors BizX, which can be accessed using the SAP IMG menu path PERSONNEL MANAGEMENT • INTEGRATION ADD-ON FOR SAP ERP HCM AND SUCCESSFACTORS BIZX • INTEGRATION SCENARIO FOR RECRUITING DATA • TRANSFER OF JOB APPLICATIONS FROM SUCCESSFACTORS BIZX TO SAP ERP.

These three BAdIs are as follows:

▶ **Determination of job requisition template from SFSF**
This BAdI can be used for custom logic for determining the appropriate ID of the job requisition template from SuccessFactors for a specific position to be staffed so that the job requisition for the position can be created. SAP ERP HCM runs through the implementation of this BAdI when executing the Create and Update Job Requisitions in SuccessFactors report (RH_SFI_TRIGGER_JOB_REQUISITION).

▶ **Mapping of SAP ERP infotype fields to SFSF fields**
This BAdI can be used for custom logic for mapping the SFSF to SAP fields. In order for SAP to run through the implementation of this BAdI, you will need to set MAPPED VIA BADI when mapping the SuccessFactors field.

▶ **Mapping of SAP ERP infotype fields to SFSF fields — changing of mapping results**
This BAdI can be used to further process the result of mapping SAP ERP HCM fields to SuccessFactors fields. For example, you can distribute the content of an SAP ERP field to multiple SuccessFactors fields.

SuccessFactors Data Tranfers

During the transfer of data to SuccessFactors, SAP ERP checks whether the SAP ERP infotype fields are assigned to SuccessFactors fields. For fields that use the mapping mode MAPPED VIA BADI, SAP ERP confirms the implementation of the BAdI mapping SAP ERP infotype fields to SFSF fields and checks all fields for a suitable implementation of this BAdI.

For this case study example, MedTron is not using any BAdIs.

This completes the SAP ERP HCM configuration setup. Now, let's discuss how to define values of a job requisition status unused in SFSF.

Define Values of Job Requisition Status Used in SFSF

In this step, the user will specify the status labels that are used in SuccessFactors HCM in the JOBREQSTATUS selection list for the STATUS field of the job requisition object. This customizing activity is only required if the statuses in SuccessFactors HCM are different from the standard statuses.

The step can be accessed using the SAP IMG menu path PERSONNEL MANAGEMENT • INTEGRATION ADD-ON FOR SAP ERP HCM AND SUCCESSFACTORS BIZX • INTEGRATION SCENARIO FOR RECRUITING DATA • TRANSFER OF JOB REQUISITION DATA

FROM SAP ERP TO SUCCESSFACTORS BIZX • DEFINE VALUES OF JOB REQUISITION STA-
TUS USED IN SFSF.

Furthermore, this information is required for the transfer of job requisition data
for positions from the SAP ERP HCM system to SuccessFactors HCM so that the
web services can set the status correctly in SuccessFactors HCM (see Figure 10.58).
Here, you will insert the status in the parameter value and save your changes.

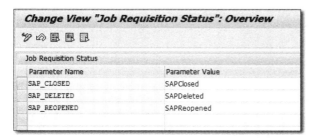

Figure 10.58 Inserting the Status Parameter

Specify Handling of Existing Vacancies during Data Transfer

In this step, the user will define how to handle existing vacancies in SAP ERP
HCM after activating the use of Infotype 1107 for job requisition transfer to SuccessFactors HCM (Infotype 1107 was discussed in Section 10.4.2).

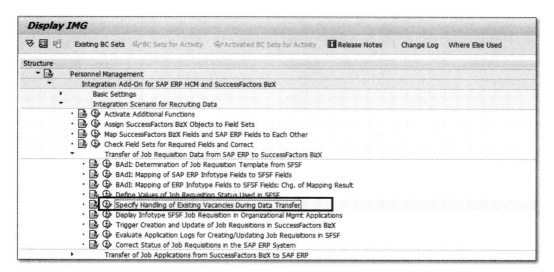

Figure 10.59 Specify Handling of Existing Vacancies during Data Transfer

The step can be accessed using the SAP IMG menu path Personnel Management • Integration Add-on for SAP ERP HCM and SuccessFactors BizX • Integration Scenario for Recruiting Data • Transfer of Job Requisition Data from SAP ERP to SuccessFactors BizX • Specify Handling of Existing Vacancies During Data Transfer, as shown in Figure 10.59.

Here, you will specify the type of transfer you want to handle current vacancies by selecting No Transfer or Standard Transfer (see Figure 10.60):

▶ No Transfer

You will make this selection if you do not want to transfer data on existing vacancies to SuccessFactors HCM. Consider the following points:

▷ When No Transfer is selected, this report will generate SFSF Job Requisition Infotype records and set the transfer mode to No Transfer.

▷ When future changes are made to the vacancy record, they will not be transferred to SuccessFactors.

▷ This option is mainly used for job requisitions that have been already created manually in SuccessFactors HCM for existing vacancies.

▶ Standard Transfer

Make this selection if you want to transfer data for existing vacancies to SuccessFactors HCM. This option is used when job requisitions have not been created in SuccessFactors for existing vacancies.

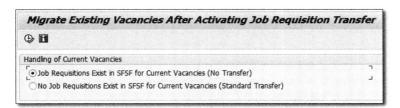

Figure 10.60 Migrate Existing Vacancies after Activating Job Requisition Transfer

For the MedTron Inc. case study, we will select the No Transfer option. Once the selection has been made, execute the report and exit the screen.

Let's now discuss how to display Infotype 1107 in Organizational Management applications.

Display Infotype 1107 in Organizational Management Applications

In this step, the user will specify whether open SuccessFactors job requisitions for positions of an organizational unit and the SFSF JOB REQUISITION tab should appear in Transactions PPOCE, PPOSE, and PPOME, which will be used by administrators who need to review and edit records for Infotype 1107 stored for the positions.

The step can be accessed using the SAP IMG menu path PERSONNEL MANAGEMENT • INTEGRATION ADD-ON FOR SAP ERP HCM AND SUCCESSFACTORS BIZX • INTEGRATION SCENARIO FOR RECRUITING DATA • TRANSFER OF JOB REQUISITION DATA FROM SAP ERP TO SUCCESSFACTORS BIZX • DISPLAY INFOTYPE SFSF JOB REQUISITION IN ORGANIZATIONAL MGMT APPLICATIONS.

On THE SCENARIO DEFINITION screen, highlight scenario OME0—ORGANIZATIONAL AND STAFFING, and double-click on the dialog structure TAB PAGE IN SCENARIO FOR EACH OBJECT TYPE.

Ensure the entries exist for the dialog structure. If they do not exist, create them as new entries:

- TAB PAGE
  SFSF_REQ
- SEQUENCE
  2
- REPORT NAME
  SAPLHRSFI_RECRUIT_1107_DETAILS
- SCREEN
  0020
- FM FOR ICONS
  HRSFI_RECRUIT_SET_TAB_ICON
- FM FOR TEXT
  Leave blank
- DO NOT DISPLAY
  Deselect

Save all changes.

Once you have saved your changes, click on the dialog structure REQUEST DEFINITION. You'll want to ensure that two entries exist for request and scenario definitions. If they do not exist, then create them as new entries:

Entry 1:

- SCENARIO
  OME0

- HIERARCHY FRAMEWORK REQUEST
  SFSF REQUISITION

- NAME
  SFSF JOB REQUISITION (Structure)

- SERVICE FOR 1ST INTERFACE OBJECT
  SFSF REQUISITIONS

- SERVICE FOR 2ND INTERFACE OBJECT
  Leave blank

- TAB PAGE
  Leave blank

Save all changes.

Entry 2:

- SCENARIO
  OME0

- HIERARCHY FRAMEWORK REQUEST
  SFSF REQUISITIONS (LIST)

- NAME
  SFSF JOB REQUISITION (LIST)

- SERVICE FOR 1ST INTERFACE OBJECT
  SFSF REQUISITIONS (LIST)

- SERVICE FOR 2ND INTERFACE OBJECT
  DETAIL (GENERAL)

- TAB PAGE
  Leave blank

Save all changes.

Once both request definitions have been defined, highlight each entry and under the REQUEST DEFINITION dialog structure, click on the sub-dialog structure REQUEST IN SCENARIO FOR EACH OBJECT TYPE. You'll want to ensure that an entry exist for each scenario request that you defined in the previous step. If they do not exist, then create them as new entries:

Entry 1:

- ▸ SCENARIO
  OME0

- ▸ OBJECT TYPE
  O

- ▸ REQUEST
  SFSF REQUISITIONS

- ▸ REQUEST IN SCENARIO FOR EACH OBJECT TYPE
  Leave blank

Save all changes.

Entry 2:

- ▸ SCENARIO
  OME0

- ▸ OBJECT TYPE
  O

- ▸ REQUEST
  SFSF REQUISITIONS (LIST)

- ▸ REQUEST IN SCENARIO FOR EACH OBJECT TYPE
  Leave Blank

Save all changes.

Now, let's discuss the correct status of job requisitions in the SAP ERP system.

Correct Status of Job Requisitions in the SAP ERP HCM System

In this step, the user runs the report to change the status of a job requisition in SAP ERP (RH_SFI_JOB_REQ_STATUS_CHANGE).

If the status is different from the one that the job requisition has in SuccessFactors HCM (e.g., a change from INITIAL to OPEN status), then this change affects the SAP ERP HCM system only. There is no communication with SuccessFactors in MedTron's case, and there were no job requisitions prior to the project that required a status change.

The step can be accessed using the SAP IMG menu path PERSONNEL MANAGE-MENT • INTEGRATION ADD-ON FOR SAP ERP HCM AND SUCCESSFACTORS BIZX • INTE-GRATION SCENARIO FOR RECRUITING DATA • TRANSFER OF JOB REQUISITION DATA FROM SAP ERP TO SUCCESSFACTORS BIZX • CORRECT STATUS OF JOB REQUISITIONS IN THE SAP ERP SYSTEM.

On the CHANGE STATUS OF JOB REQUISITIONS screen, make the following adjustments:

▶ Enter the position(s) for which you want to correct the status.

▶ Click on the EXECUTE button to review the log that tells you the number of job requisitions for which the status has been successfully changed:

  ▷ If errors occurred, then the positions in question are listed with relevant error messages.

  ▷ In these cases, double-click on the row of choice to enter the ID of the job requisition in the CHANGE STATUS OF JOB REQUISITIONS dialog box (see Figure 10.61). Click on ENTER, then on SAVE, and exit the screen.

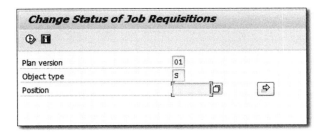

Figure 10.61 Change Status of Job Requisitions

The user must then execute the report to review the log and see the number of job requisitions for which the status has been successfully changed.

If errors occur, the positions in question are listed with the relevant error messages. In these cases, double-click on the row of choice and enter the ID of the job requisition in the CHANGE STATUS OF JOB REQUISITIONS dialog box, and press Enter.

This completes this step. We will now look at the BAdI used to transfer job applications from SuccessFactors to SAP.

BAdI for Transfer of Job Applications

SAP provides three BAdIs that support the data transfer of job applications for the recruiting integration from SuccessFactors HCM to SAP ERP HCM. For the purposes of this case study, MedTron is not using any BAdIs.

The step can be accessed using the SAP IMG menu path PERSONNEL MANAGEMENT • INTEGRATION ADD-ON FOR SAP ERP HCM AND SUCCESSFACTORS BIZX • INTEGRATION SCENARIO FOR RECRUITING DATA • TRANSFER OF JOB APPLICATIONS FROM SUCCESSFACTORS BIZX TO SAP ERP.

These BAdIs include the following uses:

▶ **Mapping of SFSF Fields to SAP ERP Infotype Fields**
This BAdI can be used for custom logic for mapping SuccessFactors fields to SAP infotype fields. You'll need a separate BAdI implementation for each field.

▶ **Mapping of SFSF Fields to SAP ERP IT Fields: Change of Mapping Result**
This BAdI can be used to further process the result of mapping SuccessFactors HCM fields to SAP ERP HCM fields. For example, you can distribute the content of a SuccessFactors HCM field to multiple SAP ERP HCM fields.

▶ **Determination of Further Data for Recruiting Scenario from SFSF**
This BAdI can be used to derive the country grouping and one or more personnel action types from recruiting data that you transfer from SuccessFactors:

  ▷ When importing data from the SuccessFactors system, the SAP ERP HCM system runs through the implementation of this BAdI and attempts to determine the chosen information from the transferred SuccessFactors field contents.

  ▷ It then uses this information to map the field contents transferred from SuccessFactors to infotype fields in the SAP ERP HCM system.

Next, we'll discuss changing the application status values used in SuccessFactors HCM.

Change Application Status Values Used in SuccessFactors HCM

In SuccessFactors HCM, the user will specify the labels for the status within the APPLICATION STATUS field of the JOB APPLICATION object in the HIRE STATUS category.

Importing recruiting data into SAP ERP HCM requires a certain status for the application so that the web services can set the status correctly in SuccessFactors

HCM. You will only need to make settings in this activity if you use a status in SuccessFactors HCM that is different from the standard delivered status.

This step can be accessed using the SAP IMG menu path Personnel Management • Integration Add-on for SAP ERP HCM and SuccessFactors BizX • Integration Scenario for Recruiting Data • Transfer of Job Applications from SuccessFactors BizX to SAP ERP • Change Application Status Values Used in SuccessFactors BizX.

In the case of MedTron, when we imported the recruiting data into SAP ERP we defined the standard statuses. If you use different settings than the standard delivered ones, then enter the values for the parameters of your choice (see Figure 10.62).

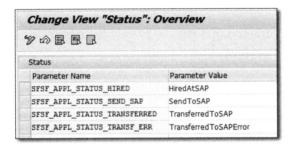

Figure 10.62 Define Status

This step is now completed. Next, we will look at defining additional display fields.

Define Additional Display Fields

In this step, the user defines the fields that are displayed as additional columns in the application for the further processing of imported applications (Transaction HRSFI_RCT_HIRE). You will only need to configure this setting if you want to display other columns in addition to the default columns. For MedTron, we did not configure this setting, because we did not want to display other columns in addition to the default columns.

If you want to display other columns, the step can be accessed using the SAP IMG menu path Personnel Management • Integration Add-on for SAP ERP HCM and SuccessFactors BizX • Integration Scenario for Recruiting Data • Trans-

FER OF JOB APPLICATIONS FROM SUCCESSFACTORS BIZX TO SAP ERP • FURTHER PRO-
CESSING OF IMPORTED APPLICATIONS • DEFINE ADDITIONAL DISPLAY FIELDS.

On the CUSTOM FIELDS screen, you will enter the technical names of the Success-
Factors fields of your choice as the values for the parameters of your choice. If
you do not require any additional columns, then make sure that the parameter
value is empty for all parameters (see Figure 10.63).

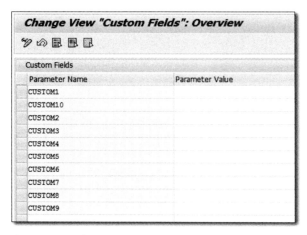

Figure 10.63 Change View Custom Fields

Headers and Field Labels

You will need to define headers and field labels for all fields that you want to display as
additional columns.

Define Names of SuccessFactors HCM Fields

In this step, the user will specify the headers and field labels for recruiting that
you transfer from SuccessFactors HCM to SAP ERP HCM to display in the Job
Applications Transferred from the SuccessFactors program (Transaction HRSFI_
RCT_HIRE) or in the data overview as a PDF document. In SuccessFactors, the
field names can have up to 255 characters.

SAP ERP HCM requires shorter versions of the field names in order to display
them; headers can consist of up to 10 characters, and field labels can consist up to
40 characters. For MedTron, we defined the names of the SuccessFactors headers

and field labels required for the recruiting data transfer within the character limits for field names.

The step can be accessed using the SAP IMG menu path Personnel Management • Integration Add-on for SAP ERP HCM and SuccessFactors BizX • Integration Scenario for Recruiting Data • Transfer of Job Applications from SuccessFactors BizX to SAP ERP • Further Processing of Imported Applications • Define Names of SuccessFactors BizX Fields. From the Attributes of SFSF Fields for Recruiting screen, ensure the following entries exist; if they do not, then create new entries as follows:

▸ SFSF Field ID
SuccessFactors field ID name

▸ Header
Column headers in the table of transferred applications

▸ SFSF Field Label
Field names in the detail view

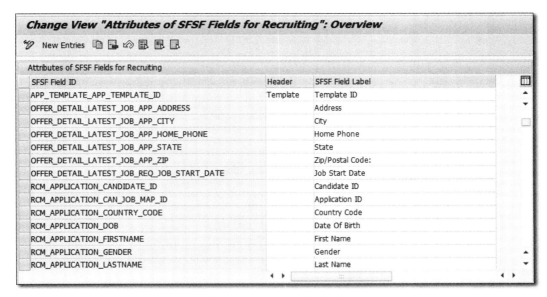

Figure 10.64 Change View—Attributes of SuccessFactors Fields for Recruiting Overview

With this step completed, we can now move onto discussing how to change print forms used for a PDF overview.

Change Print Form Used for PDF Overview

In this step, the user will specify a customer-specific PDF-based print form that the application for the further processing of imported applications (Transaction HRSFI_RCT_HIRE) will use for the PDF overview of imported data. You will need to verify that the customer-specific print form is based on the interface HRSFI_RECRUIT_APPLICATIONDATA.

The step can be accessed using the SAP IMG menu path PERSONNEL MANAGEMENT • INTEGRATION ADD-ON FOR SAP ERP HCM AND SUCCESSFACTORS BIZX • INTEGRATION SCENARIO FOR RECRUITING DATA • TRANSFER OF JOB APPLICATIONS FROM SUCCESSFACTORS BIZX TO SAP ERP • FURTHER PROCESSING OF IMPORTED APPLICATIONS • CHANGE PRINT FORM USED FOR PDF OVERVIEW.

On the PDF OVERVIEW screen, enter the form name of your choice as the value of the CUSTOM_APPLICATION_OVERVIEW parameter. Only set this value if you want to use a different print form from the standard print form. Then, save your entries (see Figure 10.65).

With respect to MedTron, we entered the form name "CUSTOM_APPLICATION_OVERVIEW" and set it as the value.

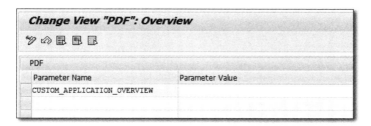

Figure 10.65 Change View PDF

Now, let's discuss choosing options for deriving the SuccessFactors user ID from SAP ERP.

Choose Option for Deriving SuccessFactors HCM User ID from SAP ERP HCM

In this step, the user will define how SAP ERP HCM derives a user ID for SuccessFactors from the SAP personnel number, if you have adopted a candidate transferred from SuccessFactors as a new employee in SAP ERP Personnel Administration.

SAP ERP HCM transfers this user ID to SuccessFactors so that a connection can be established there between the data of the external candidate who applied via SuccessFactors and that of the new employee who has been hired via Personnel Administration in the SAP ERP HCM system.

For MedTron, we defined the SuccessFactors user ID from the SAP central person number.

This step can be accessed using the SAP IMG menu path PERSONNEL MANAGEMENT • INTEGRATION ADD-ON FOR SAP ERP HCM AND SUCCESSFACTORS BIZX • INTEGRATION SCENARIO FOR RECRUITING DATA • TRANSFER OF JOB APPLICATIONS FROM SUCCESSFACTORS BIZX TO SAP ERP • TRANSFER USER ID TO SFSF AFTER ACCEPTING CANDIDATE IN SAP ERP • CHOOSE OPTION FOR DERIVING SUCCESSFACTORS BIZX USER ID FROM SAP ERP.

On the USER ID PROVISIONING OPTION screen, enter one of the following three options as the value of the PROVISIONING_OPTION parameter:

▶ PROVISIONING_OPTION = 1
Placing a "1" in the parameter value indicates that you will use the employee's Central Person (CP) ID.

▶ PROVISIONING_OPTION = 2
Placing a "2" in the parameter value indicates that you will use the ID that is stored for the employee in the EXTERNAL PERSON ID field (PERSONID_EXT) of Infotype 0709 (Person ID).

▶ PROVISIONING_OPTION = X
Placing an "X" in the parameter value indicates that you will define a customer-specific implementation. To do so, use the method GET_USERID of the Replication of Employee Data BAdI (HRSFI_B_EMPL_DATA_ REPLICATION).

For MedTron, the parameter value of 1 has been set (to use the employee's CP ID; see Figure 10.66).

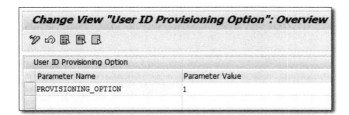

Figure 10.66 Change View—User ID Provisioning Option

Enter ID of Candidate Template from SuccessFactors HCM

In this step, the user will define which template you use for candidates in SuccessFactors HCM. SAP ERP HCM will need this information in order to transfer the user ID derived from the SAP Personnel Number to the correct applicant in SuccessFactors HCM.

For MedTron, we defined the template we used for candidates in SuccessFactors HCM so that we could transfer the user ID (derived from the SAP central person number) to the appropriate applicant in SuccessFactors.

The step can be accessed using the SAP IMG menu path PERSONNEL MANAGEMENT • INTEGRATION ADD-ON FOR SAP ERP HCM AND SUCCESSFACTORS BIZX • INTEGRATION SCENARIO FOR RECRUITING DATA • TRANSFER OF JOB APPLICATIONS FROM SUCCESSFACTORS BIZX TO SAP ERP • TRANSFER USER ID TO SFSF AFTER ACCEPTING CANDIDATE IN SAP ERP • ENTER ID OF CANDIDATE TEMPLATE FROM SUCCESSFACTORS BIZX.

On the OVERVIEW OF ADDED ENTRIES screen, insert the SuccessFactors candidate template ID that you use for candidates in SuccessFactors as the value, then save your changes (see Figure 10.67).

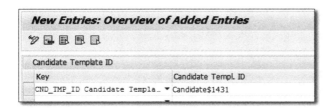

Figure 10.67 Overview of Added Entries for Candidate Template

This completes the final step for SAP ERP HCM configuration setup.

10.4.4 Step 3: SuccessFactors Configuration

We are now shifting our focus to the SuccessFactors side of the recruiting integration that we did for MedTron.

This section covers the configuration activities for MedTron that take place in the SuccessFactors Talent Management Solutions Tenant and Provisioning client to support the recruiting integration between SAP ERP HCM and SuccessFactors in the cloud.

> **Consultant Note**
>
> Your consultant must complete the *Introduction to SuccessFactors Academy* training course prior to performing the next steps.

SuccessFactors configuration settings consists of the following 12 steps:

- Activate the API
- Provide API access
- Enable Ad Hoc Report Builder
- Edit job requisition template
- Edit candidate profile template
- Edit job requisition application template
- Edit offer detail template
- Application status configuration
- Add status to candidate picklist
- Add status to job requisition status
- Map custom fields
- Create ad hoc report

Let's now discuss the first step of the SuccessFactors configuration setup: activating the API.

Activate the API

In this step, we will log in to the SuccessFactors Provisioning tool to activate the SuccessFactors API features. This step was covered in the basic settings of the employee data integration case study (see Section 10.2.2). For more information, refer to the Enable Web Services SuccessFactors API section (in Section 10.2.4).

Provide API Access

In this step, we will need to set up and grant Role-Based Permissions for the MedTron API user to gain access to recruiting objects and API login.

For SuccessFactors instances that have RBP activated, follow this step to set permissions. This step can be accessed from the Admin Tools, under Manage

EMPLOYEES • SET USER PERMISSIONS • SELECT MANAGE PERMISSION ROLES (see Figure 10.68).

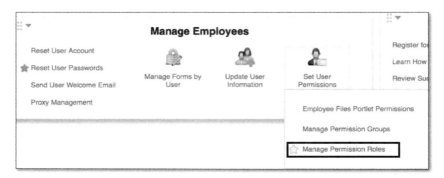

Figure 10.68 Manage Permission Roles

From the PERMISSION ROLE list, the user will need to specify the permission role. To do this, type in the role name or search through the list. Then, click on the permission role name (e.g., API_USER).

Under PERMISSION ROLE DETAIL, click on the PERMISSION button to make the following settings for the API LOGIN PRIVILEGES AND RECRUITING PERMISSIONS:

▶ API LOGIN PRIVILEGES
Make the selection under GENERAL USER PERMISSION only if you are using RBP.

▶ SFAPI USER LOGIN
Specify the SFAPI user login previously created e.g. "SAP_API_USER".

Apply Role-Based Permissions for MedTron

For MedTron, we are using RBP. The specific steps we took for MedTron are as follows.

On the PERMISSION SETTINGS screen, under RECRUITING PERMISSIONS, make the following SuccessFactors API selections only if you are using RBP:

▶ RECRUITING PERMISSIONS TO ACCESS THE RECRUITING OBJECTS VIA API

▶ SFAPI RETRIEVE CANDIDATE PERMISSION

- SFAPI INSERT CANDIDATE PERMISSION
- SFAPI UPDATE CANDIDATE PERMISSION
- SFAPI RETRIEVE JOB APPLICATION PERMISSION
- SFAPI INSERT JOB APPLICATION PERMISSION
- SFAPI UPDATE JOB APPLICATION PERMISSION
- SFAPI RETRIEVE JOB CODE PERMISSION
- SFAPI UPDATE JOB CODE PERMISSION
- SFAPI INSERT JOB CODE PERMISSION
- SFAPI UPSERT JOB CODE PERMISSION
- SFAPI RETRIEVE JOB REQUISITION PERMISSION
- SFAPI UPDATE JOB REQUISITION PERMISSION
- SFAPI INSERT JOB REQUISITION PERMISSION
- SFAPI UPSERT JOB REQUISITION PERMISSION
- SFAPI RETRIEVE JOB POSTING PERMISSION
- SFAPI RETRIEVE JOB APPLICANT PERMISSION
- SFAPI RETRIEVE ASSESSMENT ORDER PERMISSION

For Non-Role-Based Permissions

If you have a client that prefers non-Role-Based Permissions, then you will need to do take a different approach. Complete the settings in the ADMIN TOOLS • MANAGE API LOGIN PERMISSION section. If RBP is active and turned on, then MANAGE API LOGIN PERMISSIONS will not appear under Admin Tools.

Once you have completed granting permissions for all 18 SuccessFactors API functionalities, save your changes, and return to the ADMIN TOOLS page.

The final task of granting API access is setting the API login exceptions for the API user. For more information, refer to Section 10.2.4, under SuccessFactors API Login Exception.

APIs

To prevent the API user from being able to log in to the application UI, deselect USER LOGIN PERMISSION from the Admin Tools.

When setting up the API and resolving errors, it's useful to have access to the API data dictionary and API audit log. This access can be granted in the MANAGER INTEGRATION

Tools Permissions page. Note that in the API audit log the full payload data (including sensitive data) can be visible. Therefore, access should only be granted to only the appropriate users.

Let's move on to the next step, which will describe how to enable Ad Hoc Report Builder.

Enable Ad Hoc Report Builder

In this step, we will activate the Ad Hoc Report Builder for recruiting for MedTron.

This step can be accessed from the SuccessFactors Provisioning client home page; follow the menu path COMPANY • EDIT COMPANIES • COMPANY SETTINGS (see Figure 10.69).

Figure 10.69 Company Settings

On the COMPANY SETTINGS screen, under ANALYTICS AND DASHBOARD TABS & MISC REPORTING, activate the setting for RECRUITING V2 by selecting the checkbox, and save your changes to activate the Ad Hoc Report Builder for recruiting.

Edit Job Requisition Template

A job requisition template XML file defines the fields and functions for the type of requisition as well as the application status set that is to be referenced.

This step can be accessed from the SuccessFactors Provisioning home page; follow the menu path COMPANY • MANAGING RECRUITING • IMPORT/UPDATE/EXPORT JOB REQUISITION TEMPLATE.

On the COMPANY screen, you can add a new job requisition template or update an existing one. To update an existing job requisition template, select the relevant template and click on EXPORT (see Figure 10.70).

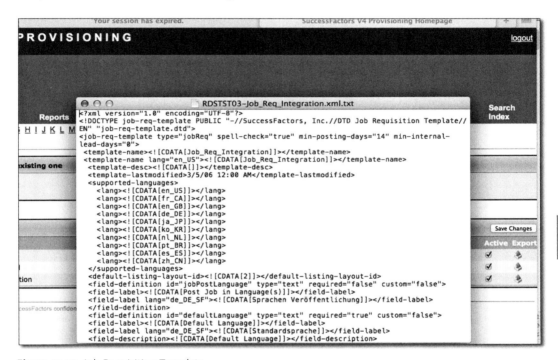

Figure 10.70 Job Requisition Template

Now, make the relevant changes and upload the XML file. Be sure to make note of the resulting template ID. Then, set the template to ACTIVE by clicking on the corresponding checkbox and saving your changes.

> **Administrator Note**
>
> An administrator will need to determine the fields that need to be added to the job requisition template based on customer requirements.

Edit Candidate Profile Template

In this step, we will log in to the SuccessFactors provisioning tool to edit the candidate profile template and add the relevant fields that MedTron requires.

This step can be accessed from the SuccessFactors Provisioning client home page; follow the menu path COMPANY • MANAGING RECRUITING • EDIT CANDIDATE PROFILE TEMPLATE.

On the COMPANY screen, on the EDIT CANDIDATE PROFILE TEMPLATE page, make the relevant edits to the candidate profile template XML to include any required fields, and save your changes (see Figure 10.71).

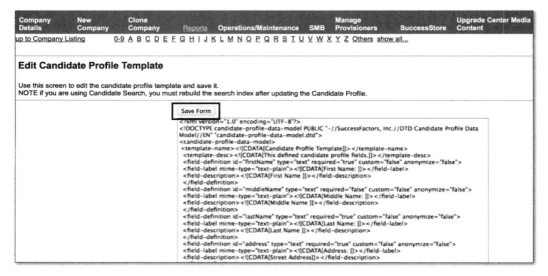

Figure 10.71 Edit Candidate Profile Template

Edit Job Requisition Application Template

In this step, we will log in to the SuccessFactors provisioning tool to edit the job requisition application template and add the relevant fields that MedTron requires. This step can be accessed from the SuccessFactors Provisioning client home page; follow the menu path COMPANY • MANAGING RECRUITING • EDIT JOB REQUISITION APPLICATION TEMPLATE.

On the COMPANIES screen, you will edit the job requisition application template or update an existing one.

For MedTron, we will update an existing job requisition application template. To open the existing template for editing, click on the Export icon (see Figure 10.72).

Figure 10.72 Edit Job Requisition Application Template (Upload)

Here, you'll want to make the relevant changes to include any required fields, and then upload the XML file. Be sure to make note of the resulting template ID. Also, set the template to Active by clicking the corresponding checkbox, and save your changes.

Let's move on to the next step.

Edit Offer Detail Template

In this step, we could either login to the SuccessFactors provisioning tool to edit the XML of an existing offer detail template or upload a new template. In the case of MedTron, we imported a new offer detail, which will be used in candidate communications, such as form letters or emails.

This step can be accessed from the SuccessFactors Provisioning client home page; follow the menu path Company • Managing Recruiting • Import/Update/Export Offer Detail Template.

On the Company screen, you will import/export a new offer detail template or update an existing one. To update an existing offer, select the relevant template and click on the Export icon (see Figure 10.73).

Then, make the relevant changes and upload the XML file. Be sure to make note of the resulting template ID. Set the template to Active by clicking the corresponding checkbox, and save your changes.

Let's move on to the application status configuration step.

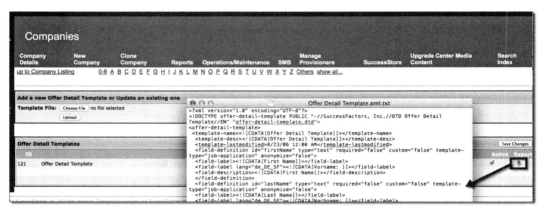

Figure 10.73 Offer Detail Template

Application Status Configuration

In this step, we will create four different application status items that will be used in MedTron's recruiting integration from SuccessFactors to SAP ERP HCM and vice versa.

This step can be accessed from the SuccessFactors Provisioning client home page; follow the menu path COMPANY • MANAGING RECRUITING • APPLICANT STATUS CONFIGURATION.

On the COMPANIES screen, you will edit the base set to make the status available for the required applicant status sets used in the recruiting integration process. To do this, click on EDIT BASE and then on ADD NEW STATUS (see Figure 10.74).

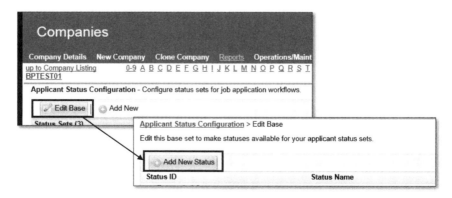

Figure 10.74 Application Status Configuration (Add New Status)

On the Status Base Details screen, enter the base status details as shown in Figure 10.75.

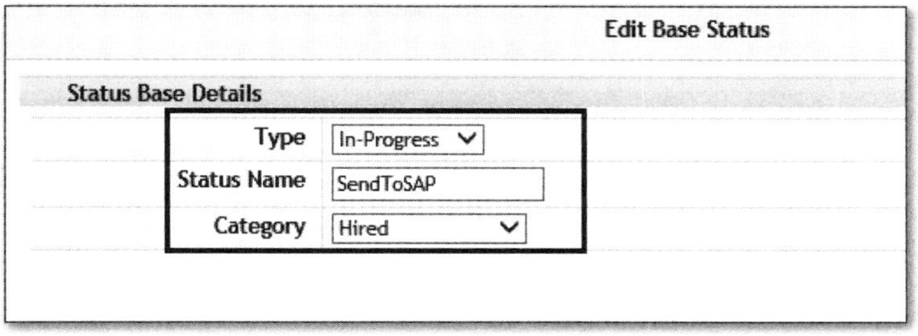

Figure 10.75 Status Base Details

At this point, save the changes you have just made. Then, you repeat the preceding steps for the following three remaining application status items:

- TransferredToSAP
  - Type: In Progress
  - Status Name: TransferredToSAP
  - Category: Hired
- TransferredtoSAPError
  - Type: In Progress
  - Status Name: TransferredtoSAPError
  - Category: Hired
- HiredAtSAP
  - Type: In Progress
  - Status Name: HiredAtSAP
  - Category: Hired

Once you are done creating all four required application status items, click on the I'm Done button near the bottom of the screen. From the Applicant Status screen, click on Applicant Status Configuration link to take you back to the Status Sets screen.

Under the Status Set list, locate the Status Set that is marked as default. Then, click on the Take Action dropdown, and select Edit (see Figure 10.76).

491

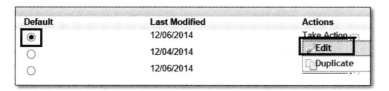

Figure 10.76 Application Status Configuration (Status Set List)

On the APPLICATION STATUS CONFIGURATION screen for the default status set, click on ADD NEW STATUS to add the four new status items you recently created. To do this, click on the checkbox next to each one. Then, click on the ADD button (see Figure 10.77) and then the I'M DONE button near the bottom of the screen.

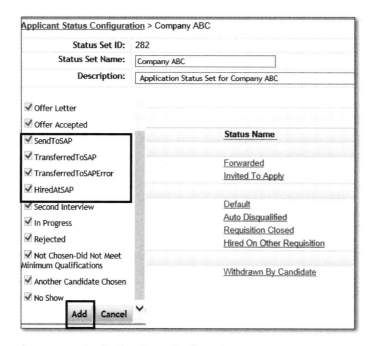

Figure 10.77 Application Status Configuration

Back on the APPLICATION STATUS CONFIGURATION screen, locate the four new application status items that were created, click on the TAKE ACTION button, then click EDIT for the status name TRANSFERREDTOSAP (see Figure 10.78).

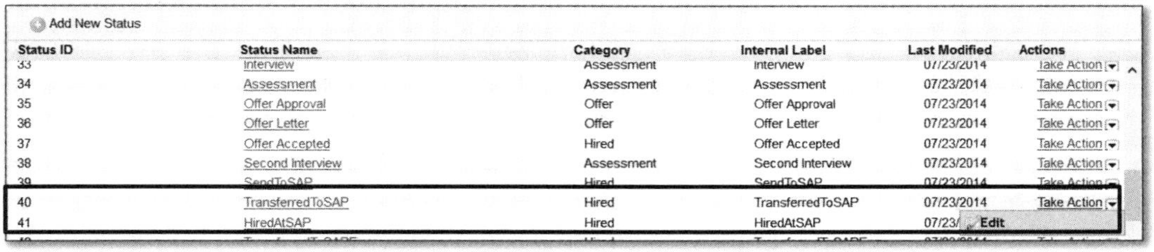

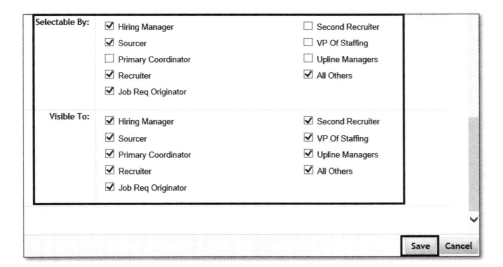

Figure 10.78 Application Status Configuration

On the EDIT BASE STATUS screen, under SELECTABLE and VISIBLE TO, verify that the base settings are correct. After validating that they are correct, click on SAVE (see Figure 10.79).

Figure 10.79 Edit Base Status

Back on the APPLICATION STATUS CONFIGURATION screen, locate the three remaining application status items that were created. Click on the TAKE ACTION button, then click on EDIT for the following status names:

▶ TRANSFERREDTOSAPERROR

▶ HIREDATSAP

▶ SENDTOSAP

When you're finished, click on the I'M DONE button near the bottom of the screen, which will complete the provisioning activity necessary to create the required application status for the recruiting integration.

You have now successfully completed this step!

Add Status to Candidate Picklist

For MedTron, in this step we added the four application statuses (SendToSAP, TransferredToSAP, TransferredtoSAPError, HiredAtSAP) to the candidate picklists in the SuccessFactors tenant.

This step can be accessed from the ADMIN TOOLS screen; go to COMPANY SETTINGS • PICKLIST MANAGEMENT (see Figure 10.80).

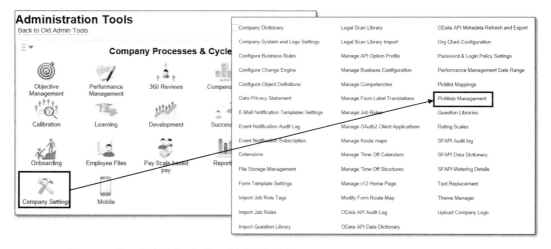

Figure 10.80 Add Status to Candidate Picklist

From the PICKLISTS screen, select the EXPORT ALL PICKLIST(S) radio button and the INCLUDE SYSTEM GENERATED JOB CODES checkbox. Then, click on SUBMIT to download the picklist CSV file (see Figure 10.81).

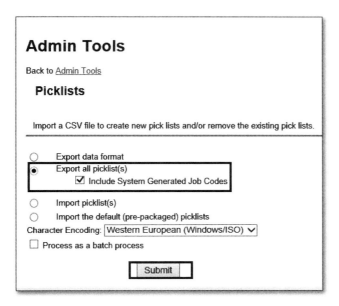

Figure 10.81 Import a CSV File to Create a New Picklist

In the picklist CSV file, ensure the following (see Figure 10.82):

▸ Only the four new statuses are in the CSV file.

▸ OptionID is blank; this ID will be allocated by the SuccessFactors system.

^picklistId	OptionId	minValue	maxValue	value	status	external_code	parentOpten_US
CandidateStatus		1	1	1	ACTIVE		-1 TransferredToSAP
CandidateStatus		1	1	1	ACTIVE		-1 HiredAtSAP
CandidateStatus		1	1	1	ACTIVE		-1 TransferredToSAPError
CandidateStatus		1	1	1	ACTIVE		-1 SendToSAP

Figure 10.82 Candidate Picklist

From the Picklists screen, select the Import Picklist(s) radio button, and choose the file via the Browse button.

The entire picklist file is not new; therefore, select No, and then click on Submit to complete the activity for adding the required application status to the candidate picklist required for the recruiting integration (see Figure 10.83).

Figure 10.83 Import Picklists

Let's move on to the next step.

Add Status to Job Requisition Status

For MedTron, in this step, we added the job requisition status (SAP closed, SAP reopened, SAP deleted) to the picklists in the SuccessFactors tenant.

Similar to the previous step, this step can be accessed from the ADMIN TOOLS screen; go to COMPANY SETTINGS • PICKLIST MANAGEMENT. From the PICKLISTS screen, select the radio button to EXPORT ALL PICKLIST(S). Then, click on SUBMIT to download the picklist CSV file.

In the picklist CSV file, ensure the following (see Figure 10.84):

▸ Only the three new status items are in the CSV file.

▸ OptionID is blank; this ID will be allocated by the SuccessFactors system.

^picklistId	OptionId	minValue	maxValue	value	status	external	parentOp	en_US	pt_BR
jobReqStatus		1	1	5	ACTIVE	null	-1	SAPClosed	SAPClosed
jobReqStatus		1	1	6	ACTIVE	null	-1	SAPDeleted	SAPDeleted
jobReqStatus		1	1	7	ACTIVE	null	-1	SAPReopened	SAPReopened

Figure 10.84 Picklist OptionID

From the PICKLISTS screen, select the IMPORT PICKLIST(S) radio button. Then, choose the file via the BROWSE button.

Let's now move on to the next step: mapping custom fields.

Map Custom Fields

In this step, you will enable MedTron's custom fields from the job requisitions to be reportable.

This step can be accessed from the Provisioning client home page; follow the menu path COMPANY • MANAGING RECRUITING • CONFIGURE REPORTABLE CUSTOM FIELDS.

On the MAP CUSTOM FIELDS TO EXTENDED FIELDS FOR REPORTING screen, click on JOB REQ, then click on the CONFIGURE CUSTOM TO EXTENDED FIELD MAPPING option.

In the TEXT section header for TEXT1 to TEXT4, enter the following XML custom field IDs:

▶ TEXT1
  sapPositionID

▶ TEXT2
  sapPositionName

▶ TEXT3
  sapOrgUnitID

▶ TEXT4
  sapOrgUnitName

In the PICKLIST section for Picklist1 to Picklist8, enter the following XML Custom Field IDs:

▶ PICKLIST1
  sapPersonnelArea

- PICKLIST2
  sapPersonnelAreaID

- PICKLIST3
  sapPersonnelSubArea

- PICKLIST4
  sapPersonnelSubAreaID

- PICKLIST5
  sapEEGroup

- PICKLIST6
  sapEEGroupID

- PICKLIST7
  sapEESubGroup

- PICKLIST8
  sapEESubGroupID

On the MAP CUSTOM FIELDS TO EXTENDED FIELDS FOR REPORTING screen, click on APPLICATION and then on the CONFIGURE CUSTOM TO EXTENDED FIELD MAPPING option.

In the TEXT section header for TEXT1, enter the following XML custom field ID: "sapError".

Save your changes to complete the activity for enabling custom fields from job requisitions and applications to be reportable.

Let's move on to the final step of the SuccessFactors configuration setup.

Create Ad Hoc Report

In this step, you will create the ad hoc report that will be used for exporting MedTron's recruiting data from SuccessFactors.

In the beginning of this chapter (in Section 10.4.2), we spoke about the ability to import metadata from SuccessFactors to SAP ERP HCM for the recruiting integration. In the DEFINE ADDITIONAL DISPLAY FIELDS area, if we choose to import the metadata, then we can see the additional columns in the application that were created upon importing the metadata.

For MedTron, we chose not to import metadata; therefore, we did not have additional columns displayed in this application.

This step can be accessed from the SuccessFactors homepage, under Main Navigation, following the menu path Analytics • Reporting • Ad Hoc Reports. On the Welcome to Reports Center screen, click on Create Report.

On the Create New Report popup, enter the following report type and definition, then click on the Create button (see Figure 10.85):

▶ Report Type
  Single Domain Report

▶ Report Definition
  Recruiting V2

On the General Info tab, enter the following details:

▶ Report Name
  For example, "Exporting Recruiting Data from SFSF"

▶ Report Description
  Free text

▶ Report Priority
  Medium

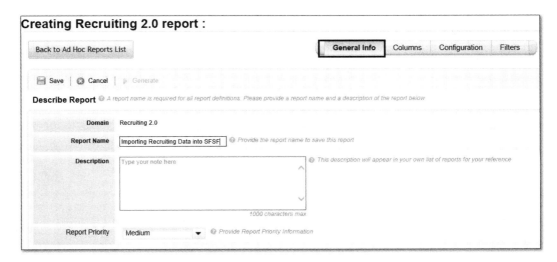

Figure 10.85 Recruiting Integration (General Info)

On the Columns tab, enter the columns shown in Table 10.13.

Folder	Columns
Application Folder	▸ Application ID ▸ Application Status ▸ Template ID ▸ First Name ▸ Last Name ▸ Gender ▸ Date of Birth ▸ SAP Position ID ▸ Any other application field the client has mapped to SAP
Last Offer Details Folder	▸ Start Date ▸ Any other application field the client has mapped to SAP
Requisition Folder	▸ Any requisition fields the client has mapped to SAP ▸ Define any of the fields as filters, with the specified filter criteria
Application Folder	▸ Application Status: SendtoSAP ▸ Template ID: whatever template ID is being used ▸ If the client uses more than one template, then create multiple versions of this report, and alter the report name to specify which report refers to Template A

Table 10.13 Recruiting Ad hoc Report Fields

The information shown in Figure 10.86 should be listed in the Configuration tab.

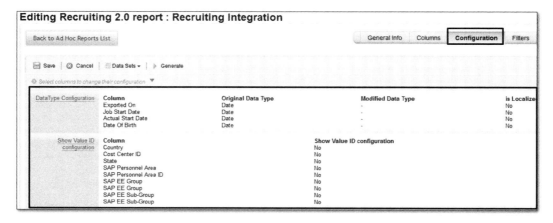

Figure 10.86 Recruiting Integration (Configuration)

The information shown in Figure 10.87 should be present on the FILTERS tab.

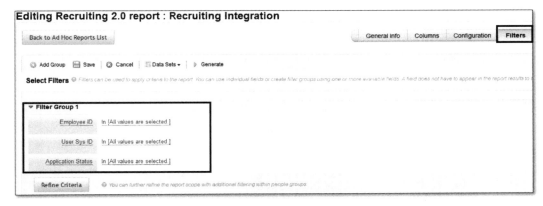

Figure 10.87 Recruiting Integration (Filters)

Be sure to save your changes to complete the activity for creating the ad hoc report for exporting recruiting data from SuccessFactors.

In this section, via the MedTron example provided, we detailed the necessary configuration and technical steps required to implement the SuccessFactors recruitment integration with SAP ERP HCM using the Talent Hybrid deployment model. The goal of this case study was to highlight the steps that you can follow as you help your clients with their SuccessFactors Recruiting module for the Talent Hybrid integration with SAP ERP HCM.

10.5   User Authentication Integration

In this section, we will discuss the user authentication integration. Specifically, we'll discuss the implementation steps necessary for both SAP ERP HCM and SuccessFactors to implement the SSO integration.

Prerequisites

There are three preliminary actions you must complete before you can begin to configure SSO:

▶ Ensure that the relevant systems are available and access requirements have been completed.

▶ Ensure that all systems have the minimum versions required:

> ▸ For SAP Netweaver, the minimum version required is 7.2 or above.
>
> ▸ For SuccessFactors, the system hosted by SuccessFactors is updated on a quarterly basis. Therefore, all SuccessFactors systems will have the minimum version for SSO.
>
> ▸ Ensure that you have the correct system access to complete the SSO setup:
>
>   ▸ In order to setup SAP Enterprise Portal as the trusted identity provider, you will need SAP Netweaver administrator access.
>
>   ▸ On the SuccessFactors system, you will need provisioning access to set it up as the service provider.
>
>   ▸ You will need SAP Enterprise Portal content administration access to be able to embed SuccessFactors transactions in the portal menu.
>
> To enable SuccessFactors to communicate securely with SAP Netweaver, during the installation you will need the SuccessFactors X509 certificate. This can be obtained by contacting your SuccessFactors implementation team.

10.5.1 Case Study Parameters

This case study focuses on a customer who desires to implement SSO between SuccessFactors and SAP ERP HCM. We'll use a client scenario to demonstrate our case. A snapshot of our client is presented next.

Client Scenario

During the preliminary presell activities, the sales team gathered that MedTron had standardized on SAP ERP HCM ECC 6.0 EHP 6 to maintain all employee data records. In addition, MedTron is running an ESS and MSS portal (SAP EP version 7.4) to allow users to access their employee and organizational information. MedTron also uses OM and PA as well as SAP PI version 7.4 Java stack.

Throughout the upfront sales consultation process, MedTron became increasingly interested in SuccessFactors, because the company appreciates the modularity of the entire SuccessFactors platform. MedTron is also very intrigued with the SSO capability of the system that makes it more user-friendly for employees to access all of their data through one single point of entry.

One piece of low-hanging fruit that the sales team identified was to immediately assist their users in removing barriers to get to their data. With that, MedTron agreed to implement SSO.

To do this, they embedded SuccessFactors transactions within the SAP portal so that users have a single user interface for both SAP and SuccessFactors transactions. In addition, we implemented SSO between SAP Netweaver and SuccessFactors so that users do not have to enter their password again when accessing SuccessFactors transactions.

Although implementing SSO is easy to execute, MedTron was concerned that this single point of entry for SAP ERP HCM and SuccessFactors could confuse users. The MedTron IT department would have to communicate this new change to all of their global users.

Specifically, IT would need to explain the benefits of SSO to the end users. These benefits include:

▶ Reducing help desk costs by decreasing the number of calls made to recover passwords.

▶ Increasing productivity (and reducing downtime) by keeping users from having to perform a unique login for both the SAP portal and SuccessFactors.

▶ Ensuring confidentiality through reliable, standards-based encryption during data transmission.

There were a couple of requirements that were also agreed to, including:

▶ Once an end user logged into the SAP portal, all SuccessFactors transactions would be embedded into the portal menu.

▶ MedTron made it clear that it did not want its users to enter their username and password again to access any SuccessFactors transactions.

This case study focuses on the necessary configuration and technical steps required to implement SSO between SAP ERP HCM and SuccessFactors.

Process Overview

This process is intended for customers using the Talent Hybrid integration who run SAP ERP HCM for Personnel Administration and Organizational Management, as well as benefits, time, and payroll, and SuccessFactors Talent Management Solutions and who desire the simplicity of SSO to access to their systems through a single point of entry.

There is only one step to complete for this specific integration: SSO set up.

The beauty of this integration is that installing SSO enables users to access both SAP and SuccessFactors pages through the SAP Enterprise Portal without having to sign in multiple times.

In order to begin this type of configuration, users will need to access transactions from both SAP ERP HCM and SuccessFactors.

SSO
SSO uses Security Assertion Markup Language (SAML) version 2.0, which is a standards-based mechanism for SSO.

10.5.2 Single Sign-On Setup

There are five steps required to setup SSO, which are itemized ahead. We'll discuss each step one-by-one in the following pages:

▸ Enable SAML 2.0 and set up SAP NetWeaver as a local provider

▸ Add the SuccessFactors system as a trusted provider

▸ Add SAP portal as a trusted identity provider in SuccessFactors (SAP Net-Weaver configuration)

▸ Add SAP Enterprise Portal as a trusted identity provider in SuccessFactors (SuccessFactors configuration)

▸ Create an SAP portal URL iView to SuccessFactors

Let's begin by enabling SAML 2.0 and setting up SAP NetWeaver as a local provider.

Enable SAML 2.0 and Set Up SAP NetWeaver as a Local Provider

SAML is the standard that SSO uses to exchange authorization and authentication between trusted systems. SAML 2.0 functionality must be activated to enable SAP NetWeaver to participate in the SSO process. Subsequently, SAP NetWeaver will also need to be set up as a local provider so that it can provide the trusted identity to request resources from SuccessFactors.

To do this, log on to the SAP NetWeaver system, and perform the following tasks:

1. Open an Internet browser.

2. Go to *<portalhost>:<port>/nwa* — for example, *dwg2131:1080/nwa*.

3. Go to the AUTHENTICATION AND SINGLE SIGN-ON screen by navigating to the CONFIGURATION tab and selecting the AUTHENTICATION AND SINGLE SIGN-ON link.

4. Select the SAML 2.0 tab, and click on the ENABLE SAML 2.0 SUPPORT button.

5. The system will then guide you through the steps to set up SAP NetWeaver as a local provider.

In the initial settings, you will need to enter a provider name. This name can be defined by the user; however, best practice is to include the system name and landscape in the name to make it more meaningful—for example, portal731ED6 for the ED6 landscape (see Figure 10.88).

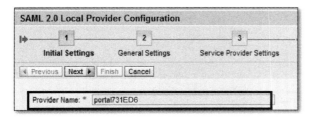

Figure 10.88 Initial Settings

The next task is to fill in the general settings. On the first screen, you need to perform the following steps:

1. In the KEYSTORE VIEW field, enter "SAML2". In the SIGNING KEY PAIR field, create a signing key pair by clicking on the BROWSE button next to the field and then clicking on the CREATE button to create a new signing key pair.

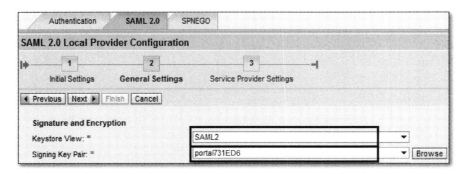

Figure 10.89 General Settings

2. At this point, you will be prompted with the steps needed to create a signing key pair. For the entry settings prompt, you will need to fill in the fields based on the information below:

▸ ENTRY NAME: <specify a entry name> for example, portal731ED6

▸ ALGORITHM: RSA

▸ KEY LENGTH: 2048

▸ VALID FROM AND VALID TO: Defaulted values

▸ STORE CERTIFICATE: Selected

Figure 10.90 Entry Settings

3. The next step required for signing the key pair is to complete the SUBJECT PROPERTIES screen. Perform the following steps (see Figure 10.91):

▸ In the COMMONNAME field, enter the ENTRY NAME defined in the entry settings step.

▸ When you have done this, click on the FINISH button to complete the signing key pair setup.

▸ Then, click on OK to go back to the SAML 2.0 provider configuration setup screen.

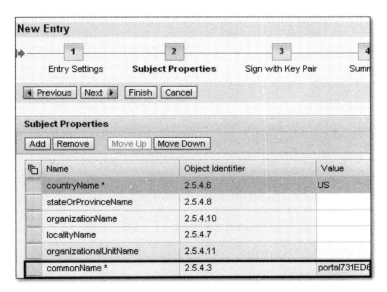

Figure 10.91 Subject Properties

4. Now that the signing key pair has been created, the signing key pair name and encryption key fields are defaulted based on the information you have just set up. Click on NEXT to go to the Service Provider Settings step. (No changes are required in the service provider settings steps.)

5. Click on FINISH to complete your setup.

You have now completed your SAP NetWeaver local provider setup. Let's now add the SuccessFactors system as a trusted provider.

Add SuccessFactors System as a Trusted Provider

In SAP NetWeaver, SuccessFactors must be set up as a trusted provider so that SAP NetWeaver can securely communicate with SuccessFactors. The SuccessFactors X509 security certificate must be loaded into SAP NetWeaver in order to authorize SAP NetWeaver to communicate securely with SuccessFactors.

To do this, log on to the SAP NetWeaver system, and perform the following steps:

1. Open an Internet browser.

2. Go to *<portalhost>:<port>/nwa*—for example, *dwg2131:1080/nwa*.

3. Go to the Authentication and Single Sign On screen by navigating to the Configuration tab and selecting the Authentication and Single Sign-On link.

4. Select the SAML 2.0 tab, and click on the Trusted Providers subtab.

Next, you will need to create a new trusted provider:

1. Click on the Add button.

2. Select the Manual button to manually add a new trusted provider.

3. On the provider step, enter the provider name for the SuccessFactors system. For example, *https://www.successfactors.com.*

4. Click on Next to continue creating a trusted provider (see Figure 10.92).

Figure 10.92 Provider Name

Now, you will need to set up the security details of the SuccessFactors system. On the Signature and Encryption screen, perform the following steps:

1. Upload the SuccessFactors certificate into the SAP NetWeaver system.

2. Next to the signing certificate, click on the Browse button.

3. Click on Import Entry to start importing the SuccessFactors certificate.

4. For Entry Type, select X509 certificate.

5. Click on the Browse button to find the path of the SuccessFactors certificate.

6. Click on Import to finish importing the certificate. The Signing Certificate field should now be filled (see Figure 10.93).

7. Click on Next to continue creating a trusted provider.

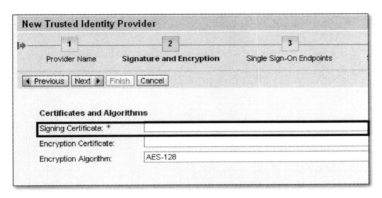

Figure 10.93 Signature and Encryption for Trusted Provider

The next task is to fill in the details of the SuccessFactors system that SAP NetWeaver must communicate with. At this point, navigate to the ENDPOINTS tab. On the SINGLE SIGN-ON ENDPOINTS screen, perform the following steps:

1. Click on the ADD button to add an SSO endpoint.

2. Enter HTTP POST for BINDING.

3. Enter the SuccessFactors consumer service URL in the LOCATION URL field.

4. Click on OK to go to the next screen.

   ▷ The consumer service URL is what you will use to log on to the SuccessFactors system. The URL address should be in the following format: *https:// <systemname.com>/saml2/SAMLAssertionConsumer?company=<companyid>*– for example: *https://performancemanager10.SuccessFactors.com/saml2/SAMLAssertionConsumer?company=ACE1234* .

5. On the NEW ENDPOINT FOR SINGLE LOGOUT screen, enter the SuccessFactors logout URL.

6. In the BINDING field, enter HTTP REDIRECT. In the LOCATION URL field, enter the global logout response handler URL, which is in the format *https://<systemname. com>/saml2/LogoutServiceHTTPRedirectResponse?company=<companyid>*–for example, *https://performancemanager10/saml2/LogoutServiceHTTPRedirectResponse? company=ACE1234* .

7. At this point, the SSO Endpoint has been created; do not enter any other end-points.

8. Click on NEXT, and then click on FINISH to complete the trusted provider setup.

Now, navigate to the next tab to the right: IDENTITY FEDERATION. On this tab, perform the following steps:

1. Click on the ADD button to add an identity federation.

2. Enter UNSPECIFIED in the FORMAT field.

3. Enter your logon ID in the SOURCE NAME field.

4. Click on SAVE.

The last task is to activate the trusted provider that has just been created. Perform the following steps:

1. Select the trusted provider *www.SuccessFactors.com*.

2. Click on ENABLE.

You have now added SuccessFactors as a trusted provider in SAP NetWeaver.

So far, you have completed two of the five steps required for setting up SSO. Now, let's discuss adding a portal as a trusted identity provider in SuccessFactors; this is an SAP NetWeaver configuration.

Add a Portal as a Trusted Identity Provider in SuccessFactors—SAP NetWeaver Configuration

SAP NetWeaver acts as a trusted identity provider to confirm the identity of the user on behalf of SuccessFactors. Specifically, SAP Netweaver validates the user by requesting a logon and password. Subsequently, when a SuccessFactors URL is requested, SAP NetWeaver identifies the user and confirms his or her identity for SuccessFactors so that the user does not need to log on again.

In this section, you will download the SAP certificate from the list provided. In the following section, you will subsequently upload this same certificate into SuccessFactors. Let's begin by first downloading the SAP certificate. To do this, log on to the SAP NetWeaver system, and perform the following steps:

1. Open an Internet browser.

2. Go to *<portalhost>:<port>/nwa*—for example, *dwg2131:1080/nwa*.

3. Go to the CERTIFICATES AND KEYS screen by navigating to the CONFIGURATION tab and clicking on the CERTIFICATES AND KEYS link.

Next, you will want to export the SAP NetWeaver certificate. Under the KEY STORAGE tab (see Figure 10.94), perform the following steps:

1. Locate and select the row named SAML2.
2. Under the VIEW ENTRIES tab:
   ▸ Locate and select the provider name you created in the ENABLING SAML 2.0 & SETTING UP SAP NETWEAVER AS A LOCAL PROVIDER section.
   ▸ Click on the EXPORT ENTRY button.
   ▸ Select the format BASE64 x 509.
   ▸ Click on DOWNLOAD to download the certificate.

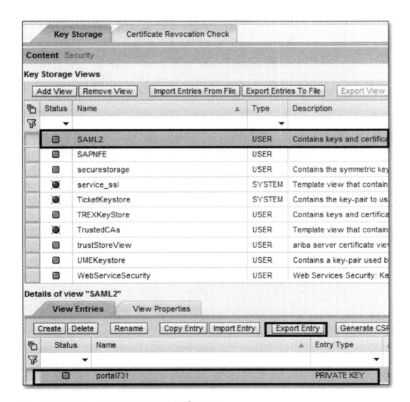

Figure 10.94 SAP NetWeaver Certificates

You have just completed the third step required for setting up SSO. Now, let's turn our attention to adding a portal as a trusted identity provider in SuccessFactors; this is a SuccessFactors configuration.

Add a Portal as a Trusted Identity Provider in SuccessFactors—SuccessFactors Configuration

In the previous section, we downloaded the SAP NetWeaver certificate. Now, it's time to upload the SAP certificate to the SuccessFactors side. Here, we'll focus on completing the SSO setup in SuccessFactors.

To do this, log on to the SuccessFactors Provisioning system, and perform the following steps (see Figure 10.95):

1. Go to COMPANY SETTINGS • SINGLE SIGN-ON (SSO) SETTINGS, and navigate to the SINGLE SIGN-ON CONFIGURATION screen.

2. In the SAML-BASED SSO section, select SAML V2 SSO to activate SAML version 2.0-based SSO.

3. In the SAML ASSERTING PARTY section, enter the following information:

   ▸ SAML ASSERTING PARTY NAME: Specify an entry name—for example, portal731ED6

   ▸ SAML ISSUER: Enter the name of the identity provider that you have set up in SAP NetWeaver

   ▸ REQUIRED MANDATORY SIGNATURE: Assertion

   ▸ ENABLE SAML FLAG: Enabled

   ▸ SAML VERIFYING CERTIFICATE: Open the signing certificate of the portal identity provider that you downloaded in the previous step in a text editor. Copy the text into the SAML VERIFYING CERTIFICATE field.

4. Once completed, click on ADD AN ASSERTING PARTY to create your entry.

5. To complete this aspect of the configuration, scroll down to the SINGLE SIGN ON FEATURES section (see Figure 10.96). Perform the following steps:

   ▸ Enter the RESET TOKEN (which can be any value).

   ▸ Click on SAVE TOKEN to activate SSO in SuccessFactors.

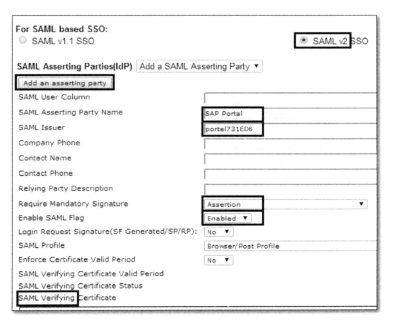

Figure 10.95 SuccessFactors Single Sign-On Settings

Figure 10.96 Single Sign-On Features

Customer Option to Set Up Partial SSO

Please note that there are some customers with a mix of both SSO and users who log on directly to SuccessFactors. For example, you might want regular employees to log on through SSO, but you may still want administrators to be able to log on directly to SuccessFactors.

6. To setup partial organization SSO, select the PARTIAL ORGANIZATION SSO checkbox under PROVISIONING • COMPANY SETTINGS in SuccessFactors Provisioning (see Figure 10.97).

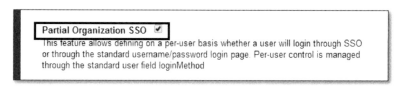

Figure 10.97 Partial Organization Single Sign-On

When creating users in a partial organization SSO scenario, you will need to fill in the login method when creating the users. This will indicate to the system whether the user is logging on with single sign on. SSO will signify users that logon via SSO, and PWD will indicate users who log on directly to SuccessFactors (see Figure 10.98).

STATUS	USERID	USERNAM	CUSTOM1	CUSTOM1	CUSTOM1	LOGIN_METHOD
STATUS	USERID	Username	Customize	Customize	Customiz	login_Method
active	50000301	MBANES				PWD
active	50000302	LOWENS				SSO

Figure 10.98 Login Method

Please note that in SuccessFactors usernames are case sensitive, whereas in SAP usernames are not case sensitive. This can cause SSO syncing problems in which usernames have been entered with mixed cases in SAP.

This can be avoided by ensuring that usernames are passed from SAP to Success-Factors as lowercase values by implementing the following in SAP:

▸ Implement BAdI definition HRSFI_B_EMPL_DATA_REPLICATION

▸ Input the ABAP code into the method IF_HRSFI_EMPL_DATA_REPLICATION~GET_USERNAME in order to convert username values to lowercase.

▸ Employee data integration (SAP program RH_SFI_SYNCHRONIZE_EMPL_DATA) will use the BAdI and pass the username as lowercase values to Success-Factors.

Let's now focus on the final step required for setting up SSO: creating an SAP portal URL iView to SuccessFactors.

Create an SAP Enterprise Portal URL iView to SuccessFactors

Now that the SSO setup is complete, the final step is to add SuccessFactors URLs into the SAP Enterprise Portal menu. To do this, you'll need to create a new SAP portal iView with an embedded SuccessFactors URL.

Log on to the SAP Enterprise Portal, and perform the following steps:

1. Go to the CONTENT ADMINISTRATOR via CONTENT ADMINISTRATION • PORTAL CONTENT MANAGER • PORTAL CONTENT.

2. Create a new URL iView with the following details:
   ▸ URL: *<hostname>/saml2/idp/sso* — for example, *https://cl1-portal2. wdf.sap.corp:50102/saml2/idp/sso*
   ▸ URL PARAMETER 1: saml2sp
   ▸ URL PARAMETER 1 (VALUE): *https://www.successfactors.com*
   ▸ URL PARAMETER 2: RelayState
   ▸ URL PARAMETER 2 (VALUE): Enter the deep link for the SuccessFactors page you want to access. For example, if the full SuccessFactors URL is *https://salesdemo4.SuccessFactors.com/sf/goals?bplte_company=xxxxxx, then the deep link is /sf/goals*

3. When you click on the newly created iView in SAP Enterprise Portal, the SuccessFactors screen will now be accessible without requiring the user to log in again.

4. Note that to make the SuccessFactors URLs look more consistent with the SAP Enterprise Portal look and feel, you can remove the SuccessFactors top menu in the SuccessFactors system.

5. Login to SuccessFactors Provisioning, and go to COMPANY SETTINGS. Select the ENABLE V12 EMBEDDABLE MODE checkbox.

You have now completed the final step required for setting up SSO.

This case study focused on the necessary configuration and technical steps to implement SSO between SAP ERP HCM and SuccessFactors. The outcome made it possible for MedTron's employees to simply and easily access both their SAP and SuccessFactors systems through the SAP Enterprise Portal via one single point of entry — without having to sign on to their systems multiple times.

The goal of sharing this example is to help you with your customers who desire to implement SSO integration and capability with their Talent Hybrid deployment model.

10.6   Summary

This chapter provided detailed case studies, which included the necessary configuration steps to implement the Talent Hybrid integration scenarios for employee data integration, compensation process integration, and recruiting process integration using SAP PI on-premise as the integration middleware. In addition, SSO integration was also covered. These case studies can be used to provide project guidance in implementing the Talent Hybrid integrations.

For customers looking to move to Employee Central, in the next and final chapter we will discuss the various data migration options available to support the migration of HR data to the cloud.

The key to a successful data migration is standardized and engineered rapid data migration content for a fast and simple go-live with valid and clean data. In this chapter, we'll explain the migration of data from an SAP ERP HCM or third-party system into Employee Central, leveraging the rapid-deployment paradigm.

11 Data Migration

As we outlined in Chapter 2, migrating to the cloud may not be the same for all customers (see Figure 11.1). Some customers may choose to move all HCM applications in one large step (Full Cloud HCM), some may choose to move talent solutions to the cloud while keeping their investment in core HR intact (Talent Hybrid), or a third type of customer may choose to move talent solutions for all employees to the cloud along with core HR for a small set of employees, usually from a subsidiary (Side-By-Side).

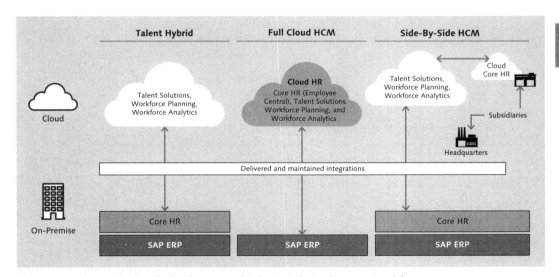

Figure 11.1 Talent Hybrid, Full Cloud HCM, and Side-By-Side Deployment Models

However, once customers have made the decision to implement Employee Central for core HR via the Full Cloud HCM, Talent Hybrid, or Side-By-Side HCM deployment model, they are faced with the challenges of migrating their data along with these integration tasks discussed earlier in this book. When moving functionality to the cloud, there may be worries about losing any legacy data when the legacy system (core HR on-premise) is retired. This is also the big difference between a data migration and the integration scenarios discussed previously: in the case of a migration, the legacy system will be switched off at some point in time and no longer used as the system of record.

The challenges facing customers migrating data to the cloud are just the same as those migrating data to an on-premise application. However, long projects with unpredictable post-implementation results and costs are no longer acceptable in the cloud world, where LOB leaders are in the driver's seat. Today, both business and IT leaders want to know upfront what they can get, how fast they can get it, and how much it will cost them.
Given that migration is an often overlooked part of an implementation project, this is especially true. To remedy this need, a new data onboarding methodology is required. The aim of this chapter is to provide insight into this data migration paradigm as it applies in the SuccessFactors space.

This chapter outlines the foundation for data migration to Employee Central (see Section 11.1) and introduces two different types of migration: simple file loads and a prepackaged data migration approach (see Section 11.2). Finally, we'll go into detail about the different migration technologies focusing on APIs (see Section 11.3).

11.1 Migration Foundation

The two sections that follow discuss the foundation of a tool-based data migration approach that includes data quality aspects and a guided implementation methodology.

11.1.1 Rapid-Deployment Solutions

SAP Rapid Data Migration is based on *SAP Rapid-Deployment Solutions* that enable a best practices methodology for the way we approach the implementation of SAP solutions today. In a nutshell, the new paradigm is based on the realization that it's faster and less risky to leverage available best business practices with rapid-deployment solutions, perform a fit/gap analysis, and restrict additional customizing, add-ons, and interfaces to only those areas of a company's operations in which significantly more business value and differentiation can be achieved.

Rapid-deployment solutions simplify the implementation of SAP solutions in the cloud, on-premise, or in hybrid landscapes, with faster, less costly, and predictable business outcomes. These solutions include best practice-based implementation content and proven, risk-reducing implementation methodologies, which accelerates the deployment of new solutions via key technology and business capabilities to help companies solve business problems and go live fast. Figure 11.2 shows how SAP Rapid-Deployment Solutions fit into the overall deployment model with its best business and implementation practices for faster time to value.

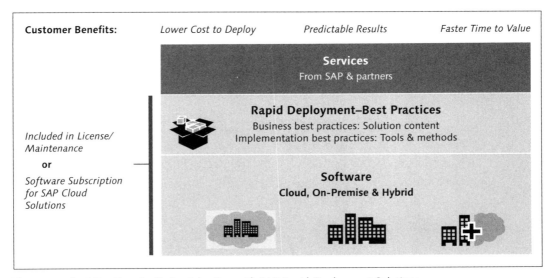

Figure 11.2 Best Practices for Faster Adoption with SAP Rapid-Deployment Solutions

With this method, customers will quickly see proposed solutions via comprehensive and seamless guidance from the evaluation to go-live, with no surprises. Modular scope options enable the assembly of end-to-end solutions, helping companies to easily adopt the right combination of best business practices and IT capabilities or to extend where necessary to meet the customer's needs.

What does this approach mean for the cloud solutions that SAP offers? It brings best practices to the cloud and makes cloud innovation adoption simple. At *http://*

service.sap.com/public/rds, you will find rapid-deployment solutions for onboarding, integration, and migration to the cloud, as outlined in Figure 11.3.

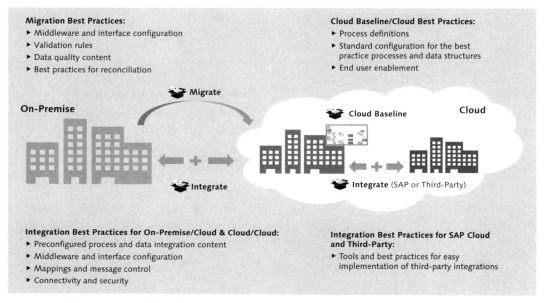

Migration Best Practices:
- Middleware and interface configuration
- Validation rules
- Data quality content
- Best practices for reconciliation

Cloud Baseline/Cloud Best Practices:
- Process definitions
- Standard configuration for the best practice processes and data structures
- End user enablement

Integration Best Practices for On-Premise/Cloud & Cloud/Cloud:
- Preconfigured process and data integration content
- Middleware and interface configuration
- Mappings and message control
- Connectivity and security

Integration Best Practices for SAP Cloud and Third-Party:
- Tools and best practices for easy implementation of third-party integrations

Figure 11.3 Rapid-Deployment Solutions for Onboarding, Integration, and Migration to the Cloud

In the next section, we will look at another foundation for data migration: SAP Data Services.

11.1.2 SAP Data Services

SAP Data Services is an ETL (extract, transform, load) tool for extracting, transforming, and loading data from one or more source systems into one or more target systems. It is a product of SAP's Enterprise Information Management portfolio. SAP Data Services lets you improve, integrate, transform, and deliver trusted data to critical business processes across the enterprise for both SAP and non-SAP systems. SAP Data Services can also be used in almost any scenario that requires you to move, enrich, transform, or cleanse data, and in this regard it functions as the technology foundation for a data migration as one of its use cases.

If all you needed for a successful data migration project was software tooling, then we wouldn't provide a separate chapter for data migration. The primary software products that you can leverage for data migration are SAP Data Services and SAP Information Steward. Data migration projects require a deep knowledge of and expertise in the target data structures. You must have the following knowledge:

▶ An understanding of the system you are migrating to

▶ The requirements for the data in the new system

▶ The expectations for the data to be successful in the new system

When migrating to SuccessFactors applications, the source system is completely unknown to the SAP Rapid Data Migration developers of SAP's rapid-deployment solutions team. You could be migrating from a homegrown application, another vendor's software solution, a mainframe application, or any other datastores that were used prior to your SuccessFactors system. Although SAP cannot provide accelerators or deep knowledge of your non-SAP legacy source systems, SAP can and certainly does provide data migration content for SAP ERP HCM as a legacy source and details of your SuccessFactors target system. This knowledge, provided for you as out-of-the-box migration content, accelerates your SuccessFactors implementation.

> **SAP Data Services Tutorial**
>
> If you're new to SAP Data Services, you might want to start by going through the SAP Data Services tutorial that is included in the documentation when you install the product.

Having looked at the foundation, let's now turn our gaze to the different types of migration available.

11.2   Types of Migration

In this section, we will look at the different types of migration to Employee Central and the technologies they entail. The two migration types are the simple *file loads* and the prepackaged SAP Rapid Data Migration content provided by SAP Rapid-Deployment Solutions.

11.2.1   File Loads

Employee Central offers an administrator tool for importing and exporting data using CSV (comma-separated values) files. While the import functionality allows you to import data objects such as metadata, foundation data, and employment data, you can also export existing data and download blank CSV templates to familiarize yourself with the required structure. The templates also include the import sequence to be used for the actual load (if necessary) and basic validations (see Figure 11.4).

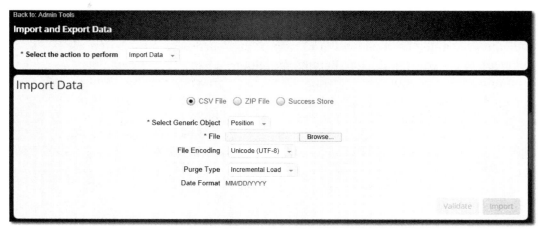

Figure 11.4 File Upload in Employee Central

Although Employee Central's file interfaces allow for full and incremental loads, this approach requires a high attention to detail (as with all file load techniques) due to its manual nature and the high error rate associated with CSV files. File encodings and security concerns can be troublesome as well. However, this approach is great for quick and dirty loads and even for delta loads while testing and setting up the system.

Automation and Data Cleansing

One of the best practices for dealing with data migration for longer periods of time is to automate as much as possible and to allow processes that enable a full data lineage during extraction, transformation, and loading.

Most companies will need to conduct a preliminary data cleanup and also look at opportunities to consolidate data. The best example of this is the job catalog, in which there may be redundant job codes that have been created over a long period of time within the legacy system. The HR representatives should go through the process of consolidating or eliminating job codes prior to the SuccessFactors cutover. Also, the conversion process must be repeatable in a limited amount of time, so it's important that there are no lengthy, time-consuming tasks included in the cutover routine.

Overall, with the file load approach it is hard to handle errors that fall out of a particular data load, because there is no built-in functionality to reprocess error records. You want to have the data in the correct format and shape and include this in the cost estimate, in case data quality checks and error handling have to be implemented. *Automation* and *data cleansing* as enhanced data verifications are rudimental only while following the file load approach. Now, let's take a look at a more sophisticated approach that also allows you to focus on data quality.

11.2.2 SAP Rapid Data Migration

In this section, we'll introduce *SAP Rapid Data Migration*, which comes with proven best practices. Migrating data using tried and tested tools that enable data cleansing and error handling lays a good foundation for migrating core HR to the cloud. We will begin by looking at the migration content and then move on to an overview of its architecture. Following this section, we will look at the migration technologies that enable these processes to function.

Migration Content

The SAP Rapid Data Migration content follows SAP's best practices methodology for data migration. It gains functionality to manage and complete six distinct activities that are critical to the transformation and migration of data (see Figure 11.5).

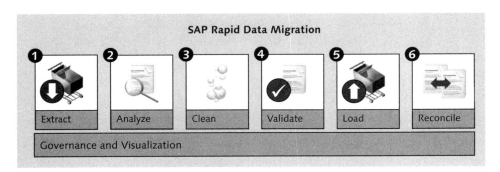

Figure 11.5 SAP Rapid Data Migration Methodology

As shown in Figure 11.5, there are six critical data migration activities:

❶ Extract the data from the source system(s).

❷ Analyze and profile the data from the source system(s).

❸ Cleanse the data records to achieve a high data quality.

❹ Validate the data against the target business context (i.e., the business rules of the target system, such as checking if there are specific fields required or if the country codes are correct).

❺ Load the data into the target SuccessFactors system.

❻ Reconcile the data between the target system and the source system.

SAP offers tools for governance and visualization to support the activities taking place in each of these stages. The governance solutions help to ensure that only authorized individuals can make changes to the data or mappings and that an audit trail exists to capture each change. The visualization tools enable you to see what is taking place during each step in the migration process.

Download the Solution

To download the latest content for SAP Rapid Data Migration to cloud solutions from SAP, go to *http://service.sap.com/rds-dm2cloud*. You will find information on how to install the software, deploy the data migration content, and use the SAP Rapid Data Migration solution. This packaged SAP Rapid-Deployment Solution can be downloaded at no additional cost.

The solution content consists of the following parts:

▶ Mapping sheets for source-to-target mapping to be used for mapping on paper or in Microsoft Excel (prefilled with the target SuccessFactors structure and also for SAP ERP HCM as the possible source)

▶ Documentation on each and every migration object, with step-by-step descriptions of how to perform mapping and migration

▶ Migration content (jobs and data flows) to be imported into SAP Data Services for mapping (*field mapping*) and validation

▶ SAP BusinessObjects Web Intelligence reports to be deployed in the SAP Business-Objects BI platform for monitoring the data migration

▶ The Migration Services tool to map source data field values to SAP business context (*value mapping*)

▶ Migration content for reconciling what was loaded in the target from the source for a full data lineage

---

With a firm understanding of the migration content that this process entails, let's now move on to the architecture.

Architecture

In this section, we will provide a detailed overview of the architecture of SAP Rapid Data Migration for Employee Central. SAP Rapid Data Migration is based on rapid-deployment solutions from SAP and uses SAP Data Services to assess and migrate your data (see Section 11.1).

There are a number of things that are included in the SAP Rapid Data Migration architecture and package. First, there are predelivered templates and content that transform the SAP Data Services data integration platform into a strong and easy-to-use migration engine. This engine comes with built-in functionality to extract and profile any legacy data directly from and on the source system. In addition, there is a new tool for value mapping called *Migration Services*, plus packaged SAP BusinessObjects Web Intelligence reports that deliver insight on the overall process and show data quality issues to the deployment team at an early stage.

Figure 11.6 shows how data migration works using SAP Data Services and the content provided with the SAP Rapid Data Migration package.

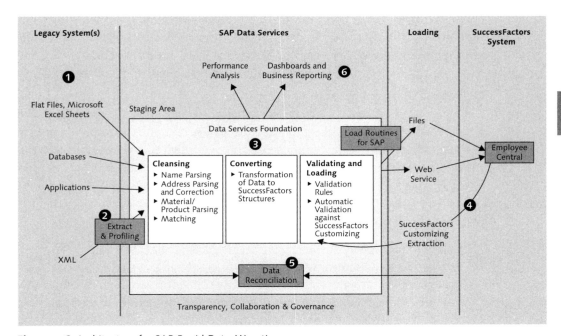

Figure 11.6 Architecture for SAP Rapid Data Migration

Each area in Figure 11.6 is explained in the following list:

❶ Legacy system

The legacy data environment refers to the source systems for the migration. The legacy environment can be any third-party source system that is supported by SAP Data Services connectivity (almost everything, because SAP Data Services supports the ODBC protocol). The legacy system can also be SAP ERP HCM. The SAP Rapid Data Migration package comes with prebuilt content for SAP ERP HCM as a source.

❷ Extract and profile

Data is extracted from the source and placed in a staging area in SAP Data Services. At this point, you can conduct technical profiling with SAP Data Services. In addition, you can start profiling very early on the source systems using SAP Information Steward, a tool that allows you to discover, assess, define, and monitor the quality of data along with SAP Data Services.

❸ Cleanse, transform, and validate

This includes updating the data so that it meets specific patterns, mapping and transforming the data according to rules, and validating data against the SuccessFactors business context. This can involve combining two fields into one, splitting fields, updating the data in a field to match certain rules (for example, telephone number formats), and validating data against required fields and lookup values from the SuccessFactors business context and configuration.

❹ SuccessFactors configuration extraction

As part of a SuccessFactors implementation, the system is configured with many values, such as cost centers and the state and country values. Mapping of the source data normally requires mapping fields that comply with the SuccessFactors configuration.

❺ Reconciliation

Reconciliation looks at what was actually loaded versus what was expected to be loaded. This functionality is the part of the SAP Rapid Data Migration package that proves the load was successful and hands it over to the business.

❻ Dashboards and business reporting

Throughout the process, dashboards are available for people involved to stay informed about the status of the migration. The validation reports can help resolve all processing errors even before the actual load to Employee Central happens. In addition, the migration project often sets data quality expectations and governance around data management.

Demo

For a complete demo of data migration, go to *http://service.sap.com/public/rds-datamigration*, and select Demo.

Once everything is installed and deployed according to the included configuration guide, you will find a predefined project in SAP Data Services. This project has jobs for each of the business objects, such as employee data or foundation data. When drilling into the job, you will see the mapping and validation that takes place (see Figure 11.7). The validation is shown against required lookup fields in the SuccessFactors system, validating mandatory fields as well as the format (e.g., whether the phone numbers all include country codes and whether the postal code is in the correct format).

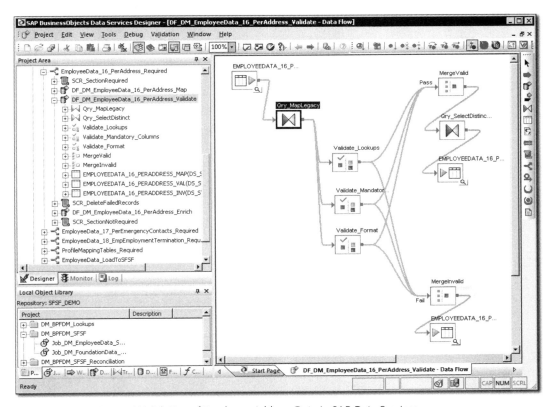

Figure 11.7 Mapping and Validation of Employee Address Data in SAP Data Services

After the mapping has been done, the SAP Data Services jobs can be started in a test mode to resolve all the remaining mapping and validation issues. Typically, this iteration can happen until all the errors have been resolved, which helps to avoid handling hundreds of conversion errors on a cutover weekend. Once the actual values have been translated, enriched, and validated successfully, the SAP Data Services job can start to load the data into the Employee Central target system using one of the APIs described in Section 11.3. The tool does not use the file load approach instead it uses either the SuccessFactors Adapter or SuccessFactors' OData interface depending on the existing interface (see Section 11.3). This approach is faster and more reliable while ensuring that the data is checked again within SuccessFactors APIs for high quality and consistent data in the target Employee Central cloud system.

In addition to the jobs, data flows, and mappings provided by SAP Rapid-Deployment Solutions, there are also reports and visualizations to keep you updated on the status of the data migration. These reports are part of the migration content and show overall project status, data quality, invalid data records, and data reconciliation. The data migration project can lay the ground work for data governance, data ownership, and ongoing data quality. Governance of data and information is a topic gaining increased interest, and data migration falls into this category, providing the first opportunity to implement governance processes around management and data quality expectations. Migration projects require iteration of data loads to better understand the data and to allow close collaboration between business and IT.

> **Download**
>
> Migration content can be downloaded from *http://service.sap.com/public/rds-dm2cloud* and loaded into SAP Data Services. This webpage also gives an overview of the existing objects that are already covered in the predefined content. A data migration object translates into an Employee Central entity that can be best interpreted as an SAP HR infotype.

The SAP Rapid Data Migration approach can be used with virtually any source system and saves time and effort by providing migration content that enables you to map sources to target data structures, as well as reports and dashboards that monitor the data migration jobs. This approach is the ideal choice for converting from an existing SAP ERP HCM system to Employee Central, because the rapid-deployment solutions package already comes with the source-to-target mapping for this scenario.

11.3   Migration Technology

In addition to the file load functionality, Employee Central offers a library of APIs that can also be used by employing ETL tools other than SAP Data Services or coding to upload data. Indeed, these existing interfaces have been used for the SAP Rapid Data Migration approach with SAP Data Services, as described in Section 11.2.2. SAP Data Services can connect either via the SuccessFactors Adapter leveraging SuccessFactors API web services or via the new OData interface.

In this section, an overview is provided of the interfaces that can be leveraged for data migration. The advantage of using interfaces for a data migration is that they provide a consistent mechanism for accessing the data on an object level rather than on a database table level.

11.3.1   Web Services

SuccessFactors API is a SOAP web service that can be used for uploading data to Employee Central (both creation and update operations are supported for the data migration use case). Working with the SuccessFactors API requires some technical understanding of the SOAP protocol, but metadata operations allow for runtime discovery of the data structure. For example, you can list the objects available to the API and also get a description of the fields in these Employee Central entities.

This generic API offers the following benefits:

▶ Provides a consistent mechanism for accessing data in the SuccessFactors platform

▶ Provides a mechanism to describe the data schema configuration, including the entities that are available and fields that appear in these entities

To get started, you will need the right web service endpoint URL, which differs from the SOAP version, and the SuccessFactors data center location—for example, *https://api.successfactors.com/sfapi/v1/soap*.

11.3.2   OData

The Open Data (OData) protocol is used as the new API for SuccessFactors. The OData technology already allows REST-based API calls for a number of Employee

Central objects. This API also allows for creating and updating operations to suit data migration use cases. OData is an open standard that will be used for future objects while most of the existing SuccessFactors APIs are still supported. The SAP Rapid Data Migration content, as described in Section 11.2.2, will be updated according to the new interfaces on a regular basis.

The endpoint URL for the OData interface also differs by data center location—for example, *https://api.successfactors.com/odata/v2*.

The OData protocol not only enables data loads via web services, it also provides much more functionality in terms of accessing the target data store, all by using simple HTTP messages. Many operations are already supported, but they vary by Employee Central entity. At the same time, OData also provides a secure and consistent data migration interface for upcoming new Employee Central objects.

The best use case for this new interface is creating complex queries by simple HTTP messages.

11.4   Summary

In this chapter, you've learned about SAP's solution for data migration to Employee Central. In addition to the cloud target systems, SAP offers Rapid Data Migration packages for SAP ERP (including Retail and SAP ERP HCM), SAP CRM, and much more. All of these packages can be downloaded in the SAP Service Marketplace free of charge as part of your license, just by visiting *http://service.sap.com/public/rds-datamigration*. All of the available content packages are based on SAP Data Services and are offered as SAP Rapid-Deployment Solutions that help to easily migrate your legacy data. You've also learned how you can take advantage of interfaces such as web service and OData APIs, which again allows for a smoother migration process.

Data Migration Community

You can find an open community for data migration topics in the SAP Community Network (SCN). Simply go to *http://scn.sap.com/community/dm*.

This is a place to discuss and share ideas and experiences as they relate to SAP Rapid Data Migration and other data migration topics. It includes blogs, videos, and a moderated forum.

This chapter also closes the *Integrating SuccessFactors with SAP* journey by adding the migration use case to the overall integration topic. You've learned about the different deployment models and the various packaged integrations they provide. You also walked through case studies and explored the best business practices for your very own integration with SuccessFactors.

Whether you're part of an implementation team or a key decision-maker in an organization, we hope this book becomes part of your toolkit for future integration endeavors.

The Authors

Vishnu Kandi currently heads the SuccessFactors HCM cloud integration practice and has been part of several integration implementations at SAP. He has an extensive background in enterprise-class software development, implementation, and management, and over 12 years of experience in integrations, and client-server and web-based technologies. He has experience in managing development teams, as well as architecting, developing, and deploying highly scalable and available systems, acquired while working on global enterprise implementations for large and multi-national companies. Prior to joining SAP in 2005, he worked in product engineering at Itreya Technologies on WorkflowDirect and eCommunix products.

Venki Krishnamoorthy is an independent SAP/SuccessFactors consultant with over 12 years of experience as a functional lead and project/program manager in the HCM space. Venki has done over 18 full lifecycle implementations of SAP, Employee Central, SuccessFactors Recruiting, SuccessFactors Onboarding, Performance and Goal Management, SuccessFactors Learning, SuccessFactors Succession and Development, and Nakisa for customers in the US and across the globe. Venki is an author of four SAP PRESS books and has been a speaker for SAP Insider, ASUG conferences, and SuccessFactors-facilitated online webinars.

You can follow Venki on twitter at *@venki_sap* or via email at *venki.krish@ymail.com*.

Donna Leong-Cohen is the co-founder and managing director of Coeus Consulting, an SAP consulting partner specializing in SAP on-premise and cloud HR implementations using best practices and rapid-deployment solutions. Prior to founding Coeus, Donna worked for several years with Deloitte Consulting in their Human Capital Division. Donna has over 16 years of experience in implementing HCM global systems and business consulting specializing in HR business process transformation. She has delivered over 30+ HCM implementation projects for a broad spectrum of global and domestic clients. Her wealth of experience in the HR systems industry has augmented her ability to work with complex global organizations and across many business sectors. Donna has worked in SAP HCM for 12 years and on SuccessFactors implementations for three years. She has considerable expertise in SAP and SuccessFactors integrations and has worked very closely with SAP's rapid-deployment solutions teams to develop packaged solutions, as well as with customers delivering complete end-to-end solutions for on-premise and cloud HR solutions. In addition, Donna has also worked to develop the curriculum for the SAP Talent Hybrid integration course with SAP Education.

Prashanth Padmanabhan is the senior director of Solution Management in the HCM group of SAP. He is an SAP Mentor as well as a solution owner for SAP/SuccessFactors integrations. Prior to January 2010, he was the global product manager for SAP Enterprise Learning, SAP's Learning Management System (LMS). In that role, he was responsible for product strategy, design, roll out, and road mapping, leading a team out of the US, Germany, and India. In addition to this book, Prashanth coauthored *SAP Enterprise Learning* (SAP PRESS, 2009) and a self-published title, *Look and Flow* (Amazon, 2012). Prashanth currently lives in the San Francisco Bay Area.

You can follow Prashanth via his product design blog at *http://productdesignjournal.blogspot.com/* and Twitter using the handle *@sprabu.*

Chinni Reddygari is a seasoned HCM expert/executive and has been with SAP (via the SuccessFactors acquisition) since 2001, gaining extensive experience in integrations and extensions. Chinni began working as an SAP consultant, later becoming the practice director of SuccessFactors Global Cloud Integration and Extension Services practice. Chinni's focus is in enterprise cloud services, an area he is excited to be a part of given the opportunities and challenges that lay ahead. Apart from his success in practice management, he regularly helps with pre-sales activities related to SuccessFactors integrations. Chinni Reddygari leads the SuccessFactors team responsible for custom integration roadmap and templates.

Contributors

Kevin Chan is an experienced SAP and SuccessFactors HCM consultant with Coeus Consulting and has over 16 years of experience working with over 35 customers across North America, Europe, and the Asian Pacific. Kevin has worked closely with SAP and SuccessFactors on various initiatives including working with SAP Education to develop their SAP and SuccessFactors integration training courses and working with SAP Packaged Solutions to co-develop their rapid-deployment solutions for SAP and Successfactors integration packages, Employee Central data migration, Employee Central integrations, and SuccessFactors Compensation. Kevin actively works with customers to implement both Talent Hybrid and Full Cloud HCM integrations. Kevin is also Dell Boomi AtomSphere Certified and SuccessFactors Associate Certified in Employee Central, SuccessFactors Compensation, Performance Management and Goals Management.

Frank Densborn is a product manager for SAP Rapid-Deployment Solutions at SAP Labs in Palo Alto, California. He works in the technology area focusing on Enterprise Information Management, data migration, and cloud integration. Frank is the package owner of SAP's Rapid Data Migration packages and is also working on integrating SAP's cloud solutions with the on-premise world. He joined SAP AG in Walldorf, Germany in 2004, holding various roles in development, education, support, and product management.

Anoop Kumar Garg is an integration solution expert with the SuccessFactors PS team at SAP, implementing end-to-end cloud HCM solutions across the product suite. He has been a trusted advisor with enterprise customers implementing SAP/SuccessFactors across multiple industries and territories, mainly based out of Europe and Asia, to deliver a large number of local/global implementation projects.

Bhargav Gogineni is an experienced and accomplished cloud integrations professional. His consulting experience spans multiple industries and cross-functional domains. He has experience working with product engineering, architecting cross-platform integrations, and managing integrations teams. Currently, he is working with SAP HCM cloud with a focus on application integrations.

Dina Hermosillo-Burrus is an experienced SAP HCM and SuccessFactors professional, specializing in Competency Management, Performance and Goals Management, and Workforce Process Management for both on-premise and cloud systems. She has domestic and international experience working with customers across North America, Europe, and the Asian Pacific. Dina has worked closely with SAP and SuccessFactors on the design, development, and implementation of the SAP Rapid-Deployment Solutions for SuccessFactors Talent Hybrid, Employee Central data migration, Full Cloud HCM, best practices for Employee Central, SuccessFactors Compensation and Recruiting modules, and SuccessFactors Talent Hybrid training content development for SAP Education.

Venkatesan Iyengar is an accomplished professional in the HCM domain. His consulting experience spans multiple industries and functional components of SAP HCM delivered globally. He has experience working with product development as well as architecting and leading the delivery of large complex solutions involving different technologies, while building a practice and developing teams. More recently, he has been focusing on cloud integration technologies while delivering large global solutions which involve integrating SAP ERP, as well as various local vendors, with a global Employee Central solution using a mixture of delivered and custom integrations.

Kiran Vuriti has been working on SAP Enterprise application integrations since 2005. As an SAP professional service team leader, he is responsible for the implementation of integrations with SuccessFactors, SAP, third-party cloud, and on-premise applications.

Rachel Leonard is a program manager at Coeus Consulting, where she consults on SuccessFactors and SAP ERP Talent Hybrid integration projects. Prior to working as a HCM consultant, she was a technical writer producing end user guides and training materials for SAP modules including SAP MM, WM, FI and HCM. She has over 15 years of experience with implementing HCM projects in the US, UK, and Australia for private, public sector, and global clients. She has worked in various project roles covering the design, configuring, and testing of HCM systems. She also has experience with team leading and project management. Her most recent project includes producing Talent Hybrid integration training materials for SAP Education.

Raja Thukiwakam is currently working as an integration architect in SAP HCM cloud technical services. He is certified in SAP Process Integration, Dell Boomi AtomSphere cloud middleware, and was twice named as Topic Leader in *scn.sap.com* for his contributions in the SAP Process Integration middleware space. He has expertise in SAP PI, SAP HCI, SAP HCM cloud solutions, and Dell Boomi AtomSphere, and is well-versed in designing integration strategies.

Ritesh Mehta has over 12 years of experience in the software industry. He started his career as a SaaS developer at SAP Labs and then moved into SAP consulting where he gained experience in managing large SAP implementations. He has managed many diverse teams including client SMEs, partner SMEs, technical leaders, and developers located across the globe. Ritesh is a certified Project Management Professional (PMP) and he has been deeply involved in program/project planning, estimations, tracking, reporting, and communications for various stakeholders such as CIOs, project sponsors, business VPs, various client IT, process owners, product owners, sales, pre-sales, professional services, customer support, and more.

Seng-Ping Gan is a technical integration expert with Coeus Consulting who specializes in SAP HCM and SuccessFactors Talent Hybrid and Full Cloud HCM integrations with SuccessFactors. Seng-Ping has over eight years of functional and technical experience in HCM working with various global companies in Asia, Europe, and the US. His area of expertise includes SAP PI, SAP HCI, ABAP, SAP HCM, and Dell Boomi AtomSphere. He is actively working with the SAP Rapid-Deployment Solutions package solutions team on several SAP/SuccessFactors integrations and data migration rapid-deployment solutions. Seng-Ping has supported the implementation of SAP HCI integrations for the Talent Hybrid training course offered by SAP Education.

Index

Interested in reading more?

Please visit our website for all new
book and e-book releases from SAP PRESS.

www.sap-press.com